THE TARYAG MITZVOT MANUAL

Second Edition

לעלוי נשמת אבי מורי אליעזר בן אביגדר

Rabbi Jonathan Rietti

The Taryag Mitzvot Manual
by Rabbi Jonathan Rietti

Copyright © 2003 Rabbi Jonathan Rietti

All rights reserved. No part of this publication may be reproduced, distributed, or transmitted in any form or by any means, including photocopying, recording, or other electronic or mechanical methods, without the prior written permission of the publisher, except in the case of brief quotations embodied in critical reviews and certain other noncommercial uses permitted by copyright law. For permission requests, write to the publisher, addressed "Attention: Permissions Coordinator," at the address below.

Breakthrough Chinuch
www.BreakthroughChinuch.com
office@breakthroughchinuch.com

Ordering Information:
Quantity sales. Special discounts are available on quantity purchases by corporations, associations, and others. For details, contact the publisher at the address above.

ISBN 9781704122458

10 9 8 7 6 5 4 3 2

1. Religion 2. Education

Second Edition

Printed in the United States of America

Table of Contents

PART I — **Taryag Mitzvos: The Road Map to the Torah**
Chapter 1 — The Mitzvah to Know Taryag Mitzvos — 1
Chapter 2 — What are the Benefits of Knowing Taryag Mitzvos? — 3
Chapter 3 — How much Does Hashem Really Love Us? — 13

PART II — **How to Teach the Taryag Mitzvos**
Chapter 4 — The Order of the Mitzvos — 18
Chapter 5 — Playing Games with the Taryag-Mitzvos Picture Cards — 26

PART III — **The Taryag Mitzvos Outline**
Chapter 6 — Introduction to the Taryag Mitzvos Outline — 36
Chapter 7 — The Taryag Mitzvos Outline — 46

PART IV — **Appendices**
Chapter 8 — Why Does Hashem Give Us So Many Mitzvos? — 129
Chapter 9 — What is the Purpose of Torah Learning? — 131
Chapter 10 — How the Torah was Taught Systematically as a Commentary to the Taryag Mitzvos — 132
Chapter 11 — Glossary of Terms — 137
Chapter 12 — How to Explain the Arayus Mitzvos to Young Children — 144

PART V — **Knowledge Maps** — 150

Knowledge Map A: Applications for Teaching Taryag Mitzvot — 152

First teach the most familiar Mitzvos — 152
How to Teach the 14 Icons for Rambam's Sefarim — 154
How to Learn the Mitzvos according to Rambam's list — 154
Practical Applications - Taryag Mitzvos Card Activities — 157
Taryag Detective - Which Mitzvah Am I? — 160
The Taryag Mitzvos Reference Book — 161
Matrix Taryag Mitzvos as they appear in Chumash — 161
Matrix Taryag Mitzvos according to the Human Anatomy — 163
Miscellaneous Matrices — 164
Students Create their own Taryag Mitzva Cards — 165
The Mitzvah Clue Game - Reveal What You Know! — 165
Taryag Chevrusos - Mitzvah Quiz Games — 166
Advanced Level for Taryag Chevrusos — 167
Mental Mapping & Mental Palaces - Memorize Where each Mitzvah is in The Torah — 167
Taryag Mitzvos Photo Cards — 171
Build your own Classroom Taryag Mitzvos Library — 172

Knowledge Map B: How to Memorize the Taryag Mitzvot According to the Rambam — 173

Step One: Memorizing Taryag Mitzvot	173
List of 122 Most Familiar Mitzvot	175
Step Two: Assign Code Names for Each Mitzvah	178
Step Three: Organize The Mitzvot	178
Memorize the names of The 14 Books of Rambam	179
Chart of 14 Icons of 14 Sefarim of Rambam 'Stacking System'	181
Step Four: Memorize Rambam's List of The Taryag Mitzvot	183
Book 1 Sefer Mada	183
Book 2 Sefer Ahava	185
Book 3 Sefer Zemanim	186
Book 4 Sefer Nashim	187
Book 5 Sefer Kedusha	188
Book 6 Sefer Hafla'ah	190
Book 7 Sefer Zeraim	191
Book 8 Sefer Avodah	193
Book 9 Sefer Korbanot	195
Book 10 Sefer Tahara	196
Book 11 Sefer Nezikin	197
Book 12 Sefer Kinyan	198
Book 13 Sefer Mishpatim	199
Book 14 Sefer Shoftim	200

Knowledge Map C: How to Memorize the Taryag Mitzvot According to the Sefer Hachinuch — 201

Mental Mapping & How to Memorize which Chapter every Mitzvah is in	201
3 Mitzvot in Sefer Bereishit	205
111 Mitzvot in Sefer Shemot	205
249 Mitzvot in Sefer Vayikra	209
50 Mitzvot in Sefer Bamidbar	216
200 Mitzvot in Sefer Devarim	218

Knowledge Map D: Anatomy of the Mitvot: Which Mitzvot are Done with Which Part of the Body — 225

Mitzvos of the Mind	- 69 Mitzvos	227
Mitzvos of the Eyes	- 19 Mitzvos	229
Mitzvos of the Ears	- 12 Mitzvos	229
Mitzvos of the Nose	- 2 Mitzvos	230
Mitzvos of the Mouth	- 219 Mitzvos	231
Mitzvos of the Hands	- 321 Mitzvos	238
Mitzvos of the Head	- 14 Mitzvos	247
Mitzvos of the legs/feet	- 118 Mitzvos	248
Mitzvos of the Bris	- 55 Mitzvos	251
Mitzvos of the Entire Body	- 46 Mitzvos	253
Mitzvos of the Mind which are Constant	- 49 Mitzvos	255
Mitzvos of the Ramban not counted by Rambam	- 70 Mitzvos	261
Mitzvos of the Smag not counted in Rambam	- 19 Mitzvos	265
Mitzvos HaSmaK not counted by Rambam, Ramban, SMaG & B'HaG	- 29 Mitzvos	266
Mitzvos of Sefer Yereim not counted by Rambam	- 50 Mitzvos	267

PART I

Taryag Mitzvos: The Road Map to the Torah

Chapter 1:

The Mitzvah to Know Taryag Mitzvos

Does the Torah Command us to know Taryag Mitzvos?[1]
Actually, dozens of times the Torah instructs us with the language of "*guard all My Mitzvos*" "*Do all My Mitzvos.*" [2]
"ושמרתם"
"ועשיתם"

Obviously, the predicate behind an instruction to *guard, observe, practice* and *Do My Mitzvos* is that one *knows* what the Mitzvos are! How else could a person be obedient to instructions if he has no familiarity with them? Clearly, the Torah assumes we know *all* of Hashem's Mitzvos.

When the Torah gives us 613 Mitzvos and some are incorporated in our daily tefila, this requires us to understand why these Mitzvos more than any others are made part of our daily verbal declarations.[3] The Mitzvah of Tzitzis stands out because the Torah offers a reason for its performance[4]:

Bamidbar 15:37
וְהָיָה לָכֶם לְצִיצִת וּרְאִיתֶם אֹתוֹ **וּזְכַרְתֶּם אֶת־כָּל־מִצְוֹת יְהוָה** וַעֲשִׂיתֶם אֹתָם
"And you will remember all My Mitzvos and you will do them."

לְמַעַן **תִּזְכְּרוּ** וַעֲשִׂיתֶם אֶת־**כָּל־מִצְוֹתָי**
"...in order that you remember and (therefore) you can do all My Mitzvos"
The purpose of the Mitzvah of Tzitzis is to remember all the Mitzvos, and the
purpose of remembering all the Mitzvos is so I will notice the opportunities to do them, to live them.

---

1. See Ex.24:12 - וַיֹּאמֶר יְהוָה אֶל־מֹשֶׁה עֲלֵה אֵלַי הָהָרָה וֶהְיֵה־שָׁם וְאֶתְּנָה לְךָ אֶת־לֻחֹת הָאֶבֶן **וְהַתּוֹרָה וְהַמִּצְוָה** אֲשֶׁר כָּתַבְתִּי לְהוֹרֹתָם. See Rashi there quoting Medrash Bamidbar Raba 13:16 - אֶת לֻחֹת הָאֶבֶן וְהַתּוֹרָה וְהַמִּצְוָה אֲשֶׁר כָּתַבְתִּי לְהוֹרֹתָם. כָּל **שֵׁם מָאֹת וּשְׁלֹשׁ עֶשְׂרֵה מִצְוֹת בִּכְלַל עֲשֶׂרֶת הַדִּבְּרוֹת הֵן**. וְרַבֵּנוּ סְעַדְיָה פֵּרַשׁ בְּאַזְהָרוֹת שֶׁיִּסֵּד לְכָל דִּבּוּר וְדִבּוּר מִצְוֹת הַתְּלוּיוֹת בּוֹ. At this point in time, Moshe Rabeynu had not written the entire Torah, only the events that occurred from Bereishit till Matan Torah (Ex.24:7, Rashi there). In Dev.31:24 the Torah tells us that Moshe Rabeynu completed the writing of the entire Torah. So it can be deduced that when he was instructed here in Ex.24:12 to receive "the Torah and the Mitzvah" it can be referring to all the 613 Mitzvos contained in the Aseret Hadibrot. The story line of the Torah was only completed in Dev.31:24.
2. See p. 192-193 in sefer Maalot HaTorah (written by the Vilna Gaon's brother, R' Avraham Kramer) citing many passukim that use the language of שמירת המצות. For example, see Dev.11:8, 5:1, 5:28, 4:6, 10:2, 5:29, 7:12, 8:1, Lev.18:5, Lev.20:8, Lev.22:31, Lev.19:37, 20:22. See also Ex.34:11. There are many more examples too.
3. For example: Shema, remembering Yetzias Mitzrayim; Lo tasuru - not to follow our eyes and thoughts; and the Mitzvah to wear Tzitzis.
4. The Torah rarely offers reasons in its text for why a Mitzvah should be performed. There are some Mitzvos which the Torah tells us their partial reward is long life, as for example Kibud Av V'Eim, Shiluach Hakaan and Mezuza. But it is still more rare for the Torah to actual offer a reason, Tzitzis is one such exception.

The first line we teach our children is תורה צוה לנו משה. Moshe rabeynu instructed us in 611 Mitzvos. The first two we heard directly from Hashem at Sinai.⁵ So the verse really can read "Moshe instructed us in 611 Mitzvos." Obviously the purpose of teaching us 613 Mitzvos is in order to do them, but that presumes I know and remember what to do. Thus again, the Torah is assuming we know Taryag Mitzvos.

Zohar Chadash:
כל התורה כולה נכלל בתוך תיבה "בראשית"
The entire Torah is hidden in the first word "Bereishis"

If it is true that knowing all Taryag Mitzvos is instructed by the Torah itself, where do we see this in the first word of the Torah?

Take the letter **ש** out of **בראשית** and you are left with the word **בראית** which has an exact numerical value of 613.

What does the letter **ש** signify? Which one word in the Torah is the source for teaching Torah to our children?
The answer is: "ושננתם"⁶
The word ושננתם starts with the letter **ש**, so now the word Bereishit - **בראשית** is really hinting to us : "Teach your children 613 Mitzvos"⁷

---

5. Makkot 23b-24a - דרש רבי שמלאי: שש מאות ושלש עשרה מצות נאמרו לו למשה, שלש מאות וששים וחמש לאוין כמנין ימות החמה, ומאתים וארבעים ושמונה עשה כנגד איבריו של אדם. אמר רב המנונא: מאי קרא? (דברים ל״ג) תורה צוה לנו משה מורשה, תורה בגימטריא **(דף כד.א)** שית מאה וחד סרי הוי, אנכי ולא יהיה לך מפי הגבורה שמענום.

   See also Devarim 5:19 - 24 where Moshe Rabeynu reminded Beney Yisrael of how they begged him to intercede between Hashem after they survived the first two of the Aseret HaDibrot and tell them what Hashem commands them instead of hearing directly from Hashem - אֶת־הַדְּבָרִים הָאֵלֶּה דִּבֶּר יְהוָה אֶל־כָּל־קְהַלְכֶם בָּהָר מִתּוֹךְ הָאֵשׁ הֶעָנָן וְהָעֲרָפֶל קוֹל גָּדוֹל וְלֹא יָסָף וַיִּכְתְּבֵם עַל־שְׁנֵי לֻחֹת אֲבָנִים וַיִּתְּנֵם אֵלָי׃ כ וַיְהִי כְּשָׁמְעֲכֶם אֶת־הַקּוֹל מִתּוֹךְ הַחֹשֶׁךְ וְהָהָר בֹּעֵר בָּאֵשׁ וַתִּקְרְבוּן אֵלַי כָּל־רָאשֵׁי שִׁבְטֵיכֶם וְזִקְנֵיכֶם׃ כא וַתֹּאמְרוּ הֵן הֶרְאָנוּ יְהוָה אֱלֹהֵינוּ אֶת־כְּבֹדוֹ וְאֶת־גָּדְלוֹ וְאֶת־קֹלוֹ שָׁמַעְנוּ מִתּוֹךְ הָאֵשׁ הַיּוֹם הַזֶּה רָאִינוּ כִּי־יְדַבֵּר אֱלֹהִים אֶת־הָאָדָם וָחָי׃ כב וְעַתָּה לָמָּה נָמוּת כִּי תֹאכְלֵנוּ הָאֵשׁ הַגְּדֹלָה הַזֹּאת אִם־יֹסְפִים ׀ אֲנַחְנוּ לִשְׁמֹעַ אֶת־קוֹל יְהוָה אֱלֹהֵינוּ עוֹד וָמָתְנוּ׃ כג כִּי מִי כָל־בָּשָׂר אֲשֶׁר שָׁמַע קוֹל אֱלֹהִים חַיִּים מְדַבֵּר מִתּוֹךְ־הָאֵשׁ כָּמֹנוּ וַיֶּחִי׃ כד קְרַב אַתָּה וּשֲׁמָע אֵת כָּל־אֲשֶׁר יֹאמַר יְהוָה אֱלֹהֵינוּ וְאַתְּ ׀ תְּדַבֵּר אֵלֵינוּ אֵת כָּל־אֲשֶׁר יְדַבֵּר יְהוָה אֱלֹהֵינוּ אֵלֶיךָ וְשָׁמַעְנוּ וְעָשִׂינוּ׃

6. Dev. 6:5

7. See Medrash Aggadah, Parshas Bereishis. The letter שׁין in its 2 letter root means שׁן. שׁן has two meanings, "tooth" and "twice." What's the connection between the two? The tooth does the constant act of repetition, breaking the food down till it is ready for digestion, a process that is latent, hidden. When we repeat our learning again and again, we are preparing the Torah for digestion, a hidden process of changing our persona. שׁן is also the two letter root of 'change,' because by *repeating* one's learning, we *sharpen* (the tooth is sharp in order to break the food down) our understanding of it, and ultimately, the learning is meant to *change* us for the better.

Chapter 2:
What are the Benefits of Knowing Taryag Mitzvos?

We will now provide a list of 29 sources describing the great value and benefits of learning Taryag Mitzvos. Perhaps this list will help bring the learning of Taryag Mitzvos into a more prominent place in the daily lives of both our children and all klal Yisrael, Amen.

#1
Sefer Kitzur Chareidim: Hakdama
וכי אפשר להיות עבד למלך אם לא ידע חקיו וגזרותיו ?

The Divrei Chayim committed Taryag Mitzvos to memory well before Bar Mitzvah and when asked why he put so much effort into their memorization he gave the following analogy: *"How could a loyal soldier do his duty if he doesn't know the instructions of his general. So too, every Jew is a soldier in the Army of Hashem, it is inconceivable that I can do my duty without knowing what I'm supposed to do, and I want to be a good soldier."*

#2
Messilas Yesharim[8] *puts it even more strongly:*
If I want to have the best possible marriage, how can I not want to know all the ways that make my spouse happy and feel appreciated. Hashem defined 613 ways in which He wants me to give Him pleasure, how can I not want to know them all? Or at least all the Mitzvos which apply today? So studying the Taryag Mitzvos is a demonstration of our desire to know and love Hashem.

#3
Sefer Chereidim Hakdama:
If I don't know all the לאוים how can I properly do Teshuva? Obviously the Mitzvah to do Teshuva is predicated on my knowing what the Torah forbids me to do, so I have to know all the 'Lo Ta'asehs' of the Torah and all the 'Asehs' in order to know what teshuva to do on violations or Mitzvos not performed.

#4
Messilas Yesharim:
The Mitzvos are Hashem's plan for giving us eternity:
If I don't know what is a Mitzvah I'll pass opportunities for preparing my place in Olam Haba.[9]

#5
Rambam: Hilchos Lulav 8:15
השמחה שישמח אדם בעשיית המצוה ובאהבת האל שצוה בהן, עבודה גדולה היא וכל המונע עצמו משמחה זו ראוי להפרע ממנו שנאמר: "תחת אשר לא עבדת את ה' אלקיך בשמחה ובטוב לבב מרב כל"

---
8. See beginning of Chapter 19
9. Chapter 1

Hashem instructed us in His Mitzvos, the simcha and ahava for the Mitzvah is part of that instruction. The avoda of being happy in doing His Mitzvos and feeling love for Hashem and His Mitzvos is tremendous. If a person is held accountable for being happy as the Torah says (Dev. 28:47) after the long list of curses, the Torah inserts the reason for the terrible consequences that would come upon us "...because you did not serve Hashem with joy, with a good attitude of gratitude from the abundant good he gave you." (translation based upon Rashi).

So I have to know the Mitzvos in order to know when I must engage in this great avoda of being B'Simcha in its performance and use it to demonstrate my love to Hashem.

#6

Rambam: Hilchos Temura, 4:13
I need the Mitzvos to win against the Yetser Hara:
רוב דיני התורה אינן אלא עצות מרחוק מגדול העצה לתקן הדעות וליישר כל המעשים
'The majority of the halachos of the Torah are strategies and directives to correct our thoughts and thus correct our actions too.' So I need to know Taryag Mitzvos because they are my weapons, Hashem gifted me, to fight against the Yetser Hara.

#7

Hakdama to Sefer Mitzvos HaKatser of The Chafetz Chaim
Shulchan Aruch Siman 60:4 - מצות צריכות כונה - Mishna Berura ס"ק י'
מצות צריכות כונה מדאורייתא - ומי שעשה מצוה מן התורה בלי כונה לא יצא ידי חובתו וחייב לחזור ולקיימה שנית עם כונה....וחבל שאנחנו מפסידים כל כך הרבה מצות דאורייתא מחמת חוסר כונה
'The obligation to pay attention while performing the Mitzvos of the Torah is a D'Oraissa, a Torah mandated requirement. So if one does Mitzvos without kavana, he does not fulfil the Mitzvah! He must then repeat the Mitzvah with Kavana.....what a shame that we lose out on so many Mitzvos of the Torah because we do not have Kavana!'

Obviously, Mishna Berura is assuming one needs to know the Mitzvos of the Torah in order to know when one needs Kavana. Mishna Berura gives a list of just some Mitzvos we need to be aware of. They are Mitzvos not addressed in Shulchan Aruch that we should be familiar with because they are constant occurances in our lives:[10]

#1 To be Davuk to Chachamim
#2 To Love every Jew, speak his praise, avoid hurting others with words.
#3 Not to have hatred in one's thoughts.
#4 To love a convert.
#5 To give loving words of correction, tochacha.
#6 To be extremely careful not to hurt widows and orphans
#7 Not speak words of gossip, rechilus.
#8 Not to speak lashon Hara.
#9 To avoid telling a sheker, lies.
#10 Not to defame a person's reputation, motzi Shem ra.

---

10. See *Mishna Berura* ש"ע ס' קנו : ס"ק ד

#11 Not to be seduced into Machlokes, arguments or disputes.

#12 Not to have thoughts of begrudging, anger or resentment.

#13 Not to take revenge.

#14 To do Teshuva.

#15 A Katan should not eat like a gluten זולל וסובה[11]

#16 Don't give misleading advice.

#17 Don't undermine items of Kedusha or people's kavod. Avoid לצנות.

#18 Don't flatter, give compliments with a hidden agenda to take advantage of the person you are flattering - וחניפות.

#19 Mitzvah to interpret people's seemingly negative behavior favorably.

#20 Not to speak דברים בטלים

#21 To emulate Hashem's virtues and follow Hashem's ways והלכת בדרכיו

...ועוד יש הרבה הרבה שלא הובאו בש"ע ונמצאים בספרי מוני המצות ונכון מאד שילמד אותם כל אדם ויהיה בקי בהן ועל ידי זה יהיה ביכלתו לקיימם

Continues the Mishna Berura with very emphatic words:

"....and there are many, many more Mitzvos not addressed in Shulchan Aruch and can be found in the various Seforim which list the Taryag Mitzvos[12] and it is extremely worthwhile for every Jew to learn them and commit them till he is is really familiar with them (the Taryag Mitzvos) so that by knowing them all he will be able to do them."

Mishna Berura offers how one can take a simple Mitzvah in the Torah, such as the Mitzvah to pay a worker on time מצות "ביומו תתן שכרו" and as he is about to pay his worker he should literally say out loud to himself:

הריני מקיים מצות בוראי לשלם לשכיר בזמנו

"Behold I am fulfilling the Mitzvah of My Creator to pay a worker his wage in its correct time."

#8

The Mitzvah of Tzitzis

This Mitzvah literally specifies the need to know and remember all 613 Mitzvos. I cannot relegate memorizing the Mitzvos to "when I have time." The Torah commands me to know there is a specific Mitzvah to remember all 613 Mitzvos and do them: "וראיתם אותו וזכרתם את כל מצות ה' ועשיתם אותם"[13]

What is the message here? Chazal tell us that by remembering the Mitzvos, we will be able to do them - שזכירה מביאה לידי עשיה. Indeed, Shulchan Aruch emphasizes this in hilchos Tzitzit:[14]

יכוין בהתעטפו שציונו הקב"ה להתעטף בו כדי שנזכור כל מצותיו לעשותם

'When wearing one's Tzitzis, one should have in mind to wear them in order to remember ALL Hashem's MITZVOS to be able to do them.'

This entire Halacha is predicated on the assumption that I know all 613 Mitzvos!

---

11. Ramban, Vayikra 19:2 - Kedoshim Tiyahu
12. Sefer HaChinuch, Smag, Smak, Chareidim, Poel Tzedek of the Shach, etc.
13. במדבר טו: לט
14. ש"ע ס' ח

#9

Sefer Charedim[15] asks:

Why does the Passuk start 'וזכרתם את כל מצות ה

"You shall remember all the Mitzvos of Hashem" and then writes:

למען תזכרו ועשיתם את כל מצותי...? - in order that you remember and do all My Mitzvos." ?

Answers Sefer Chareidim:

למען תזכרו means לזכרם בלב and וזכרתם את כל מצות ה' means לזכרם בפה

Thus, the Torah is instructing us in two practises:

1. To remember all 613 Mitzvos in my memory, and
2. To verbally list them.[16]

#10

Sefer Charedim:

"וראוי לכל ירא ה' להקדים כל יום לזכור בלב ולהוציא בפה המצות...."

"It is correct for every G-d fearing Jew to start his day by remembering both by heart and verbally the Mitzvos..."

This recommendation of Sefer Chareidim is also found in Poel Tzedek (Shach), Smak, Smag, Radvaz, Shelah Hakadosh, R' David Vital, Sefer Yereyim, Sefer HaChinuch, the Chayey Adam in Zichru Toras Moshe: **They all recommend that a Jew recite the Mitzvos each day, or at least once a week.**

#11

The **Smak**[17] wrote in his introduction:

כי יש הרבה מצות שאין אדם חייב לעשותם עד שבאו לידו, וכשהוא קוראם ומעלה בלבו לעשותם, מעלה הכתוב כאילו עשה, וזה השכר גדול לאין קץ.

"There are many Mitzvos a person has no obligation to fulfil till the opportunity presents itself. However, when a person reads the list of Mitzvos and intends to fulfil them, the Torah counts it as though he actually did them. The reward is thus without end!" The SMaK continues to recommend that one should learn two or three Mitzvos each day in some depth in addition to his recital of all the Taryag Mitzvos daily.

#12

Rabeynu Chaim Vital, Shaar HaGilgulim, Hakdama #11

"A Jew has the mission to fulfil all 613 Mitzvos on three levels.

1. With his actions,
2. With his words and
3. With his thoughts.

When he learns the 613 Mitzvos, he is counted as having actually done them all, just in the same way our sages tell us that when we learn about the Korban Olah we are counted as though we actually brought a Korban Olah.[18] Failure to fulfil all 613 Mitzvos on all three levels requires a person to return as a Gilgul till he fulfills them all in action, speech and thought."

---

15. Sefer Chareidim, in the Hakdama, introduction.
16. Perhaps this is a pshat in the passuk Dev.31:19 וְעַתָּה כִּתְבוּ לָכֶם אֶת־הַשִּׁירָה הַזֹּאת וְלַמְּדָהּ אֶת־בְּנֵי־יִשְׂרָאֵל **שִׂימָהּ בְּפִיהֶם** לְמַעַן תִּהְיֶה־לִּי הַשִּׁירָה הַזֹּאת לְעֵד בִּבְנֵי יִשְׂרָאֵל, the words שִׂימָהּ בְּפִיהֶם refers to verbalizing the Taryag Mitzvos while the verse in Dev.32:46 - וַיֹּאמֶר אֲלֵהֶם **שִׂימוּ לְבַבְכֶם** לְכָל־הַדְּבָרִים אֲשֶׁר אָנֹכִי מֵעִיד בָּכֶם הַיּוֹם אֲשֶׁר תְּצַוֻּם אֶת־בְּנֵיכֶם לִשְׁמֹר לַעֲשׂוֹת אֶת־כָּל־דִּבְרֵי הַתּוֹרָה הַזֹּאת, the words שִׂימוּ לְבַבְכֶם - refer to memorizing all Taryag Mitzvos.
17. Sefer Smak, Sefer Mitzvos Katan, was written by Rabeynu Yitschak M'Kubril, he was a talmid of the baaley Tosfos. He wrote it for people to complete once a week.
18. Menachos 110a

#13

Sefer Ohr HaYashar, Rebi Meir Popears[19]

"One must fulfil all 613 Mitzvos in action, in words and in thoughts. That is why one should learn the Yad Hazaka of the Rambam, or his Sefer HaMitzvos which explain the 613 Mitzvos."

#14

The **Shach** wrote a sefer called **Poel Tzedek** in which he lists all the 613 Passukim of the Taryag Mitzvos and states in his introduction that he wrote it because he noticed how so few amongst our people have bothered to commit Taryag Mitzvos to memory. The Shach then makes the shocking claim that he believes the fact that the vast majority of Hashem's people do not know Taryag Mitzvos is indeed what was predicted by Chazal when they said:[20]

כשנכנסו רבותינו בכרם ביבנה, אמרו: עתידה תורה שתשכח מישראל,

They meant that Taryag Mitzvos would be forgotten as a formal learning. He therefore wrote the list of Taryag Mitzvos for himself, his children and for his generation in the hope that others would read them from beginning to end every single day. He wrote that in reciting them each day, one would be counted as fulfilling the instruction from Yehoshua[21] to never stop learning Torah by day or night[22] - לֹא־יָמוּשׁ סֵפֶר הַתּוֹרָה הַזֶּה מִפִּיךָ וְהָגִיתָ בּוֹ יוֹמָם וָלָיְלָה. The Shach then adds, that if it is too much for some to recite all Taryag Mitzvos every single day, he should at least finish them once a week by learning some every day.[23] The Shach concludes his hakdama with the following amazing insight.

Quoting the last verse in Chumash Vayikra:[24]

אֵלֶּה הַמִּצְוֺת אֲשֶׁר צִוָּה יְהוָה אֶת־מֹשֶׁה אֶל־בְּנֵי יִשְׂרָאֵל בְּהַר סִינָי

"These are the Mitzvos which Hashem instructed Moshe on Mount Sinai to give to Beney Yisrael."

Explains the Shach, the word מִצְוֺת when written out in full (each letter is spelled in full), this is what you get:

מם

צדי

ואו

תיו

The exact Gematria of all these letters combined is 613.

---

19. Talmid of the Arizal
20. Shabbos 139b.
21. Yehoshua 1:8. See also Yishayahu 59:21 - וַאֲנִי זֹאת בְּרִיתִי אוֹתָם אָמַר יְהוָה רוּחִי אֲשֶׁר עָלֶיךָ וּדְבָרַי אֲשֶׁר־שַׂמְתִּי בְּפִיךָ **לֹא־יָמוּשׁוּ מִפִּיךָ וּמִפִּי זַרְעֲךָ וּמִפִּי זֶרַע זַרְעֲךָ אָמַר** יְהוָה מֵעַתָּה וְעַד־עוֹלָם. This is a nevua that Torah will never be forgotten, a promise to the nation of Beney Yisrael, but individuals have bechira to not be part of this promise.
22. The remainder of the Passuk reveals the purpose of learning Torah day and night: לְמַעַן תִּשְׁמֹר לַעֲשׂוֹת כְּכָל־הַכָּתוּב בּוֹ כִּי־אָז תַּצְלִיחַ אֶת־דְּרָכֶךָ וְאָז תַּשְׂכִּיל. "This Sefer Torah should not leave your mouth and you should review it day and night (Radak defines וְהָגִיתָ as a lashon of repetition - Sefer Hasherashim L'Radak) in order that you guard and do all that is written in it, then you will be successful in your ways and you will also be successful in your decisions (Malbim, Nachalat Yehoshua).
23. In his sefer, Poel Tzedek, he divides the entire 613 passukim into seven sections, one to be finished each day for those who cannot complete it once a day.
24. Vayikra 27:34

#15

Rabeynu Yitzchak Katz wrote:[25]

"וכל בר ישראל צריך להיות מגלגל עד שיקים כל תרי"ג מצות, ומי הירא וחרד לדבר ה' שלא ירצה לתקן נשמתו בדבר שהוא בנקל בלתי סגופים ותעניתים, כידוע מה אמרו חז"ל אצל קרבנות "זאת תורת העולה" כל העוסק בכל יום בפרשת הקרבנות כאלו הקריב קרבן. וכן בכל המצות שאי אפשר לקיימם, אמירתם חשובה ומקובלת לפני המקום כאילו קיימם בכל התיקונים...."

Every person has to return to this world as a Gilgul if he did not fulfil all 613 Mitzvos. Who among those who are concerned to do Hashem's will would not want to rectify his soul? Specially if he can come to his Tikkun without self-inflicted suffering and fasting. Our sages famously claim that one who studies the Korbanos each day is counted as though he actually offered that Korban! This applies to all Mitzvos one is unable to perform. Just reciting the Mitzvos counts in Hashem's eyes as though he did all of them!

#16

The Chidda z"l [26]

" Shach wrote a Kitzur of the Mitzvos according to Rambam's listing,[27] and divided them into seven parts, for a person to learn one part a day and finish all Taryag Mitzvos once a week. Happy is the one who consistently reads them every week. This learning will count as though he did all the Mitzvos that he is not able to do....Indeed, it is good to listen to the Kohen Gadol (Baal HaShach) and not let the Mitzvos leave his eyes."

#17

The Radvaz[28]

The Radvaz carried with him everywhere a list of Taryag Mitzvos which he wrote for himself. He wrote a remez for each Mitzvah and would daily review them all.

#18

Shlah HaKadosh, Masechta Shavuos.

"Anyone who dedicates himself to loving Hashem should commit Taryag Mitzvos to memory. He should recite them every day till he knows them by heart with immediate retrieval of the Passuk of the Mitzvah."

#19

Shlah HaKadosh, Sefer Torah Sh'Bichtav

The Shlah writes extensively of the value of learning Taryag Mitzvos because a person can only complete the Tikkun to his 365 איברים and 248 גידים by learning and performing all Taryag Mitzvos. He also adds:

"רק צריך ללמוד תחילה תרי"ג מצות והתלמוד (כלומר למודם של תרי"ג מצות) יביאנו לידי מעשה ויהיה ירא חטא"

"One needs to first learn Taryag Mitzvos because that learning will bring him to doing, and he will be a Yereh Chet."

---

25. He was the son of Rav Moshe Katz who was the son of the Shach.
26. Sefer Shem Hagedolim in reference to the Shach's sefer Poel Tzedek on the listing of Taryag Mitzvos.
27. He means the choice of Passukim of the 613 Mitzvos is based on Rambam, the actual sequence of the Shach's listing as as they appear in the Torah, similar to the Chinuch's sequence.
28. In Teshuvas HaRadvaz.

#20

Sefer Derech Chaim[29]

One should learn one hundred Mitzvos a day so that he learns 600 Mitzvos before Shabbos and 13 on Shabbos. This way one will constantly have Taryag Mitzvos at his fingertips and will have them before his eyes at all times.

#21

Shulchan Aruch HaRav, Hilchos Talmud Torah, Ch.#1, halacha #4

וכן אמרו חכמי האמת שכל נפש מישראל צריכה לבוא בגלגולים רבים עד שתקים כל התרי"ג מצות במעשה בדבור ובמחשבה...ולכן אמרו חז"ל "אשרי מי שבא לכאן ותלמודו בידו" כדי שלא יצטרך לבוא בגלגול לעולם הזה."

"...And so our the Mekubalim say that every Jewish soul has to return numerous times through Gilgul till he performs all 613 Mitzvos with his actions, his words and his thoughts....and that's why our sages say "Happy is the one who comes here (into the world to come) with his learning in his hand,[30] in order that he will not have to return to this world again."

#22

Rav Aryeh Leib Epstein in his sefer Ohr HaShanim[31]

Writes: 'Every single Melamed should should learn this sefer (on Taryag Mitzvos) from beginning to end and teach it to their students. He should teach every single Aseh and Lo Ta'aseh in Chumash and learn very thoroughly all of Rashi's comments on each Mitzvah so that the student will know all the Mitzvos clearly. Or at the very least, every rebbe should teach the Mitzvos which still apply nowadays, and as Shlomo Hamelech stated[32] חֲנֹךְ לַנַּעַר עַל־פִּי דַרְכּוֹ גַּם כִּי־יַזְקִין לֹא־יָסוּר מִמֶּנָּה 'Train the student according to his way, so that when he reaches old age, he will not deviate from it.'

#23

Hanhagos R' Moshe Leib M'Sassov

"...Learning Torah has to begin with mastering the Taryag Mitzvos and their explanation and not learn for the sake of pilpul. Only after you have clarity of all the Taryag Mitzvos and their explanations, then you can delve into pilpul, analysis of the Torah...."

#24

R' Moshe Chassid of Prague

Wrote in his will to his children: First take the short route by learning all the main points about the Taryag Mitzvos, learn them well till you know them all by heart. I recommend you learn Taryag Mitzvos for one to two hours a day and the remainder of your learning time, learn whatever your heart desires and your mind has the capacity for. Once you know Taryag Mitzvos really well and by heart, you never have to worry about bitul Torah because you can so easily review the Mitzvos at any time, between tasks, after Davening, after your meals, even during your meals, you can easily review just a few Mitzvos in order to fulfil the obligation of learning Torah during mealtimes.[33] Take three Mitzvos review them again and again for two or three days and keep doing this every single day of your life! Eventually, the Taryag Mitzvos will be so ingrained in your mind and on the tip of your tongue so you will never forget them.

---

29. From the Gedolei Hakadmaei
30. "In his hand" is an expression for mastery of the learning.
31. Rav Epstein was the rebbe of the mechaber of Yesod V'Shoresh Ha'avoda. Rav Epstein was so outstanding a Talmid Chacham and Tzadik that he was one of the only two people to ever have a written haskama from the Vilna Gaon where the Gaon extolled the praises of Rav Epstein.
32. Mishley 22:6
33. Avot. 3:3

#25

Rebi Yaakov Yechezkel Greenwald from Poppa

Offers the following advice for remembering Taryag Mitzvos: A way to remember the Taryag Mitzvos is to mechadesh, find some new insight of your own in each Mitzvah.

#26

The Chafetz Chaim in Shmiras Halashon[34]

Without knowing Taryag Mitzvos, we are not able to completely fulfil the Mitzvah of wearing Tzitzis.

"We recite every day וְהָיָה לָכֶם לְצִיצִת וּרְאִיתֶם אֹתוֹ **וּזְכַרְתֶּם אֶת־כָּל־מִצְוֹת ה'** וַעֲשִׂיתֶם אֹתָם. But how will reciting the words of the third parsha of Shema help us if we don't actually know the Taryag Mitzvos? How will wearing Tzitzis help me remember the Mitzvos if I have not learned them to start with? Therefore, every Jew should learn either Sefer Mitzvos Hashem or at least Kitzur Sefer Chareidim in order to know Taryag Mitzvos and then he will be able to completely observe the Mitzvah of Tzitzis."

The Chafetz Chaim now offers a brilliant moshol to explain his point:
"When a business merchant travels to a market to buy merchandise, he makes a sign for him to remember all the items he needs to buy and he looks at the sign or simanim he made ever so often till he remembers all the items he needs to buy. But if he does not know what merchandise he needs in the first place, what help will his signs and simanim be to him? So first, obviously he needs to be clear about what he needs to buy. So too, a Jew has Tzitzis which the Torah tells us is worn "in order to remember all My Mitzvos for you to do them" but what will wearing Tzitzis help if he does not know all Hashem's Mitzvos? He can look at Tzitzis all day long but he will not know what Mitzvos he needs 'to buy' at every opportunity that arises today! This is why we need to know all Taryag Mitzvos by heart.

#27

Harav from Petisberg in Hadras Melech[35]

We know that all the Kedoshim and Geonim, Yirei Hashem were involved in identifying the 613 Mitzvos. They learned and reviewed the Mitzvos every month and counted them again and again till they knew them by heart. I myself can testify that I saw the Rav Hagaon, Moreinu Naftali Zilberberg of Warsaw spend his time from his learning studying in depth Sefer HaMitzvos. I would frequently see him counting the Taryag Mitzvos on his fingers and indeed, he told me on his death bed when he no longer had the mind to learn Torah b'iyun, that "a Jew still has an obligation to learn Torah while he is dyeing as it says אדם כי ימות באהל upon which Chazal say אפילו בשעת מיתה תהא עוסק בתורה, even in the last hour of one's life, one should be busy learning Torah. I am now fulfilling this Chazal by counting the Taryag Mitzvos on my fingers." That is why it is a Mitzvah to know them by heart. Indeed, in his very last seconds of his life, he was so weak, yet his fingers were still busy counting Taryag Mitzvos.

---

34. End of the Sefer, Chatima Gimel.
35. In his introduction to the Mitsvos.

#28

The Rav, haTzadilk, R' Mottel Slonimer זצ"ל

He would review every single day the entire Taryag Mitzvos and he knew them so well that he was able to recite them by heart in the gaps of time between his many duties. He would constantly emphasize the importance of teaching children to know all Taryag Mitzvos by heart. He claimed in the name of Rabbi Mendel of Vitebsk זי"ע that this is the meaning of שימה בפיהם, "place it your mouths"[36] refers to Taryag Mitzvos.[37]

#29

Hagaon Rav Yosef Chaim Zonnenfeld זצ"ל

Instead of teaching his son to recite a *drasha* at his bar-Mitzvah, Rabbi Zonnenfeld learned with him Taryag Mitzvos and declared: "A soldier who does not know the Kings instructions will not be able to serve the King. How can my son enter עול המצות without knowing the Mitzvos Hashem has given him?

Summary:

#1 **Sefer Charedim & Divrei Chayim**: "I want to be a good Soldier"

#2 **Messilas Yesharim**: If I really Love my beloved, I will search out every nuance that makes him happy. Demonstrate my love for Hashem

#3 **Sefer Charedim**: How else can I do Teshuva if I don't know all the Lavim?

#4 **Messilas Yesharim**: I will not lose the countless opportunities to earn Olam Haba

#5 **Rambam, Hilchos Lulav**: Being Happy and In love with Hashem

#6 **Rambam, Hilchos Temura**: To be cognizant that the Mitzvos have the power to help me overcome the Yetser Hara and refine my character.

#7 **Sefer HaMitzvos Hakatzer**: מצות דאורייתא צריכות כונה, so one has to know all the Mitzvos D'Oraissa to have kavana for them.

#8 **Num.15:39 Mitzvos Tzitzit**: predicated on knowing the 613 Mitzvos to do them.

#9 **Sefer Chareidim**: One should recite the Taryag Mitzvos every day /week in order to be aware of the opportunities to do Hashem's Mitzvos and one should learn them by heart.

#10 **Sefer Chareidim**: Start the day with a verbal reading of the entire Taryag Mitzvos and then reciting them from memory.

#11 **The Smak**: Reciting Taryag Mitzvos is counted as having done them! Learn two or three Mitzvos a day in depth.

#12 **R' Chaim Vital** z"l: A Jew has to fulfil all 613 Mitzvos in thought, words and action. When reciting all 613, he is fulfilling all three!

#13 **Ohr HaYashar**: Learn Rambam's Mishnah Torah or his Sefer HaMitzvos in order to know Taryag Mitzvos in depth too.

#14 **The Shach in Poel Tzedek**: reciting Taryag Mitzvos each day counts as fulfilling the instruction from Yehoshua to never stop learning Torah by day or night - לֹא־יָמוּשׁ סֵפֶר הַתּוֹרָה הַזֶּה מִפִּיךָ וְהָגִיתָ בּוֹ יוֹמָם.

#15 **Rabeynu Yitzchak Katz**: If one did not fulfil Taryag Mitzvos in his life, he has to return as a Gilgul, a recycled soul. But reciting all 613 Mitzvos counts as though one did them, so he saves himself from Gilgul with such a simple recital!

---

36. Dev. 31:19
37. When offering a verse for an action, one is elevating that action to a D'oraissa!

#16 **The Chidda** z"l: Follow the advice of the Shach, recite all Taryag Mitzvos, at least once a week and it literally counts as though he did them all!

#17 **The Radvaz:** Carry a pocket version of Taryag Mitzvos wherever you go and review them daily.

#18 **Shlah HaKadosh**: Anyone who loves Hashem should commit TaryagMitzvos to memory till he has immediate retrieval of the Passuk of the Mitzvah.

#19 **Shlah HaKadosh**: Only by learning all Taryag Mitzvos can one complete the Tikkun to his 365 איברים and 248 גידים. One first needs to only learn Taryag Mitzvos in order to bring him to do them and become a ירא חטא.

#20 **Sefer Derech Chaim**: Learn 100 Mitzvos per day and 13 on Shabbos, thus completing them all once a week.

#21 **Shulchan Aruch HaRav**: Happy is the one who comes here (into the world to come) **with his learning in his hand**, in order that he will not have to return to this world again. '**with his learning in his hand**' refers to Taryag Mitzvos.

#22 **Ohr HaShanim**: Every Melamed should teach his students all Taryag Mitzvos inside the passukim with Rashi. Or at least the Mitzvos applicable today.

#23 **R' Moshe Leib M'Sassov**: Start teaching all Taryag Mitzvos thoroughly, only then learn pilpul, in great depth.

#24 **R' Moshe Hassid of Prague**: Once you know Taryag Mitzvos really well and by heart, you never have to worry about bitul Torah because you can so easily review the Mitzvos at any time. Review three Mitzvos every day for two or three days and keep doing this every day of your life! Eventually, the Taryag Mitzvos will be so ingrained in your mind and on the tip of your tongue so you will never forget them.

#25 **Rabbi Greenwald from Poppa**: A way to remember the Taryag Mitzvos is to mechadesh, find some new insight of your own in each Mitzvah.

#26 **The Chafetz Chaim in Shmiras Halashon**: Without knowing Taryag Mitzvos, we are not able to completely fulfil the Mitzvah of wearing Tzitzis.

#27 **R' Mottel Slonimer**: Teach children to know all Taryag Mitzvos by heart. He claimed this is the meaning of שימה בפיהם, "place it your mouths" refers to Taryag Mitzvos.

#28 **Harav from Petisberg in Hadras Melech**: Learn and review the Mitzvos every month till you know them by heart. Count the Taryag Mitzvos on your fingers, it helps to remember them.

#29 **Rav Yosef Chaim Zonnenfeld**: Taught his son Taryag Mitzvos in place of a Bar Mitzvah drasha because he exclaimed: How can my son enter the עול המצוות without knowing What Hashem instructs him?

Chapter 3:
How Much Does Hashem Really Love Us?

The answer is related to Taryag Mitzvos. Why does Hashem give us so many Mitzvos with literally thousands of details related to many of them?[38] Because He loves us so! Yes, His love for is infinite,[39] He gave us many Mitzvos in order to give us unlimited chances to gain merit, both in this world and the next. We remind ourselves of this great love each time we recite the Mishna before Kaddish after learning Torah together:

רַבִּי חֲנַנְיָא בֶּן עֲקַשְׁיָא אוֹמֵר,
רָצָה הַקָּדוֹשׁ בָּרוּךְ הוּא לְזַכּוֹת אֶת יִשְׂרָאֵל, לְפִיכָךְ הִרְבָּה לָהֶם תּוֹרָה וּמִצְוֹת, שֶׁנֶּאֱמַר (ישעיה מב) יְיָ חָפֵץ לְמַעַן צִדְקוֹ יַגְדִּיל תּוֹרָה וְיַאְדִּיר:

Hashem Loves us so much that He credits us with the reward for a Mitzvah even before it's done!

Shaarey Teshuva or Rabeynu Yona, Shaar Sheni, Paragraph #10.
שערי תשובה, שער שני, אות י

"In the moment a Jew commits with all his heart to do a Mitzvah, Hashem does not wait to give him the שכר *for that Mitzvah after he does it, Hashem gives him the reward in the moment of commitment!!"* [40]

Rabeynu Yona offers the following proof for this amazing love Hashem has for us, that He wants to give us reward as soon as we intend to do a Mitzvah. He quotes Shemos 12:28 - "וילכו ועשו בני ישראל" " Beney Yisrael went and did (the Mitzvah of shechting the Korban Pesach)." Asks the Mechilta[41] 'But did they really do the Mitzvah of slaughtering the Pesach immediately after they were commanded? וכי מיד עשו? They did not slaughter it till the fourteenth of Nissan! והלא לא עשו עד ארבעה עשר לחודש. So why does the Torah write that they did the Mitzvah immediately? The answer is because as soon as they accepted to do the Mitzvah, the Torah writes it as though they had immediately performed the Mitzvah.

אלא, כיון שקבלו עליהם לעשות, מעלה עליהם הכתוב כאילו עשו מיד

---

38. For example, the one Mitzvah in the Torah to not do Melacha on Shabbos (Ex. 20:5) only states a mere four words - לֹא־תַעֲשֶׂה כָל־מְלָאכָה yet there are literally tens of thousands of details related to the 39 forbidden Melachos. This is a typical example of just one of the 613 Mitzvos which itself has thousands upon thousands of details related to its performance.
39. As we declare every Shachris in the Beracha before Shem Yisrael אַהֲבָה רַבָּה אֲהַבְתָּנוּ and again in Maariv where the entire Beracha is about Hashem's unlimited love for us, in both the opening and closing words, and in between, the entire text is all about how His Mitzvos are what we rejoice in because He loves us so: אַהֲבַת עוֹלָם בֵּית יִשְׂרָאֵל עַמְּךָ אָהָבְתָּ, תּוֹרָה וּמִצְוֹת, חֻקִּים וּמִשְׁפָּטִים אוֹתָנוּ לִמַּדְתָּ. עַל כֵּן יְיָ אֱלֹהֵינוּ, בְּשָׁכְבֵנוּ וּבְקוּמֵנוּ נָשִׂיחַ בְּחֻקֶּיךָ, וְנִשְׂמַח בְּדִבְרֵי תוֹרָתֶךָ וּבְמִצְוֹתֶיךָ לְעוֹלָם וָעֶד. כִּי הֵם חַיֵּינוּ וְאֹרֶךְ יָמֵינוּ, וּבָהֶם נֶהְגֶּה יוֹמָם וָלַיְלָה, וְאַהֲבָתְךָ אַל תָּסִיר מִמֶּנּוּ לְעוֹלָמִים. בָּרוּךְ אַתָּה יְיָ, אוֹהֵב עַמּוֹ יִשְׂרָאֵל
40. The Torah reveals this concept in the story of the sale of Yosef HaTzadik. It was Reuven suggested they throw him into a pit instead of killing him. His intent was to return later (after his turn taking care of his father) and remove Yosef and return him to his father. However when he did return to the pit and found it empty, it was then he learned that his brothers sold Yosef in his absence. Yet the Torah itself reports Reuven as having actually saved Yosef! (Gen.37:21) וַיִּשְׁמַע רְאוּבֵן **וַיַּצִּלֵהוּ מִיָּדָם**
Then the Torah tells us Reuven's intent was to return Yosef to his father: וַיֹּאמֶר אֲלֵהֶם רְאוּבֵן אַל־תִּשְׁפְּכוּ־דָם הַשְׁלִיכוּ אֹתוֹ אֶל־הַבּוֹר הַזֶּה אֲשֶׁר בַּמִּדְבָּר וְיָד אַל־תִּשְׁלְחוּ־בוֹ **לְמַעַן הַצִּיל אֹתוֹ מִיָּדָם לַהֲשִׁיבוֹ אֶל־אָבִיו**
41. Mechilta on Ex.12:2

That's proof for one Mitzvah, but what if a person told himself he wants to commit to all the Mitzvos? does he get rewarded in one moment with all 613 Mitzvos? Does Hashem's love for us extend so far?

Rabeynu Yona quotes Avos D'Rebi Natan:[42]
כל שמעשיו מרובים מחכמתו, חכמתו מתקיימת שנא' "נעשה ונשמע"
"Whoever has more deeds than wisdom, his wisdom will endure."
Asks Rabeynu Yona: how could it ever be possible for a person to have more deeds than wisdom? We always plan to accomplish much more than we actually do? So how is this ever possible? Rabeynu Yona answers that indeed, it is possible to have more deeds than wisdom because Hashem counts our intent to do good as though it was already done!

באור הדבר, כי האיש אשר קבל על נפשו בלב נאמן לשמור ולעשות על פי התורה אשר יורוהו ועל פי המשפט אשר יאמרו לו היושבים על המשפט, יש בידו מן היום הזה שכר על כל המצות...וכענין מה שאמרו ישראל בסיני נעשה ונשמע, שהקדימו קבלת המעשה על נפשם לפני השמיעה. ובענין אחר לא יתכן שיהיו מעשי האדם מרובים ממה שהוא יודע.

"One who sincerely commits with all his intent to live according to the Torah, both as is stated in the Torah and the Torah Sh'b'al Peh, from that moment onward, Hashem gives him the reward for all the Mitzvos....and this is equivalent to what happened at Matan Torah when we declared "We Shall do and listen" נעשה ונשמע, we committed to do the Mitzvos before we actually did them. There is no other way that a person can do more than his actual wisdom."

This still leaves open a simple question, how can a Jew have intent to perform every Mitzvah in the Torah, not all Mitzvos will ever apply to him? For example, if he is not a Kohen, he can never do the Mitzvos specific to a Kohen. If he is not a Judge, all the mitzvos pertaining to judges will not apply to him, if he never loses a brother in order to perform Yibum, etc. So even if he intends to do all the Mitzvos, he will never be able to. So how can he get rewarded for Mitzvos he cannot do just because he intends to? It just will not help to say "I intend doing all the Mitzvos" and thus be rewarded as Rabeynu Yona just described?

The astonishing answer to this question will demonstrate yet an even higher level of Hashem's love for us. The Ben Ish Chai[43] gives the following answer:[44]

...וידוע שאי אפשר לאדם אחד לקיים כל התרי"ג מצות בפועל, אך על ידי המחשבה שהוא יושב ומצפה "אימתי תבא לידי מצוה זו ואקיימנה או הלואי שהייתי שייך במצוה זו ואקיימנה, נחשב לו כאלו קיים כולם. ולפי זה, אפשר שביום אחד יקיים האדם כל תרי"ג מצות אם יהיה מחשב על כל מצוה בפני עצמה...הנה בזה תרויח אפילו ביום אחד בלבד נחשב לך כאילו עשיתם בפועל.

"It is obvious that one person cannot possibly fulfil all 613 Mitzvos in reality. However, through his intent in his mind whereby he sits down and says "When will I have the opportunity to have this Mitzvah come my way so I can do it?" If he has that intent with all 613 Mitzvos, then Hashem counts

---

42. אבות דרבי נתן פ' כב

43. Famous Kabbalist of 19th Century, In Bagdad. 1839 - 1909. He has been dubbed the 'Baal Shem Tov of the Sefardim' He knew all nigla and nistar and his popularity increases throughout the Torah world. He wrote many responsa, a peirush on all the Aggadata of Shass, he was probably the greatest expert in the writings of the Arizal. He is revered by the entire Torah world as a giant in Tzidkus and Torah. It is said that he learned from Eliyahu HaNavi every Motzei Shabbos. He was a towering personality in Kedusha and Tahara. In fact he only ate chulin b'Tahara!

44. ספר בן איש חי פרשת ואתחנן בהקדמה

is as though he did all Taryag Mitzvos! Accordingly, it is possible for a person to fulfil all 613 Mitzvos in a single day! All he has to do is think about wanting to do each and every one, and Hashem literally counts his intention as though he did all of them in reality!

But Hashem's love for us does not stop there!

The Gemora in Shabbos[45] tells us that when a person is angry, it is equivalent to serving Avoda Zara! Yet another Chazal tells us:

וכל הכופר בע"ז כאילו מקיים כל התורה כולה

"Anyone who denies the validity of Avoda Zara, it is as though he kept the entire Torah!"

How often are you persuaded to serve Avoda Zara and refuse, to then win the reward of having done all the Mitzvos? Do you know anyone who was forced to serve Avoda Zara and refused? Explains the Arizal, how often are we provoked to anger and refuse to be angry? In other words, In one moment of controlling anger one attains 613 Mitzvos!! Is that a good deal? But what if controlling one's anger is hard, surely the reward is greater when a Mitzvah is done with difficulty!

Indeed, Chazal tell us[46] **לפום צרה אגרא**, according to the difficulty is the compensation. How much more reward does one receive for a Mitzvah done with difficulty? Chazal give us the answer to this too:[47]

מוטב מצוה אחת בצער ממאה מצות שלא בצער

One Mitzvah done with difficulty is worth more than a hundred Mitzvos done without difficulty. Wow!

So let's look again at our case of being provoked to anger and refusing to give in, we said that is equivalent to fulfilling 613 Mitzvos in one moment. But if one succeeds in controlling one's anger and it is hard, that is 613 X 100 = 61,000 Mitzvos in one moment! Is that a good deal?

Does Hashem hate us when He sends us difficult people to provoke our anger, or is He inviting us to earn thousands of Mitzvos in a single moment?

Hashem's love for us does not stop there! When you do a Mitzvah with joy, besimcha, is it worth the same as any other Mitzvah not done בשמחה, or is it worth more?

---

45. Shabbos 105. See also Sifri on Devarim 11:28 for the a similar statement. See also Rashi Devarim. 11:28 quoting this Sifri. הָא לָמַדְתָּ שֶׁכָּל הַכּוֹעֵס כְּעוֹבֵד עֲבוֹדַת כּוֹכָבִים הֲרֵי הוּא סַר מִכָּל הַדֶּרֶךְ שֶׁנִּצְטַוּוּ יִשְׂרָאֵל, מִכָּאן אָמְרוּ, כָּל הַמּוֹרֶה בַּעֲבוֹדַת כּוֹכָבִים כּוֹפֵר בְּכָל הַתּוֹרָה כֻּלָּהּ

46. Avos: 5:22
47. Avos D'Rebi Nasan, Ch. #3

Of course it is worth more. How much more? According to Orchot Tzadikim,[48] when doing a Mitzvah with joy, it is worth one thousand times more than a Mitzvah without joy! So now, if a person is being provoked to anger, it is not easy and he conquers his anger with a smile, that is 61,000 X 1,000 which equals sixty one million, three hundred thousand Mitzvos in one moment! Is that a good deal? Does Hashem love us?

But it does not stop there!

When we do a Mitzvah on Shabbos, is it worth the same as a weekday Mitzvah or more because of the infused kedusha of Shabbos? Of course, it is worth more. How much more? Claims the Ben Ish Chai, Mitzvos done on Shabbos are worth one thousand times more! Now do the math! It's Shabbos and you are provoked to anger, you conquer the urge to be enraged, and do so with a smile, so now that is 61 Million, three hundred thousand Mitzvos times 1000!! That equals 61 BILLION, THREE HUNDRED MILLION Mitzvos in one moment!! Does Hashem love us?

---

48. Orchot Tzadikim, Shaar Simcha

PART II

How to Teach the Taryag Mitzvos

Chapter 4:

The Order of the Mitzvos:

The most popular lists of Taryag Mitzvos are:
1. **Rambam's** list in the Mishnah Torah[49]
2. **Rambam's** list of all the Aseh and lo Ta'aseh in Sefer HaMitzvos.
3. The **Chinuch's** list of Taryag Mitzvos as they appear sequentially in the Chumash.
4. Sefer **Chareidim's** list of Mitzvos as they pertain to different parts of the body.

We will be focusing on Rambam's list of Mitzvos as found in the Mishnah Torah. This list lends itself to memorization because the Mitzvos are listed in categories which Rambam carefully organized to facilitate memorization. But first we want to show you how you can teach children about 100 Mitzvos in less than an hour! Then we will teach you how you can teach the children the Taryag Mitzvos as they appear in Rambam's list.

Follow the Child

Shlomo Hamelech, חכם מכל אדם, states:[50] "Train the student according to his way." So how can I teach Taryag Mitzvos עַל־פִּי דַרְכּוֹ according to his way?

STEP ONE:
Teach the Mitzvos the child is already familiar with.

We have provided below some of the more familiar Mitzvos as well as others that are very easy to teach if you are using the Taryag Picture cards that come with this manual.[51] There are many Mitzvos that are less familiar, but a simple picture will create a deep enough impression that the student will immediately remember that Mitzvah when he sees the picture again.

(In the list below there is a number after the Code Name to indicate which Picture Card to find this Mitzvah in the second half of this manual).

---

49. This list sequences the 613 Mitzvos according to categories. For example, all Mitzvos spread throughout the Torah that are relevant to Avoda Zara are organized in one category called Hilchos Avodas Kochavim.
50. Mishley 22:6 - חֲנֹךְ לַנַּעַר עַל־פִּי דַרְכּוֹ גַּם כִּי־יַזְקִין לֹא־יָסוּר מִמֶּנָּה
51. See www.breakthroughchinuch.com for a list of products under the Taryag Mitzvos category.

#	Mitzvah	Page
1.	Hashem is One	3
2.	Love Hashem	4
3.	Have Emuna in Hashem	1
4.	Love other Jews	13
5.	Love the convert	14
6.	Tzitzit	84
7.	Tefilin shel Rosh	79
8.	Tefilin Shel Yad	80
9.	Shema	76
10.	Tefila	77
11.	Kiddush & Havdala	91
12.	Mezuza	81
13.	Live in a Sukkahh seven days	117
14.	Listening to the Shofar	116
15.	Shake the Lulav	118
16.	Learn and Teach Torah	22
17.	Show Kavod to Talmidey Chachamim	23
18.	Don't hate another Jew	15
19.	Don't speak Lashon Hara	19
20.	Don't embarrass someone	17
21.	Kibud Av V'Em	584
22.	Keep your promises	214
23.	Don't wear Shaatnez. (wool and linen together)	238
24.	Give Tzedaka	250
25.	Don't refuse to give Tzedaka	251
26.	Do Teshuva for Aveiros	75
27.	Return lost object to its owner	480
28.	Return a stolen object	478
29.	Don't harm someone else's body	481
30.	Don't hurt people with words	501
31.	Don't hurt a convert with words	503
32.	Take chala from the dough	273
33.	Don't kill	482
34.	Don't kidnap	473
35.	Don't steal	467
36.	Don't rob	474
37.	Don't serve Avoda Zara	28
38.	Destroy Avoda Zara	53
39.	Don't let a Witch or Wizard live	552
40.	Lend money to the poor	526
41.	Don't do Melacha on Shabbos	88
42.	Don't do Melacha on the 1st day of Pesach	97
43.	Don't do Melacha on the 7th day of Pesach	99

44.	Don't do Melacha on Shavuos	101
45.	Don't do Melacha on Rosh Hashana	103
46.	Don't do Melacha on Yom Kippur	93
47.	Fast on Yom Kippur	94
48.	Don't do Melacha on the 1st day of Sukkos	105
49.	Don't do Melacha on the 7th day of Sukkos	107
50.	Rest on Shabbos	87
51.	Rest on the 1st day of Pesach	96
52.	Rest on the 7th day of Pesach	98
53.	Rest on Shavuos	100
54.	Rest on Rosh Hashana	102
55.	Rest on Yom Kippur	92
56.	Rest on 1st day of Sukkos	104
57.	Rest on 7th day of Sukkos	107
58.	Count the Omer	384
59.	Destroy Chametz on Erev Pesach	109
60.	Eat Matza on first night of Pesach	114
61.	Don't eat Chametz 7 days	110
62.	Tell the story of Yetzias Mitzrayim on the 1st night of Pesach	115
63.	Don't cut Peos of the head	68
64.	A man cannot wear women's clothes	70
65.	A woman cannot wear men's clothes	71
66.	Don't make a tattoo on your skin	72
67.	Birkas Kohanim	78
68.	Birkas Hamazon	85
69.	Write a Sefer Torah	82
70.	A King must write his own Sefer Torah	83
71.	Bris Mila	86
72.	Don't eat Treif meat	190
73.	Know which animals are Kosher	176
74.	Know which birds are Kosher	177
75.	Know which fish are kosher	178
76.	Know which locusts are kosher	179
77.	Don't eat blood	192
78.	Don't eat flying insects	183
79.	Don't eat crawling insects	184
80.	Don't eat water insects	187
81.	Don't eat worms in fruit	186
82.	Don't eat maggots	185
83.	Don't eat milk and meat together	195
84.	Don't cook meat and milk together	196
85.	Shecht an animal in a kosher way	204
86.	Don't marry a non-Jew	162
87.	Don't steal someone elses wife (adultery)	160

88.	Don't marry a father (Mishkav Zachur)	158
89.	Don't marry another man	157
90.	Don't marry an uncle	159
91.	Don't marry your mother	139
	(We use the word 'marry' here in reference to arayus, and all the next 17 examples below)	
92.	Don't marry your step-mother	140
93.	Don't marry a sister	141
94.	Don't marry a half-sister	142
95.	Don't marry a granddaughter (son's daughter)	143
96.	Don't marry a granddaughter (daughter's daughter)	145
97.	Don't marry a daughter	144
98.	Don't marry a mother and daughter	146
99.	Don't marry a mother and granddaughter (mother and her son's daughter)	147
100.	Don't marry a mother and granddaughter (mother and daughter's daughter)	148
101.	Don't marry your aunt (father's sister)	149
102.	Don't marry your aunt (mother's sister)	150
103.	Don't marry your aunt (Uncle's wife)	151
104.	Don't marry your daughter-in-law	152
105.	Don't marry your sister-in-law (brother's wife)	153
106.	Don't marry your sister-in-law (your wife's sister)	154
107.	A man cannot marry an animal	155
108.	A woman cannot marry an animal	156
109.	Make a Ma'aka (fence around a flat roof)	494
110.	Don't leave things in places a person could trip	493
111.	Help another Jew unload heavy things	496
112.	Help others to load their heavy things.	497
113.	Do business honestly, according to Torah law	499
114.	Don't cheat in business	500
115.	Don't cheat a convert in business	502
116.	Pay your day worker on time	518
117.	Don't delay paying your worker	519
118.	Don't muzzle an animal while it is ploughing	523
119.	A Jewish King cannot have more than 18 wives	591
120.	A Jewish King cannot have too many horses	594
121.	A Jewish King cannot have too much money	595

Because many of the Mitzvos above are part of the child's cultural environment and Jewish calendar, you are maximizing the likelihood of the child remembering the Mitzvah and enjoying learning about them.

Using the picture cards of Taryag Mitzvos you will be able to teach many more Mitzvos than just those the child is familiar with. That's because the picture 'speaks a thousand words,' meaning it prints the information in the mind of the child at a much deeper level of penetration than just teaching the information verbally.

Using the Taryag Picture cards, the children will:
1. Remember the Mitzvos more easily,
2. They will receive a massive head start with being able to learn easily a hundred Mitzvos in just a couple of sessions.
3. Teaching familiar Mitzvos and easy to remember Mitzvos with the Picture cards will help motivate the children to want to know more.
4. Learning with pictures helps convince the child that learning Taryag Mitzvos is easy and not hard.

STEP TWO:
Challenge the students to organize the Mitzvos themselves.

Bring to class the following Seforim:
1. *Sefer HaMitzvos of the Rambam*
2. *One of the Sefarim of Rambam's Yad Chazaka, Mishnah Torah*
3. *One copy of Sefer HaChinuch*
4. *One copy of Sefer Chareidim*

Once you have taught the children about a hundred Mitzvos or more with the pictures, and they know them really well,[52] you can then ask the children to think of ways to organize the Mitzvos. Let them surprise you...and they will!

For example, ask: 'Children, what ways can you think of to help us sort the Mitzvos? Are their some piles we could make of one type of Mitzvah and another pile for a different type of Mitzvah?"

One kid will probably tell you that we can separate the Mitzvos into two piles, one pile of the dos and another of the dont's. Then you can say *"Wow, Moshe! You just had the same idea as Rambam!"* Now walk to the 6,000-year time line [53] on the classroom wall and show them where Rambam lived. if you can have an actual **Sefer HaMitzvos** of the Rambam for this lesson, pull it out in view of the children and show the class how the Rambam thought of the same idea as Moshe over here. Moshe will feel so happy and he will feel a personal connection to Rambam.

---

52. On the back of each picture card of Taryag Mitzvos is a short essay of essential information on that Mitzvah. See also how to teach 'Which Mitzvah Am I Cards' showing how to teach each Mitzvah in more detail.
53. See Contextual Education Teacher's Manuals Part 1 & 2 by Jonathan Rietti.

Another student might suggest sequencing the Taryag Picture cards in the order of the Mitzvos as they appear in the Torah. That is your cue to say *"Wow! Mordecai, you have the same idea as Sefer HaChinuch!* And show the class your **Sefer HaChinuch**. Again, walk over to the Time Line and show them when the Author of Sefer HaChinuch lived and where.[54] He lived soon after the Rambam and also from Spain.

Next, ask the students if there are any other ways they can think of to sort and arrange the Mitzvos. At some point, one student will offer to sort them out according to bunches, or categories. Then you can show them how Rambam did exactly that in his other, much bigger work on Taryag Mitzvos, the **Mishnah Torah**. Again, pull out a copy or show them an entire set and again, walk to the Time Line reminding where and when Rambam lived.

Don't be surprised if eventually one student figures out how to make piles of Mitzvos according to the part of the body which does that Mitzvah. That's your cue to introduce **Sefer Chareidim**,[55] which indeed, lists the Mitzvos of the Torah according to the body part it is performed by.

Listed below are the four main ways to organize the Mitzvos:
1. Two Piles of Cards, one pile of Asehs and one pile of Lo Ta'asehs.[56]
2. Piles of Cards for that weeks Parsha.[57]
3. Pile the Picture Cards in bunches. (We will cover this in more detail below)
4. Pile the Mitzvos according to the body parts.

Now we can teach them a system for memorizing the Mitzvos.

STEP THREE:
How to memorize Taryag Mitzvos
The two most popular systems of listing Taryag Mitzvos are the Rambam's Mishnah Torah and Sefer HaChinuch. How to memorize the Rambam' list is fully outlined in the Taryag Mitzvah Codes in the other half of this manual. We will give a brief summary here:

After the children learn a new Mitzvah, using the Taryag Picture cards, we assign a 'Hebrew Code Word' for each Mitzvah. The full listing of the code words is in the end of this manual. Sometimes we assign two words for a Mitzvah. So, for example, the Mitzvah of Tzitzis has one code word, yes! You guessed correctly - ציצית. The code word for Love of Hashem is אהבת ה', the code word for the Mitzvah to live in a Sukkah is simply סוכה.

---

54. The author lived in Barcelona, Spain and the most compelling evidence suggests it was written in the years 1252-1256. Though the actual authors name and identity is not certain, the amazing work of Minchas Chinuch reveals that the author had the mind and mastery of Talmud and legal codes to be one of the Rishonim. See translators preface to the English edition of Sefer HaChinuch by Charles Wengrov, Feldheim Publishers, second edition 1992.
55. Written by Rabbi Elazar Azikri (1533-1600). The author was a great mekkubal and leader in Tzefat during the time of the Arizal, Rabbi Yitzchak Luria. Sefer Chareidim was later condensed into an abridged version called Kitzur Chareidim by the author of the Chayey Adam, Rabbi Avraham Danzig from Vilna.
56. As is the system of Sefer HaMitzvos, Smag and Smak.
57. For example, Parshas Bo will have 20 Taryag Mitzvah cards, Beshalach has one, Yisro has 17, etc,.

The point here is that the child is being taught to memorize 613 words associated to the Mitzvos and their Picture. In Rambam's listing of the Mitzvos, he has categorized them under 14 books, and then subdivided those books into a total of 83 sub-sections.

All Taryag Mitzvos are then categorized under one of those 83 sub-sections. So, for example, Rambam lists the first ten Mitzvos under the section called Yesodey HaTorah, they are the fundamental Mitzvos upon which the entire Torah depends. They are:

1. Know Hashem (the Mitzvah of Emuna)
2. There are no other powers beside Him
3. He is ONE
4. Love Hashem
5. Fear Hashem
6. Be a Kiddush Hashem
7. Don't be a Chillul Hashem
8. Don't destroy His Name
9. Listen to His Prophets
10. Don't over-test the Prophet

The assigned code word/s for each of the above Mitzvos is the following:[58]

1. אמונה
2. זולתו
3. אחד

Notice how these three Mitzvos are so closely related;
- To know Hashem Exists - אמונה;
- No other power exists besides Him - זולתו; and
- He is One - אחד.

So we grouped them together and this becomes an even easier way to memorize the Mitzvos because you are only memorizing 1-3 Mitzvos in sequence at a time.[59]

See what happens to the next four Mitzvos and how obvious it is that they are bunched together because of their immediate association:

4. אהבת ה'

---

58. Before every sub-section, Rambam gives a very clear list of the Mitzvos he is dealing with in that section and numbers them, we are quoting for you his exact words in his introduction to the first sub-section of the Book of Mada, called Yesodey HaTorah:
הלכות יסודי התורה. יש בכללן עשר מצות, שש מצות עשה, וארבע מצות לא תעשה. וזהו פרטן: (א) לידע שיש שם אלוה. (ב) שלא יעלה במחשבה שיש שם אלוה אחר זולתי ה'. (ג) ליחדו. (ד) לאהבו. (ה) ליראה ממנו. (ו) לקדש שמו. (ז) שלא לאבד דברים שנקרא שמו עליהם. (ח) שלא לחלל שמו. (ט) לשמוע מן הנביא המדבר בשמו. (י) שלא לנסותו. וביאור כל המצות האלו בפרקים אלו.

59. In fact the reason why phone numbers are divided into groups of 3 or 4 numbers is because research has demonstrated that the average mind does not need a system to memorize between 1-5 items in perfect sequence. From 5-8 items, the average mind can remember in sequence if it is important to them to really remember, but beyond 8 items, the vast majority of minds need a system to connect the items. So phone numbers are broken down into groupings of 3-4 numbers! When I first learned this in Page a Minute Memory Book by Harry Lorraine and Jerry Lucus, I then reviewed the Taryag Mitzvos of the Rambam and found that almost always, there was an obvious bunching, grouping of Mitzvos within every one of the 83 categories, and that the vast majority of the time it was 2-3 Mitzvos and only 5 times were there 5 Mitzvos obviously associated and only 3 times were there 6 Mitzvos bunched together, but never more than six! I am under the impression that Rambam knew he was listing them in a sequence that made it easier for the student to memorize the Mitzvos by heart.

5. **יראת ה'**

And the next two:

6. **קדוש ה'**
7. **חלול ה'**

And next to Chilul Hashem is:

8. **לאבד** (don't destroy any item with Hashem's Name on it. This Mitzvah is associated to Chilul Hashem, not to desecrate Hashem's Name).

Then again, 9 and 10 are grouped together:

9. **לשמוע** (Listen to Hashem's Navi)
10. **לנסות** (Don't over-test the Navi)

There you are! The first ten Mitzvos of Rambam, organized and 'grouped' together in a way that helps memorization.[60]

We suggest teaching only 1-3 new Mitzvos a day, and quickly review with the children all the Mitzvos learned till now. (Reviewing the code names only takes minutes!)

---

60. See the last paragraph of Rambam's introduction to his Mishneh Torah where he spells out the reason he wrote his work in this format, according to the listing of Taryag Mitzvos as grouped in the divisions he selected:

וראיתי לחלק לחבור זה הלכות הלכות בכל ענין וענין. ואחלק ההלכות לפרקים שבאותו ענין. וכל פרק ופרק אחלק אותו להלכות קטנות כדי שיהיו סדורים על פה....מפני שחילוק חיבור זה לפי הענינים לא לפי המצות כמו שיתבאר לקורא בו. ומנין מצות התורה הנוהגת לדורות שש מאות ושלש עשרה מצות. מהם מצות עשה מאתים וארבעים ושמונה, סימן להם - מנין אבריו של אדם. ומהם מצות לא תעשה שלש מאות וששים וחמש, סימן להם - מנין ימי שנת החמה.

Chapter 5:

Playing Games with the Taryag Picture Cards

1. Which Mitzvah Is This Picture?

When using the Taryag Picture cards[61], pull out different Picture Cards (that they have learned) and ask them "which Mitzvah is this?" They can answer in their own words (so if you pull out a picture of Tefilin Shel Rosh, they might answer "It's a Mitzvah to wear Tefilin on the head").

2. Team Games for 'Which Mitzvah is this Picture?'

Divide class into two teams or groups. Give out a stack of picture cards (they have already learned) to one group and another stack to another group and have them quiz each other. The same can be done with pairs of students, each student holds a stack of about 10 Taryag Picture cards and they take turns pulling out one at a time and asking their partner "which Mitzvah is this?"

3. Teaching some details about each Mitzvah

As they gradually master the picture on each card, you can introduce more information about each Mitzvah. On the back of each Taryag Mitzvah card is a short description of the Mitzvah in both Hebrew and English, plus the Torah source for the Mitzvah. We have separate cards with short essays giving some basic halachos, information and Hashkafa about the Mitzvah.

4. Hebrew Code Name Strips

With this program comes the 'Hebrew Code Name' strips. These are strips of cards with the Hebrew Code Name for each Mitzvah. These strips have the code name on one side and the number it corresponds to in the listing of the Rambam on the other side. This number is for the child to self-correct[62] so that when he places the Code Name Strip beneath the Mitzvah, he can check if he is right by turning over the strip to see if its number corresponds to the Picture Card he matched it to. You can give a child a number of strips and ask him to find the Taryag Picture cards that match the Code Name Strip and have him lay out the picture cards with their code Name strip beneath the picture. You can have the class split into teams or 'chevrusas' and one team or partner has a bunch of say 10 strips, while the other partner or team have the picture cards and they take turns reading out a Code Name and the other partner or team have to pull out its corresponding Picture. For example, the 'Code Name' strip 'השם אחד' is matched with the Taryag Picture Card with the Number 1 on it, and the 'Code Name' 'אהבת ה'' is matched with the Picture card with a heart and the letter 'ה' inside the heart.

5. English Code Word Strips.

These are the same as the Hebrew Code Name Strips, just in English. So, for example you will have the English Code Name 'ONE' and match it with the Picture Card which has the number 1 on it, referring to the Mitzvah that Hashem is One. The English Code Name strip 'Love Hashem' is matched with the picture of the heart with 'ה' inside the heart referring to the Mitzvah to love

---

61. We have created picture cards and many other educational products that help reinforce the memory of the Taryag Mitzvot. They are effective for children and adults alike. Please see the back of this book for a full list of products or visit our website: www.breakthroughchinuch.com
62. For him to check that he got the right code word for the right picture.

Hashem. You can do the same games and activities described above where one student pulls out a picture and his partner or other team has to pull out its equivalent code name.

6. Passukim Strips

As the children are learning the Mitzvos from the Taryag Picture Cards and their equivalent Hebrew Code Name, eventually they will be ready to learn the Passuk that is the source of that Mitzvah in the Torah. For this, we have provided Passuk Strips for you to have the children learn the passuk associated with the Picture Card and match it to the picture. Engage the children in the same activities suggested above for the Hebrew Code Words and English Code Names. You are gradually building their knowledge of Taryag Mitzvos, each day learning 1-3 new Mitzvos and then adding those new ones to the daily review, and each day learn some more details about the Mitzvos with lots of review.

7. Which Mitzvah Am I Cards

This is a very exciting component of the Taryag Mitvos Program. The 'Which Mitzvah Am I Cards' are one card per Mitzvah, each card has a list of clues on one side of the card. Each clue is easier than the previous clue till finally you ask "Which Mizvah Am I?" to the child. On the other side of the card is the answer. For example, here is a list of clues:

- I am a garment
- I have a hole in the middle
- I have four corners
- I have five knots at the end of each corner
- I have eight strings at the end of the five knots
- My name has the Gematria of 600
- Add my 5 knots and 8 strings and it equals 13
- When you look at me you are reminded of all the Taryag Mitzvos
- Which Mitzvah Am I ?

Then on the back of the card is the answer **Tzitzit**.

The purpose of putting the information about a Mitzvah into 'Clue' format is to make the child an 'active learner.' He is being challenged to think. Now he is learning the information in an active way as opposed to passively listening to halachos about a Mitzvah. The clues also make it more engaging for the child and more enjoyable. Each clue being successively easier helps the child be able to get the right answer. Thus increasing the child's ability to be successful.

Initially the teacher will read out the Which Mitzvah Am I Cards. But once the students know how to read English well enough to read these cards themselves, they can take a pack of Which Mitzvah Am I Cards and quiz each other in pairs or groups. A set of simple instructions come with the set of Which Mitzvah Am I Cards.

6. Knowing Where the Mitzvah is in the Torah

The Memorization of Taryag Mitzvos as listed by Sefer HaChinuch works by memorizing the chapter in which each Mitzvah can be found. We are not going to learn the Mitzvos according the number assignment of the Chinuch. The Chinuch lists the Mitzvos as they appear in sequence in the

Torah. He assigns a number to each Mitzvah to a total of 613 Mitzvos. It is possible to memorize them in this sequence, however there are two reasons we are not using this method:

Firstly, to memorize 613 Mitzvos in sequence according numbers 1-613 takes more effort to associate a specific Mitzvah to a number for 613 numbers than to remember which Chapter the Mitzvah is in.[63]

Secondly, though it is certainly worth the investment of time to memorize the Mitzvos in their number format from 1-613, it does not yield the same usefulness as knowing where the Mitzvah is in the Torah.[64] This is doubly true when you consider that there is not a single reference to the Mitzvos in this numbered format beside Sefer HaChinuch and the Minchas Chinuch. All other systems of reference[65] relate to the chapter number in which the Mitzvah appears or the parsha it appears in.

To know where each Mitzvah is in the Chumash is much more useful, and is easier to memorize than knowing its number as referenced in the Chinuch. Consider that the highest number of chapters you will ever find in all Chumash is 50 (in Bereishis).[66] You only need a system to memorize up to 50 numbers. To this goal, we offer two methods:

Method #1 for memorizing where Taryag Mitzvos are in Chumash

Adapting a classical memory system that substitutes the 9 digits 1-9 and 0 for actual letters from the Alphabet, we have presented here a simple method for taking 50 words corresponding to 1-50. Each word assigned to that number is also a picture in the mind. Now we take that word/picture (which is also a number) and make a story that contains that word/picture and associate that story with the equivalent chapter number and information contained in that chapter.[67] The entire system is outlined in the Memory System Manual which is 'Building Block of Chinuch' #6. So for example, the first 9 chapter numbers of every Chumash are assigned a word that rhymes with that number.

1 = Sun

2 = Glue

3 = Tree

4 = Door

5 = Hive

6 = Sticks

7 = Heaven

8 = Gate

9 = Wine

---

63. For example, between just two parshios, Mishpatim and Ki Tetzey, there are 133 Mitzvos shared between only 6 Chapters. So instead of having to memorize 133 numbers for 133 Mitzvos, you only have to remember 6 numbers! Pretty good deal!
64. If you ask the question 'why did Sefer HaChinuch and others list the Mitzvos 1-613 and not according to the chapters, that is for a very simple reason, the Chapter number divisions were not in existence till the 13th Century! We need to appreciate that before printing presses, all texts were scrolls and if you wanted to find information, you had to have pretty much memorized the contents in order to be able to navigate the text. The problem of the texted scroll before the index and table of contents was that for all the information contained in a scroll, it was impossible to navigate. Our Torah was learned and reviewed both from childhood and read publicly so that a person would have a decent chance of finding information based on the break down of Parshios, but there are no actual parsha headings in the Torah scroll, the reader had to know how to navigate the petuchos and s'tumos and deliberate gaps in margins to find information.
65. Meaning to say, whenever the Mishna or Gemora or any sefer quotes a passuk that is a one of the Taryag Mitzvos, it quotes the chapter you will find it in, it NEVER quotes which number Mitzvah it is according to Sefer HaChinuch! So memorizing the numbers 1-613 has no useful applications in being able to reference the Mitzvos elsewhere other than Sefer HaChinuch itself and the Minchas Chinuch.
66. Shemos has 40 chapters, Vayikra has 27, Bamidbar 36 and Devarim 34. So if you have a memory system that is like having 50 files in your mind, you can use the same system to cover the entire Chumash. Actually, all the books of Nevi'im Rishonim are also less than 50 chapters, so the same filing system can be used for all of Yehoshua, Shoftim, Shmuel I & II and Melachim I & II.
67. See Building Block of Chinuch #6, Memory Systems. You can order the memory system from www.breakthroughchinuch.com

Now we summarize the essential information in each chapter into a simple 'one line summary.' Then we associate the summary line with the number. So for example, in Chapter #1 (Sun) Hashem created the universe. So we make an association with that information and the Sun. When Hashem created the universe He created ONE SUN in our local solar system. In chapter #3, for example, is the story of the snake enticing Chava and in turn both Adam and Chava ate from the TREE and were cursed with the Snake. So as a summary of that Chapter, we will say 'the story of the snake.' Now we take that summary and associate it with our number-word assigned to that chapter. In this case it is 3 - TREE, so just imagine the snake in the tree persuading Chava to eat from the TREE in Chapter THREE.

After chapter nine, we switch to another method[68] where each number from 1-9 and Zero are assigned a letter, similar to Gematria.

1 = T or D[69]
2 = N[70]
3 = M[71]
4 = R[72]
5 = L[73]
6 = J or Sh or Ch[74]
7 = K[75]
8 = F or Ph[76]
9 = P[77] or b
0 = Z[78]

---

68. You cannot find single words to rhyme with numbers in the teens and beyond.
69. This is a phonetic system which means that very similar sounding letters are the same numeric value, so because T and D are similar in sound, they both equal the number 1. A simple way to remember T and D are one is because they each have one down stroke.
70. Turn N on its side and it has a similar shape to 2. Also, N has TWO down strokes.
71. Turn M on its side and it looks like the number 3.
72. A way to remember R is 4 is to count how many letters in the word FOUR, and which is the 4th letter? R.
73. When the cops stop the traffic, what shape letter do they make with their 5 fingers? That's right, they make the letter L shape with their FIVE fingers. So, L is 5.
74. Again, because this is a phonetic system, the letters which sound very similar share the same number value. Thus, J which is 6 (Turn 6 around and it resembles the shape of a J) has a similar sound to Ch and Sh. So Ch and Sh also have a numeric value of 6.
75. Look carefully at the letter K and see how many shapes of 7 inside the K? K is the exact same sound as hard C and very similar in sound to G so both hard C and hard G are 7 as well.
76. When you write an F in script, it is similar in shape to 8. F has the exact same sound as Ph and is also very similar in sound to V. So both Ph and V are also 8.
77. If you put a mirror in front of the number 9, you will have a P as its reflection, and because b is a similar sound to P, both P and b are the number 9. If you invert the 9 you will get a b shape.
78. You can remember Z is a ZERO because Zero begins with a Z. S and soft c are very close in sound to the sound of a Z and therefore have the same value 0.

There are very few rules in this memory system. Beside memorizing these 9 digits and Zero with their equivalent number value, the only major rule to remember is:

Rule #1
All vowels have no numeric value, so **a**, **e**, **i**, **o** and u mean nothing at all. Neither do **h**, **y** and **x**.

So if you have the word DaTe. D = 1 and 'a' is a vowel, so it does not count, T is also 1 and 'e' is a vowel so the number DaTe is 11. TiN is 12 because T is 1, 'a' does not count, and N is 2.

Rule #2
If you have a word that has a letter repeated twice together, you only count one. So, for example, TuMmy, has M twice, but you only count one, so TuMmy is 13, not 133.

The entire list of words that have a value of 10-50 are listed in the Memory System Manual. Here they are for fast reference.
11 = DaTe or TeDdy
12 = TiN
13 = TuMmy
14 = TiRe
15 = TaLe
16 = DiSH or TiSH
17 = DoC. (as in Doctor) or DocK
18 = DoVe
19 = TuB
20 = NoSe
21 = NuT
22 = oNioN
23 = NaMe
24 = NeRo
25 - NaiL
26 = NoSH
27 = NecK
28 = kNiFe[79]
29 = NoB or NiB
30 = MouSe
31 = MaT
32 = MooN
33 = MuMmy
34 = MoweR
35 = MuLe
36 = MatCH
37 = MucK (as in Mud) or MiC. as in short for Microphone.
38 = MuFf

---

79. Again, because this is a phonetic memory system, we do not count a letter than cannot be heard, so in this example of 'knife' where the 'k' of knife is not pronounced, one does not count it as a number, so kNiFe is 28.

39 = MoP

40 = RoSe

41 = RoD

42 = RaiN

43 = RaM

44 = RoweR or RR for Rolls Royce (exensive car)

45 = RaiL

46 = RaSH

47 = RocK or RaKe

48 = RooF

49 = RoPe

50 = LiCe or LaCe

Because we are using rhyming words for the first nine numbers 1-9, you only need to memorize the numbers from 10 to 35 because there are no mitzvos in chapters beyond 35 [80] in all of Chumash.[81] Here are some examples of how to memorize Mitzvos in the Torah according to their chapter number:

The Mitzvah to Shecht the Korban Pesach is in chapter #12 of Shemos, parshas Bo. In the system just described above, 12 = TiN. So you would now associate the Mitzvah of Shechting a Korban Pesach with TiN. You could have a TiN can whose sharp lid was used to Shecht the korban pesach. On the TiN you could see in your imagination a list of halachos of the Korban pesach. Another example could be 'Ahavas Yisrael' as in the Mitzvah of ואהבת לרעך כמוך as found in Chapter #19 of Parshas Kedoshim in Vayikra. The picture for number 19 is TuB. (T = 1 and B = 9). So you could imagine standing by a bath TuB in the street for all Jews who need to wash their faces from dirt.

---

80. The entire Chumash Bereishis has 50 chapters, however, there are only three Mitzvos of all 613 in the entire Bereishis, (the Mitzvah of P'ru U'rvu in Chapter #1, the Mitzvah of Bris Milah in Chapter #17 and Gid Hanasheh in Chapter #32). The Most number of chapters in Shemos is 40 (the last Mitzvah in entire Shemos is in Vayakhel, Chapter #35 not to judge cases of capital punishment on Shabbos). Vayikra only has 27 Chapters, Bamidbar has 36 Chapters of which the last Mitzvah in all Bamidbar is in Chapter #35 (don't take Kofer (ransom money to release an unintenional manslaughterer from going to an Arey Miklat). Devarim has a total of 34 Chapters of which the last Mitzvah in Devarim is in Chapter #31, to write a Sefer Torah). So really you only need to know the numbers 10 through 35 in the list above. That's just 25 words and their associated picture and number in order to remember where all the 613 Mitzvos are located in Chumash.

81. See footnote #78 above.

Method #2 for memorizing where Taryag Mitzvos are in Chumash

If you prefer to use a memory system that works with the letters of the Aleph Bais, you can use the list below to create files in your mind to then associate the Mitzvah in that chapter to the picture of that chapter number:

א = Chief (Aluf in Hebrew is a Chief. (see picture of an Indian Chief)

ב = Bayit (see picture of a house with chimney, windows and front door)

ג = Gamal (see picture of camel)

ד = door

ה = Hay, see a stack of Hay

ו = Hook, see Vav in the shape of a hook ו

ז = Weapon (a כלי זין is a weapon in Hebrew) see a sword.

ח = See a Gate, Chess has the shape of a gate.

ט = See a smiley face[82]

י = See a hassidish YiD - יָד with streimel and peios, you need 10 YiDin to make a Minyan.

יא = See a 10 Amos high Ladder. יא stands for יְ אַמּוֹת

יב = See the giant YishBee יִשְׁבִּי (he was the brother of Goliat) or see a Bee which is יב read backwards.

יג = See bottle of wine יג stands for יין גפן

יד = Yud, see a hand

טו = Trumpet, see a trumpet going TOOO TOOO as in "טו טו"

טז = TieS / ToeS / ToyS

יז = See a Clock, יש זמן , or Yo Yoz (as in Yo Yoos)

יח = See Siddur open at Shomeh Esrei. יח = שמונה עשרה.

יט = Matza as a symbol of Yom Tov - יוֹם טוֹב

כ = Cup of Coffee or CuFF (as in Cuffs at the bottom of one's trousers, pants)

כא = Kibud Av - כַּבוּד אָב (see a son bringing tray of food to his father)

כב = Hammer - כְּלִי בַּרְזֶל or CaB as in taxi CAB - כב

כג = See Kohen Gadol, כ"ג - כהן גדול

כד = Barrel - כַּד in Hebrew is a Barrel

כה = Kiseh Hakavod, a throne, כסה הכבוד

כו = Periscope, see the vav atop the end of the chaff.

כז = Golden Cup - כלי זהב or KeyS or an olive - KZayis - כזית

---

[82]. The first time the letter ט is found in the Torah at the beginning of a word is in the word טוב (Bava Kama 55) so we are using a smiley face to denote ט.

כח = See strong man holding up bar of weights. The weights at the end of the bars are כלי חרס

כט = Scissors (cut - כַּט) or CaT or CoaT

ל = Lightening, see lightening come down in shape of a Lamed ל

לא = See a STOP sign. לא means no! or stop!

לב = See a Heart - Lev - לֵב

לג = LoG, see a long log of wood. Or an Eraser, as in לא גרסינן

לד = LiD or LOD airport

לה = see sign for NO LASHON HORA

לו = is gematria 36, see 36 Tzadikim hiding, 36 hidden tzadikim.

לז = Grave Stone with Z"L on it. לז backward is זכרונו לברכה - ז"ל

לח = Sponge, because it is a דבר לח. לח means 'wet,' thus a sponge.

לט = LighT

מ = Water[83] (see water coming out of the spout of the מ like a watering can)

מא = Megilas Ester - מְגִילַת אֶסתר or Mateh Aharon - מטה אַהרן

מב = MoB (as in a riot) or מַכַּת בְרד

מג = MuG or מַעלה גֵרה

מד = MuD (as in muck)

מה = MaH is a Mummy, as in ancient Egyptian Mummy. Or Malach Hamaves - מַלאך הַמות

מו = Mooo as in a cow going "mooo."

מז = MaZe

מח = Brain as in מֹחַ

מט = MaT as in door mat

נ = Fish (Aramaic, נִין is a fish).

7. Matrices for Taryag Mitzvos according to the Chinuch:

Match the Hebrew and English Name Words with their corresponding Picture card, then place the Passuk Strip with its Chapter # beneath the code names. Place these cards vertically in the order in which they appear in the Torah under the Parsha of the Torah in which they appear. The Children will see the distribution of the Mitzvos within the Torah. The Matrix Chart for this could go horizontally from right to left with Parshas Bereishis being on the far left with only one Mitzvah under it (Mitzvas P'ru Urvu) all the way to Zos HaBracha to the far right with the one Mitzvah of כתיבת ס"ת under it. For example, first place down the picture of the Mitzvah, say Bris Mila, then beneath the picture place the Hebrew Code Name ברית מילה and beneath that card, place the English

---

83. The first appearance of מ in the Torah at the beginning of a word is מים. According to the Vilna Gaon on Bava Kama 55, מים is the essence of מ. See footnote 94 above.

Code Name 'Circumcision' and then place the passuk strip beneath that. Do this with each Mitzvah in a parsha or perek of a parsha for the children to see how the Mitzvos unfold in front of them according to their appearance in the Torah.

8. Matrices for Taryag Mitzvos according to Rambam[84]

Similar to the Matrix of Mitzvos according to the Chinuch above, take the same materials; Hebrew and English Code Names, the Taryag Picture Cards and the Passuk Strips and match them together. This time, the order of the Mitzvos will be according to how Rambam lists them in his Mishnah Torah. So the first ten Mitzvos will be laid down in a vertical row under the heading of Yesodei HaTorah with the picture of Emuna and its matching Hebrew English Code Names and Passuk Strip, followed by the Picture for זולתו and then אחד each with their matching code words and passuk strips. Please call us for the name cards for all 14 books of Yad Hazakah and name cards for all 83 sub-categories of the 14 books, together with the symbols for the 14 books and symbols for the 83 sub-categories. The children line up the Mitzvos vertically in the order they are listed under each sub-category.

9. Matrices for Taryag Mitzvos לפי ספר חרדים (according to body parts) :

Make a large outline of the human body on cardboard, or a large piece of paper. Then have the children go through one Taryag Mitzvah card at a time, identifying which body part that Mitzvah is performed by. You can print labels of the body parts, (both in English and Hebrew) brain, hands, legs, etc, and place those on the outline of the human body. The Picture cards can be stacked in a pile next to the body part label or you can make the body part labels with an arrow shape at one end of the card for the child to match it against its corresponding body part.

Another way to do this is pin the outline onto the wall and stick envelopes on the various body parts and then have the children place the Taryag Picture cards in the relevant envelope. You can buy Sefer Chareidim or the Kitzur version as a reference for all the body parts and their corresponding Mitzvos.

10. Taryag Mitzvah Books

Have children make their own Taryag Mitzvah book. They would take one of the Taryag Mitzvah Cards to copy (the stick picture version of the Taryag Mitzvos, they are very easy for the child to copy). The student draws a one Mitzvah per page and labels it (using the Hebrew and/or English Code Name), you collect the pages and collate them into books i.e. first 30 Mitzvos would be volume one, till he has his own version of Taryag Mitzvos. He can make this a project over the entire school year. The student can choose to make his book in the order of the Rambam, Chinuch or Chareidim.

11. Taryag Mitzvah Scroll

Another application can be making a scroll of the pictures he makes instead of a book. Have the student tape the pictures he makes into a scroll.

---

84. In his Yad Hazakah.

PART III

The Taryag Mitzvos Outline

Chapter 6:

Introduction to the Taryag Mitzvos Outline

The entire spectrum of Torah finds its roots in the 613 Mitzvot.

The Purpose of the Outline:
This section lists the 613 Mitzvot in abbreviated form so that one can memorize 613 abbreviations of all the Mitzvot.

How to Use the Outline:
To accomplish this, one or two key words have been selected to represent each Mitzva. The list of Mitzvot is according to Rambam (as found in his table of contents to the Mishnah Torah). Rambam divided the 613 Mitzvot under 83 headings.

To increase the efficiency of the memorization, the Mitzvot have been bunched according to their immediate association with the other Mitzvot in each category.

In this section you will find a list containing three parallel columns. The first column gives a simple description in English of the Mitzva. The second column gives a simple description in Hebrew. The third column contains the one word in Hebrew that represents that Mitzva, or as we are calling it a 'Code Name' for that Mitzvah.

The easiest way to memorize the 613 Mitzvot is accomplished in 3 stages:
1. Study two to five Mitzvot each day.
2. The following day, review the past Mitzvot you committed to memory and then learn another two to five Mitzvot.
3. Each day you review the previous Mitzvot, read through the list of 'Code Names' till the Mitzva you are up to.

If each Code Name triggers in your mind the Mitzva represented by that word, your review is working, if the corresponding Mitzva does not come into your mind by use of the 'one word' trigger, then, simply review that Mitzva in the first listing. If the information in the first list is not sufficient to understand that Mitzva, research more information about that Mitzva[85] till the one-word representation triggers off the memory of that Mitzva.

---

85. If you are unfamiliar with a Mitzva and the English and Hebrew descriptions in the first list are not sufficient description, then refer to the more full description found in Sefer HaMitzvot of the Rambam, or the listing of the Taryag Mitzvot in Sefer HaChinuch. You can also refer to the English translations available. There is 'The Taryag Mitzvot' published by CIS in Lakewood, and 'The Mitzvot' by Rabbi Abraham Chill (Keter Books, Jerusalem). Rabbi Wax of The Taryag Foundation (732-942-3420) has produced a wonderful rendering of the Taryag Mitzvot on 613 Mitzva Cards, offering the essential information for each Mitzva. In preparation is an encyclopedic work in English of the Taryag Mitzvot also written by Rabbi Wax. Artscroll has published Sefer HaChinuch with complete translation and extensive footnotes. The Yahadus Curriculum has provided an excellent resource for learning more details about Tarayg Mitzvot. Each volume is beautifully illustrated and it follows the listing of Rambam's Yad Chazaka. Their contact information is 1-347-709-8660 or www.livinglessons.com and info@livinglessons.com.

As the days turn into weeks, the accumulative review will result in you memorizing hundreds and hundreds of the Mitzvot in sequence till you memorize all six hundred and thirteen. Once you have committed them all to memory, you will still find it helpful to review the Mitzvot once a week from the second 'one-word' listing. You will find that it takes about eight minutes to review the entire 613 Mitzvot by memorizing the one-word representations!

Your success is not dependent on your intelligence,
Your success depends on your discipline and persistence!

Even if you find yourself distracted or your daily review of the Taryag Mitzvot is interrupted, start again and keep going, just two to five new Mitzvot each day till you commit them all to memory. You are not in a race, you are building a foundation upon which to organize all your future learning (and past learning!). Once you have memorized Taryag Mitzvot you will have the awesome ability to think about them in the many pockets of time during your day, waiting on line in a store, in traffic (keep your eye on the road!), even while you chew your food! removing your Tefilin, walking to Shul on Shabbat and back, etc,. As you reinforce your memory with each review, you will find it easier to think about the Mitzvot at will.

May our efforts to memorize the Taryag Mitzvot give Hashem great Nachat Ruach and bring us special heavenly assistance in our Torah learning and may we all merit to see the גאולה שלימה speedily in our days, Amen.

THE 14 CATEGORIES OF THE TARYAG MITZVOT				
Instructions on How to Know G-d	Mada	מדע		1
Instructions on How to Love G-d	Ahava	אהבה		2
Instructions Performed at Designated Times	Zemanim	זמנים		3
Instructions for Marriage and Divorce	Nashim	נשים		4
Instructions that Make a Jew Kadosh	Kedusha	קדושה		5
Instructions Pertaining to the Power of Speech	Hafla'ah	הפלאה		6
Instructions Pertaining to Agriculture	Zera'im	זרעים		7
Instructions Pertaining to the Temple Service	Avoda	עבודה		8
Instructions Pertaining to the Temple Offerings	Korbanot	קרבנות		9
Instructions for Spiritual Purity	Tahara	טהרה		10
Instructions Pertaining to all types of Damages	Nezikin	נזיקין		11
Instructions for Acquisitions	Kinyan	קנין		12
Instructions for Rentals, Borrowing, Loans & Litigations	Mishpatim	משפטים		13
Instructions for the Judicial System	Shoftim	שופטים		14

83 Sub-Divisions of the Taryag Mitzvot

Book 1: מדע
Instructions on How to Know G-d

Laws of the Fundamentals of Monotheism	יסודי התורה	1
Laws of Thinking & Excellence in Character	דעות	2
Laws of How to Learn Torah	תלמוד תורה	3
Laws of Idol Worship	עובדי כוכבים	4
Laws of Personal Transformation	תשובה	5

Book 2: אהבה
Instructions on How to Love G-d

Laws of Reciting the Shema Yisrael	קריאת שמע	1
Laws of Prayer & the Priestly Blessing	תפלה וברכת כהנים	2
Laws of Tefilin, Mezuzot & Torah Scrolls	תפילין, מזוזות, וספר תורה	3
Laws of Tzitzit	ציצית	4
Laws of Blessings	ברכות	5
Laws of Circumcision	מילה	6

Book 3: זמנים
Instructions Performed at Designated Times

Laws of the Shabbat	שבת	1
Laws of Eruvin (Rabbinical)	עירובין	2
Laws of Yom Kippur	שביתת עישור	3
Laws of Festivals	שביתת יום טוב	4
Laws of Chametz & Matzah	חמץ ומצה	5
Laws of Blowing the Shofar	שופר	6
Laws of Living in the Sukkah	סוכה	7
Laws of the Lulav	לולב	8
Laws of the Shekalim Tax	שקלים	9
Laws of Sanctifying the New Moon	קידוש החודש	10
Laws of Fast Days	תענית	11
Laws of Megilla and Chanuka (Rabbinical)	מגילה וחנוכה	12

Book 4: נשים
Instructions for Marriage and Divorce

Laws of Marriage	אשות	1
Laws of Divorce	גירושין	2
Laws of Yibum & Chalitza	יבום וחליצה	3
Laws of a Besula	נערה בתולה	4
Laws of a Sota	סוטה	5

Book 5: קדושה
Instructions that Make a Jew Kadosh

Laws of Forbidden Relationships	איסורי ביאה	1
Laws of Forbidden Foods	מאכלות אסורות	2
Laws of Ritual Slaughter	שחיטה	3

Book 6: הפלאה
Instructions Pertaining to the Power of Speech

Laws of Oaths	שבועות	1
Laws of Promises	נדרים	2
Laws of the Nazir	נזירות	3
Laws of Evaluations & Dedications	ערכין וחרמים	4

Book 7: זרעים
Instructions Pertaining to Agriculture

Laws of Forbidden Mixtures	כלאים	1
Laws of Gifts to the Poor	מתנות עניים	2
Laws of Agricultural Tithes to the Kohen	תרומות	3
Laws of Agricultural Tithes to the Levi	מעשר ראשון	4
Laws of Tithes to Oneself & 4th Year Plantings	מעשר שני ונטע רבעי	5
Laws of First Fruits	ביכורים	6
Laws of Shemita & the Jubilee Years	שמיטה ויובל	7

Book 8: עבודה
Instructions Pertaining to the Temple Service

Laws of the Temple	בית בחירה	1
Laws of Temple Furnishings & Its Workers	כלי המקדש והעובדים בו	2
Laws of Entering the Temple Site	ביאת המקדש	3
Laws of Forbidden Offerings	איסורי מזבח	4
Laws of Offerings	מעשה הקרבנות	5
Laws of Daily & Additional Offerings	תמידין ומוספים	6
Laws of Offerings that Become Invalid	פסולי המוקדשים	7
Laws of the Yom Kippur Service	עבודת יום הכיפורים	8
Laws of Misuse of Temple Property	מעילה	9

Book 9: קרבנות
Instructions Pertaining to the Temple Offerings

Laws of the Pascal Lamb	קרבן פסח	1
Laws of the Festival Offering	חגיגה	2
Laws of First-Born	בכורות	3
Laws of Offerings for Unintentional Sins	שגגות	4
Laws of People Who Need Atonement	מחוסרי כפרה	5
Laws of Exchanged Animal Offerings	תמורה	6

Book 10: טהרה
Instructions for Spiritual Purity

Laws of Contact with a Corpse	טומאת מת	1
Laws of the Red Hefer	פרה אדומה	2
Laws of Tzara'as	טומאת צרעת	3
Laws of Mishkav U'Moshav	טומאת משכב ומושב	4
Laws of Other Major Causes of Tumah	שאר אבות הטומאה	5
Laws of Tumah Contracted with Food & Drink	טומאת אוכלין	6
Laws of Tumah Through Vessels (Rabbinic)	כלים	7
Laws of The Mikveh	מקואות	8

Book 11: נזיקין
Instructions Pertaining to all Types of Damages

Laws of Monetary Compensation for Damage	נזקי ממון	1
Laws of Stealing	גניבה	2
Laws of Theft, Lost & Found	גזילה ואבידה	3
Laws of Physical Harm and Damage	חובל ומזיק	4
Laws of Murder & Protecting Lives	רוצח ושמירת הנפש	5

Book 12: קנין
Instructions for Acquisitions

Laws of Sales	מכירה	1
Laws of Bequeathing and Gifting (Rabbinic)	זכיה ומתנה	2
Laws Relating to Neighbors (Rabbinic)	שכנים	3
Laws for Appointing Agents and Partnerships (Rabbinic)	שלוחים ושותפים	4
Laws relating to Treatment of Servants	עבדים	5

Book 13: משפטים
Instructions for Rentals, Borrowing, Loans & Litigations

Laws Relating to Rentals	שכירות	1
Laws of Borrowing and Collateral	שאלה ופקדון	2
Laws of Lending and Borrowing	מלוה ולוה	3
Laws of Claims and Defense	טוען ונטען	4
Laws of Inheritance	נחלות	5

Book 14: שופטים
Instructions for the Judicial System

Laws Relating to the Supreme Court	סנהדרין	1
Laws of Witnesses	עדות	2
Laws of Obedience to Authority	ממרים	3
Laws of Mourning	אבל	4
Laws of Kings and Warfare	מלכים ומלחמותיהם	5

Taryag Mitzvos Cards Icons

Icon	Hebrew / English	Icon	Hebrew / English
✓	מצות עשה — Mitzvos one must do	✗	מצות לא תעשה — Mitzvos one must not do
	אנשים — Mitzvos for Men		אנשים — Mitzvos for Men
	נשים — Mitzvos for women		נשים — Mitzvos for women
	מצות לכהנים — Mitzvos for *kohanim*		מצות לכהנים — Mitzvos for *kohanim*
	סקילה — Death by Stoning		שריפה — Death by Burning
	הרג (סייף) — Death by the sword		חנק — Death by Choking
	מלקות — Lashes		כרת — Early Death
	מצות ארץ ישראל — Performed in Israel Only		מיתה בידי שמים — Death by the Hand of Heaven
	מצות תמידיות — Constant Mitzvos		ירושלים — Performed in Jerusalem Only

Key

List of Mitzvos According to the Rambam

סֵפֶר מַדָּע	1-75	
סֵפֶר אַהֲבָה	76-86	
סֵפֶר זְמַנִּים	87-121	
סֵפֶר נָשִׁים	122-138	
סֵפֶר קְדוּשָׁה	139-208	
סֵפֶר הַפְלָאָה	209-233	
סֵפֶר זְרָעִים	234-300	
סֵפֶר עֲבוֹדָה	301-403	
סֵפֶר קָרְבָּנוֹת	404-442	
סֵפֶר טָהֳרָה	443-462	
סֵפֶר נְזִיקִין	463-498	
סֵפֶר קִנְיָן	499-516	
סֵפֶר מִשְׁפָּטִים	517-539	
סֵפֶר שׁוֹפְטִים	540-613	

Chapter 7:

The Taryag Mitzvos Outline

Book 1: Instructions on How to Know Hashem : סֵפֶר מַדָּע

Section 1: Laws of The Fundamentals of The Torah : יְסוֹדֵי הַתּוֹרָה
(10 Mitzvos)

1	אֱמוּנָה	לֵידַע שֶׁיֵּשׁ שָׁם אֱלוֹקַ	Know Hashem exists
2	זוּלָתוֹ	לֹא יַעֲלֶה בְּמַחֲשָׁבָה שֶׁיֵּשׁ זוּלָתוֹ	Know there is no other power except Hashem
3	אֶחָד	לְיַחֲדוֹ	Know that Hashem is One

4	אַהֲבַת ה׳	לְאַהֲבוֹ	Love Hashem
5	יִרְאַת ה׳	לְיִרְאָה מִמֶּנּוּ	Be in awe of Hashem

6	קִדּוּשׁ ה׳	לְקַדֵּשׁ אֶת שְׁמוֹ	Be a Kiddush Hashem
7	חִלּוּל ה׳	לֹא לְחַלֵּל אֶת שְׁמוֹ	Don't be a chillul Hashem
8	לְאַבֵּד	שֶׁלֹּא לְאַבֵּד דְּבָרִים שֶׁשְּׁמוֹ עֲלֵיהֶם	Don't destroy an item with Hashem's Name on it

9	לִשְׁמֹעַ	לִשְׁמֹעַ מִן הַנָּבִיא הַמְדַבֵּר בִּשְׁמוֹ	Listen to a real Navi of Hashem
10	לְנַסּוֹת	שֶׁלֹּא לְנַסּוֹתוֹ	Don't over-test Hashem or His Navi

Book 1: Instructions on How to Know Hashem: סֵפֶר מַדָּע

Section 2: Laws of Thinking & Excellence in Character: דֵּעוֹת
(11 Mitzvos)

11	לְהִדַּמּוֹת	לְהִדַּמּוֹת בִּדְרָכָיו	Learn and copy Hashem's ways
12	לְהִדָּבֵק	לְהִדָּבֵק בְּיוֹדְעָיו	Be close to Hashem by being close to Tzadikim & Talmidei Chachamim
13	אַהֲבָה	לֶאֱהֹב אֶת יִשְׂרָאֵל	Love every Jew
14	אַהֲבָה	לֶאֱהֹב אֶת הַגֵּרִים	Love a Ger Tzedek
15	שִׂנְאָה	שֶׁלֹּא לִשְׂנֹא יִשְׂרָאֵל	Don't hate other Jews
16	תּוֹכֵחָה	לְהוֹכִיחַ	Gently correct another Jew
17	הַלְבָּנָה	שֶׁלֹּא לְהַלְבִּין פָּנִים	Don't embarrass others
18	עִנּוּי	שֶׁלֹּא לְעַנּוֹת אֻמְלָלִים	Don't hurt children or adults who have nobody to defend them
19	רְכִילוּת	שֶׁלֹּא לֵילֵךְ רָכִיל	Don't speak Lashon Hara
20	לִנְקֹם	שֶׁלֹּא לִנְקֹם	Don't take revenge
21	לִנְטֹר	שֶׁלֹּא לִנְטֹר	Don't keep remembering other people's mistakes

Book 1: Instructions on How to Know Hashem: סֵפֶר מַדָּע

Section 3: Laws of How to Learn Torah: תַּלְמוּד תּוֹרָה

(2 Mitzvos)

Learn & Teach Torah	לִלְמֹד וּלְלַמֵּד תּוֹרָה	לִלְמֹד וּלְלַמֵּד	22
Respect Torah teachers	לְכַבֵּד מְלַמְּדֶיהָ וְיוֹדְעֶיהָ	לְכַבֵּד	23

Book 1: Instructions on How to Know Hashem: סֵפֶר מַדָּע

Section 4: Laws of Avodah Zara: עוֹבְדֵי כּוֹכָבִים
(51 Mitzvos)

English	Hebrew	Key Word	#
Don't think about Avoda Zara or find out how to do it	שֶׁלֹּא לִפְנוֹת אַחַר עֲבוֹדָה זָרָה	לִפְנוֹת	24
Don't trust everything you think and see	לֹא לָתוּר אַחַר הַלֵּב וְהָעֵינַיִם	תָּתוּרוּ	25
Don't curse Hashem	שֶׁלֹּא לְגַדֵּף	לְגַדֵּף	26
Don't serve Avoda Zara even to throw stones at it	שֶׁלֹּא יַעֲבֹד אוֹתָהּ כְּדֶרֶךְ עֲבוֹדָתָהּ	כְּדַרְכּוֹ	27
Don't serve idols in the 4 ways we serve Hashem	שֶׁלֹּא יִשְׁתַּחֲוֶה לַעֲ"ז	הִשְׁתַּחֲוָה	28
Don't make Avoda Zara for yourself	שֶׁלֹּא לַעֲשׂוֹת פֶּסֶל לְעַצְמוֹ	פֶּסֶל	29
Don't make Avoda Zara to sell to others	שֶׁלֹּא לַעֲשׂוֹת פֶּסֶל אֲפִלּוּ לַאֲחֵרִים	פֶּסֶל	30
Don't make full human statues even for decorations	שֶׁלֹּא לַעֲשׂוֹת צוּרוֹת אֲפִלּוּ לְנוֹי	צוּרוֹת	31
Don't persuade a city to follow Avoda Zara	שֶׁלֹּא לְהַדִּיחַ אֲחֵרִים אַחֲרֶיהָ	לְהַדִּיחַ	32
Burn an עִיר הַנִּדַּחַת, a city which served Avoda Zara	לִשְׂרֹף עִיר הַנִּדַּחַת	לִשְׂרֹף	33
Don't rebuild an עִיר הַנִּדַּחַת	שֶׁלֹּא לִבְנוֹתָהּ	לִבְנוֹת	34
Don't benefit from an עִיר הַנִּדַּחַת	שֶׁלֹּא לֵהָנוֹת מִכָּל מָמוֹנָהּ	לֵהָנוֹת	35

Book 1: Instructions on How to Know Hashem : סֵפֶר מַדָּע

Section 4: Laws of Avodah Zara : עוֹבְדֵי כּוֹכָבִים
(continued)

Don't persuade anyone to serve Avoda Zara	שֶׁלֹּא לְהָסִית יָחִיד לְעָבְדָהּ	לְהָסִית	36
Don't love a missionary	שֶׁלֹּא לֶאֱהֹב הַמֵּסִית	לֶאֱהֹב	37
Don't stop hating a missionary	שֶׁלֹּא לַעֲזֹב שִׂנְאָתוֹ	לִשְׂנֹא	38
Don't save a missionary's life	שֶׁלֹּא לְהַצִּילוֹ	לְהַצִּיל	39
Don't say anything in a missionary's defence	שֶׁלֹּא לְלַמֵּד עָלָיו זְכוּת	זְכוּת	40
Don't avoid giving testimony against a missionary	שֶׁלֹּא יִמָּנַע מִלְּלַמֵּד עָלָיו חוֹבָה	חוֹבָה	41

Don't say Nevua in the name of Avoda Zara	שֶׁלֹּא לְהִתְנַבֵּא בְּשֵׁם ע״ז	לְהִתְנַבֵּא	42
Don't listen to a Navi Sheker	שֶׁלֹּא לִשְׁמֹעַ מִן הַמִּתְנַבֵּא בִּשְׁמָהּ	לִשְׁמֹעַ	43
Don't give false Nevua in Hashem's Name	שֶׁלֹּא לְהִתְנַבֵּא בְּשֶׁקֶר אֲפִלּוּ בְּשֵׁם הַשֵּׁם	שֶׁקֶר	44
Don't be afraid to kill a Navi Sheker	שֶׁלֹּא לָגוּר מֵהֲרִיגַת נְבִיא שֶׁקֶר	לַהֲרֹג	45
Don't swear in the name of Avoda Zara	שֶׁלֹּא לְהִשָּׁבַע בְּשֵׁם ע״ז	לְהִשָּׁבַע	46

Don't do an act of Ov	שֶׁלֹּא לַעֲשׂוֹת מַעֲשֵׂה אוֹב	אוֹב	47
Don't do an act of Yidoni	שֶׁלֹּא לַעֲשׂוֹת מַעֲשֵׂה יִדְּעוֹנִי	יִדְּעוֹנִי	48
Don't pass children in the fire of Molech	שֶׁלֹּא לְהַעֲבִיר לַמֹּלֶךְ	מֹלֶךְ	49

Book 1: Instructions on How to Know Hashem :סֵפֶר מַדָּע
Section 4: Laws of Avodah Zara :עוֹבְדֵי כּוֹכָבִים
(continued)

Don't build a stand for Avoda Zara	שֶׁלֹּא לְהָקִים מַצֵּבָה	מַצֵּבָה	50
Don't bow down on smooth stone	שֶׁלֹּא לְהִשְׁתַּחֲווֹת עַל אֶבֶן מַשְׂכִּית	אֶבֶן	51
Don't plant trees in the courtyard of the Bais Hamikdash	לֹא לִטַּע אֲשֵׁרָה	אֲשֵׁרָה	52
Destroy Avoda Zara	לְאַבֵּד ע״ז וְכָל הַנַּעֲשֶׂה בִּשְׁבִילָהּ	לְאַבֵּד	53
Don't benefit from Avoda Zara	שֶׁלֹּא לֵהָנוֹת בְּע״ז וּמִשַּׁמְּשֶׁיהָ	לֵהָנוֹת	54
Don't benefit from ornaments of Avoda Zara	שֶׁלֹּא לֵהָנוֹת בְּצִפּוּי נֶעֱבָד	צִפּוּי	55
Don't make agreements with people who serve Avoda Zara	שֶׁלֹּא יִכְרֹת בְּרִית לְעוֹבְדֵי ע״ז	בְּרִית	56
Don't show favor to those who serve Avoda Zara	שֶׁלֹּא יָחֹן עֲלֵיהֶם	יָחֹן	57
Don't let anyone who serves Avoda Zara live in Eretz Yisrael	שֶׁלֹּא יֵשְׁבוּ בְּאַרְצֵנוּ	יֵשְׁבוּ	58
Don't copy the customs or clothing of people who serve Avoda Zara	שֶׁלֹּא לִנְהֹג כְּמִנְהֲגֵיהֶם וּכְמַלְבּוּשֵׁיהֶם	חֻקֹּת	59
Don't be superstitious	שֶׁלֹּא לְנַחֵשׁ	לְנַחֵשׁ	60
Don't go into a trance to see the future	שֶׁלֹּא לִקְסֹם (מְגַלֶּה עֲתִידוֹת)	לִקְסֹם	61
Don't read the future using astrology	שֶׁלֹּא לְעוֹנֵן (אַסְטְרוֹלוֹגְיָה)	לְעוֹנֵן	62
Don't say magic spells	שֶׁלֹּא לַחְבֹּר חָבֶר	לַחְבֹּר	63
Don't try to contact the dead	שֶׁלֹּא לִדְרֹשׁ אֶל הַמֵּתִים	לִדְרֹשׁ	64

Book 1: Instructions on How to Know Hashem: סֵפֶר מַדָּע

Section 4: Laws of Avodah Zara: עוֹבְדֵי כּוֹכָבִים

(continued)

65	אוֹב	שֶׁלֹּא לִשְׁאֹל בְּאוֹב	Don't consult an Ov
66	יִדְעוֹנִי	שֶׁלֹּא לִשְׁאֹל בְּיִדְעוֹנִי	Don't consult a Yidoni
67	לְכַשֵּׁף	שֶׁלֹּא לְכַשֵּׁף	Don't perform acts of magic
68	פְּאַת הָרֹאשׁ	שֶׁלֹּא לְהַקִּיף פְּאַת הָרֹאשׁ	Men must not shave the hair from the sides of their head
69	פְּאַת הַזָּקָן	שֶׁלֹּא לְהַשְׁחִית פְּאַת הַזָּקָן	Men must not shave any of the 5 corners of their beard
70	נָשִׁים	שֶׁלֹּא יִלְבַּשׁ אִישׁ בִּגְדֵי אִשָּׁה	Men must not wear women's clothing
71	אֲנָשִׁים	שֶׁלֹּא תִלְבַּשׁ אִשָּׁה בִּגְדֵי אִישׁ	Women must not wear men's clothing
72	קַעֲקַע	שֶׁלֹּא לִכְתֹּב קַעֲקַע	Don't tattoo the skin
73	לְהִתְגּוֹדֵד	שֶׁלֹּא לְהִתְגּוֹדֵד (לִשְׂרֹט עוֹרוֹ כְּשֶׁמִּתְאַבֵּל)	Don't tear the skin in mourning
74	קָרְחָה	שֶׁלֹּא לַעֲשׂוֹת קָרְחָה עַל הַמֵּת	Don't tear out hair and make a bald spot in mourning

Book 1: Instructions on How to Know Hashem — סֵפֶר מַדָּע

Section 5: Laws of Personal Transformation — תְּשׁוּבָה

(1 Mitzvah)

| 75 | תְּשׁוּבָה | שֶׁיָּשׁוּב הַחוֹטֵא מֵחֶטְאוֹ לִפְנֵי הַשֵּׁם וְיִתְוַדֶּה | Admit mistakes and correct them |

Book 2: Instructions on How to Love Hashem: סֵפֶר אַהֲבָה

Section 1: The Laws of Reciting Shema Yisrael (1 Mitzvah)

Say the Shema every morning and night	לִקְרֹא ק"ש פַּעֲמַיִם בְּכָל יוֹם	קְרִיאַת שְׁמַע	76

Section 2: The Laws of Tefila & Birkas Kohanim (2 Mitzvos)

Thank, praise & ask things from Hashem every day	לַעֲבֹד ה' בִּתְפִלָּה בְּכָל יוֹם	תְּפִלָּה	77
Kohanim bless the Jewish people daily	לְבָרֵךְ כֹּהֲנִים אֶת יִשְׂרָאֵל בְּכָל יוֹם	בִּרְכַּת כֹּהֲנִים	78

Section 3: The Laws of Tefilin, Mezuzot & Torah Scrolls (5 Mitzvos)

Wear Tefilin on the head	לִהְיוֹת תְּפִלִּין עַל הָרֹאשׁ	תְּפִלִּין	79
Strap Tefilin on the arm	לְקָשְׁרָן עַל הַיָּד	תְּפִלִּין	80
Fix a Mezuza on each door post	לִקְבֹּעַ מְזוּזָה בְּפִתְחֵי הַשְּׁעָרִים	מְזוּזָה	81
Each Jewish man has to write a Sefer Torah	לִכְתֹּב כָּל אִישׁ סֵפֶר תּוֹרָה לְעַצְמוֹ	סֵפֶר תּוֹרָה	82
The king must write a second Sefer Torah	לִכְתֹּב הַמֶּלֶךְ סֵפֶר תּוֹרָה שֵׁנִי לְעַצְמוֹ וְיִהְיֶה לוֹ שְׁנֵי ס"ת	סֵפֶר תּוֹרָה	83

Section 4: The Laws of Tzitzit (1 Mitzvah)

Tie Tzitzis on clothing with four corners	לַעֲשׂוֹת צִיצִית עַל כַּנְפֵי הַכְּסוּת	צִיצִית	84

Section 5: The Laws of Blessings (1 Mitzvah)

Bless Hashem after eating bread	לְבָרֵךְ אֶת שְׁמוֹ אַחַר אֲכִילָה	בְּרָכוֹת	85

Section 6: The Laws of Circumcision (1 Mitzvah)

Do Bris Mila on the 8th day of every Jewish baby boy	לָמוּל אֶת הַזְּכָרִים בַּיּוֹם הַשְּׁמִינִי	מִילָה	86

Book 3: Mitzvos Designated to Time :סֵפֶר זְמַנִים

Section 1: Laws of Shabbos: שַׁבָּת
(5 Mitzvos)

Rest on Shabbos	לִשְׁבֹּת בַּשְּׁבִיעִי	לִשְׁבֹּת	87
Don't do Melacha on Shabbos	שֶׁלֹּא לַעֲשׂוֹת בּוֹ מְלָאכָה	מְלָאכָה	88
Bais Din cannot give the death penalty on Shabbos	שֶׁלֹּא לַעֲנשׁ בְּשַׁבָּת	עֹנֶשׁ	89
Don't walk outside city boundary	שֶׁלֹּא לָצֵאת חוּץ לַגְּבוּל בְּשַׁבָּת	תְּחוּם	90
Declare Shabbos special with Kiddush and Havdalah	לְקַדֵּשׁ הַיּוֹם בִּזְכִירָה	קִדּוּשׁ	91

Section 2: Laws of Eruvin: עֵרוּבִין
(1 Mitzvah - Rabbinical)

Eruvin - Rabbinical	מִדְּרַבָּנָן	עֵרוּבִין

Book 3: Mitzvos Designated to Time: סֵפֶר זְמַנִים
Section 3: Laws of Yom Kippur: שְׁבִיתַת עָשׂוֹר

(4 Mitzvos)

Rest on Yom Kippur from Melacha	לִשְׁבֹּת בּוֹ מִמְּלָאכָה	לִשְׁבֹּת	92
Don't do Melacha on Yom Kippur	שֶׁלֹּא לַעֲשׂוֹת בּוֹ מְלָאכָה	מְלָאכָה	93

Fast on Yom Kippur	לְהִתְעַנּוֹת בּוֹ	עִנּוּי	94
Don't eat or drink on Yom Kippur	שֶׁלֹּא לֶאֱכֹל וְלִשְׁתּוֹת בּוֹ	אֲכִילָה	95

Book 3: Mitzvos Designated to Time :סֵפֶר זְמַנִים
Section 4: Laws of Festivals :שְׁבִיתַת יוֹם טוֹב
(12 Mitzvos)

Rest on the first day of Pesach	לִשְׁבֹּת בָּרִאשׁוֹן שֶׁל פֶּסַח	פֶּסַח לִשְׁבֹּת	96
Don't do Melacha 1st day of Pesach	שֶׁלֹּא לַעֲשׂוֹת בּוֹ מְלָאכָה	פֶּסַח מְלָאכָה	97

Rest on 7th day of Pesach	לִשְׁבֹּת בַּשְּׁבִיעִי שֶׁל פֶּסַח	פֶּסַח לִשְׁבֹּת	98
Don't do Melacha 7th day of Pesach	שֶׁלֹּא לַעֲשׂוֹת בּוֹ מְלָאכָה	פֶּסַח מְלָאכָה	99

Rest on Shavuos	לִשְׁבֹּת בְּיוֹם חַג שָׁבוּעוֹת	שָׁבוּעוֹת לִשְׁבֹּת	100
Don't do Melacha on Shavuos	שֶׁלֹּא לַעֲשׂוֹת בּוֹ מְלָאכָה	שָׁבוּעוֹת מְלָאכָה	101

Rest on Rosh Hashana	לִשְׁבֹּת בְּרֹאשׁ הַשָּׁנָה	ר"ה לִשְׁבֹּת	102
Don't do Melacha on Rosh Hashana	שֶׁלֹּא לַעֲשׂוֹת בּוֹ מְלָאכָה	ר"ה מְלָאכָה	103

Rest on 1st day of Succos	לִשְׁבֹּת בָּרִאשׁוֹן שֶׁל חַג הַסֻּכּוֹת	סֻכּוֹת לִשְׁבֹּת	104
Don't do Melacha on 1st day of Sukkos	שֶׁלֹּא לַעֲשׂוֹת בּוֹ מְלָאכָה	סֻכּוֹת מְלָאכָה	105

Rest on Sh'mini Atzeres	לִשְׁבֹּת בַּשְּׁמִינִי שֶׁל חַג	שְׁמִינִי לִשְׁבֹּת	106
Don't do Melacha on Sh'mini Atzeres	שֶׁלֹּא לַעֲשׂוֹת בּוֹ מְלָאכָה	שְׁמִינִי מְלָאכָה	107

Book 3: Mitzvos Designated to Time: סֵפֶר זְמָנִים
Section 5: Laws of Chametz and Matzah: חָמֵץ וּמַצָּה
(8 Mitzvos)

Don't eat chametz from midday of the 14th of Nissan	לֹא לֶאֱכֹל חָמֵץ בְּיוֹם י״ד מֵחֲצוֹת הַיּוֹם	ו׳ שָׁעוֹת	108
Destroy all chametz Erev Pesach	לְהַשְׁבִּית שְׂאוֹר בְּי״ד	הַשְׁבָּתָה	109
Don't eat chametz all 7 days	שֶׁלֹּא לֶאֱכֹל חָמֵץ כָּל שִׁבְעָה	ז׳ יָמִים	110
Don't eat mixtures of chametz	שֶׁלֹּא לֶאֱכֹל תַּעֲרוֹבוֹת חָמֵץ כָּל שִׁבְעָה	תַּעֲרוֹבוֹת	111
Chametz should not be seen	שֶׁלֹּא יֵרָאֶה חָמֵץ כָּל שִׁבְעָה	לֹא יֵרָאֶה	112
Chametz should not be found	שֶׁלֹּא יִמָּצֵא חָמֵץ כָּל שִׁבְעָה	לֹא יִמָּצֵא	113
Eat Matzah on 1st night of Pesach	לֶאֱכֹל מַצָּה בְּלֵיל פֶּסַח	מַצָּה	114
Tell the story of Yetzias Mitzrayim on the 1st night of Pesach	לְסַפֵּר בִּיצִיאַת מִצְרַיִם בְּאוֹתוֹ הַלַּיְלָה	לְסַפֵּר	115

Book 3: Mitzvos Designated to Time : סֵפֶר זְמַנִים

Section 6: Laws of Blowing the Shofar (1 Mitzvah)

Hear the shofar blown on the 1st day of Tishrei	לִשְׁמוֹעַ קוֹל שׁוֹפָר בְּאֶחָד בְּתִשְׁרֵי	שׁוֹפָר	116

Section 7: Laws of Living in the Sukkah (1 Mitzvah)

Live in a Succah for 7 days	לֵישֵׁב בְּסֻכָּה שִׁבְעַת יְמֵי הֶחָג	סֻכָּה	117

Section 8: Laws of the Lulav (1 Mitzvah)

Shake Lulav and Esrog all 7 days of Sukkos in the Beis Hamikdash.	לִטֹּל לוּלָב בַּמִּקְדָּשׁ כָּל שִׁבְעַת יְמֵי הֶחָג	לוּלָב	118

Section 9: Laws of the Shekalim Tax (1 Mitzvah)

Give donation of half a shekel every year	לִתֵּן כָּל אִישׁ מַחֲצִית הַשֶּׁקֶל בְּכָל שָׁנָה	מַחֲצִית הַשֶּׁקֶל	119

Section 10: Laws of Sanctifying the New Moon (1 Mitzvah)

Calculate the beginning of every Rosh Chodesh	לַחֲשֹׁב וְלֵידַע וְלִקְבֹּעַ בְּאֵיזֶה יוֹם הוּא תְּחִלַּת כָּל חֹדֶשׁ וְחָדְשֵׁי הַשָּׁנָה	חֹדֶשׁ	120

Section 11: Laws of Fast Days (1 Mitzvah)

Fast and cry out in times of trouble	לְהִתְעַנּוֹת וְלִזְעֹק לִפְנֵי ה' בְּעֵת כָּל צָרָה גְדוֹלָה שֶׁלֹּא תָבוֹא עַל הַצִּבּוּר	תַּעֲנִית	121

Section 12: Laws of Megilla and Chanuka (Rabbinical)

Chanukah - Rabbinical	מִדְּרַבָּנָן	חֲנֻכָּה
Purim - Rabbinical	מִדְּרַבָּנָן	מְגִלָּה

Book 4: Instructions for Marriage and Divorce: סֵפֶר נָשִׁים

Section 1: Laws of Marriage: אִישׁוּת

(4 Mitzvos)

Marry a lady with a Kesuba & Kiddushin	לִישָׂא אִשָּׁה בִּכְתֻבָּה וְקִדּוּשִׁין	כְּתֻבָּה	122
Don't marry without a Kesuba & Kiddushin	שֶׁלֹּא תִבָּעֵל אִשָּׁה בְּלֹא כְּתֻבָּה וְקִדּוּשִׁין	כְּתֻבָּה	123
A husband must not hold back food, clothes and time from his wife	שֶׁלֹּא יִמְנַע שְׁאֵר כְּסוּת וְעוֹנָה	שְׁאֵר כְּסוּת וְעוֹנָה	124
A Jewish man has to father children	לִפְרוֹת וְלִרְבּוֹת מִמֶּנָּה	פְּרוּ וּרְבוּ	125

Book 4: Instructions for Marriage and Divorce: סֵפֶר נָשִׁים
Section 2: Laws of Divorce: גירושין
(2 Mitzvos)

126	גֵּט	שֶׁיְגָרֵשׁ הַמְגָרֵשׁ בְּסֵפֶר	Divorce only with a kosher Get
127	יַחֲזִיר	שֶׁלֹּא יַחֲזִיר גְּרוּשָׁתוֹ מִשֶּׁנִשֵּׂאת לְשֵׁנִי	Don't remarry one's ex-wife after she divorced her 2nd husband

Book 4: Instructions for Marriage and Divorce: סֵפֶר נָשִׁים
Section 3: Laws of Yibum and Chalitza : יִבּוּם וְחֲלִיצָה
(3 Mitzvos)

Do Yibum	לְיַבֵּם	יִבּוּם	128
Do Chalitzah	לַחֲלוֹץ	חֲלִיצָה	129
A widow must not remarry outside her husband's brothers until Chalitzah	לֹא תִנָּשֵׂא יְבָמָה לְאִישׁ זָר עַד שֶׁתָּסִיר רְשׁוּת הַיָּבָם מֵעָלֶיהָ	זָר	130

Book 4: Instructions for Marriage and Divorce: סֵפֶר נָשִׁים

Section 4: Laws of a Besula: נערה בתולה

(5 Mitzvos)

A Mefateh must pay 3 fines	לִקְנוֹס הַמְפַתֶּה	**מְפַתֶּה**	131
A Ma'aness must marry her	שֶׁיִּשָּׂא הָאוֹנֵס אֲנוּסָתוֹ	**אוֹנֵס**	132
A Ma'aness cannot divorce her	שֶׁלֹּא יְגָרֵשׁ הָאוֹנֵס אֶת אֲנוּסָתוֹ	**אוֹנֵס**	133
A מוֹצִיא שֵׁם רַע must remain married	שֶׁתֵּשֵׁב אֵשֶׁת מוֹצִיא שֵׁם רַע תַּחַת בַּעְלָהּ לְעוֹלָם	**מוֹצִיא שֵׁם רַע**	134
A מוֹצִיא שֵׁם רַע cannot divorce his wife	שֶׁלֹּא יְגָרֵשׁ מוֹצִיא שֵׁם רַע אֶת אִשְׁתּוֹ	**מוֹצִיא שֵׁם רַע**	135

Book 4: Instructions for Marriage and Divorce: סֵפֶר נָשִׁים

Section 5: Laws of a Sota: סוֹטָה

(3 Mitzvos)

Follow the laws of Sotah	לַעֲשׂוֹת לְסוֹטָה כַּדִּין קְנָאוֹת הַסְּדוּרוֹת בַּתּוֹרָה	סוֹטָה	136
Don't add oil to a Sota's Mincha	שֶׁלֹּא לִתֵּן שֶׁמֶן עַל קָרְבָּנָהּ	שֶׁמֶן	137
Don't add Levona spices to a Sota's Mincha	שֶׁלֹּא לִתֵּן עָלָיו לְבוֹנָה	לְבוֹנָה	138

Book 5: Instructions that Make a Jew Kadosh סֵפֶר קְדוּשָׁה
Section 1: Laws of Forbidden Relationships: אִסּוּרֵי בִּיאָה
(37 Mitzvos)

Mother	שֶׁלֹּא לָבוֹא עַל הָאֵם	אֵם	139
Step-mother	שֶׁלֹּא לָבוֹא עַל אֵשֶׁת אָב	אֵשֶׁת אָב	140
Sister	שֶׁלֹּא לִבְעֹל אָחוֹת	אָחוֹת	141
Half-sister	שֶׁלֹּא לִבְעֹל בַּת אֵשֶׁת אָב	בַּת אֵשֶׁת אָב	142
Granddaughter, a son's daughter	שֶׁלֹּא לִבְעֹל בַּת הַבֵּן	בַּת הַבֵּן	143
Daughter	שֶׁלֹּא לִבְעֹל בַּת	בַּת	144
Granddaughter, a daughter's daughter	שֶׁלֹּא לִבְעֹל בַּת הַבַּת	בַּת הַבַּת	145
Mother and her daughter	שֶׁלֹּא לִשָּׂא אִשָּׁה וּבִתָּהּ	אִשָּׁה וּבִתָּהּ	146
Mother and her granddaughter	שֶׁלֹּא לִשָּׂא אִשָּׁה וּבַת בְּנָהּ	אִשָּׁה וּבַת בְּנָהּ	147
Mother and her granddaughter	שֶׁלֹּא לִשָּׂא אִשָּׁה וּבַת בִּתָּהּ	אִשָּׁה וּבַת בִּתָּהּ	148
Aunt - father's sister	שֶׁלֹּא לִבְעֹל אֲחוֹת אָב	אֲחוֹת אָב	149
Aunt - mother's sister	שֶׁלֹּא לִבְעֹל אֲחוֹת אֵם	אֲחוֹת אֵם	150
Aunt - uncle's wife	שֶׁלֹּא לִבְעֹל אֵשֶׁת אֲחִי הָאָב	אֵשֶׁת אֲחִי הָאָב	151
Daughter-in-law	שֶׁלֹּא לִבְעֹל אֵשֶׁת הַבֵּן	אֵשֶׁת הַבֵּן	152
Sister-in-law - brother's wife	שֶׁלֹּא לִבְעֹל אֵשֶׁת אָח	אֵשֶׁת אָח	153
Sister-in-law - wife's sister	שֶׁלֹּא לִבְעֹל אֲחוֹת אִשְׁתּוֹ	אֲחוֹת אִשְׁתּוֹ	154
A man cannot marry an animal	שֶׁלֹּא יִשְׁכַּב עִם בְּהֵמָה	בְּהֵמָה	155
A woman cannot marry an animal	שֶׁלֹּא תָּבִיא אִשָּׁה בְּהֵמָה עָלֶיהָ	בְּהֵמָה	156

Book 5: Instructions that Make a Jew Kadosh סֵפֶר קְדוּשָׁה
Section 1: Laws of Forbidden Relationships אִסּוּרֵי בִּיאָה:
(continued)

157	מִשְׁכַּב	שֶׁלֹּא לִשְׁכַּב עִם זָכָר	A man cannot marry a man
158	אָב	שֶׁלֹּא לְגַלּוֹת עֶרְוַת אָב	A man cannot marry his father
159	אֲחִי הָאָב	שֶׁלֹּא לְגַלּוֹת עֶרְוַת אֲחִי הָאָב	A man cannot marry his uncle, his father's brother

160	אֵשֶׁת אִישׁ	שֶׁלֹּא לִבְעֹל אֵשֶׁת אִישׁ	Don't marry another man's wife
161	נִדָּה	שֶׁלֹּא לִבְעֹל נִדָּה	Don't be close to a Nidah

162	חֲתָנוּת	שֶׁלֹּא לְהִתְחַתֵּן בְּעַכּוּ״ם	Don't marry a non-Jew

163	עַמּוֹן וּמוֹאָב	שֶׁלֹּא יָבֹא עַמּוֹנִי וּמוֹאָבִי בִּקְהַל ה׳	A Jewess must not marry a man from Amon and Moav
164	מִצְרִי	שֶׁלֹּא לְהַרְחִיק דּוֹר שְׁלִישִׁי מִצְרִי מִלָּבוֹא בִּקְהָל	A Jew must not marry an Egyptian convert till he is a 3rd generation convert
165	אֱדוֹם	שֶׁלֹּא לְהַרְחִיק דּוֹר שְׁלִישִׁי אֲדוֹמִי מִלָּבוֹא	A Jew must not marry a convert from Edom till he is a 3rd generation convert

166	מַמְזֵר	שֶׁלֹּא יָבֹא מַמְזֵר בִּקְהַל ה׳	A Mamzer must not marry a Jew

167	סָרִיס	שֶׁלֹּא יָבֹא סָרִיס בִּקְהַל ה׳	A Sariss cannot marry a Jew
168	לְסָרֵס	שֶׁלֹּא לְסָרֵס זָכָר אֲפִלּוּ בְּהֵמָה חַיָּה וָעוֹף	Don't make a person or animal a Sariss

169	כ״ג אַלְמָנָה	שֶׁלֹּא יִשָּׂא כ״ג אַלְמָנָה	A Kohen Gadol cannot marry a widow
170	כ״ג אַלְמָנָה	שֶׁלֹּא יִבְעֹל כ״ג אַלְמָנָה אֲפִלּוּ בְּלֹא נִשּׂוּאִין	A Kohen Gadol may not act as married to a widow even if they don't get married
171	כ״ג בְּתוּלָה	שֶׁיִּשָּׂא כ״ג בְּתוּלָה בִּנְעָרוּתָהּ	A Kohen Gadol must only marry a Besula

Book 5: Instructions that Make a Jew Kadosh סֵפֶר קְדוּשָׁה
Section 1: Laws of Forbidden Relationships אִסּוּרֵי בִּיאָה
(continued)

A Kohen may not marry a divorcee	שֶׁלֹּא יִשָּׂא כֹהֵן גְּרוּשָׁה	גְּרוּשָׁה	172
A Kohen may not marry a Zonah	שֶׁלֹּא יִשָּׂא כֹהֵן זוֹנָה	זוֹנָה	173
A Kohen may not marry a Challala	שֶׁלֹּא יִשָּׂא כֹהֵן חֲלָלָה	חֲלָלָה	174
Don't have physical contact with any forbidden women	שֶׁלֹּא יִקְרַב אָדָם לְאַחַת מִכָּל הָעֲרָיוֹת אֲפִלּוּ שֶׁלֹּא בָּעַל	יִקְרַב	175

Book 5: Instructions that Make a Jew Kadosh סֵפֶר קְדוּשָׁה
Section 2: Laws of Forbidden Foods : מַאֲכָלוֹת אֲסוּרוֹת
(28 Mitzvos)

Learn to identify kosher animals	לִבְדֹּק סִימָנֵי בְּהֵמָה וְחַיָּה וּלְהַבְדִּיל בֵּין טָמֵא לְטָהוֹר	בְּהֵמָה חַיָּה	176
Learn to identify kosher birds	לִבְדֹּק סִימָנֵי עוֹף וּלְהַבְדִּיל בֵּין טָמֵא לְטָהוֹר	עוֹף	177
Learn to identify kosher fish	לִבְדֹּק סִימָנֵי דָּגִים וּלְהַבְדִּיל בֵּין טָמֵא לְטָהוֹר	דָּגִים	178
Learn to identify kosher locust	לִבְדֹּק סִימָנֵי חֲגָבִים וּלְהַבְדִּיל בֵּין טָמֵא לְטָהוֹר	חֲגָבִים	179

Don't eat non-kosher animals	שֶׁלֹּא לֶאֱכֹל בְּהֵמָה וְחַיָּה טְמֵאָה	בְּהֵמָה חַיָּה	180
Don't eat non-kosher birds	שֶׁלֹּא לֶאֱכֹל עוֹף טָמֵא	עוֹף	181
Don't eat non-kosher fish	שֶׁלֹּא לֶאֱכֹל דָּגִים טְמֵאִים	דָּגִים	182

Don't eat flying insects	שֶׁלֹּא לֶאֱכֹל שֶׁרֶץ הָעוֹף	שֶׁרֶץ הָעוֹף	183
Don't eat crawling creatures	שֶׁלֹּא לֶאֱכֹל שֶׁרֶץ הָאָרֶץ	שֶׁרֶץ הָאָרֶץ	184
Don't eat maggots	שֶׁלֹּא לֶאֱכֹל רֶמֶשׂ הָאָרֶץ	רֶמֶשׂ הָאָרֶץ	185
Don't eat worms in fruit	שֶׁלֹּא לֶאֱכֹל תּוֹלַעַת הַפֵּרוֹת	תּוֹלַעַת	186
Don't eat water insects	שֶׁלֹּא לֶאֱכֹל שֶׁרֶץ הַמַּיִם	שֶׁרֶץ הַמַּיִם	187

Don't eat kosher animals not slaughtered according to Halacha	שֶׁלֹּא לֶאֱכֹל נְבֵלָה	נְבֵלָה	188
Don't eat a condemned ox	שֶׁלֹּא לֵהָנוֹת מִשּׁוֹר הַנִּסְקָל	שׁוֹר	189
Don't eat a Treifa animal	שֶׁלֹּא לֶאֱכֹל טְרֵפָה	טְרֵפָה	190

Book 5: Instructions that Make a Jew Kadosh סֵפֶר קְדוּשָׁה
Section 2: Laws of Forbidden Foods מַאֲכָלוֹת אֲסוּרוֹת:
(continued)

Don't eat a limb torn from a living animal	שֶׁלֹּא לֶאֱכֹל אֵבֶר מִן הַחַי	אֵבֶר	191
Don't eat blood	שֶׁלֹּא לֶאֱכֹל דָּם	דָּם	192
Don't eat Chelev - certain animal fats	שֶׁלֹּא לֶאֱכֹל חֵלֶב בְּהֵמָה טְהוֹרָה	חֵלֶב	193
Don't eat the Gid Hanasheh sinew of the thigh	שֶׁלֹּא לֶאֱכֹל גִּיד הַנָּשֶׁה	גִּיד	194
Don't eat milk and meat together	שֶׁלֹּא לֶאֱכֹל בָּשָׂר בְּחָלָב	בָּשָׂר וְחָלָב	195
Don't cook milk and meat together	שֶׁלֹּא לְבַשֵּׁל בָּשָׂר בְּחָלָב	בָּשָׂר וְחָלָב	196
Don't eat bread from new grain called Chadash	שֶׁלֹּא לֶאֱכֹל לֶחֶם תְּבוּאָה חֲדָשָׁה	חָדָשׁ	197
Don't eat parched grain Kali, from new grain	שֶׁלֹּא לֶאֱכֹל קָלִי מִן הֶחָדָשׁ	קָלִי	198
Don't eat early ripened grain called Karmel	שֶׁלֹּא לֶאֱכֹל כַּרְמֶל מִן הֶחָדָשׁ	כַּרְמֶל	199
Don't eat Orla - fruit of a tree in its first 3 years	שֶׁלֹּא לֶאֱכֹל עָרְלָה	עָרְלָה	200
Don't eat Kilayim seeds planted in a vineyard	שֶׁלֹּא לֶאֱכֹל כִּלְאֵי הַכֶּרֶם	כִּלְאֵי הַכֶּרֶם	201
Don't eat Tevel foods	שֶׁלֹּא לֶאֱכֹל טֶבֶל	טֶבֶל	202
Don't drink wine used for Avoda Zara	שֶׁלֹּא לִשְׁתּוֹת יֵין נֶסֶךְ	יַיִן	203

Book 5: Instructions that Make a Jew Kadosh סֵפֶר קְדוּשָׁה
Section 3: Laws of Ritual Slaughter: שְׁחִיטָה
(5 Mitzvos)

Must Shecht an animal before eating its meat	לִשְׁחֹט וְאח"כ לֶאֱכֹל	לִשְׁחֹט	204
Don't Shecht a mother animal & her child on the same day	לֹא לִשְׁחֹט אוֹתוֹ וְאֶת בְּנוֹ בְּיוֹם אֶחָד	אוֹתוֹ	205
Cover the blood after Shechita of a Chaya or bird	לְכַסּוֹת דַּם חַיָּה וְעוֹף	כִּסּוּי	206
Don't take a mother bird from her chicks	לֹא לָקַח הָאֵם עַל הַבָּנִים	שִׁלּוּחַ	207
Send away the mother bird before taking the chicks	לְשַׁלֵּחַ הָאֵם אִם לְקָחָהּ עַל הַבָּנִים	שִׁלּוּחַ	208

Book 6: Instructions Pertaining to the Power of Speech: סֵפֶר הַפְלָאָה

Section 1: Laws of Oaths: שְׁבוּעוֹת

(5 Mitzvos)

209	שֶׁקֶר	שֶׁלֹּא לְהִשָּׁבַע בִּשְׁמוֹ לְשֶׁקֶר	Don't swear falsely in Hashem's Name
210	שָׁוְא	שֶׁלֹּא יִשָּׂא אֶת שְׁמוֹ לַשָּׁוְא	Don't mention Hashem's Name for no reason

211	פִּקָּדוֹן	שֶׁלֹּא לִכְפֹּר בְּפִקָּדוֹן	Don't deny possession of collateral or money or objects belonging to others

212	מָמוֹן	שֶׁלֹּא לְהִשָּׁבַע עַל כְּפִירַת מָמוֹן	Don't make a Shevua to deny a monetary claim

213	אֱמֶת	לְהִשָּׁבַע בִּשְׁמוֹ הָאֱמֶת	Confirm the truth with a Shevua

Book 6: Instructions Pertaining to the Power of Speech: סֵפֶר הַפְלָאָה

Section 2: Laws of Promises: נְדָרִים

(3 Mitzvos)

214	לְקַיֵּם	שֶׁיִּשְׁמֹר מוֹצָא פִּיו וִיקַיֵּם נִדְרוֹ	Keep your promise
215	יַחֵל	שֶׁלֹּא יַחֵל דְּבָרוֹ	Don't break a promise
216	מֵפֵר	שֶׁיּוּפַר הַנֶּדֶר אוֹ הַשְּׁבוּעָה כַּדִּין הֲפָרַת נְדָרִים	Follow the laws of how to cancel a Neder or Shavua

Book 6: Instructions Pertaining to the Power of Speech : סֵפֶר הַפְלָאָה

Section 3: Laws of the Nazir : נָזִיר

(10 Mitzvos)

A Nazir must let his hair grow	שֶׁיְּגַדֵּל הַנָּזִיר פֶּרַע	שְׂעָרוֹ	217
A Nazir must not cut his hair	שֶׁלֹּא יְגַלַּח שְׂעָרוֹ כָּל יְמֵי נִזְרוֹ	לְגַלֵּחַ	218
A Nazir must not drink wine	שֶׁלֹּא יִשְׁתֶּה יַיִן, תַּעֲרֹבֶת יַיִן וַאֲפִלּוּ חֹמֶץ יַיִן	יַיִן	219
A Nazir must not eat grapes	שֶׁלֹּא יֹאכַל עֲנָבִים לַחִים	עֲנָבִים	220
A Nazir must not eat raisins	שֶׁלֹּא יֹאכַל צִמּוּקִים	צִמּוּקִים	221
A Nazir must not eat grape seeds	שֶׁלֹּא יֹאכַל חַרְצַנִּים	חַרְצַנִּים	222
A Nazir must not eat grape skins	שֶׁלֹּא יֹאכַל זַגִּים	זַגִּים	223
A Nazir must not be under same roof with a dead body	שֶׁלֹּא יִכָּנֵס לְאֹהֶל הַמֵּת	אֹהֶל	224
A Nazir must not touch a dead body	שֶׁלֹּא יִטָּמֵא לַמֵּתִים	טָמֵא	225
A Nazir must shave all his body hair when he brings his Korban Nazir	שֶׁיְּגַלַּח עַל הַקָּרְבָּנוֹת כְּשֶׁיַּשְׁלִים נְזִירוּתוֹ אוֹ כְּשֶׁיִּטָּמֵא	לְגַלֵּחַ	226

Book 6: Instructions Pertaining to the Power of Speech: סֵפֶר הַפְלָאָה
Section 3: Laws of Evaluations and Dedications: עֲרָכִין וַחֲרָמִים

(7 Mitzvos)

Estimate human value as a money gift to Bais Hamikdash	דִּין עֶרְכֵי אָדָם כִּמְפֹרָשׁ בַּתּוֹרָה	אָדָם	227
Estimate animal value as a money gift to Bais Hamikdash	דִּין עֶרְכֵי בְּהֵמָה	בְּהֵמָה	228
Estimate house value as a money gift to Bais Hamikdash	דִּין עֶרְכֵי בָּתִּים	בָּתִּים	229
Estimate field's value as a money gift to Bais Hamikdash	דִּין עֶרְכֵי שָׂדוֹת	שָׂדֶה	230
Follow laws of Cherem, dedicated property	דִּין מַחֲרִים נְכָסָיו	נְכָסִים	231
Don't sell property donated to Hekdesh	שֶׁלֹּא יִמְכֹּר חֵרֶם	יִמָּכֵר חֵרֶם	232
Don't redeem property donated to Hekdesh	שֶׁלֹּא יִגָּאֵל חֵרֶם	יִגָּאֵל חֵרֶם	233

Book 7: Instructions Pertaining to Agriculture: סֵפֶר זְרָעִים
Section 1: Laws of Forbidden Mixtures: כִּלְאַיִם
(5 Mitzvos)

Don't plant two different seeds together	שֶׁלֹּא לִזְרֹעַ זְרָעִים כִּלְאַיִם	שָׂדֶה	234
Don't plant different grains or greens together in a vineyard	שֶׁלֹּא לִזְרֹעַ תְּבוּאָה אוֹ יֶרֶק בְּכֶרֶם	תְּבוּאָה	235
Don't crossbreed animals	שֶׁלֹּא לְהַרְבִּיעַ בְּהֵמָה כִּלְאַיִם	בְּהֵמָה	236
Don't work different animals together	שֶׁלֹּא לַעֲשׂוֹת מְלָאכָה בְּכִלְאֵי בְּהֵמָה	מְלָאכָה	237
Don't wear Shaatnez, a mixture of wool and linen together	שֶׁלֹּא לִלְבּוֹשׁ כִּלְאַיִם	שַׁעַטְנֵז	238

Book 7: Instructions Pertaining to Agriculture: סֵפֶר זְרָעִים
Section 2: Laws of Gifts to the Poor : מַתְּנוֹת עֲנִיִּים
(13 Mitzvos)

Leave Peah, a corner of the field for the poor	לְהָנִיחַ פֵּאָה	פֵּאָה	239
Don't harvest Peah, the corner of the field	שֶׁלֹּא יְכַלֶּה הַפֵּאָה	פֵּאָה	240
Leave Leket of the field for the poor	לְהָנִיחַ לֶקֶט	לֶקֶט	241
Don't collect Leket of the field	שֶׁלֹּא יְלַקֵּט הַלֶּקֶט	לֶקֶט	242
Leave Ollelos, small bunches of unformed or unripe grapes of the vineyard for the poor	לַעֲזֹב עוֹלְלוֹת בַּכֶּרֶם	עוֹלְלוֹת	243
Don't gather Ollelos, small bunches of unformed or unripe grapes of the vineyard	שֶׁלֹּא יְעוֹלֵל הַכֶּרֶם	עוֹלְלוֹת	244
Leave Peret, fallen or unformed grapes for the poor	לַעֲזֹב פֶּרֶט הַכֶּרֶם	פֶּרֶט	245
Don't pick up Peret, fallen or unformed grapes	שֶׁלֹּא יְלַקֵּט פֶּרֶט הַכֶּרֶם	פֶּרֶט	246
Leave forgotten bundle of stalks of grain for the poor	לְהָנִיחַ הַשִּׁכְחָה	שִׁכְחָה	247
Don't go back to collect a forgotten bundle of stalks of grain	שֶׁלֹּא יָשׁוּב לָקַחַת הַשִּׁכְחָה	שִׁכְחָה	248
Give Maaser Oni to the poor	לְהַפְרִישׁ מַעֲשֵׂר לָעֲנִיִּים	לְהַפְרִישׁ	249
Give charity	לִתֵּן צְדָקָה כְּמַתְּנַת יָד	צְדָקָה	250
Don't refuse to give charity	שֶׁלֹּא יְאַמֵּץ אֶת לְבָבוֹ עַל הֶעָנִי	יִמָּנַע	251

Book 7: Instructions Pertaining to Agriculture: סֵפֶר זְרָעִים
Section 3: Laws of Agricultural Tithes to the Kohen: תְּרוּמָה
(8 Mitzvos)

Give Terumah Gedola to a Kohen	לְהַפְרִישׁ תְּרוּמָה גְדוֹלָה	תְּרוּמָה גְדוֹלָה	252
The Levi must give Terumus Maaser to a Kohen	לְהַפְרִישׁ תְּרוּמַת מַעֲשֵׂר	תְּרוּמַת מַעֲשֵׂר	253
Don't give Teruma and Maaser in the wrong order	שֶׁלֹּא יַקְדִּים תְּרוּמוֹת וּמַעַשְׂרוֹת זֶה לָזֶה	יַקְדִּים	254
A Zar, a non-Kohen cannot eat Terumah	שֶׁלֹּא יֹאכַל זָר אוֹ שְׂכִירוֹ תְּרוּמָה	זָר	255
Hired workers of the Kohen cannot eat Terumah	שֶׁלֹּא יֹאכַל תּוֹשָׁב כֹּהֵן אוֹ שְׂכִירוֹ תְּרוּמָה	שָׂכִיר	256
A Kohen Arel must not eat Teruma	שֶׁלֹּא יֹאכַל עָרֵל תְּרוּמָה	עָרֵל	257
A Kohen Tameh must not eat Terumah	שֶׁלֹּא יֹאכַל כֹּהֵן טָמֵא תְּרוּמָה	טָמֵא	258
A Challala must not eat Terumah	שֶׁלֹּא תֹּאכַל חֲלָלָה תְּרוּמָה	חֲלָלָה	259

Book 7: Instructions Pertaining to Agriculture : סֵפֶר זְרָעִים
Section 4: Laws of Agricultural Tithes to the Levi : מַעֲשֵׂר רִאשׁוֹן
(1 Mitzvah)

A farmer gives Maaser Rishon to a Levi each year	לְהַפְרִישׁ מַעֲשֵׂר רִאשׁוֹן בְּכָל שָׁנָה וְשָׁנָה	מַעֲשֵׂר רִאשׁוֹן	260

Book 7: Instructions Pertaining to Agriculture: סֵפֶר זְרָעִים

Section 5: Laws of Tithes to Oneself and 4th Year Plantings: מַעֲשֵׂר שֵׁנִי וְנֶטַע רְבָעִי

(9 Mitzvos)

261	מַעֲשֵׂר שֵׁנִי	לְהַפְרִישׁ מַעֲשֵׂר שֵׁנִי	A farmer has to separate Ma'aser Sheni for himself
262	יִפָּדֶה	שֶׁלֹּא לְהוֹצִיא דָמָיו בִּשְׁאָר צָרְכֵי הָאָדָם חוּץ מֵאֲכִילָה, שְׁתִיָּה וְסִיכָה	If a farmer buys back Maaser Sheni with money, he must not spend it on anything except food, drink & oil in Yerushalayim
263	טְמֵאָה	שֶׁלֹּא לְאָכְלוֹ בְּטֻמְאָה	Don't eat Ma'aser Sheni if Tameh
264	אֲנִינוּת	שֶׁלֹּא לְאָכְלוֹ בַּאֲנִינוּת	Before burial, an Onen mourner must not eat Ma'aser Sheni
265	דָּגָן	לֹא לֶאֱכֹל מַעֲשֵׂר שֵׁנִי דָּגָן חוּץ לִירוּשָׁלַיִם	Don't eat Ma'aser Sheni grains outside Yerushalayim
266	תִּירוֹשׁ	שֶׁלֹּא לֶאֱכֹל מַעֲשֵׂר שֵׁנִי תִּירוֹשׁ חוּץ לִירוּשָׁלַיִם	Don't drink Ma'aser Sheni wine outside Yerushalayim
267	יִצְהָר	שֶׁלֹּא לֶאֱכֹל מַעֲשֵׂר שֵׁנִי יִצְהָר חוּץ לִירוּשָׁלַיִם	Don't eat Ma'aser Sheni oil outside Yerushalayim
268	נֶטַע רְבָעִי	נֶטַע רְבָעִי קֹדֶשׁ יֹאכַל בִּירוּשָׁלַיִם לִבְעָלָיו כְּדִין מַעֲשֵׂר שֵׁנִי	Neta Revai - 4th year produce can only be eaten in Yerushalayim like Maaser Sheni
269	וִדּוּי מַעֲשֵׂר	לְהִתְוַדּוֹת וִדּוּי מַעֲשֵׂר	Say Vidui Maaser in 4th & 7th years of Shemitta

Book 7: Instructions Pertaining to Agriculture: סֵפֶר זְרָעִים
Section 6: Laws of First Fruits בִּכּוּרִים וּשְׁאָר מַתְּנוֹת כְּהוּנָה:
(9 Mitzvos)

Separate Bikkurim, First Fruits for the Kohanim in the Bais Hamikdash	לְהַפְרִישׁ בִּכּוּרִים וּלְהַעֲלוֹתָן לַמִּקְדָּשׁ	בִּכּוּרִים	270
Kohanim must not eat Bikkurim outside Yerushalayim	שֶׁלֹּא יֹאכַל הַכֹּהֵן בִּכּוּרִים חוּץ לִירוּשָׁלַיִם	חוּץ	271
Read Torah portion when you bring Bikkurim	לִקְרֹא עֲלֵיהֶם	לִקְרֹא	272
Separate the Challa portion of dough for a Kohen	לְהַפְרִישׁ חַלָּה לַכֹּהֵן	חַלָּה	273
Gift the shoulder, two cheeks and stomach for a Kohen	לִתֵּן זְרוֹעַ וּלְחָיַיִם וְקֵבָה לַכֹּהֵן	זְרוֹעַ	274
Gift Reishis Hagez, the first sheering of sheep to a Kohen	לִתֵּן לוֹ רֵאשִׁית הַגֵּז	רֵאשִׁית הַגֵּז	275
Do Pidyon Haben for a first-born son with money to a Kohen	לִפְדּוֹת בְּכוֹר הַבֵּן וְלִתֵּן פִּדְיוֹנוֹ לַכֹּהֵן	פִּדְיוֹן	276
Buy back a firstborn donkey with a lamb to a Kohen	לִפְדּוֹת פֶּטֶר חֲמוֹר וְלִתֵּן פִּדְיוֹנוֹ לַכֹּהֵן	פִּדְיוֹן	277
Break the first born donkey's neck if it's not redeemed	לַעֲרֹף פֶּטֶר חֲמוֹר אִם לֹא רָצָה לִפְדּוֹתוֹ	לַעֲרֹף	278

Book 7: Instructions Pertaining to Agriculture: סֵפֶר זְרָעִים
Section 7: Laws of Shmita and Yovel שְׁמִיטָה וְיוֹבֵל
(22 Mitzvos)

279	תִּשְׁבֹּת	שֶׁתִּשְׁבֹּת הָאָרֶץ מִמְּלַאכְתָּהּ בַּשְּׁבִיעִית	Rest the land in Shemitta, the 7th year
280	תַּעֲבֹד	שֶׁלֹּא יַעֲבֹד עֲבוֹדַת הָאָרֶץ בַּשָּׁנָה זוֹ	Don't work the land in Shemitta
281	אִילָן	שֶׁלֹּא יַעֲבֹד עֲבוֹדַת הָאִילָן בַּשָּׁנָה זוֹ	Don't work trees in Shemitta
282	יִקְצֹר	שֶׁלֹּא יִקְצֹר הַסָּפִיחַ כְּדֶרֶךְ הַקּוֹצְרִים	Don't harvest Sefichim, wild crops in the usual way in Shemitta
283	יִבְצֹר	שֶׁלֹּא יִבְצֹר הַנְּזִירִים כְּדֶרֶךְ הַבּוֹצְרִים	Don't collect Nezirim, wild grapes, in the usual way in Shemitta
284	נִשְׁמָט	שֶׁיַּשְׁמִיט מַה שֶּׁתּוֹצִיא הָאָרֶץ	Disown your produce grown in Shemitta
285	נִשְׁמָט	שֶׁיַּשְׁמִיט כָּל הַלְוָאוֹתָיו	Cancel all loans in Shemitta
286	תּוֹבֵעַ	שֶׁלֹּא יִגֹּשׂ וְלֹא יִתְבַּע הַלֹּוֶה	Don't pressure the borrower to pay back the loan in Shemitta
287	יִמָּנַע	שֶׁלֹּא יִמָּנַע מִלְּהַלְווֹת קֹדֶם הַשְּׁמִיטָה	Don't refuse to lend money Erev Shemitta, in the 6th year
288	לִסְפֹּר	לִסְפֹּר שָׁנִים שֶׁבַע שֶׁבַע	Sanhedrin count 7 groups of 7 years till Yovel
289	לְקַדֵּשׁ	לְקַדֵּשׁ שְׁנַת חֲמִשִּׁים	Sanhedrin must declare Yovel, the 50th year as Kadosh
290	לִתְקֹעַ	לִתְקֹעַ בְּשׁוֹפָר בַּעֲשִׂירִי לְתִשְׁרֵי	Blow Shofar on the 10th of Tishrei of the Yovel year

Book 7: Instructions Pertaining to Agriculture: סֵפֶר זְרָעִים
Section 7: Laws of Shmita and Yovel שְׁמִיטָה וְיוֹבֵל:
(continued)

Don't work the land in Yovel, the 50th year	שֶׁלֹּא יַעֲבֹד אֲדָמָה בִּשְׁנַת יוֹבֵל	תַּעֲבֹד	291
Don't harvest wild crops in the usual way in Yovel	שֶׁלֹּא יִקְצֹר סְפִיחֶיהָ כְּדֶרֶךְ הַקּוֹצְרִים	יִקְצֹר	292
Don't pick wild grown grapes in usual way in Yovel	שֶׁלֹּא יִבְצֹר נְזִירֶיהָ כְּדֶרֶךְ הַבּוֹצְרִים	יִבְצֹר	293

Return land and homes to original owners in Yovel	לִתֵּן גְּאֻלָּה לָאָרֶץ בִּשְׁנַת יוֹבֵל וְהוּא דִּין שְׂדֵה אֲחֻזָּה וּשְׂדֵה מִקְנֶה	גְּאֻלָּה	294
Don't sell land in Eretz Yisrael as a permanent sale	שֶׁלֹּא תִמָּכֵר הָאָרֶץ לִצְמִיתוּת	נֶצַח	295
Follow the law of houses in walled cities, 1 year right to buy back	דִּין בָּתֵּי עָרֵי חוֹמָה	בָּתִּים	296

Shevet Levi has no portion in the land of Israel	שֶׁלֹּא יִנְחַל כָּל שֵׁבֶט לֵוִי בְּאֶרֶץ יִשְׂרָאֵל אֶלָּא נוֹתְנִים לָהֶם עָרִים מַתָּנָה לָשֶׁבֶת בָּהֶם	נַחֲלָה	297
Shevet Levi have no share in spoils of war	שֶׁלֹּא יִקַּח שֵׁבֶט לֵוִי חֵלֶק בַּבִּזָּה	בִּזָּה	298

Give Shevet Levi 48 cities & surrounding fields	לִתֵּן לַלְוִיִּם עָרִים לָשֶׁבֶת וּמִגְרְשֵׁיהֶם	עָרִים	299
The fields of shevet Levi cannot be sold. They must remain theirs before and after Yovel	שֶׁלֹּא יִמָּכֵר מִגְרְשֵׁי עָרֵיהֶם אֶלָּא גּוֹאֲלִים בֵּין לִפְנֵי הַיּוֹבֵל בֵּין לְאַחַר הַיּוֹבֵל	עָרִים	300

Book 8: Instructions Pertaining to the Temple Service: סֵפֶר עֲבוֹדָה

Section 1: Laws of the Temple: בֵּית הַבְּחִירָה

(6 Mitzvos)

Build a Bais Hamikdash	לִבְנוֹת בֵּית הַמִּקְדָּשׁ	לִבְנוֹת	301
Don't build the Mizbayach with stones cut with metal	שֶׁלֹּא לִבְנוֹת הַמִּזְבֵּחַ גָּזִית	גָּזִית	302
Don't ascend the Mizbayach using steps	שֶׁלֹּא לַעֲלוֹת בְּמַעֲלוֹת עָלָיו	מַעֲלוֹת	303
Show Yirah, reverence for the Bais Hamikdash	לִירָא מִן הַמִּקְדָּשׁ	לִירָא	304
Guard the Bais Hamikdash	לִשְׁמֹר אֶת הַמִּקְדָּשׁ סָבִיב	לִשְׁמֹר	305
Don't leave The Bais Hamikdash unguarded	שֶׁלֹּא לְהַשְׁבִּית שְׁמִירַת הַמִּקְדָּשׁ	לִשְׁמֹר	306

Book 8: Instructions Pertaining to the Temple Service : סֵפֶר עֲבוֹדָה

Section 2: Laws of the Temple Furnishings & Its Workers : כְּלֵי הַמִּקְדָּשׁ וְהָעוֹבְדִים בּוֹ:

(14 Mitzvos)

Prepare the Shemen Hamishcha anointing oil	לַעֲשׂוֹת שֶׁמֶן הַמִּשְׁחָה	שֶׁמֶן	307
Don't reproduce the exact same formula of Shemen Hamishcha	שֶׁלֹּא לַעֲשׂוֹת כָּמוֹהוּ	כָּמוֹהוּ	308
Don't use Shemen Hamishcha on a non-Kohen	שֶׁלֹּא לָסוּךְ מִמֶּנּוּ זָר	זָר	309
Don't reproduce the exact same formula of Ketores	שֶׁלֹּא לַעֲשׂוֹת כְּמַתְכֹּנֶת הַקְּטֹרֶת	קְטֹרֶת	310
Don't burn anything else except Ketores on the Golden Mizbayach	שֶׁלֹּא לְהַקְטִיר בְּמִזְבַּח הַזָּהָב חוּץ מִן הַקְּטֹרֶת	זָהָב	311
The Levi'im transport the Aron on their shoulders	לָשֵׂאת הָאָרוֹן עַל הַכָּתֵף	אָרוֹן	312
Don't remove poles from the ark	שֶׁלֹּא יָסֻרוּ הַבַּדִּים מִמֶּנּוּ	בַּדִּים	313
Levi'im must work in the Bais Hamikdash	שֶׁיַּעֲבֹד הַלֵּוִי בַּמִּקְדָּשׁ	לֵוִי	314
A Levi cannot do the Avoda of another Levi or Kohen	שֶׁלֹּא יַעֲשֶׂה אֶחָד בִּמְלֶאכֶת חֲבֵרוֹ בַּמִּקְדָּשׁ	חֲבֵרוֹ	315
A Kohen must be treated special	לְקַדֵּשׁ הַכֹּהֵן לַעֲבוֹדָה	לְקַדֵּשׁ הַכֹּהֵן	316
All 24 shifts of Kohanim work on all 3 Yomim Tovim	שֶׁיִּהְיוּ כָּל הַמִּשְׁמָרוֹת שָׁווֹת בָּרְגָלִים	מִשְׁמָרוֹת	317
Kohanim must wear Bigdei Kehuna during their Avoda	לִלְבּוּשׁ בִּגְדֵי כְהֻנָּה לַעֲבוֹדָה	לִלְבּוּשׁ	318
Don't tear the Me'il gown	שֶׁלֹּא יִקָּרֵעַ הַמְּעִיל	מְעִיל	319
The Choshen must not be loose	שֶׁלֹּא יִזַּח הַחֹשֶׁן מֵעַל הָאֵפוֹד	חֹשֶׁן	320

Book 8: Instructions Pertaining to the Temple Service :סֵפֶר עֲבוֹדָה
Section 3: Laws of Entering the Temple Site :בִּיאַת הַמִּקְדָּשׁ
(15 Mitzvos)

A drunk Kohen must not enter the Bais Hamikdash area.	שֶׁלֹּא יִכָּנֵס שִׁכּוֹר לַמִּקְדָּשׁ	שִׁכּוֹר	321
A long haired Kohen must not enter the Bais Hamikdash	שֶׁלֹּא יִכָּנֵס פְּרוּעַ רֹאשׁ	פְּרוּעַ	322
A Kohen must not enter the Bais Hamikdash with torn clothes	שֶׁלֹּא יִכָּנֵס קָרוּעַ בְּגָדִים	קָרוּעַ	323

A Kohen cannot enter the Heichal if not doing Avoda	שֶׁלֹּא יִכָּנֵס כֹּהֵן בְּכָל עֵת אֶל הַהֵיכָל	יִכָּנֵס	324
Don't leave the Bais Hamikdash during the Avoda	שֶׁלֹּא יֵצֵא כֹּהֵן מִן הַמִּקְדָּשׁ בִּשְׁעַת עֲבוֹדָה	יֵצֵא	325

Anyone Tameh has to leave the Bais Hamikdash	לְשַׁלֵּחַ טְמֵאִים מִן הַמִּקְדָּשׁ	יְשַׁלַּח טָמֵא	326
Someone Tameh cannot enter the Bais Hamikdash	שֶׁלֹּא יִכָּנֵס טָמֵא לַמִּקְדָּשׁ	יִכָּנֵס טָמֵא	327
Someone Tameh cannot enter the Har Habayis	שֶׁלֹּא יִכָּנֵס טָמֵא לְהַר הַבַּיִת	יִכָּנֵס טָמֵא	328
A Kohen Tameh must not do Avoda	שֶׁלֹּא יַעֲבֹד טָמֵא	יַעֲבֹד טָמֵא	329
Kohen Tameh who Toveled still can't enter the Bais Hamikdash till after sundown	שֶׁלֹּא יַעֲבֹד טְבוּל יוֹם	טְבוּל יוֹם	330

A Kohen must wash his hands and feet before doing Avoda	לְקַדֵּשׁ יָדָיו וְרַגְלָיו	רְחִיצָה	331

A wounded Kohen cannot enter the Bais Hamikdash	שֶׁלֹּא יִכָּנֵס בַּעַל מוּם לַהֵיכָל וְלַמִּזְבֵּחַ	בַּעַל מוּם יִכָּנֵס	332
A wounded Kohen cannot do any Avoda	שֶׁלֹּא יַעֲבֹד בַּעַל מוּם	בַּעַל מוּם יַעֲבֹד	333
Even a temporarily wounded Kohen cannot do any Avoda	שֶׁלֹּא יַעֲבֹד בַּעַל מוּם עוֹבֵר	בַּעַל מוּם עוֹבֵר	334
Non-Kohen must not do any Avoda	שֶׁלֹּא יַעֲבֹד זָר	זָר	335

Book 8: Instructions Pertaining to the Temple Service: סֵפֶר עֲבוֹדָה

Section 4: Laws of Forbidden Offerings אִסּוּרֵי מִזְבֵּחַ:
(14 Mitzvos)

Only bring Korbanos with no wounds	לְהַקְרִיב כָּל הַקָּרְבָּנוֹת תְּמִימִים	תָּמִים	336
Don't reserve a wounded animal for a Korban	שֶׁלֹּא לְהַקְדִּישׁ בַּעַל מוּם לַמִּזְבֵּחַ	מוּם	337
Don't schecht a wounded animal for a Korban	שֶׁלֹּא יִשְׁחֹט בַּעַל מוּם	יִשְׁחֹט	338
Don't sprinkle the blood of a wounded Korban	שֶׁלֹּא יִזְרֹק דָּמוֹ	יִזְרֹק	339
Don't burn the fats of a wounded korban	שֶׁלֹּא יַקְטִיר חֶלְבּוֹ	יַקְטִיר	340
Don't bring a temporarily wounded animal for a Korban	שֶׁלֹּא יַקְרִיב בַּעַל מוּם עוֹבֵר	עוֹבֵר	341
Don't bring a wounded Korban of Goyim	שֶׁלֹּא יַקְרִיב בַּעַל מוּם אֲפִלּוּ בְּקָרְבְּנוֹת הַגּוֹיִם	גּוֹיִם	342
Don't make a wound on a Korban	שֶׁלֹּא יָטִיל מוּם בַּקֳּדָשִׁים	יָטִיל	343
Buy back Korbanos which became Passul	לִפְדּוֹת פְּסוּלֵי הַמֻּקְדָּשִׁים	לִפְדּוֹת	344
A Korban must be at least 8 days old	לְהַקְרִיב מִיּוֹם הַשְּׁמִינִי וְהָלְאָה וְקֹדֶם זְמַן זֶה נִקְרָא מְחֻסַּר זְמַן	שְׁמִינִי	345
Don't bring an animal used to pay a Zona or an animal traded for a dog	שֶׁלֹּא לְהַקְרִיב אֶתְנָן וּמְחִיר	אֶתְנָן וּמְחִיר	346
Don't burn Se'or or D'vash on the Mizbayach	שֶׁלֹּא לְהַקְטִיר שְׂאֹר וּדְבָשׁ	שְׂאֹר וּדְבָשׁ	347
All Korbanos must be salted	לִמְלֹחַ כָּל הַקָּרְבָּנוֹת	מֶלַח	348
Don't leave out salt from any Korban	שֶׁלֹּא לְהַשְׁבִּית מֶלַח מֵעַל הַקָּרְבָּנוֹת	מֶלַח	349

Book 8: Instructions Pertaining to the Temple Service: סֵפֶר עֲבוֹדָה
Section 5: Laws of Offerings מַעֲשֵׂה הַקׇּרְבָּנוֹת
(23 Mitzvos)

Follow the laws for the Korban Olah	לַעֲשׂוֹת הָעוֹלָה כְּמַעֲשֶׂיהָ הַכְּתוּבִים עַל הַסֵּדֶר	עוֹלָה	350
Don't eat meat of the Korban Olah	שֶׁלֹּא לֶאֱכֹל בְּשַׂר הָעוֹלָה	בָּשָׂר	351
Follow the laws for the Korban Chatos	סֵדֶר הַחַטָּאת	חַטָּאת	352
Don't eat meat of the Chatos Hapenimi whose blood is brought in the Kodesh	שֶׁלֹּא לֶאֱכֹל מִבְּשַׂר חַטָּאת הַפְּנִימִי	פְּנִימִי	353
Don't completely split the Chatos Ha'off	שֶׁלֹּא יַבְדִּיל בְּחַטַּאת הָעוֹף	יַבְדִּיל	354
Follow the laws for the Korban Asham	סֵדֶר הָאָשָׁם	אָשָׁם	355
Kohanim must eat Kodshei Kodshim meat of the Chatos & Asham in the Azara	שֶׁיֹּאכְלוּ הַכֹּהֲנִים בְּשַׂר ק"ק בַּמִּקְדָּשׁ	ק"ק	356
Don't eat the Kodshei Kadshim meat of the Chatos and Asham outside the Azara	שֶׁלֹּא יֹאכְלוּם חוּץ לָעֲזָרָה	חוּץ	357
Non-Kohen cannot eat Kodshei Kadshim meat	שֶׁלֹּא יֹאכַל זָר מִקׇּדְשֵׁי הַקֳּדָשִׁים	זָר	358
Follow the laws of the Korban Shelamim	סֵדֶר הַשְּׁלָמִים	שְׁלָמִים	359
Don't eat Kodshei Kalim meat before sprinkling their blood	שֶׁלֹּא לֶאֱכֹל מִבְּשַׂר קׇדָשִׁים קַלִּים קֹדֶם זְרִיקַת דָּמָם	יִזְרֹק	360
Follow the laws of the Korban Mincha	לַעֲשׂוֹת כׇּל מִנְחָה כְּסֵדֶר מַעֲשֶׂיהָ הַכְּתוּבִים בַּתּוֹרָה	מִנְחָה	361
Don't add oil to a Minchas Choteh	שֶׁלֹּא יָשִׂים שֶׁמֶן עַל מִנְחַת חוֹטֵא	שֶׁמֶן	362
Don't add Levona to a Minchas Choteh	שֶׁלֹּא לִתֵּן עָלֶיהָ לְבוֹנָה	לְבוֹנָה	363

Book 8: Instructions Pertaining to the Temple Service: סֵפֶר עֲבוֹדָה

Section 5: Laws of Offerings: מַעֲשֵׂה הַקָּרְבָּנוֹת

(continued)

The Mincha of a Kohen cannot be eaten	שֶׁלֹּא תֵּאָכֵל מִנְחַת כֹּהֵן	מִנְחַת כֹּהֵן	364
Don't bake a Mincha as Chametz (only Matza)	שֶׁלֹּא תֵּאָפֶה מִנְחָה חָמֵץ	חָמֵץ	365
Kohanim must eat the remains of a Korban Mincha	שֶׁיֹּאכְלוּ הַכֹּהֲנִים שְׁיָרֵי מְנָחוֹת	שְׁיָרֵי	366
Bring to the Bais Hamikdash every Korban Neder & Nadava on the first available Yom Tov	שֶׁיָּבִיא כָּל נְדָרָיו וְנִדְבוֹתָיו בָּרֶגֶל שֶׁפָּגַע רִאשׁוֹן	נְדָרָיו	367
Don't delay bringing a Korban Neder or Nedava	שֶׁלֹּא יְאַחֵר נִדְרוֹ וְנִדְבָתוֹ וּשְׁאָר דְּבָרִים שֶׁחַיָּב בָּהֶן	יְאַחֵר	368
Bring all Korbanos to the Bais Hamikdash	לְהַקְרִיב כָּל הַקָּרְבָּנוֹת בְּבֵית הַבְּחִירָה	בֵּית הַבְּחִירָה	369
Bring all Korbanos from outside Eretz Yisrael to the Bais Hamikdash	לְהָבִיא קָדְשֵׁי חוּצָה לָאָרֶץ לְבֵית הַבְּחִירָה	חוּץ לָאָרֶץ	370
Don't Shecht Korbanos outside the Azara	שֶׁלֹּא לִשְׁחֹט קָרְבָּנוֹת חוּץ לָעֲזָרָה	לִשְׁחֹט חוּץ	371
Don't bring Korbanos outside the Azara	שֶׁלֹּא לְהַקְרִיב קָרְבָּן חוּץ לָעֲזָרָה	לְהַקְרִיב חוּץ	372

Book 8: Instructions Pertaining to the Temple Service: סֵפֶר עֲבוֹדָה
Section 6: Laws of Daily and Additional Offerings: תְּמִידִין וּמוּסָפִים
(19 Mitzvos)

Offer two lambs for the Korban Tamid every day	לְהַקְרִיב שְׁנֵי כְבָשִׂים בְּכָל יוֹם	תָּמִיד	373
Light a fire on the Mizbayach every day	לְהַדְלִיק אֵשׁ עַל הַמִּזְבֵּחַ בְּכָל יוֹם	אֵשׁ	374
Don't extinguish the fire on the Mizbayach	שֶׁלֹּא לְכַבּוֹתָהּ	לְכַבּוֹתָהּ	375
Remove ashes from the Mizbayach every day	לְהָרִים אֶת הַדֶּשֶׁן בְּכָל יוֹם	דֶּשֶׁן	376
Burn Ketores every day	לְהַקְטִיר קְטֹרֶת בְּכָל יוֹם	לְהַקְטִיר	377
Light the Menorah every day	לְהַדְלִיק נֵרוֹת בְּכָל יוֹם	נֵרוֹת	378
The Kohen Gadol must bring a Korban Mincha every morning and afternoon	שֶׁיַּקְרִיב כֹּהֵן גָּדוֹל מִנְחָה בְּכָל יוֹם וְהִיא הַנִּקְרֵאת חֲבִתִּין	מְנָחוֹת כ"ג	379
Bring Korban Mussaf on Shabbos of two extra lambs	לְהוֹסִיף שְׁנֵי כְבָשִׂים עוֹלוֹת בְּשַׁבָּת	מוּסָף שַׁבָּת	380
Bake the Lechem Hapanim	לַעֲשׂוֹת לֶחֶם הַפָּנִים	לֶחֶם הַפָּנִים	381
Bring Korban Mussaf on Rosh Chodesh	מוּסָף רָאשֵׁי חֳדָשִׁים	מוּסָף ר"ח	382
Bring Korban Mussaf on Pesach	מוּסָף הַפֶּסַח	מוּסָף פֶּסַח	383
Bring the Omer on 2nd day of Pesach	לְהַקְרִיב עֹמֶר הַתְּנוּפָה	עֹמֶר	384
Count 7 weeks from 2nd day of Pesach till Shavuos	לִסְפֹּר כָּל אִישׁ וָאִישׁ שִׁבְעָה שָׁבוּעוֹת מִיּוֹם הַקְרָבַת הָעֹמֶר	לִסְפֹּר	385
Bring Korban Mussaf on Shavuos	מוּסָף עֲצֶרֶת	מוּסָף שָׁבוּעוֹת	386
Bring Shtei HaLechem with the Korban Mussaf on Shavuos	לְהָבִיא שְׁתֵּי הַלֶּחֶם עִם הַקָּרְבָּנוֹת הַבָּאוֹת בִּגְלַל הַלֶּחֶם בְּיוֹם עֲצֶרֶת	שְׁתֵּי הַלֶּחֶם	387

Book 8: Instructions Pertaining to the Temple Service: סֵפֶר עֲבוֹדָה

Section 6: Laws of Daily and Additional Offerings: תְּמִידִין וּמוּסָפִים

(continued)

Bring Korban Mussaf on Rosh Hashana	מוּסָף רֹאשׁ הַשָּׁנָה	מוּסָף ר״ה	388
Bring Korban Mussaf on Yom Kippur	מוּסָף יוֹם כִּפּוּר	מוּסָף יוה״כ	389
Bring Korban Mussaf on Succos	מוּסָף הֶחָג	מוּסָף סֻכּוֹת	390
Bring Korban Mussaf on Shemini Chag Atzeret	מוּסָף שְׁמִינִי עֲצֶרֶת	מוּסָף שְׁמִינִי ח״ע	391

Book 8: Instructions Pertaining to the Temple Service: סֵפֶר עֲבוֹדָה

Section 7: Laws of Offerings that Become Invalid: פְּסוּלֵי הַמֻּקְדָּשִׁין

(8 Mitzvos)

Don't eat a Korban which is Passul or has a wound	שֶׁלֹּא לֶאֱכֹל קׇרְבָּנוֹת שֶׁהִפְסְלוּ וְשֶׁהוּטַל בָּהֶם מוּם	פָּסוּל	392
Don't eat a Korban brought with the wrong thoughts, called Pigul	שֶׁלֹּא לֶאֱכֹל פִּגּוּל	פִּגּוּל	393

Don't let a Korban become Notar, left on Mizbayach after final burning time	שֶׁלֹּא יוֹתִיר קׇדָשִׁים אַחַר זְמַנָּם	נוֹתָר	394
Don't eat Notar after the allowed time	שֶׁלֹּא יֹאכַל נוֹתָר	נוֹתָר	395

Don't eat Korbanos that become Tameh	שֶׁלֹּא יֹאכַל קׇדָשִׁים שֶׁנִּטְמְאוּ	ק׳ טָמֵא	396
Somone Tameh must not each Kodshim	שֶׁלֹּא יֹאכַל אָדָם שֶׁנִּטְמָא אֶת הַקֳּדָשִׁים	אָדָם טָמֵא	397

Burn Notar, left over Korbanos	לִשְׂרֹף אֶת הַנּוֹתָר	לִשְׂרֹף	398
Burn all Korbanos which became Tameh	לִשְׂרֹף אֶת הַטָּמֵא	לִשְׂרֹף	399

Book 8: Instructions Pertaining to the Temple Service: סֵפֶר עֲבוֹדָה

Section 8: Laws of the Yom Kippur Service: עֲבוֹדַת יוה"כ

(1 Mitzvah)

| 400 | עֲבוֹדַת יוה"כ | שֶׁיַּעֲשֶׂה מַעֲשֵׂה יוה"כ כֻּלּוֹ עַל סֵדֶר כְּמוֹ שֶׁכָּתוּב בְּפָרָשַׁת אַחֲרֵי מוֹת, הַקָּרְבָּנוֹת וְהַוִּדּוּיִין, שִׁלּוּחַ הַשָּׂעִיר, וּשְׁאָר הָעֲבוֹדָה | Follow the order of Avoda on Yom Kippur |

Book 8: Instructions Pertaining to the Temple Service: סֵפֶר עֲבוֹדָה

Section 9: Laws of Misuse of Temple Property: מְעִילָה

(3 Mitzvos)

Misuse of Hekdesh property pays fine of full price plus 1/5	לְשַׁלֵּם הַמּוֹעֵל אֲשֶׁר חָטָא בְּתוֹסֶפֶת חֹמֶשׁ וְקָרְבָּן וְזֶהוּ דִּין הַמּוֹעֵל	הַמּוֹעֵל	401
Don't do Melacha with animals reserved for Korbanos	שֶׁלֹּא לַעֲבֹד בַּקֳּדָשִׁים	מְלָאכָה	402
Don't sheer the wool of sheep reserved for Korbanos	שֶׁלֹּא לָגֹז קָדָשִׁים	לָגֹז	403

Book 9: Instructions Pertaining to the Temple Offerings : סֵפֶר קָרְבָּנוֹת
Section 1: Laws of the Korban Pesach : פֶּסַח
(16 Mitzvos)

Shecht the Korban Pesach on 14th of Nissan after midday	לִשְׁחֹט אֶת הַפֶּסַח בִּזְמַנּוֹ	זְמַנּוֹ	404
Don't Shecht the Korban Pesach while you still own Chametz	שֶׁלֹּא לִזְבֹּחַ אוֹתוֹ עַל הֶחָמֵץ	חָמֵץ	405
Don't leave the Emurim fats of the Korban Pesach overnight	שֶׁלֹּא לָלִין אֵמוּרָיו	אֵמוּרָיו	406
Shecht the Korban Pesach Sheni	לִשְׁחֹט פֶּסַח שֵׁנִי	שֵׁנִי	407
Eat meat of the Korban Pesach with Matza & Maror	לֶאֱכֹל בְּשַׂר הַפֶּסַח עַל מַצָּה וּמָרוֹר בְּלֵיל ט"ו	אֲכִילָה	408
Eat meat of Korban Pesach Sheni on the 15th of Iyar	לֶאֱכֹל בְּשַׂר פֶּסַח שֵׁנִי בְּלֵיל ט"ו לַחֹדֶשׁ הַשֵּׁנִי	אֲכִילָה	409
Don't eat Korban Pesach meat raw or boiled	שֶׁלֹּא יֵאָכֵל נָא וּמְבֻשָּׁל	נָא	410
Don't remove Korban Pesach meat from group area	שֶׁלֹּא יוֹצִיא בְּשַׂר פֶּסַח חוּץ לַחֲבוּרָה	חוּץ	411
A Mumar cannot eat the Korban Pesach	שֶׁלֹּא יֹאכַל מִמֶּנּוּ מוּמָר	מוּמָר	412
A Toshav or hired worker cannot eat the Korban Pesach	שֶׁלֹּא יֹאכַל מִמֶּנּוּ תּוֹשָׁב אוֹ שָׂכִיר	שָׂכִיר	413
An Arel cannot eat the Korban Pesach	שֶׁלֹּא יֹאכַל מִמֶּנּוּ עָרֵל	עָרֵל	414
Don't break any bones of the Korban Pesach	שֶׁלֹּא יִשְׁבֹּר בּוֹ עֶצֶם	עֶצֶם	415
Don't break bones of the Korban Pesach Sheni	שֶׁלֹּא יִשְׁבֹּר עֶצֶם בְּפֶסַח שֵׁנִי	עֶצֶם	416
Don't leave any meat of the Korban Pesach till morning	שֶׁלֹּא יַשְׁאִיר מִמֶּנּוּ לַבֹּקֶר	תּוֹתִירוּ	417
Don't leave any meat of the Korban Pesach Sheni till morning	שֶׁלֹּא יַשְׁאִיר מִפֶּסַח שֵׁנִי לַבֹּקֶר	תּוֹתִירוּ	418
Don't leave meat of Korban Chagiga later than 16th of Nissan	שֶׁלֹּא יַשְׁאִיר מִבְּשַׂר חֲגִיגַת י"ד עַד הַיּוֹם הַשְּׁלִישִׁי	תּוֹתִירוּ	419

Book 9: Instructions Pertaining to the Temple Offerings: סֵפֶר קָרְבָּנוֹת
Section 2: Laws of the Korban Chagiga: חֲגִיגָה
(6 Mitzvos)

Be seen in the Bais Hamikdash on Pesach, Shavuos and Sukkos	לְהֵרָאוֹת אֶת פְּנֵי ה'	לְהֵרָאוֹת	420
Celebrate every Yom Tov in the Bais Hamikdash with the Korban Chagiga	לָחֹג בַּג' רְגָלִים	לָחֹג	421
Be B'Simcha on Pesach, Shavuos & Sukkos	לִשְׂמֹחַ בָּרְגָלִים	לִשְׂמֹחַ	422
Don't come to the Bais Hamikdash all 3 times a year without a Korban Olas Riya	שֶׁלֹּא יֵרָאֶה רֵיקָם	רֵיקָם	423
Don't avoid giving the Levi'im their Maaseros on Yom Tov	שֶׁלֹּא לַעֲזֹב לֵוִי מִלְּשַׂמְּחוֹ וְלִתֵּן לוֹ מַתְּנוֹתָיו בָּרְגָלִים	לַעֲזֹב	424
Every single Jew must gather inside the Azara on Motzei Yom Tov Rishon of Succos at end of Shemitta	לְהַקְהִיל אֶת הָעָם בְּחַג הַסֻּכּוֹת בְּמוֹצָאֵי שְׁמִיטָה	לְהַקְהִיל	425

Book 9: Instructions Pertaining to the Temple Offerings: סֵפֶר קָרְבָּנוֹת

Section 3: Laws of the First-Born: בְּכוֹרוֹת

(5 Mitzvos)

A 1st born sheep, goat or cow is reserved for the Kohen	לְהַפְרִישׁ בְּכוֹרוֹת	לְהַפְרִישׁ	426
A Kohen cannot eat a 1st born sheep, goat or cow outside Yerushalayim	שֶׁלֹּא יֹאכַל בְּכוֹר תָּמִים חוּץ לִירוּשָׁלַיִם	חוּץ	427
Don't buy back the first born sheep, goat or cow	שֶׁלֹּא יִפְדֶּה הַבְּכוֹר	יִפְדֶה	428
Separate Maaser Beheima from sheep, goats and cows, and eat them in Yerushalayim	לְהַפְרִישׁ מַעֲשֵׂר בְּהֵמָה	מַעֲשֵׂר	429
Don't buy back Maaser Beheima	שֶׁלֹּא יִגְאַל מַעֲשֵׂר בְּהֵמָה	יִגְאַל	430

Book 9: Instructions Pertaining to the Temple Offerings: סֵפֶר קָרְבָּנוֹת

Section 4: Laws of Offerings for Unintentional Sins: שְׁגָגוֹת

(5 Mitzvos)

431	חַטָּאת	קָרְבָּן חַטָּאת קָבוּעַ עַל שִׁגְגָתוֹ	Bring a Korban Chatos for an accidental Chet
432	אָשָׁם	סָפֵק אִם חָטָא אוֹ לֹא, יַקְרִיב אָשָׁם תָּלוּי	Bring an Asham Talu'i if he is not sure he did a Chet
433	אָשָׁם	עַל עֲבֵרוֹת יְדוּעוֹת יַקְרִיב אָשָׁם וַדַּאי	Bring an Asham Vadai if for sure he did a Chet
434	עוֹלֶה וְיוֹרֵד	עַל עֲבֵרוֹת יְדוּעוֹת אִם עָשִׁיר בְּהֵמָה וְאִם הָיָה עָנִי, מֵבִיא עוֹף אוֹ עֲשִׂירִית הָאֵיפָה	For 4 known Aveiros, bring a Korban Oleh V'yored. If wealthy - a sheep or goat, if poor a bird or Korban Mincha
435	חַטָּאת ב"ד	סַנְהֶדְרִין טָעוּ וְהוֹרוּ לֹא כַּהֲלָכָה יַקְרִיבוּ קָרְבָּן	Sanhedrin brings a Chatos Bais Din for a mistaken ruling

Book 9: Instructions Pertaining to the Temple Offerings: סֵפֶר קָרְבָּנוֹת
Section 5: Laws of People Who Need Atonement: מְחֻסְרֵי כַּפָּרָה
(4 Mitzvos)

A Zava brings a Korban Zava	שֶׁתַּקְרִיב הַזָּבָה כְּשֶׁתִּטְהַר קָרְבָּן	זָבָה	436
After giving birth, a mother brings a Korban Yoledes	שֶׁתַּקְרִיב הַיּוֹלֶדֶת כְּשֶׁתִּטְהַר קָרְבָּן	יוֹלֶדֶת	437
A Zav brings a Korban Zav	שֶׁיַּקְרִיב הַזָּב קָרְבָּן כְּשֶׁיִּטְהַר	זָב	438
A Metzorah brings a Korban Metzora	שֶׁיַּקְרִיב הַמְּצֹרָע קָרְבָּן כְּשֶׁיִּטְהַר	מְצֹרָע	439

Book 9: Instructions Pertaining to the Temple Offerings: סֵפֶר קָרְבָּנוֹת
Section 6: Laws of People Who Need Atonement: תְּמוּרָה
(3 Mitzvos)

Don't substitute a new animal for an already reserved Korban	שֶׁלֹּא יָמִיר	יָמִיר	440
Both a new animal and the original Korban are Kadosh	שֶׁתְּהֵא תְּמוּרָה קֹדֶשׁ אִם הֵמִיר	שְׁנֵיהֶם	441
Don't switch one Korban for another type of Korban	שֶׁלֹּא יְשַׁנֶּה הַקֳּדָשִׁים מִקְּדוּשָׁה לִקְדוּשָׁה	יְשַׁנֶּה	442

Book 10: Instructions for Spiritual Purity: סֵפֶר טַהֲרָה
Section 1: Laws of Contact with a Corpse: טֻמְאַת מֵת
(1 Mitzvah)

| 443 | טֻמְאַת מֵת | דִּין טֻמְאַת מֵת | Follow the laws of Tumas Meis |

Book 10: Instructions for Spiritual Purity: סֵפֶר טַהֲרָה
Section 2: Laws of the Red Hefer: פָּרָה אֲדֻמָּה
(2 Mitzvos)

Follow the laws of the Parah Aduma	דִין פָּרָה אֲדֻמָּה	פָּרָה	444
Follow the laws of sprinkling Mei Nidda water to make Tahor someone who is Tamei Meis	דִין טֻמְאַת מֵי נִדָּה וְטִהֲרָתָם	טִהֲרָתָם	445

Book 10: Instructions for Spiritual Purity: סֵפֶר טָהֳרָה
Section 3: Laws of Tzara'as: טֻמְאַת צָרַעַת
(8 Mitzvos)

Follow the laws of Tzara'as	לְהוֹרוֹת בְּצָרַעַת אָדָם כַּדִּין הַתּוֹרָה	לְהוֹרוֹת	446
A Metzorah must not remove signs of Tzara'as	שֶׁלֹּא יָקֹץ סִימָנֵי טֻמְאָה	יְסַלֵּק	447
A Metzorah must not shave signs of Tzara'as from his skin	שֶׁלֹּא יְגַלַּח הַנֶּתֶק	יְגַלֵּחַ	448
A Metzorah must publicize his Tumah	קְרִיעַת בְּגָדָיו, פְּרִיעַת רֹאשׁוֹ וְגִדּוּל שְׂפָמוֹ וִיפַרְסֵם צָרַעְתּוֹ	לְפַרְסֵם	449
Follow the rules to make a Metzorah Tahor	טָהֳרַת הַמְּצֹרָע	טָהֳרָתוֹ	450
Shave all hair of a Metzorah before Tahara in a Mikvah	שֶׁיְּגַלַּח הַמְּצֹרָע כָּל שְׂעָרוֹ כְּשֶׁיִּטְהַר	יְגַלֵּחַ	451
Follow the laws of Tzara'as on clothing	דִּין צָרַעַת בֶּגֶד	בֶּגֶד	452
Follow the laws of Tzara'as on houses	דִּין צָרַעַת בַּיִת	בַּיִת	453

Book 10: Instructions for Spiritual Purity: סֵפֶר טָהֳרָה
Section 4: Laws of Mishkav U'Moshav: טְמֵאֵי מִשְׁכָּב וּמוֹשָׁב
(4 Mitzvos)

Follow the laws of Niddah	דִּין טֻמְאַת נִדָּה	נִדָּה	454
Follow the laws of Tumah caused by childbirth	דִּין טֻמְאַת יוֹלֶדֶת	יוֹלֶדֶת	455
Follow the laws of Tumah of a Zava	דִּין טֻמְאַת זָבָה	זָבָה	456
Follow the laws of Tumah of a Zav	דִּין טֻמְאַת זָב	זָב	457

Book 10: Instructions for Spiritual Purity: סֵפֶר טַהֲרָה
Section 5: Laws of Other Major Causes of Tumah: שְׁאָר אֲבוֹת הַטֻּמְאָה
(3 Mitzvos)

Follow laws of Tumah caused by contact with a Neveila	דִּין טֻמְאַת נְבֵלָה	נְבֵלָה	458
Follow laws of Tumah caused by contact with the 8 Sheratzim	דִּין טֻמְאַת שֶׁרֶץ	שֶׁרֶץ	459
Follow laws of Tumah caused by Shichvas Zera	דִּין טֻמְאַת שִׁכְבַת זֶרַע	שִׁכְבַת זֶרַע	460

Tumah caused by contact with Idols have same status as 8 Sheratzim - Rabbinical	מִדְּרַבָּנָן: מַגָּע עִם ע״ז מְטַמֵּא כְּמוֹ טֻמְאַת ח׳ שְׁרָצִים	ע״ז מְטַמֵּא

Book 10: Instructions for Spiritual Purity: סֵפֶר טַהֲרָה

Section 6: Laws of Tumah Contracted with Food and Drink: אֲכָלִין
(1 Mitzvah)

| 461 | טֻמְאַת אֳכָלִים | דִין טֻמְאַת אֳכָלִים וּמַשְׁקִין וְהֶכְשֵׁרָן | Follow laws of Tumah from foods and liquids |

Section 7: Laws of Tumah Through Vessels (Rabbinical): כֵּלִים
(1 Mitzvah)

| כֵּלִים | מִדְּרַבָּנָן: כֵּלִים הַמְקַבְּלִין טֻמְאָה וְכֵלִים שֶׁאֵינָם מְקַבְּלִים טֻמְאָה וְכֵיצַד מְטַמְּאִים | Follow the Laws of Tumah from contact with Keilim - Rabbinical |

Book 10: Instructions for Spiritual Purity :סֵפֶר טַהֲרָה
Section 8: Laws of the Mikveh :מִקְוָאוֹת
(1 Mitzvah)

| 462 | מִקְוָאוֹת | שֶׁיִּטְבֹּל כָּל טָמֵא בְּמֵי מִקְוֶה וְאַחַר כָּךְ יִטְהַר | Every Tameh person must immerse in the mikvah |

Book 11: Instructions Pertaining to All Types of Damages: סֵפֶר נְזִיקִין

Section 1: Laws of Monetary Compensation for Damages: נִזְקֵי מָמוֹן

(4 Mitzvos)

Judge the cost of damage caused by a goring ox	דִּין הַשּׁוֹר	שׁוֹר	463
Judge the cost of damage caused by animal eating others property	דִּין הַהֶבְעֵר	שֵׁן	464
Judge the cost of damages to an animal or person who fell into a pit	דִּין הַבּוֹר	בּוֹר	465
Judge the cost of damage caused by fire	דִּין הַבְעֵרָה	אֵשׁ	466

Book 11: Instructions Pertaining to All Types of Damages: סֵפֶר נְזִיקִין

Section 2: Laws of Stealing: גְּנֵבָה
(7 Mitzvos)

Don't steal money or property	שֶׁלֹּא לִגְנֹב מָמוֹן	לִגְנֹב	467
Bais Din must enforce consequences for stealing	דִּין הַגַּנָּב	גַּנָּב	468
Make sure your scales & weights are exact	לְצַדֵּק הַמֹּאזְנַיִם עִם הַמִּשְׁקָלוֹת	לְצַדֵּק	469
Don't cheat with scales & weights	שֶׁלֹּא יַעֲשֶׂה עָוֶל בְּמִדּוֹת וּבְמִשְׁקָלוֹת	עָוֶל	470
Don't even own inaccurate scales & weights even if not used	שֶׁלֹּא יִהְיֶה בְּיַד אָדָם אֶבֶן אֵיפָה אַף עַל פִּי שֶׁאֵינוֹ לוֹקֵחַ וְנוֹתֵן בָּהֶם	בְּיָדוֹ	471
Don't move a boundary marker	שֶׁלֹּא יַסִּיג גְּבוּל	גְּבוּל	472
Don't kidnap	שֶׁלֹּא יִגְנֹב נְפָשׁוֹת	נְפָשׁוֹת	473

Book 11: Instructions Pertaining to All Types of Damages : סֵפֶר נְזִיקִין
Section 3: Laws of Theft, Lost and Found : גְּזֵלָה וַאֲבֵדָה

(7 Mitzvos)

474	לִגְזֹל	שֶׁלֹּא לִגְזֹל	Don't rob
475	לַעֲשֹׁק	שֶׁלֹּא לַעֲשֹׁק	Don't hold onto your worker's salary or refuse to pay a debt
476	לַחְמֹד	שֶׁלֹּא לַחְמֹד	Don't even think of ways to get what belongs to others
477	לְהִתְאַוּוֹת	שֶׁלֹּא לְהִתְאַוּוֹת	Don't desire anything belonging to someone else
478	לְהָשִׁיב	לְהָשִׁיב אֶת הַגְּזֵלָה	Return a stolen item or its value to its owner
479	לְהִתְעַלֵּם	שֶׁלֹּא יִתְעַלֵּם מִן הָאֲבֵדָה	Don't ignore a lost object
480	לְהָשִׁיב	לְהָשִׁיב הָאֲבֵדָה	Return a lost object

Book 11: Instructions Pertaining to All Types of Damages: סֵפֶר נְזִיקִין

Section 4: Laws of Physical Harm and Damage: חוֹבֵל וּמַזִּיק

(1 Mitzvah)

| 481 | חוֹבֵל | דִּין חוֹבֵל בַּחֲבֵרוֹ אוֹ מַזִּיק מָמוֹן חֲבֵרוֹ | Bais Din must judge cases of bodily harm & damage to property |

Book 11: Instructions Pertaining to All Types of Damages: סֵפֶר נְזִיקִין

Section 4: Laws of Murder and Protecting Lives: רוֹצֵחַ וּשְׁמִירַת נֶפֶשׁ

(17 Mitzvos)

Don't murder	שֶׁלֹּא לִרְצֹחַ	רוֹצֵחַ	482
Don't accept money to free a convicted murderer	שֶׁלֹּא לָקַח כֹּפֶר לְנֶפֶשׁ רוֹצֵחַ	כֹּפֶר	483
An unintentional killer must escape to a city of safety	לְהַגְלוֹת רוֹצֵחַ בִּשְׁגָגָה	גָּלוּת	484
Don't accept money from the accidental murderer instead of him going to a city of safety	שֶׁלֹּא לָקַח כֹּפֶר לִמְחֻיָּב גָּלוּת	כֹּפֶר	485
Don't execute a murderer before he stands trial	שֶׁלֹּא יוּמַת הָרוֹצֵחַ קֹדֶם עֲמִידָה בַּדִּין	קֹדֶם	486
Save the person being chased even by taking the life of the Rodef	לְהַצִּיל הַנִּרְדָּף בְּנַפְשׁוֹ שֶׁל רוֹדֵף	לְהַצִּיל	487
Don't pity the Rodef	שֶׁלֹּא לָחוּס עַל הָרוֹדֵף	לָחוּס	488
Don't stand by and do nothing when someone's life is in danger	שֶׁלֹּא לַעֲמֹד עַל דָּם	דָּם	489
Set aside cities of safety and clearly mark the roads to the nearest Arei Miklat	לְהַפְרִישׁ עָרֵי מִקְלָט וּלְהָכִין לוֹ הַדֶּרֶךְ	מִקְלָט	490
Break the Egla Arufa's neck after an unsolved murder	לַעֲרֹף אֶת הָעֶגְלָה בַּנַּחַל	עֶגְלָה	491
Don't work or plant the ground where the Egla Arufa was killed	שֶׁלֹּא יַעֲבֹד בְּאוֹתוֹ הַקַּרְקַע וְלֹא יִזָּרַע	עֲבוֹדָה	492
Don't leave objects lying around which could be dangerous	שֶׁלֹּא לָשִׂים דָּמִים	מִכְשׁוֹל	493
Make a guard rail around flat roofs	לַעֲשׂוֹת מַעֲקֶה לְגַגּוֹ	מַעֲקֶה	494
Don't put a stumbling block in front of the blind or take advantage of someone's ignorance	שֶׁלֹּא יַכְשִׁיל תָּמִים בַּדָּבָר	תָּמִים	495

Book 11: Instructions Pertaining to All Types of Damages: סֵפֶר נְזִיקִין

Section 4: Laws of Murder and Protecting Lives: רוֹצֵחַ וּשְׁמִירַת נֶפֶשׁ
(continued)

Help remove a heavy load from an animal even though it belongs to someone you hate	לִפְרֹק עִם מִי שֶׁנִּכְשַׁל בַּדֶּרֶךְ	לִפְרֹק	496
Help others load their animal	לִטְעֹן עִמּוֹ	לִטְעֹן	497
Don't pass by without helping unload an animals heavy packages and help re-loading it	שֶׁלֹּא יָנִיחֶנּוּ בַּדֶּרֶךְ נִבְהָל בְּמַשָּׂאוֹ וְיֵלֶךְ לוֹ	חֲבֵרוֹ	498

Book 12: Instructions for Acquisitions: סֵפֶר קִנְיָן
Section 1: Laws of Sales: מְכִירָה
(5 Mitzvos)

Buy and sell according to the Torah laws of business	דִּין מִקָּח וּמִמְכָּר	מִקָּח וּמִמְכָּר	499
Don't overcharge or underpay for merchandise	שֶׁלֹּא יוֹנֶה בְּמִקָּח וּמִמְכָּר	אוֹנָאַת־מָמוֹן	500
Don't hurt anybody with words	שֶׁלֹּא יוֹנֶה בִּדְבָרִים	אוֹנָאַת־דְּבָרִים	501

Don't cheat a Ger Tzedek in business	שֶׁלֹּא יוֹנֶה גֵּר צֶדֶק בְּמָמוֹנוֹ	גֵּר – מָמוֹן	502
Don't insult a Ger Tzedek with words	שֶׁלֹּא יוֹנֶה גֵּר צֶדֶק בִּדְבָרִים	גֵּר – דְּבָרִים	503

Endowments & Gifts - Rabbinical	מִדְּרַבָּנָן	זְכִיָּה וּמַתָּנָה
Neighbors' boundaries - Rabbinical	מִדְּרַבָּנָן	שְׁכֵנִים
Agents & business partners - Rabbinical	מִדְּרַבָּנָן	שְׁלוּחִים וְשֻׁתָּפִים

Book 12: Instructions for Acquisitions: סֵפֶר קִנְיָן
Section 5: Laws Relating to Treatement of Servants: עֲבָדִים
(13 Mitzvos)

English	Hebrew Description	Hebrew Name	#
Follow the laws of buying an Eved Ivri	דִין קִנְיַן עֶבֶד עִבְרִי	עֶבֶד עִבְרִי	504
Don't sell an Eved Ivri the same way a slave is sold	שֶׁלֹּא יִמָּכֵר מִמְכֶּרֶת עֶבֶד	מְכִירַת	505
Don't give an Eved Ivri harsh work	שֶׁלֹּא יַעֲבְדוּהוּ בְּפָרֶךְ	פָּרֶךְ	506
Don't allow a non-Jew to give an Eved Ivri harsh work	שֶׁלֹּא נַנִּיחַ גֵּר תּוֹשָׁב לִרְדוֹת בּוֹ בְּפָרֶךְ	לִרְדוֹת	507
Don't give degrading work to an Eved Ivri	שֶׁלֹּא נַעֲבֹד בּוֹ עֲבוֹדוֹת עֶבֶד	עֶבֶד	508
Give an Eved Ivri generous gifts when he goes free	לְהַעֲנִיק לוֹ בְּצֵאתוֹ חָפְשִׁי	לְהַעֲנִיק	509
Don't send an Eved Ivri away empty handed	שֶׁלֹּא יֵצֵא רֵיקָם	רֵיקָם	510
Buy back a Jewish girl servant to return to her family	לִפְדּוֹת אָמָה עִבְרִיָּה	לִפְדּוֹת	511
The buyer of a Jewish maidservant must marry her or marry her to his son	לִיעָדָהּ	לִיעָדָהּ	512
A master cannot sell his Jewish maidservant	שֶׁלֹּא תִמָּכֵר	לִמְכֹּר	513
An Eved Canaani must work forever, he does not go free after 6 years or Yovel	לַעֲבֹד ע׳ כְּנַעֲנִי לְעוֹלָם אֶלָּא אִם הִפִּיל לוֹ אֲדוֹנָיו אֶחָד מֵרָאשֵׁי אֵבָרָיו	לְעוֹלָם	514
Don't send back a non-Jewish slave who fled to Eretz Yisrael for safety	שֶׁלֹּא לְהַסְגִּיר עֶבֶד שֶׁבָּרַח מֵחוּ״ל לְאָ״י	לְהַסְגִּיר	515
Don't hurt a runaway non-Jewish slave with words	שֶׁלֹּא לְהוֹנוֹת עֶבֶד זֶה הַנִּצָּל אֵלֵינוּ	לְהוֹנוֹת	516

Book 13: Instructions for Acquisitions: סֵפֶר מִשְׁפָּטִים
Section 1: Laws Relating to Rentals: שְׂכִירוּת
(7 Mitzvos)

Follow the laws of a hired worker & hired guard	דִּין שָׂכִיר וְשׁוֹמֵר שָׂכִיר	שָׂכִיר	517
Pay your worker's salary on time	לִתֵּן שְׂכַר שָׂכִיר בְּיוֹמוֹ	בְּיוֹמוֹ	518
Don't delay payment of your worker's salary	שֶׁלֹּא יְאַחֵר שְׂכַר שָׂכִיר אַחַר זְמַנּוֹ	יְאַחֵר	519
Allow workers to eat from grown produce while they walk between rows	שֶׁיֹּאכַל הַשָּׂכִיר מִן הַמְחֻבָּר שֶׁעָשָׂה בּוֹ	אֲכִילָה	520
While at work, a worker may not eat from the crops	שֶׁלֹּא יֹאכַל הַשָּׂכִיר מִן הַמְחֻבָּר בִּשְׁעַת מְלָאכָה	אֲכִילַת שָׂכִיר	521
A worker must not take more than he can eat	שֶׁלֹּא יוֹלִיךְ בְּיָדוֹ יוֹתֵר מִמַּה שֶּׁיָּכוֹל לֶאֱכֹל	פּוֹעֵל יוֹלִיךְ	522
Don't muzzle an ox while it's treading grain	שֶׁלֹּא יַחְסֹם שׁוֹר בְּדִישׁוֹ וְכֵן בִּשְׁאָר בְּהֵמָה	יַחְסֹם	523

Book 13: Instructions for Acquisitions: סֵפֶר מִשְׁפָּטִים

Section 2: Laws of Borrowing and Collateral: שְׁאֵלָה וּפִקָּדוֹן

(2 Mitzvos)

Follow the laws of a borrower	דִּין שׁוֹאֵל	שׁוֹאֵל	524
Follow the laws of an unpaid guard	דִּין שׁוֹמֵר חִנָּם	שׁוֹמֵר חִנָּם	525

Book 13: Instructions for Acquisitions: סֵפֶר מִשְׁפָּטִים
Section 3: Laws of Lending and Borrowing: מַלְוֶה וְלֹוֶה
(12 Mitzvos)

Lend money to the poor	לְהַלְוֹות לְעָנִי וּמָךְ	לְהַלְוֹות	526
Don't pressure him for payment if you know he does not have money to pay you back yet	שֶׁלֹּא יִגּשׁ אוֹתוֹ	יִגּשׁ	527
Pressure a non-Jew to pay back a loan	לִגּשׁ אֶת הַנָּכְרִי	נָכְרִי	528
Someone owed money cannot take a Mashkon by force	שֶׁלֹּא יְמַשְׁכֵּן בַּעַל חוֹב בִּזְרוֹעַ	מַשְׁכּוֹן בִּזְרוֹעַ	529
Return a Mashkon when it's needed by its owner	לְהַחֲזִיר הַמַּשְׁכּוֹן לִבְעָלָיו בִּזְמָן שֶׁהוּא צָרִיךְ לוֹ	מַשְׁכּוֹן לְהַחֲזִיר	530
Don't delay returning a Mashkon	שֶׁלֹּא יְאַחֵר הַמַּשְׁכּוֹן מִבְּעָלָיו	מַשְׁכּוֹן יְאַחֵר	531
Don't demand a Mashkon from a widow	שֶׁלֹּא יַחֲבֹל אַלְמָנָה	אַלְמָנָה	532
Don't demand Keilim used for food as a Mashkon	שֶׁלֹּא יַחֲבֹל כֵּלִים שֶׁעוֹשִׂים בָּהֶם אֹכֶל נֶפֶשׁ	כְּלִי	533
Don't lend and charge Ribis	שֶׁלֹּא יִתֵּן הַמַּלְוֶה בְּרִבִּית	רִבִּית	534
Don't borrow money and pay Ribis	שֶׁלֹּא יִלְוֶה הַלֹּוֶה בְּרִבִּית	רִבִּית	535
Don't even be a witness, a guarantor, Sofer or middle man on a loan of Ribis	שֶׁלֹּא יִתְעַסֵּק אָדָם בֵּין מַלְוֶה וְלֹוֶה בְּרִבִּית וְלֹא יָעִיד בֵּינֵיהֶן וְלֹא יַעֲרֹב וְלֹא יִכְתֹּב שְׁטָר	יִתְעַסֵּק	536
Borrow and lend money with Ribis to non-Jews	לִלְוֹות מִגּוֹי וּלְהַלְוֹות לוֹ בְּרִבִּית	נָכְרִי	537

Book 13: Instructions for Acquisitions: סֵפֶר מִשְׁפָּטִים
Section 4: Laws of Claims and Defense: טוֹעֵן וְנִטְעַן
(1 Mitzvah)

#			
538	טוֹעֵן	דִּין טוֹעֵן וּמוֹדֶה אוֹ כּוֹפֵר	Bais Din must judge all types of cases of one person making a claim against another

Book 13: Instructions for Acquisitions: סֵפֶר מִשְׁפָּטִים
Section 5: Laws of Inheritance: נְחָלוֹת
(1 Mitzvah)

539	נְחָלוֹת	דִין סֵדֶר נְחָלוֹת	Follow the laws of Yerusha and the order of who inherits first, second, etc.

Book 14: Instructions for the Judicial System: סֵפֶר שׁוֹפְטִים
Section 1: Laws Relating to the Supreme Court: סַנְהֶדְרִין
(30 Mitzvos)

Select judges for Bais Din	לִמְנוֹת שׁוֹפְטִים	לִמְנוֹת	540
Don't select judges who are not expert Talmidei Chachamim	שֶׁלֹּא לִמְנוֹת דַּיָּן שֶׁאֵינוֹ יוֹדֵעַ דֶּרֶךְ הַמִּשְׁפָּט	לִמְנוֹת	541
If judges disagree, decide the case by a majority vote	לִנְטוֹת אַחֲרֵי הָרַבִּים אִם נֶחְלְקוּ הַשּׁוֹפְטִים	רֹב	542
Don't give the death penalty with a majority vote of one judge	שֶׁלֹּא לַהֲרֹג אִם רֻבּוּ הַמְחַיְּבִין בְּאִישׁ אֶחָד עַד שֶׁיִּהְיוּ יֶתֶר שְׁנַיִם	ב׳	543
A judge cannot switch verdict from innocent to guilty	שֶׁלֹּא יְלַמֵּד חוֹבָה מִי שֶׁלִּמֵּד זְכוּת בְּדִינֵי נְפָשׁוֹת	זְכוּת–חוֹבָה	544
Follow the laws of the death penalty of Skila	לַהֲרֹג בִּסְקִילָה	סְקִילָה	545
Follow the laws of the death penalty of Sereifa	לַהֲרֹג בִּשְׂרֵפָה	שְׂרֵפָה	546
Follow the laws of the death penalty of Sayif	לַהֲרֹג בְּסַיִף	סַיִף	547
Follow the laws of the death penalty by Cheneck	לַהֲרֹג בְּחֶנֶק	חֶנֶק	548
Somone who curses Hashem or worships Avoda Zara gets Skila followed by Hanging	לִתְלוֹת	לִתְלוֹת	549
Bury the executed on the same day of execution	לִקְבֹּר הַנֶּהֱרָג בְּיוֹם הֲרִיגָתוֹ	לִקְבֹּר	550
Don't delay burial overnight	שֶׁלֹּא תָלִין נִבְלָתוֹ	לְהָלִין	551
Bais Din must not let a witch or wizard live	שֶׁלֹּא לְהַחֲיוֹת מְכַשֵּׁף	מְכַשֵּׁף	552
Bais Din must whip the Choteh	לְהַלְקוֹת לָרָשָׁע	מַלְקוֹת	553
Don't whip more than the number of lashes decided by Bais Din	שֶׁלֹּא יוֹסִיף בְּהַכָּאַת הַלּוֹקֶה	יוֹסִיף	554

Book 14: Instructions for the Judicial System: סֵפֶר שׁוֹפְטִים
Section 1: Laws Relating to the Supreme Court: סַנְהֶדְרִין
(continued)

Don't give the death penalty only based on circumstantial evidence	שֶׁלֹּא יַהֲרֹג נָקִי בְּאֹמֶד דַּעַת	נָקִי	555
Don't punish an Anuss	שֶׁלֹּא לַעֲנֹשׁ אָנוּס	אָנוּס	556
A Judge must not pity a murderer at trial by giving a lesser punishment	שֶׁלֹּא לָחוּס עַל הוֹרֵג חֲבֵרוֹ אוֹ חוֹבֵל בּוֹ	לָחוּס	557
A judge must not show any favor to a poor man at a trial	שֶׁלֹּא לְרַחֵם עַל הַדַּל בַּדִּין	דַּל	558
A judge must not show favor to a rich or powerful man at a trial	שֶׁלֹּא לְהַדֵּר גָּדוֹל בַּדִּין	גָּדוֹל	559
A judge must not decide a guilty verdict because the accused is a Choteh	לֹא לְהַטּוֹת הַדִּין לְרָשָׁע אע"פ שֶׁהוּא חוֹטֵא	רָשָׁע	560
A Judge must not pervert justice	שֶׁלֹּא לְעַוֵּת מִשְׁפָּט	לְעַוֵּת	561
A judge must not favor a convert or orphan in a trial	שֶׁלֹּא לְהַטּוֹת מִשְׁפַּט גֵּר וְיָתוֹם	גֵּר יָתוֹם	562
A judge must treat both sides equally in court	לִשְׁפֹּט בְּצֶדֶק	בְּצֶדֶק	563
A judge must not let fear of threats from a violent offender sway his decision	שֶׁלֹּא לִירָא בַּדִּין מֵאִישׁ זְרוֹעַ	אִישׁ זְרוֹעַ	564
A judge must not accept bribes	שֶׁלֹּא יִקַּח שֹׁחַד	שֹׁחַד	565
A judge must not listen to a testimony till both sides are present	שֶׁלֹּא לִשָּׂא שֵׁמַע שָׁוְא	שֵׁמַע שָׁוְא	566
Don't curse judges	שֶׁלֹּא לְקַלֵּל הַדַּיָּנִים	לְקַלֵּל דַּיָּן	567
Don't curse a king or Nasi	שֶׁלֹּא יְקַלֵּל הַנָּשִׂיא	לְקַלֵּל מֶלֶךְ	568
Don't curse another Jew	שֶׁלֹּא לְקַלֵּל אָדָם מִשְּׁאָר בְּנֵי יִשְׂרָאֵל הַכְּשֵׁרִים	לְקַלֵּל יְהוּדִי	569

Book 14: Instructions for the Judicial System: סֵפֶר שׁוֹפְטִים
Section 2: Laws of Witnesses: עֵדוּת
(8 Mitzvos)

Whoever knows evidence must testify in Bais Din	לְהָעִיד בְּב"ד לְמִי שֶׁיּוֹדֵעַ לוֹ עֵדוּת	לְהָעִיד	570
Carefully examine the witnesses	לִדְרֹשׁ וְלַחֲקֹר הָעֵדִים	לִדְרֹשׁ	571
A witness cannot also be the judge in a case which could have the death penalty	לֹא יוֹרֶה בַּדִּין זֶה שֶׁהֵעִיד עָלָיו בְּדִינֵי נְפָשׁוֹת	עֵד–דַּיָּן	572
Don't accept the testimony of one witness	שֶׁלֹּא יָקוּם דָּבָר בְּעֵדוּת אֶחָד	א'	573
A Baal Aveira cannot testify	שֶׁלֹּא יָעִיד בַּעַל עֲבֵרָה	בַּעַל עֲבֵרָה	574
Relatives cannot testify	שֶׁלֹּא יָעִיד קָרוֹב	קָרוֹב	575
Don't give a false testimony	שֶׁלֹּא יָעִיד בְּשֶׁקֶר	שֶׁקֶר	576
Give false witnesses the same punishment they would have caused the accused	לַעֲשׂוֹת לְעֵד זוֹמֵם כַּאֲשֶׁר זָמַם	זוֹמֵם	577

Book 14: Instructions for the Judicial System: סֵפֶר שׁוֹפְטִים
Section 3: Laws of Obedience to Authority: מַמְרִים
(9 Mitzvos)

A Jew must follow the rulings of the Sanhedrin	לַעֲשׂוֹת עַל פִּי הַתּוֹרָה שֶׁיֹּאמְרוּ ב"ד הַגָּדוֹל	סַנְהֶדְרִין	578
Don't act differently from the rulings of the Sanhedrin	שֶׁלֹּא יָסוּר מִדִּבְרֵיהֶם	לָסוּר	579

Don't add to the 613 Mitzvos	שֶׁלֹּא לְהוֹסִיף מִצְוֹת הַתּוֹרָה שֶׁבִּכְתָב וּבְע"פ	לְהוֹסִיף	580
Don't delete any of the 613 Mitzvos	שֶׁלֹּא לִגְרֹעַ מִכָּל הַמִּצְוֹת	לִגְרֹעַ	581

Don't curse your father or your mother	שֶׁלֹּא לְקַלֵּל אָב וָאֵם	קַלֵּל או"א	582
Don't hit your father or your mother	שֶׁלֹּא לְהַכּוֹת אָב וָאֵם	לְהַכּוֹת	583
Respect your father and your mother	לְכַבֵּד אָב וָאֵם	לְכַבֵּד	584
Fear your father and your mother	לִירָא אָב וָאֵם	לִירָא	585

Don't be a Ben Sorer Umoreh	שֶׁלֹּא יִהְיֶה הַבֵּן סוֹרֵר עַל קוֹל אָבִיו וְאִמּוֹ	סוֹרֵר	586

Book 14: Instructions for the Judicial System: סֵפֶר שׁוֹפְטִים

Section 4: Laws of Mourning: אָבֵל

(4 Mitzvos)

587	ז׳ קְרוֹבִים	לְהִתְאַבֵּל עַל הַקְּרוֹבִים וַאֲפִלּוּ כֹּהֵן מִתְטַמֵּא וּמִתְאַבֵּל עַל קְרוֹבִים, וְאֵין אָדָם מִתְאַבֵּל עַל הֲרוּגֵי ב״ד	Mourn close relatives. Even Kohanim can become Tameh for their closest relatives
588	כ״ג	שֶׁלֹּא יִטַּמֵּא כֹּהֵן גָּדוֹל לַקְּרוֹבִים	A Kohen Gadol must not become Tameh even for his closest relatives
589	כ״ג	שֶׁלֹּא יִכָּנֵס עִם הַמֵּת בָּאֹהֶל	Kohen Gadol cannot to be under the same roof as a dead body
590	כֹּהֵן	שֶׁלֹּא יִטַּמֵּא כֹּהֵן הֶדְיוֹט בְּנֶפֶשׁ אָדָם אֶלָּא לַקְּרוֹבִים בִּלְבַד	A Kohen must not become Tameh except for his closest relatives

Book 14: Instructions for the Judicial System: סֵפֶר שׁוֹפְטִים
Section 5: Laws of Kings and Warfare: מְלָכִים וּמִלְחֲמוֹתֵיהֶם:
(23 Mitzvos)

Only select a Jewish king	לְמַנּוֹת מֶלֶךְ מִיִּשְׂרָאֵל	מֶלֶךְ	591
Don't select a convert to be a king	שֶׁלֹּא יְמַנֶּה מִקְּהַל גֵּרִים	גֵּר	592
A king must not have too many wives	שֶׁלֹּא יַרְבֶּה לוֹ נָשִׁים	נָשִׁים	593
A king must not have too many horses	שֶׁלֹּא יַרְבֶּה לוֹ סוּסִים	סוּסִים	594
A king must not have too much gold and silver	שֶׁלֹּא יַרְבֶּה לוֹ כֶּסֶף	כֶּסֶף	595
Destroy the seven nations of Canaan	לְהַחֲרִים שִׁבְעָה עֲמָמִים	לְהַחֲרִים	596
Don't let any of the Seven Nations of Canaan remain alive	שֶׁלֹּא לְהַחֲיוֹת מֵהֶם נְשָׁמָה	נְשָׁמָה	597
Wipe out descendants of Amalek	לִמְחוֹת זַרְעוֹ שֶׁל עֲמָלֵק	לִמְחוֹת	598
Remember what Amalek did to the Jewish people when we came out of Egypt	לִזְכֹּר מַה שֶּׁעָשָׂה לָנוּ עֲמָלֵק	לִזְכֹּר	599
Don't forget Amalek's evil attack on Benei Yisrael	שֶׁלֹּא לִשְׁכֹּחַ מַעֲשָׂיו הָרָעִים וְאָרְבָתוֹ בַּדֶּרֶךְ	לִשְׁכֹּחַ	600
Don't live in Egypt permanently	שֶׁלֹּא לִשְׁכֹּן בְּאֶרֶץ מִצְרַיִם	לָשׁוּב	601
Offer a peace agreement to a city under siege	לִשְׁלוֹחַ שָׁלוֹם לְיוֹשְׁבֵי הָעִיר כְּשֶׁצָּרִים עָלֶיהָ	שָׁלוֹם	602
Don't offer peace to Ammon or Moav during a siege	שֶׁלֹּא לִדְרֹשׁ שָׁלוֹם מֵעַמּוֹן וּמוֹאָב בִּלְבַד כְּשֶׁצָּרִים עֲלֵיהֶם	עַמּוֹן וּמוֹאָב	603

Book 14: Instructions for the Judicial System: סֵפֶר שׁוֹפְטִים
Section 5: Laws of Kings and Warfare: מְלָכִים וּמִלְחֲמוֹתֵיהֶם
(continued)

Description	Hebrew Keyword	Hebrew Text	#
Don't destroy fruit trees during a siege	אִילָנֵי	שֶׁלֹּא לְהַשְׁחִית אִילָנֵי מַאֲכָל בְּמָצוֹר	604
Prepare bathroom areas when going to war	לְתַקֵּן	לְהַתְקִין יָד שֶׁיֵּצְאוּ בּוֹ בַּעֲלֵי הַמַּחֲנֶה לְהִפָּנוֹת	605
Every soldier must have a small shovel to dig with	לְתַקֵּן	לְהַתְקִין יָתֵד לַחְפֹּר בּוֹ	606
Select a special Kohen to speak to the soldiers before battle	כֹּהֵן	לִמְשֹׁחַ כֹּהֵן לְדַבֵּר בְּאָזְנֵי אַנְשֵׁי הַצָּבָא בִּשְׁעַת מִלְחָמָה	607
A soldier who just married, built a house or planted a vineyard must return home	שָׁנָה א׳	לִהְיוֹת מְאָרֵשׂ וּבוֹנֶה בִּנְיָן וְנוֹטֵעַ כֶּרֶם שְׂמֵחִים בְּקִנְיָנָם שָׁנָה תְּמִימָה וּמַחֲזִירִין אוֹתָם מִן הַמִּלְחָמָה	608
In the first year of marriage, a husband does no military service or communal service	שָׁנָה א׳	שֶׁלֹּא יַעֲבֹר עֲלֵיהֶם לְכָל דָּבָר וְלֹא יֵצְאוּ אֲפִלּוּ לְצָרְכֵי צִבּוּר וּלְצָרְכֵי הַגְּדוּד וְהַדּוֹמֶה לָהֶם	609
Don't panic and retreat during battle	לַעֲרֹץ	שֶׁלֹּא לַעֲרֹץ וְלַחֲזֹר לְאָחוֹר בִּשְׁעַת מִלְחָמָה	610
A Jewish soldier must follow the laws of a Yafes Toar	יְפַת	דִּין יְפַת תֹּאַר	611
Don't sell a Yafes Toar into slavery	תִּמְכֹּר	שֶׁלֹּא תִמְכֹּר יְפַת תֹּאַר	612
Don't keep a Yafes Toar to be your maid. Either marry her or free her	לְהַעֲבִידָהּ	שֶׁלֹּא יִכְבְּשֶׁנָּה לְעַבְדוּת אַחַר שֶׁנִּבְעֲלָה	613

PART IV

Appendices

Chapter 8:

Why Does Hashem Give Us So Many Mitzvos?

This question has many possible answers. We will answer it with another question: How much does Hashem really love us? The answer is obviously so important because Chazal have us reminding ourselves every morning and evening in our daily davening of how much Hashem loves us: In Shachris before Shema we recite אַהֲבַת עוֹלָם אֲהַבְתָּנוּ "Your love for us is unlimited..." and in Maariv we say before Shema אַהֲבַת עוֹלָם בֵּית יִשְׂרָאֵל עַמְּךָ אָהָבְתָּ - "Your love for the House of Israel is eternal..." and then we connect this declaration of Hashem's constant and eternal love for us with the biggest reason why He loves us - תּוֹרָה וּמִצְוֹת, חֻקִּים וּמִשְׁפָּטִים אוֹתָנוּ לִמַּדְתָּ, - "You taught us Torah, Mitzvos, Statutes and Mishpatim." In other words, the greatest demonstration of Hashem's love for us is in the very fact He has given us so many Mitzvos to practise so that He can reward us accordingly.

Hashem's love for us as revealed in His gifting us so many Mitzvos is echoed in the Mishna - **Makos, 3:16**

רַבִּי חֲנַנְיָא בֶּן עֲקַשְׁיָא אוֹמֵר,
רָצָה הַקָּדוֹשׁ בָּרוּךְ הוּא לְזַכּוֹת אֶת יִשְׂרָאֵל, לְפִיכָךְ הִרְבָּה לָהֶם תּוֹרָה וּמִצְוֹת, שֶׁנֶּאֱמַר (ישעיה מב) יְיָ חָפֵץ לְמַעַן צִדְקוֹ יַגְדִּיל תּוֹרָה וְיַאְדִּיר:

"Because Hashem desires to give us merit (demonstrating His unlimited love for us), He thus increased the opportunities to fulfil His Torah with a multitude of Mitzvos...."[86]

The Vilna Gaon's brother, Rabbi Avraham Kramer, in his sefer Maalot HaTorah quoting his brother the Vilna Gaon explains that in reality the number of Mitzvos in the Torah is unlimited. The actual number 613 is the number of sherashim, root directories that have unlimited connections to every situation and encounter in life.[87]

"I heard from my brother the Gaon z"l, that it is irrational to say that there are only 613 Mitzvos and not more, because if that were the case, then from Parshas Bereishis till Parshas Bo there are only three Mitzvos, beside the many other parshios in the Torah without any Mitzvos, this belief is unacceptable. Rather, in reality, every single word that HaShem spoke in the Torah is a Mitzvah. Even with a little insight and understanding, it becomes evident that the smallest detail of everyday living, no matter how great or seemingly insignificant the event, encounter or detail, there exists multiple Mitzvos that apply to a person in every given moment in time and every possible circumstance. Just studying the lives of the Tannaim and Amoraim, their statements in the Medrash

---

86. The Rav Bartenura explains what it means that Hashem wants to give us merit: He wants to make us righteous and give us merit. להצדיק את ישראל ולזכות אותן
87. Sefer Maalot HaTorah P.188

and Gemarah reveal that their every action was saturated with the fulfillment of many Mitzvos. Not only is every moment saturated with unlimited opportunities for Mitzvah fulfillment dictated from the Torah itself, but every word in the Torah contains within it all the other Mitzvos in the Torah and all their details."

Chapter 9:

What is the Purpose of Torah Learning?

The simple answer is to know the Ratzon HaBoreh, the desire of our Creator.

But to be a Boki and Charif, even in Kol HaTorah Kula,[88] would not be the full goal of learning. The full goal of learning is demonstrated when we are be Besimcha, filled with happiness that we are His עם נבחר chosen nation to live His Torah.

We see this recorded in Shulchan Aruch:[89] ברכת התורה צריך לזהר בה מאד.
"One should be exceedingly careful when reciting Birkas HaTorah."

The Mishna Brura explains:

> שיברך אותה בשמחה גדולה וליתן הודאה על שבחר בנו ונתן לנו כלי חמדתו
> גם אמרו חז"ל שאינו זוכה ה"ו להיות לו בן תלמיד חכם עבור זה שאינו נזהר בברכת התורה

"One should be exceedingly careful to recite the blessing with tremendous happiness and gratitude for being chosen to live His Torah, Hashem's precious gift. In addition, our sages state that one might not be deserving of a Talmid Chacham for a son (G-d forbid) if one does is not careful to recite Birkas HaTorah (with happiness)."

The Torah is without limit to its depths and breadth. So how could it be transmitted…?

---

88. to be an expert in the entire Torah.
89. ש"ע ס' מ"ו: א

Chapter 10:

How the Torah was Taught Systematically as a Commentary to the Taryag Mitzvos

The entire Chumash can be defined as containing two types of information:
1. **A Story Line**,[90] and inside the story line are located....
2. **The Taryag Mitzvos**.[91]

How the Chumash is organized:

Once the Torah was completed, we studied the text of the Torah and all its missing information, the Oral Torah, which was transmitted from teacher to student, father to son. Moshe Rabeynu divided the Torah into 54 readings which we call the weekly parsha. Each reading is subdivided into Parshiot (paragraphs, not to be confused with the term 'weekly parsha').[92] So, throughout the year every Jew would review all Taryag Mitzvos found throughout the Torah. But the Torah gives no details to enable a Jew to apply a single Mitzvah! All the missing information is in the Oral Law which was taught by Moshe Rabeynu throughout the forty years in the Midbar.[93]

How the Mishna is organized:

When Rabeynu HaKadosh, Rebbi Yehuda HaNassi, edited and formulated the Mishna, it was extremely organized. Essentially, he took all Taryag Mitzvos of the Torah and provided all the main details of Taryag Mitzvos under six sections known as Shisha Sedarim. So that all of the 613 Mitzvos relevant to agricultural laws were placed under the first Seder called Zeraim (literally 'seeds'). All Mitzvos related to time were located under the title Moed, etc,. Then Rabeynu Hakadosh divided all six sections of the Mishna into 63 sub-sections, known as Masechtas, or tractates. Each tractate was

---

90. Starting with the story of creation of the universe, man, the flood, the lives of the Avos, the sons of Yaakov, sons go down to Egypt for grain and find Yosef, reunited with Yosef, Egyptian slavery, the Exodus, Matan Torah and then the forty year trek in the wilderness. This is the skeletal outline of the story line.
91. The 613 Mitzvos are found throughout the story line without any apparent sequence. The Rishonim organized the Mitzvos into different lists. The Mitzvos still remain the foundation from which the Mishna, the Gemora and later the halacha are all built.
92. See Eruvin 53b
93. See Eruvin 53b-54. How did Moshe Rabeynu teach the Torah Sh'Baal Peh? He taught one parsha of the Torah at a time to Aron HaKohen with the Oral Law on that parsha (or 'paragraph,' or what we call 'Petuchos Ustumos.' see the first Rashi in Vayikra citing Toras Kohanim, parsha 1:8-9, who explains it thus: ומה היו הפסקות משמשות, לתן רוח למשה להתבונן בין פרשה לפרשה ובין ענין לענין, קל וחמר להדיוט הלומד מן הדיוט, in other words, Moshe Rabeynu would pause between the paragraphs of the Torah in order to think about the Oral Law on that paragraph). Then Moshe Rabeynu taught that same paragraph to Aron HaKoehens' sons, with the Oral Law explanation and then he taught it a third time to the Zekenim, and a fourth time to the Shevatim. In all, Moshe Rabeynu taught every parsha of the Torah four times. Then Aron would teach the exact same paragraph to the Shevatim, then Aron's sons would teach it and finally the Zekenaim, so in total, everyone heard the Oral law at least once from Moshe Rabeynu directly and between Aron, Aron's sons and the Zekenim, all Klal Yisrael heard each parsha with its Oral Law four times. The remainder of the day, the fathers reviewed the Torah they learned with their children, that is the literal and accurate meaning of ושננתם לבניך which really means to 'repeat to your children.' See foot note 7 above.

further divided into numbered and named Chapters and every chapter was broken down into numbered paragraphs, each one called a Mishna. All the Mishnayos cover the entire 613 Mitzvos.

The writing of the Mishna was extremely organized concise. Mishnayos are headlines for much more information, and that information is really the details of Taryag Mitzvot. **The Mishna is really a commentary to the Taryag Mitzvos.** The Rav Bartenura on Avot 1.1 actually defines Avot as a unique Masechta because all the rest of Mishnayos are commentary to the Mitzvot, while Avot is a combination of different Mitzvot related to בין אדם לחברו and בין אדם למקום.

How the Gemara is organized:

Rabyenu Hakodesh wrote the Mishna so that students were forced to ask questions from their teachers to learn the missing information. The concise language of the Mishna forces questions which in turn create dialogue between the teacher and student and thus engage the minds of the students in the learning process. Within three hundred years of the Mishna being written, our sages saw it necessary to write down the missing information in the Mishna, known as Gemara or Talmud.

The Gemara is a commentary to the Mishna, it goes through each Mishna in the sequence of the information as it appears in the Mishna. The Gemara was written to explain the obvious questions that the Mishna forces a student to ask. The format of the Gemara is constant questions and answers, problems and solutions. In this way, the student studying Gemara is forced to engage his mind in the back and forth discussion of the Gemara. Indeed, the Gemara is a flow of dialogue between the Amoraim discussing each Mishna. Rarely does the Gemara give us legal rulings. So in conclusion, the Mishna is an explanation of the Taryag Mitzvos and the Gemara is an explanation to the Mishna.

How Legal Codes, Halacha on Gemara was organized:

Later,[94] the legal authorities give us precise legal rulings based on the discussions of the Gemara so that a Jew would know how to live the Taryag Mitzvos. This means to say that if a child knows all Taryag Mitzvos to some level of detail, he actually has the amazing advantage of having 613 files in his mind for all his future learning to be filed in! Whatever he learns of the legal side of Torah - Mishna, Gemara, Halacha, Shaalos Uteshuvos, his brain will file that legal information under one or more of the Taryag Mitzvos. So Mishna fills in the details to the Taryag Mitzvos while the Gemara explains the reasoning, but the ultimate goal of all this learning is to come to the הלכה למעשה, to know how to apply the Mitzvos in our lives. To that end, the Rishonim began reforming the Gemara's information.

The Rif[95]

The Rif was the first to make Gemara more accessible as an halachic work. He actually rewrote the Gemara by removing much of the machlokes of the Amoraim and excluding most non-legal statements, allegory, mashalim, stories and anecdotes. He also 'updated' the Gemara text by adding halachic rulings of Gaonim and his own contemporaries, but most outstanding, are his halachic conclusions inside the text. The Rif's work was called the 'Talmud Katan' for its reduced size of the original Shass Bavli.

---

94. After about 500 years after the closing of the Talmud. Mostly after the Gaonim.
95. Acronym for Rabeynu Itzchak alFasi, 11th Century (1013-1103), from Fez, Morocco. He was 25 years old when the last of the Gaonim, Rav Chai Gaon died.

The Rambam[96]

The Rambam reorganized the entire Torah sh'baal Peh by taking all the Taryag Mitzvos and listing them under 14 major books, known as the Mishneh Torah. He then divided these 14 into 83 topics and plotted the 613 Mitzvos under these 83 topics. Each chapter of each topic is broken into numbered Halachos. His intent was to give the widest range of Jews immediate access to Halacha, legal applications. Something that till now, only an exceptional Talmid Chacham could do, because to know a single halacha in any area, meant you needed to know the entire Talmud Bavli, Yerushalmi, Tosefta, Sifri, Sifra, Mechilta and more.[97] The reason was because there is so much cross referencing in any single page of Talmud to so many other sources that you had to know all the Talmud in order to fully understand a single halacha in depth. Rambam sought to make halacha immediately accessible by taking the entire gamut of Torah ShBal Peh, both the Bavli and Yerushalmi Talmuds, all the Braisos, Tosefta, Sifri, Sifra, Mechilta, and offer one digest of halacha using Taryag Mitzvos as the table of contents. In other words, the *Rambam's Mishneh Torah is indeed a legal digest of legal applications to the Taryag Mitzvos.*

The S'MaG[98]

The Smag wrote an halachic work and again, used Taryag Mitzvos as the format. He divided his Sefer into two sections, listing all the Mitzvos Aseh in one section and all the 'lo ta'aseh' in the second. He then gave a short essay for each Mitzvah, giving many halachic rulings as well as spicing each essay with either Aggadata or an insight that adds meaning to the performance of that mitzvah. Both the Rambam's Mishneh Torah and the Smag cover all 613 Mitzvos.

Arba Turim[99]

Though both the Rambam and the Smag each gave legal rulings on the Taryag Mitzvos, the majority of the Mitzvos no longer applied because we were in Galus. So the vast majority of agricultural laws did not apply, neither all the halachos relevant to the Bais Hamikdash, Tumah and Tahara, the Korbanos, Avoda and of course Yoval and Shemitta. Also, so many shaalos and teshuvos had been written and were still being written that there was room for a new legal work that would focus only on the 279 Mitzvos still applicable since the Churban Bayis Sheni and the subsequent Galus. And such a work could also incorporate new situations that arose which needed legal rulings applied. Thus the Tur, written by Rabeynu Yaakov, covered all areas of life in Galus. He divided his sefer into four parts, the Arba Turim, or four rows. Orach Chaim being the first, dealing with daily life (from awakening till going to sleep) and the Jewish Calendar (Shabbos, Rosh Chodesh, Pesach, Rosh Hashana, etc,). Each topic was assigned a number called a Siman. Yoreh Deah is the second section, dealing with all areas of Kashrus, Shechita, Tereifus, milk & meat mixtures, etc. As well as laws of Tzedaka, kibud av v'em, Nidda, etc,. The third section deals with all laws pertaining to marriage and divorce, known as Even HaEzer, and lastly, the fourth section is Choshen Mishpat dealing with laws of courts, witnesses, Dayanim, buying and selling, real estate, contracts, litigations, etc,. The Tur essentially became a legal digest to access all the Taryag Mitzvos which apply since the beginning of Galus Edom.

---

96. Acronym for Rabeynu Moshe Ben Maimon, 12th Century, Spain. 1135-1204. Born in Spain, moved to Egypt and died in Tiveria, Eretz Yisrael.
97. Very few Rabbis even had access to the copied manuscripts of all these works as the Printing Press had not yet been invented.
98. Sefer Mitzvos Gedolos of R' Moshe From Cucy, also known as the Sar M'Cucy, he was one of the Baaley Tosfos.
99. Rabeynu Yaakov, author of the Arba Turim was the son of the Rosh, Rabeynu Asher who himself had written legal rulings at the end of every masechta in Talmud Bavli.

Shulchan Aruch

The most prominent and arguably most thorough commentary on both the Rambam and the Tur was Rabeynu Yosef Caro.[100] He had written his 'Kesef Mishna' on the Rambam and the 'Bais Yosef' commentary on the Tur. Now he set out to write a definitive halachic work that was to become the standard legal code for all the communities in the entire Diaspora, the Shulchan Aruch, or 'set table.' He actually based his work on the same outline as the Arba Turim, using the exact 'four sections' and the numbering system of his 'Simanim' for easy reference. But R' Caro also added sub-sections to every Siman, meaning, he broke down every numbered Siman (section) into numbered halachos known as S'ifim. Rav Yosef Caro's work was essentially accepted amongst all the great legal minds and Torah leaders of the generation, despite the fact that Rabeynu Yosef Caro was Serfadi and based his rulings upon those of the Rambam, the Rif and the Rosh.[101] The famous Rema, Rabbi Moshe Isserlis, from Cracow, Poland, was planning on writing such a work himself, and seeing that the Shulchan Aruch accomplished his vision, he decided that he would add his 'side comments' wherever the Ashkenazi minhagim differed, and in a few places, he would openly disagree. His work is known as the 'Mapah'[102] and usually referred to as the Rema.[103] The main point once again, is that the Shulchan Aruch is a legal digest to all the Taryag Mitzvos which apply today so that Taryag Mitzvos is still central to the learning of halacha.

Mishna Brura[104]

Written by the famous Tzadik, Rabbi Yisrael Meir Kagan, popularly known as the Chafetz Chaim. The Mishna Berurah covers all of Orach Chaim, the first section of Shulchan. His commentary is really a digest of halachic rulings and variations of situations that arose since the writing of Shulchan Aruch. The Chafetz Chaim saw a need to give a short summary of the literally dozens of Nosey Keilim, commentaries to the Shulchan Aruch so that the vast majority of Jews trying to fulfil Hashem Mitzvos as they apply to him would be able to find the halacha fast and efficiently instead of laboring through the many and often long legal explanations of the commentaries to Shulchan Aruch. So many new situations had arisen in the past 400 years since Shulchan Aruch was first printed, and so many legal authorities had been printed around the text of Shulchan Aruch, that its learning was no longer easy, because there were so many commentaries and hundreds of thousands of piskey halachos in the thousands of Shaalos and Teshuvos (legal responsa written since Shulchan Aruch) that a short digest of the main points of rulings was in place. Rabbi Kagan was actually planning on writing the same type of digest for Yoreh Deah. The Chofetz Chaim was himself so aware of the need for Jews around the world to know Taryag Mitzvos that he himself wrote a sefer called Sefer Mitzvos HaKatzer, where he lists all 279 Mitzvos that apply nowadays and wrote a very short essay on each Mitzvah, encouraging the reader to complete his book once a week!

So all in all, the purpose of the last few pages listing the major legal codes is to demonstrate how they are all commentaries to the Taryag Mitzvos! So, even though we do not look at Taryag Mitzvos as

---

100. He completed it in 1563 and it was first published two years later in venice. He was born in Toledo, Spain in 1488 and died in Safed, Eretz Yisrael in 1575.
101. The Rosh was Rabeynu Asher who was the Gadol Hador in Spain and was the father of Rabeynu Yaakov, author of the Arba Turim. Though himself Ashkenaz, his rulings were for the Sefardi world he served and so Rabbi Caro's rulings were based on three Sefardi legal rulings, whereas the Rema based his rulings on the Rosh & Mordecai.
102. Literally 'table cloth' meaning to say, the table cloth added to the 'set table' which is the meaning of Shulchan Aruch.
103. Rema in Hebrew is רמא which is the acronym for רבינו משה אסרליס
104. Born 1838, died 1933. Lived in Radin, Poland, was recognized as the Tzadik of the generation. He spent 18 years writing the Mishnah Berura.

central to conventional Yeshiva Curricula, it really is pivotal to all the child's future learning, from Mishna to Gemara, and indeed every single one of the legal codes.

Chapter 11:
Glossary of Terms

Hebrew Term	Meaning
Amalek	Descendants of Esav.
Amon	An enemy nation on the east side of the Yarden (Jordan River).
Anuss	A lady forced to do an aveira. She is not punished.
Aron	The transportable box containing the two stones of the Ten Commandments.
Arei Miklat	Cities of Safety where an accidental murderer can flee till trial.
Arel	Someone who does not have circumcision.
Asham Vadai	An offering for an intentional violation of the Torah.
Avoda	Service
Avoda Zara	Idol worship. Literally 'worship of [something] weird/strange. Because anything mistakenly assumed to have power of its own outside of Hashem's Power is considered weird and strange.
Azara	Temple Courtyard.
B'Simcha	State of happiness.
Ba'al Aveira	Someone with a reputation for doing Aveiros, violations of the Torah.
Bais Din	Either 3, 23 or 71 Judges in a Jewish court of law.
Bais Hamikdash	The Temple in Jerusalem.
Ben Sorer Umoreh	A rebellious son who steals meat and wine of his parents and eats and drinks out of control.
Besula	A virgin
Bigdei Kehuna	Clothing of the Kohanim when on duty in the Bais Hamikdash.
Bikurim	First fruit of seven species grown in Eretz Yisrael.
Bris Mila	Circumcision
Canaan	The land of Israel before it was conquered in the time of Joshua.
Chadash	New grain.
Chalitza	Ritual whereby the brother of the deceased releases himself from marrying the widow.

Hebrew Term	Meaning
Challa	A gift of dough to a Kohen.
Challala	A lady who is the daughter of a Kohen and was born to a mother who is forbidden to marry a Kohen.
Chametz	Flour and water mixed together and left for 18 or more minutes without kneading becomes 'leavened' or Chametz.
Chatos Ha'off	Bird offering
Chatos Hapenimi	Offering whose blood was sprinkled inside the Temple building on the Golden Altar.
Chaya	Non-domesticated kosher animal.
Chelev	Forbidden fats of a kosher animal.
Cheneck	Death penalty of strangulation.
Chet	A mistake. A violation of the Torah done unintentionally
Chilul Hashem	When a Torah Jew misbehaves, he makes people say how bad it is to be a Torah Jew.
Choshen	Breastplate only worn by the High Priest.
D'vash	Honey
Edom	Enemy nation of Amalek, south east of Eretz Yisrael, in the region of Mt. Sair.
Egla Arufa	Calf whose neck is severed in the place of an unsolved murder.
Eretz Yisrael	The Land of Israel.
Eved Canaani	A non-Jewish servant.
Eved Ivri	Jewish servant who either sold himself or was sold by Bais Din.
Ger Tzedek	A non-Jew who converted to Judaism.
Get	Divorce document.
Gid Hanasheh	Sciatic nerve sinew of the thigh.
Goyim	Gentiles/Nations
Havdala	Words said on wine at the end of Shabbos.
Ir Hanidachas	A City which was persuaded to serve Avoda Zara.
Kali	Parched grain.
Karmel	Early ripened grain.
Kesuba	Marriage contract.
Ketores	Specially prepared formula of spices called Ketores.

Hebrew Term	Meaning
Keylim	Vessels, containers, bowels, cups, utensils, etc.
Kiddush	Words said on wine before the Friday night Shabbos meal.
Kiddush Hashem	When a Jew behaves in ways which makes people say how special it is to be a Torah Jew.
Kiddushin	Marriage ritual.
Kilayim	Forbidden mixtures.
Kohen	Plural - Kohanim - Jewish Priests, descendants of Aron HaKohen.
Kohen Gadol	High Priest officiating in The Temple.
Korban	An offering. A Korban could be an animal, bird or grain offering depending on the type of Korban.
Korban Asham	Offering brought for a deliberate violation of the Torah.
Korban Chagiga	A Festival Offering brought to the Temple on each of the three festivals.
Korban Chatos	Offering brought for many different accidental violations of the Torah.
Korban Metzora	Three Lamb offerings, one Olah, one Chatos and one Asham.
Korban Olah	Offering that was totally burned on the Altar.
Korban Olas Riya	An Offering brought to the Temple whenever one sees the Temple. The literal meaning of the word 'Olas Riya' is an 'offering of appearing' that is brought up (to be completely burned on the Altar) whenever one is seen in the Temple.
Korban Oleh V'Yored	A Sliding Scale Offering. A rich man brings a lamb, a poor man can bring either two doves or a grain offering.
Korban Pesach Sheni	For anyone Tameh or too far to bring the Pascal Lamb on the 14th of Nissan, he gets a second chance to bring a Pesach offering in the following month of Iyar, called the Korban Pesach Sheni, or 'Second' Pascal Lamb.
Korban Shelamim	Offering whose meat was partly burned on the Altar and partly eaten by both the officiating Kohanim and the owners of the animal offered.
Korban Yoledes	An offering of a lamb and two turtle doves for a Yoledes after she is Tahor.
Korban Zav	An offering of two turtle doves brought by Zav after he is Tahor.
Korban Zava	An offering of two turtle doves brought by a Zava after she is Tahor.
Leket	One or two stalks of wheat left in the field which the owner has to leave for the poor.
M'aness	Rapist
Maaser Beheima	One tenth of one's domestic animals.

Hebrew Term	Meaning
Maaser Oni	An agricultural tax of one tenth of the farmers produce given to the poor in years 3 and 6 of the Shemitta cycle.
Maaser Rishon	An agricultural tax of 1/10 of the produce given to the Levi after the farmer gave Teruma Gedola to the Kohen.
Maaser Sheni	A second tithe. In years 1,2, 4 and 5 of Shemitta, the farmer takes 1/10 of his produce to the Bais Hamikdash to eat it there. This is called Maaser Sheni.
Maaseros	Agricultural Taxes or Tithes.
Mamzer	Child born from adulteration.
Mashkon	Collateral, an item used as security pledge against a loan.
Me'il	Sky blue gown only worn by the High Priest.
Mefateh	Seducer.
Mei Nidda	Water mixed with the ashes of the Red Hefer to purify someone who is Tameh Meis.
Melacha	One of 39 forbidden activities on Shabbos. Sometimes Melacha is an activity related to working the land in the year of Shemitta or work related to animals.
Metzora	Someone with a skin condition caused by certain Aveiros, especially Lashon Hara.
Mezuza	Two paragraphs of Shema written on parchment and rolled up and affixed to the door posts in a Jewish home.
Mincha	Grain offering.
Minchas Choteh	Grain offering for certain unintentional violations.
Mizbayach	Altar
Moav	An enemy nation on the East side of the Yarden (Jordan River).
Molech	Name of Avoda Zara which burns children in fire.
Motzi Shem Ra	Husband who claims his wife was not loyal during engagement.
Mumar	Someone who denies the Divine Origin of the Torah.
Nasi	Head of the Sanhedrin or President of the Jewish People.
Navi	Someone who is known to people to be a great Talmid Chacham and Tzadik from a very young age and who Hashem gives messages to him for the Jewish people.
Navi Sheker	Someone who lies and pretends Hashem spoke to him.
Nazir	A man or lady who promises not to drink wine for 30 days.
Neder	A verbal promise.

Hebrew Term	Meaning
Neta Reva'i	Fourth year produce.
Nezirim	Wild grapes.
Niddah	A lady who sees blood during menstrual period.
Ollelos	Small bunches of grapes left for the poor.
Onen	A Mourner of any of his 7 closest relatives on the first day after death.
Orla	Fruit grown in the first three years after a tree was planted.
Ov	Name of Avoda Zara which uses a skull to speak to the dead.
Parah Aduma	Red Cow, also called a Red Hefer.
Peah	Corner (can refer to the corner of the head or corner of a field).
Peret	Either fallen individual grapes or fallen unformed grapes.
Pidyon Haben	A first born son automatically belongs to the Kohanim. The father buys his son back in a ceremony called Pidyon Haben, redeeming the son.
Reishit Hagez	A gift of wool sheering to the Kohen.
Ribis	Interest on a loan.
Rishon	First
Rodef	Someone in pursuit of another person with intent to harm or kill.
Rosh Chodesh	New Month.
Sanhedrin	Jewish Supreme Court, consisting of 71 of the highest caliber judges.
Sariss	Someone unable to have children.
Sayif	Death penalty of decapitation by the sword.
Se'or	Yeast
Sefer Torah	Torah Scroll
Sefichim	Wild crops (ownerless).
Sereifa	Death penalty of having molten lead poured down the throat.
Shaatnez	A mixture of wool and linen in a garment.
Shabbos	Jewish day of rest, the seventh day after Hashem created the universe in 6 days and rested on the Seventh, Shabbos.
Shavua	An oath using Hashem's Name.
Shecht	Ritual slaughter by a trained Shochet with a blade about 5 times the sharpness of a razor blade and insures the slaughter of the animal in the least painless way.

Hebrew Term	Meaning
Shekel	Coin
Shema	The Shema Yisrael prayer.
Shemen Hamishcha	Specially prepared anointing oil made.
Shemitta year	The Seventh year in Eretz Yisrael.
Sheratzim	Eight specific reptiles listed by the Torah whose dead body causes Tumah upon contact.
Shevet	Tribe
Shichvas Zera	Liquid that exits from a man and makes him Tameh.
Shofar	Horn of a Ram.
Skila	Death penalty of being thrown from a two story structure.
Sota	Married lady accused by her husband of being alone with another man.
Talmid Chacham	Someone who knows all 24 Sefarim of Tanach as well as Mishna and Talmud. (Plural: Talmidei Chachamim)
Tameh	A state of spiritual contamination usually caused by contact with a dead body that transmits Tumah, or with a person or object which can transmit Tumah.
Tefilin	Black boxes of leather with Shema Yisrael written inside. They are worn on head and arm of every man above Bar Mitzvah.
Teruma Gedola	An agricultural tax of any amount that is given to the Kohen. Rabbinically the Jewish farmer gives 1/50th of his produce.
Tevel	Produce which has not yet had agricultural taxes removed (Teruma, Ma'aser have not been taken from this produce).
Tishrei	Name of first month in Jewish Calendar.
Toshav	A Gentile living in Eretz Yisrael who promises not to serve Avoda Zara. He does eat Neveilos.
Treifa	A Kosher animal with a physical defect which means it will die within 12 months.
Tumas Meiss	Spiritual contamination caused by contact with a human corpse.
Tzadik	Someone who behaves correctly according to the Torah. (Plural – Tzadikim)
Tzitzis	Eight fringes of wool tied to the four corners of a garment.
Viduy Maaser	A recitation of the Jewish Farmer declaring he has separated all his agricultural taxes correctly.
Yafes Toar	Non-Jewish captive lady of war.

Hebrew Term	Meaning
Yerusha	Inheritance.
Yetzias Mitzrayim	The Exodus from Egypt.
Yibum	Leverite right where the closest in age brother of the deceased marries the childless widow.
Yidoni	Name of Avoda Zara which uses the bone of a bird called the Yidoni to tell the future.
Yirah	Reverence or fear.
Yoledes	A lady who just gave birth becomes Tameh.
Yomim Tovim	The three festivals of Pesach, Shavuos and Sukkos.
Yovel	The fiftieth year also called Jubilee year.
Zav	A man who has a flow of liquid from his body making him Tameh.
Zava	A lady who has a flow of liquid from her body making her Tameh.
Zonah	A lady who takes money or other compensation for her services.

Chapter 12:
How to Explain the Arayus Mitzvos to Young Children

The New Challenge:
Generally speaking, young children do not need details of any the Mitzvos pertaining to Arayus. On the other hand, we do not want our children learning any corrupted impressions about relationships from the street. We are also faced with the additional challenge that the street has infiltrated almost everyone's lives through technology. The invasion of technology and our dependency on it has reached a point where it is all but impossible to insulate our children's pure Neshamos and protect their Temimus. The infiltration is so overwhelming that if we are not open and honest with our children about what the Torah has to say about forbidden relationships, we are almost inviting the street to offer its version.

The goal of this short explanation of how to approach these Mitzvos is to give enough information for now. The goal here is not give details, but just enough information for the child to know the Torah is not scared to talk about anything. As the child matures, the parent can be more open as the situation merits.

Resource for more information:
At www.breakthroughchinuch.com we have an mp3 lecture entitled 'When and How to Talk to Your Children about the Birds & the Bees.' The lecture is available for download. We recommend you listen to that lecture in preparation for if/when your child asks for more specifics.

How the Picture Cards illustrate Issurei Arayos.
The actual prohibition of Arayos in the Torah refer to **איסורי ביאה**. We have depicted this with a Chuppa and a red X, denoting they are not allowed to marry. This is not accurate to the actual Aveira referred to by the Torah, but this was considered by veritable Gedolei Yisrael as an acceptable way to show young minds that these relationships are forbidden without going into further detail.

As one of the consultants on the Taryag Project of the Taryag Foundation, I am familiar with how the Gedolim consulted (notably Rav Chaim Kanievsky shlita, Reb Eliyashav z"l) responded to the question of how to describe **איסורי ביאה** to children in both picture format and words, one version they agreed to was '**not to live as married with...**' and then name the specific forbidden relationship, either a mother, sister, aunt, etc. Thus, the picture of the Chuppa with a red X in our stick figure version.[105]

Naming the specific Issur:
In the stick figure version we have simply listed the name of the person under the general title of forbidden relationships. So, in a picture of a bride standing under the Chuppa, we have written the

---
105. In our photo version of the Taryag Mitzvos, we have also used this expression 'not to live as married with....'

name of the person forbidden in this relationship. See pictures 139-168 as examples of 16 forbidden relationships illustrated this way. Included in that range of pictures are a man and lady 'forbidden to be married' to an animal. Again, the actual issur in the Torah refers to ביאה with an animal. We have followed the same idea with the issur of משכב זכור where two stick figures of men are under a Chuppa with the red X going through the Chuppa. Usually this is enough for young children to understand without details.

How to answer ' questions on איסורי ביאה.
If a child does ask 'how does a man marry a dog?' Or 'how does a man marry another man?' I have found that for young children, the best way to answer is to tell the child or class "that is an excellent question and the Mishna and Gemora write all about it and when we get there, we will learn about them."

The danger of not answering how we will address this topic:
It is important to give yourself credit in the eyes of the children by specifically referencing where the Torah talks about the details. This disarms the children from the wrong impression or damaging impression that this entire subject is taboo and forbidden to know or learn about. We want to avoid the wrong message. If we do not tell them anything, their question will not go away, they will simply know the teacher or parent is the wrong address for the answer. The non- response almost becomes the invitation for the 'street' to reach them instead.

Sample response #1
A simple example of how to respond would be to point to a specific Sefer, for example, Sefer HaChinuch, or tell them about this Sefer if you do not have it in the classroom. Tell the students that "when we learn this Sefer, we will learn more details."

Sample answer #2
Consider another option: "When we reach Mitzvos 188-212 (where all the Arayus are discussed) we will learn this in more detail."

Sample answer #3
Another option would be to point to a Sefer of Rambam or to the picture of the Rambam on the History time line in the classroom and tell them "When we get to Rambam's 5th book, Sefer Kedusha, section #1, we will learn this in more detail."
Even tell the children the number of that Mitzvah or range of Mitzvos of forbidden relationships (in Rambam, Hilchos Issurei Bi'ah, its 139-175).

You are not giving details, you are simply being honest that the Torah teaches us all we need to know and we will get to the details of the Issur later.

A Torah way to view this topic:
Consider the following: Pirkei Avot (5:21) gives us a list of milestones in a person's life. Children learn the entire Tanach from ages five till ten, בן חמש שנים למקרא.[106] This means they encounter the stories of many serious Issurei Arayos.[107]

---

106. Shulchan Aruch follows the same age guidelines as found in Yorah Deah, Siman #245, S'if #4, the Mechaber rules a father has to teach or hire a rebbe to teach his son the entire Torah Sh'bichtav which both the Shach and Taz explain means all TaNaCh.
107. Chapter 19:4-10, the men surrounding Lot's house want to commit Mishkav Zachor with Lot's guests and in the same chapter 19:30-38, the story

See the footnote below for the specific references to Mishkav Zachor in Sdom; the episode of Lots' daughters; the stories of Dina; Er and Onan; Yehuda and Tamar; Potifar's wife; Zimri, the leader of Shevet Shimon took the Moabite princess, Kozbi. These are all glaring examples where some level of pashut pashat has to be taught to the children. Clearly, the Torah itself is not shying away from informing our children of these sordid episodes in the age period between 5-10 years old! It's difficult to argue that we are not meant to teach children these stories before ten years old because both the Mishna[108] and Shulchan Aruch[109] clearly instruct us to be teaching all Tanach before ten years old.

The Torah obviously wants us to know who is forbidden to us, and lists them in Vayikra Chapters 18 and 20, as well as other places throughout Tanach. In Nach, stories abound of forbidden relationships. This would include the Pilegesh in Givah (Shoftim Ch.19) and the story of Shimshon in Shoftim Chapters 13-16, then of Amnon and Tamar in Shmuel I, Chapter 13, and with the rebellion of Avshalom who took ten wives of David Hamelech, etc. Though we can get away without teaching specific details of these stories, they are obviously written to be taught, at the very least, in a general sense.

The Chazon Ish on when to teach these topics:
I heard from Rabbi Yaakov Greenwald,[110] Shlita who heard from the Chazon Ish who was asked when to teach children about עניני עריות and his response was "when the child learns Chumash and Nach." I take this to mean that as one is learning these subjects in the context of the Torah learning, that is the opportunity to learn about these subjects with our children and students. It is simply healthy for children to learn about these subjects in the safe context of a parent learning Torah with their child and for the child to realize that the Torah is not afraid of reality, that terrible Aveiros exist and people have made poor choices. The Torah instructs against these choices and encourages us to live with Kedusha and avoid behaviors which destroy our lives in this world and and possibly the next, רח"ל. When learning of the greatness of Yosef HaTzadik in Bereishis Chapter 37-40, and specifically his Nissayon with the wife of Potifar, the children are learning within the Torah context that Yosef refused to do an Aveira with Zelusha, Potifar's wife. Yosef was only seventeen turning eighteen at the time. Ask the child: "Why is Yosef called Yosef 'HaTzadik?" "Oh, he refused to do the terrible Aveira of living as married with another man's wife!" Yaakov Avinu describes his Bracha to Reuven in Bereishis 49:3 - רְאוּבֵן בְּכֹרִי אַתָּה כֹּחִי **וְרֵאשִׁית אוֹנִי** יֶתֶר שְׂאֵת וְיֶתֶר עָז. Rashi (quoting Chazal[111]) explains the meaning of the words **וְרֵאשִׁית אוֹנִי**, 'the Raishis of my strength' as - הִיא טִפָּה רִאשׁוֹנָה שֶׁלּוֹ, שֶׁלֹּא רָאָה קֶרִי מִיָּמָיו, אוֹנִי. כֹּחִי. The beginning of my strength means the very first drop of semen he ever produced was what conceived Reuven because he had never seen Keri his entire life till then (Yaakov Avinu married when he was 84 years old!).

A Reality Check - Today's Generation:
In a generation when children are going to find out sooner or later from the street, or perhaps, more

---

with Lot's daughters mothering their father's sons. Ch. 34:1-31, the story of Shem, the son of Chamor abusing Dina. Ch.38:2-11, the story of Er and Onan spilling Zera l'vatala. Then later in Ch. 38:12-30 with Yehuda and Tamar. Ch. 39:7-20 the story of Potifar's wife and her attempt to seduce Yosef HaTzadik. In Bamidbar, Chapter 22 you find the story of Bilam and his donkey, while in Chapter 25:1-9 is the episode of Beney Ysirael's promiscuity at Shittim, and in Ch. 26:14-15, the open decadence of Zimri Ben Salu, the Nasi if Shimon with the Moabite princess Kozbi Bat Tzur.
108. Avot 5:21.
109. Yoreh Deah, 245:2.
110. Mechaber of Etzos V'Hadrachos, written with the Steipler Gaon.
111. Medrash Raba (Bereishis) 98:4 & Yevamos 76a.

accurately, 'sooner *than* later' from the street, we have more urgency than ever to reach our children first. What better way to first talk about these subjects than when they appear in the weekly parsha or when learning with our children!?

We parents and teachers are our children's frame of reference. We are the shapers of their reality. Till they form their own independent minds and learn to think for themselves, they totally depend on us to give meaning to what they see, hear and experience. A child who innocently sees two אנשים in an embrace on the city streets is confusing at the very least, and is peeling away layers of insulation of Kedusha. The exposure alone to a 'duty free magazine' on a plane, or an unclean scene in a movie, requires that we give Torah clarity to their experiences, or else suffer the worse alternative of the consequences of our silence. Our silence creates a void which the street, internet, magazine pictures and movies will easily fill. Perhaps we could argue that *our silence invites the street* to fill in the blanks of our silence! The best way to win our children's confidence is to be honest with them.

The best way to win our children's confidence is to be honest with them.
The Torah is honest with us about reality of horrific Aveiros committed from day one of Man's existence. So how do we respond? We suggest two levels of answers; one for young minds, and the second level answer for slightly older children.

Answers for young minds.[112]
Most young children's natural curiosity is satisfied when we tell them we are going to learn more about this when we get to that part of Chumash or Sefer Ploni. They are happy to know an answer exists without knowing the specifics now.

Answers for children who need more information:
When children ask questions which need more detailed answers, we have a bigger obligation to give more information because if not, they will either seek it outside the confines of our homes or will be more receptive to the street's version since we did not not respond satisfactorily. One approach is to offer a metaphor.

Explaining the Mitzvah of פְּרוּ וּרְבוּ:
Give the analogy of a fruit bearing tree. Show the child the passuk in the Torah which uses the language of being 'fruitful' when instructing Adam to have children.[113] Here is a suggested metaphor: Hashem makes a seed which is planted in the ground. The seed grows inside the ground from the nutrients in the soil, the rain and the sunshine. Gradually the seed grows into a fruit bearing tree of its own. Each fruit on the tree has its own seeds which too can be planted and become another generation of fruit bearing trees. So too, Hashem created man to be able to give a seed which is planted into the lady he marries. That seed grows inside a special place in her body called the 'womb,' or רֶחֶם. The food eaten by the lady goes into the seed in her womb till the seed grows into a baby. The food the mummy eats nourishes the baby till the baby is ready to come out her womb, it takes about

---

112. There is no set age to the term 'young minds.' In chazal, a child has the din of a child till Bar Mitzvah or Bat Mitzvah. Then they are adults. So 'young child' is either till Bar Mitzvah or earlier. If a young child has the maturity or the need for a more forthright response than 'we will learn about this in more detail when we learn Sefer Ploni, or Masechta Ploni, then such a young child will need the type of response in the next paragraph.

113. Bereishit 1:28 וַיְבָרֶךְ אֹתָם אֱלֹהִים וַיֹּאמֶר לָהֶם אֱלֹהִים **פְּרוּ וּרְבוּ** וּמִלְאוּ אֶת־הָאָרֶץ

nine months for the seed to grow into a baby who is ready to come out. While in the womb, Hashem makes the perfect temperature for the baby to grow. Hashem makes the womb protect the seed and keep it safe while it grows into a baby.

If a child then asks "how does a father plant a seed in the mother?" You can have a Masechta Kiddushin close by and respond: "we will learn all about that when we learn Mishnayos Kiddushin[114] and Gemora Kesubos.[115]

The main message:
The main message to the child is that the Torah is not silent on the matter. The Torah is clear and unafraid to discuss these topics, but the context is Torah, therefore it is in the context of Kedusha and Tahara.

In explaining forbidden relationships using this analogy, one would explain that Hashem only wants us to plant seeds in a lady we are permitted to marry.

Any more details than this can be communicated one on one between a father and son, a mother and daughter.[116]

Explaining The Mitzvah of a Mefateh, Seducer.
Some rebbeim asked for guidance specifically on Mitzvah #131, regarding a Mefateh. We just used the Hebrew name of a מפתה instead of the more sophisticated term 'seducer.' The rebbe explaining the Mitzvah can define a Mefateh as a man who convinces a young unmarried girl to live as married, and because he persuaded her when she really did not want to, he has to pay a penalty of 50 silver coins unless he agrees to marry her properly. If he does not marry her properly, then Bais Din make him pay the 50 silver coins and another fine of money for embarrassment to the family called Boshes, and yet another fine called Pegum for making it harder for her to find a really good husband (loss of desirability).

Explaining The Mitzvah of a M'Aness, Rapist.
Another Mitzvah, #132, a M'Aness, rapist, has to marry the lady he hurt. The simplest way to explain this Mitzvah is to say someone who forces a lady to live as married has to marry her properly and stay married. (If she does not want to marry him, of course, she does not have to).

---

114. Chapter. #1 Mishna #1. There are 4 methods of Kiddushin, one of them is Bi'ah.
115. The first 10 pages of the Gemora.
116. We recommend the lecture 'How & When to Talk to your Children about the Birds and the Bees' which can be downloaded at BreakthroughChinuch.com. It covers more details and approaches to this topic.

Explaining a Sariss, Castrated Person or Animal.

In Mitzvah #167 a Jewish lady is not allowed to marry a Sariss and in Mitzvah #168 we are not allowed to cause a person or animal to become a Sariss. How do we explain Sariss to children? The simple explanation for #167 is that A man who cannot have children is called a Sariss. This Mitzvah means a Jewish lady is not allowed to marry a Sariss, a man who is not able to have children. For Mitzvah #168, we can simply explain: we not allowed to do anything that will make a man or animal into a Sariss. Hashem created a perfect world, Hashem blessed Adam with the Mitzvah to make a family and fill the world with people.[117] Hashem also blessed the animals, birds, fish and insects to have children and fill the world.[118]

Don't forget to open the Shefa of Siyata Dishmaya:

Lastly, put a peruta in Tzedaka before talking to your children and say a brief Tefila asking the Ribbono Shel Olam to give you the right words and for your child to be receptive to only taking what you have to say bikdusha u'b'tahara, Amen.

In the zchus of only wanting to guard our children from a society which has been saturated with decadence throughout the media, may we all be zoche to much nachas from all our children and talmidim, Amen.

---

117. Bereishis 1:28, וַיְבָרֶךְ אֹתָם אֱלֹהִים וַיֹּאמֶר לָהֶם אֱלֹהִים פְּרוּ וּרְבוּ וּמִלְאוּ אֶת־הָאָרֶץ וְכִבְשֻׁהָ וּרְדוּ בִּדְגַת הַיָּם וּבְעוֹף הַשָּׁמַיִם וּבְכָל־חַיָּה הָרֹמֶשֶׂת עַל־הָאָרֶץ. And again after Noach departed from the Teiva, Bereishit 9:1 - וַיְבָרֶךְ אֱלֹהִים אֶת־נֹחַ וְאֶת־בָּנָיו וַיֹּאמֶר לָהֶם פְּרוּ וּרְבוּ וּמִלְאוּ אֶת־הָאָרֶץ. And yet again mankind is commanded in this Mitzvah in Bereishis 9:7 - וְאַתֶּם פְּרוּ וּרְבוּ שִׁרְצוּ בָאָרֶץ וּרְבוּ־בָהּ.

118. See Berishis 1:22 - וַיְבָרֶךְ אֹתָם אֱלֹהִים לֵאמֹר פְּרוּ וּרְבוּ וּמִלְאוּ אֶת־הַמַּיִם בַּיַּמִּים וְהָעוֹף יִרֶב בָּאָרֶץ.

PART IV

The Knowledge Maps

Welcome to **The Knowledge Map for** Taryag Mitzvot.

What is a Knowledge Map?

A conventional map gives you a geographical description of name places, where they are and the distance between one location and another. Maps give your orientation too, that means at an given place, you can identify where is North, South, West and East so you know exactly where you are in relation to where you want to go.

A 'Knowledge Map' is really the same idea, it is a map of information that is designed to give you definitions of the information you are learning and how it relates to all the other connected information. A Knowledge Map shows you all the incremental steps of knowledge you need to acquire on your way to mastery of that subject.

We want to deliver into your mind a 'Map of Chumash.' This means you will learn how to have a map in your mind of the two components of Chumash:
1. The Story Line of Chumash[119] and
2. Taryag Mitzvot.

Credits for Certification

If you are taking our certification program, you need to learn through the entire knowledge map 'mapped' out below. If you are learning this without certification, you can just be a few steps ahead of your students and teach each of the items below as you yourself are learning through the knowledge map.

---

119. This is outlined in the Knowledge Map for Building Block #3 - The Story Line of Chumash.

The Knowledge Map as you Lesson Plans

The knowledge map of Taryag Mitzvos is not only what you, the teacher, are expected to know in order to teach your student, it is actually the curriculum of what you are teaching! You can literally use this map for your lesson plans. In this Knowledge Map for 'Taryag Mitzvot,' you have over 400 units of instruction, which translates into over 400 lesson plans.

Please note that there three 'Knowledge Maps' for Taryag Mitzvot. They are 2A (this document, how to memorize Taryag Mitzvot according to Rambam's list of 14 Sefarim. Knowledge 2B is the practical applications of how to learn Taryag Mitzvot with all the supporting materials. This is also explained in detail in DVDs #3, 4 & 5 of the Tarayg Mitzvot Training DVDs. The you have document 2C which is how to memorize Taryag Mitzvot as they appear in Chumash. This is according to the listing of Sefer HaChinuch where we give a memory system for remembering which Perek in Chumash every Mitzvah appears in.

Because this entire teaching method is based upon Al Pi Darko, you are not actually expected to do all the teaching. You will show your students how to use the Taryag Mitzvot Cards and materials, and the students will have to go through each unit of instruction at their own pace. In the training DVDs of Building Block #2[120] of Taryag Mitzvot, you will be shown how to use the materials in conjunction with this Knowledge Map.

By delivering a map of Taryag Mitzvot into the mind of your students, you are giving them a filing system for all their future learning.

We will begin with teaching you a memory system committing 613 files in your brain for Taryag Mitzvot.

The Chumash Knowledge Map is really a memory system. It is based upon learning Simanim[121] for all the 178 Chapters of Chumash. The memory system for Taryag Mitzvot is based on Rambam's categorization of the Mitzvot as outlined in his Mishne Torah. We will also teach you another memory system for knowing where every Mitzvah is in Chumash based on the chapter numbers each Mitzvah is found. This will give you a filing system in your brain for the Story of Chumash and its 613 Mitzvot. Don't be afraid of the wealth of information you are about to commit to memory, just remember, a thousand mile journey begins with the first step! Also, how do you eat an entire cow ? One bite at a time?

Bon Voyage! Enjoy the journey through Chumash and Taryag Mitzvot, the skeleton of the entire Torah!

---

120. Building Block #2 have the following DVD Training Videos: #1 The Value of learning Taryag Mitzvot. #2 How to Teach 100 + Mitzvot in less than an Hour! #3 & 4 - Practical Applications, many activities using the Taryag Mitzvos materials to learn all 613 Mitzvot in various levels of detail. #3 & #4 have their own Knowledge Map.
121. A Siman is a 'trigger' word, or 'sign' or mnemonic for remembering information.

Knowledge Map A:

Applications for Teaching Taryag Mitzvot

1.0 First teach the most familiar Mitzvos

1.1 Teach 122 Familiar Mitzvos as found in Chapter 4 of the Taryag Manual.[122]

We have used three criterion for selecting these 122 Mitzvos.
1. These 122 Mitzvos are selected because they appear in the daily lives of the children.
2. These Mitzvos are familiar to the children in their annual performance throughout the Jewish calendar (Sukka, Lulav, Shofar, etc.).
3. Some of these 122 are less familiar but are selected nevertheless because the 'Picture Card' is so simple that once taught, the child will easily remember the Mitzvah from seeing the picture again.

1. Examples of daily Mitzvos are a picture of Tefilin shel Rosh and Yad, Mezuza, Tzitzit, etc.
2. Examples of Calendar Mitzvos are pictures for Shabbos, Yom Tov, eating Matzah, shaking Lulav, blowing Shofar, living in a Sukkah, etc.
3. Examples of a Picture being printed on the mind of the child are writing a Sefer Torah (probably a Mitzvah the child is not familiar with, but after seeing the picture of the Mitzvah, he will remember that Mitzvah each time he sees the card). Similarly, the Mitzvah for a Jewish King to write a second Sefer Torah for himself is not a familiar Mitzvah but once he learned the Mitzvah Picture Card, he will easily recall this Mitzvah.

Teaching the children Mitzvos they are either familiar with or will easily remember from the Picture Card has three major benefits. Firstly, this is real Al Pi Darko, because we begin with *their* starting point, Mitzvos they already know, and build upon that. Secondly, by teaching easier Mitzvos, we are setting them up for success. Thirdly, by teaching Mitzvos they know and adding Mitzvos easy to remember because of the Picture Card, the children become more easily endeared to wanting to know more Mitzvos since they do not find this hard.

It is only once they have a critical mass of over 100 Mitzvos do we then identify different ways to organize the Mitzvos and only then do we follow the listing of Rambam in Yad Chazaka which is the most organized of all lists of the Rishonim. These 122 Mitzvos can be taught in a very short period. On the Teacher Training DVD, Disc #2, we show how this can be accomplished in literally an hour or two. We recommend the rebbe teaching these 122 Mitzvos in the space of a week and making a Siyum on the first 100 with the expectation that there will be a Siyum celebration for each hundred Mitzvos. The final Siyum can be a finale with parents and grandparents.

---

122. This is explained fully in the DVD (Part 2) on how to teach 100 Mitzvos in less than an hour.

1.2

Ask the students to organize the 122 Mitzvos they already know.

Guide the students to identify (without actually telling them) **the four main methods for organizing Taryag Mitzvos**[123] (as listed below). According to their responses, guide the students to make piles of the cards in the ways they said we can organize the Mitzvos.

1. Two Piles of Cards, one pile of Asehs and one pile of Lo Ta'asehs.[124]
2. A Pile of Cards for that week's Parsha.[125]
3. Pile the Picture Cards in categories.[126]
4. Pile the Mitzvos according to the body parts.[127]

After the students explored some of the ways to organize the Mitzvos. We will now focus specifically on Rambam's list of Taryag Mitzvos. Rambam organized all 613 under 14 Sefarim with 83 sub-sections. He then plotted all 613 under their category of those 14 major and 83 minor categories.

The following activities in 2.0 are recommended for students ready for this level of sorting and categorization.

Please Note: sorting, piling and categorizing the Mitzvos should be done as and when the students are ready. This may be in second or third grade, but of course, it really depends on when the student himself is ready.

The first step would be to teach the 14 icons we created for the 14 Sefarim of Rambam. In Disc #3 we show how to teach the students these icons using a memory system known as 'stacking.' An illustrated chart of the icons can be found on the back of the Taryag Mitzvos Manual and is available for schools in digital format should they want to put them on Smart Boards or computer screens or to print their own size icons.

If your students are not ready for learning the icons, then skip 2.0 and go straight to 3.0 which is 'Learn the Taryag Mitzvos according to the list of Rambam.' When the students are ready you can teach them the icons in 2.0.

---

123. What is below is for Building Block #2 how to teach Taryag Mitzvos (not covered in Building Block Memory)
124. As is the system of Sefer HaMitzvos of Rambam, Smag (R' Moshe of Coucy) and Smak.
125. For example, Parshas Bo will have 20 Taryag Mitzvah cards, Beshalach has one, Yisro has 17, etc,. The students could also elect to make piles of Mitzvah cards for each chapter of that Parsha, so Bo would have a pile of 14 cards for Chapter 12 and a pile of 6 cards for Chapter 13. Etc.
126. As in Rambam's 14 Sefarim of Mishneh Torah and its 83 sub-sections.
127. As Sefer Chareidim lists the Mitzvos. Note that Sefer Chareidim lists those Mitzvos which apply nowadays, not all 613. For a more comprehensive list of all 613 according to the Human Anatomy, see the Appendices to the Taryag Manual or Taryag Reference Book.

2.0

Teach the 14 Icons for Rambam's Sefarim[128]

Now we will learn a system for memorizing the Mitzvos according to Rambam's Yad Chazaka, 14 Books starting with the 14 Icons.

2.1 Teach the children the 14 Icons for the 14 Books of Rambam.[129]

2.2 Ask the children to lay out the Icons for Ahava, Zemanim and Nashim on a table and place under each Icon the Mitzvos they think relate to the category defined by that Icon.

2.3 Ask the children to tell you their reasons for why they placed those Mitzvos under that Icon.

2.4 Ask the students to do the same (as 2.2 above) with the Icons for Kedusha, Haflaah and Zeraim. Then repeat the question in 2.3 above.

2.5 Ask the students to do the same (as 2.2 above) with the Icons for Avoda, Korbanot and Avoda. Then repeat the question in 2.3 above.

2.6 Ask the students to do the same (as 2.2 above) with the Icons for Tahara, Nezikin and Kinyan. Then repeat the question in 2.3 above.

2.7 Ask the students to do the same (as 2.2 above) with the Icons for Mishpatim and Shoftim. Then repeat the question in 2.3 above.

3.0 Learn the Taryag Mitzvos according to the list of Rambam:

3.1

Familiarize yourself with the many supporting materials for teaching Taryag Mitzvos.[130]
You need the following supporting materials for the activities in 4.0 - 4.15.

1. The Taryag Mitzvos Manual
2. The Taryag Mitzvos Outline: Student Edition
3. Taryag Mitzvos Teacher Training DVDs[131]
4. The 613 Picture Cards[132]
5. The Matching Hebrew Code Name Card
6. The Matching Hebrew Description Card[133]
7. The Matching English Description Card
8. The Matching Passuk Card
9. The 83 Icon Cards (for the Picture Cards)
10. The 613 Photo Cards

---

128. Your students may not be ready for this step. Teaching the 14 Icons does not hold you back from continuing to teach the remainder of Taryag Mitzvos in the order of the Rambam. If your students are not ready, then go straight to 3.0 below and you can always return to organizing the Mitzvos

129. You will find a full explanation of how to do this on Disc #3 of Taryag Mitzvos (The practical applications of teaching Taryag Mitzvos) with a memory system for the 14 Icons in sequence.

130. These materials allow for a variety of activities as will soon be described in 4.1-4.15. For most of the activities the students will work with 3-10 Picture Cards at a time and their equivalent matching cards. This means 3 or more Cards for each Mitzvah & the following: 1. The Picture Card, 2. The Hebrew Code Name Card, 3. The Hebrew Description Card, 4. The English Description Card and 5. The Passuk Card. So if two students are learning 5 Mitzvos at a time, that would mean they will have 25 cards in a shuffled pile, or they will lay out the cards face up on a table at random to sort and match.

131. There are 5 DVDs. Disc.# 1 demonstrates the value of learning Taryag Mitzvos. Disc.# 2 demonstrates how it is possible to teach over 100 Mitzvos in less than an hour using those Mitzvos which children are already familiar with. Discs.# 3, 4 & 5 show the many practical applications, activities and 'hands-on' ways for children to learn the Taryag Mitzvos using the materials listed here.

132. This refers to the 'stick-figure' version. Not to be confused with the 'photo' version.

133. This follows the wording of Rambam with only a handful of exceptions.

11. The 83 Icon Cards (for the 613 Photo Cards)
12. The Taryag Detective: Which Mitzvah Am I ?
13. 613 Short Essays
14. 613 Animations
15. Sefer Mitzvos HaMishna[134]
16. The Taryag Mitzvos Reference Book
17. 5 Volumes of Yahadus: Comprehensive Curriculum of all 613 Mitzvos.
18. Assessment Sheets for Taryag Mitzvos

3.2 Teach 1-3 Mitzvos daily.[135]

3.3 Watch the first 1-3 Mitzvah Animations & Learn the first 3 Mitzvah Picture Cards.

3.4 Learn the next 2 Mitzvah Animations and their Picture Cards (Ahavas & Yirat Hashem)

3.5 Review first 5 Mitzvos (Animations and Picture Cards).

3.6 Learn the next 2 Mitzvos (Kiddush and Chilul Hashem)

3.7 Review all 7 Mitzvos learned so far.

3.8 Learn the next Mitzvah (Don't erase Hashem's Name)

3.9 Learn the last 2 Mitzvos in Yesodei HaTorah.

3.10 Introduce the first five Icons for the 83 sub-sections of Rambam.[136]

3.11 Review all 10 Mitzvos in Yesodei HaTorah.

3.12 Ask the students to tell you what they know from each picture.

3.13 Ask the students to explain why they think Rambam put these 10 in Yesodei HaTorah.

3.14 Instruct them to learn the Code Name for the first 3 Mitzvos.

3:15 Instruct them to learn the Code Names of the next 4 Mitzvos.

3.16 Instruct them to learn the last 3 Code Names of the last 3 Mitzvos.

3.17 Review all 10 Mitzvos with their Code Name.

3.18 The next step is to continue learning the Mitzvos in Hilchos Deos, but note that 4.0 below outlines activities that you can introduce to the students which will review and deepen their understanding of the first ten Mitzvos just learned in Yesodei HaTorah.

3.19 Learn the next 1-2 Mitzvos in Hilchos Deos and go through the same steps as 3.3 - 3.18 above and continue through all 83 sub-sections this way.

---

134. This Sefer lists every single Mitzvah found in each Mishna in all Mishnayos. The Rebbe teaching Mishna need only tell the students which Taryag Mitzvos they have to review in preparation for learning the Mishna together later. Most Rebbeim spend anywhere between 30-50% of the learning time teaching the needed background information for each Mishna. Rav Bartenura claims that all Mishnayos is a commentary to Taryag Mitzvos (Avot.1:1) so if children learn all Taryag Mitzvos in the first three grades, the Rebbe can tell them which Mitzvos to review in preparation for learning the next Mishna in class.
135. There is no hard fast rule here, go at the pace that works for you as the teacher and the pace which works for the students. We suggest you follow as closely as possible the 'grouping/bunching' of the Mitzvos as found within each sub-section. That means to say, we have made a slight gap on the page between every 'grouping' of Mitzvos within each category as explained on the DVD. For example, the first three Mitzvos are grouped/bunched together because they are obviously closely related, Emuna, Zulato and Echad. Then the next two, Ahavas Hashem and Yirat Hashem are 'twins' and so we grouped/bunched them together.
136. Watch DVD #3 of Taryag Mitzvos Training where this is fully explained and illustrated.

The introduction to each Mitzvah includes three items:
1. The Taryag Animations
2. The Picture Cards
3. The Code Name for each Mitzvah

Each Picture Card contains 7 pieces of information:
1. Picture of the Mitzvah
2. Code Name
3. Aseh/Lo Ta'aseh Icon
4. English Description of the Mitzvah
5. Hebrew Description of the Mitzvah (taken word for word from Rambam)[137]
6. The Passuk of the Mitzvah
7. The Torah Reference (Chapter Number and Verse)

Please note that all the Taryag Mitzvos Cards are available in digital version for the teacher to use on a smart board or screen or for the children to learn the Mitzvos themselves or for review.

Additional details of the Mitzvos can be found in the photo version of the Taryag Mitzvos. The photo version includes 12 icons[138] for :
1. Men
2. Women
3. Kohen
4. Kohen Gadol
5. Malkus
6. Death Penalty of Skila
7. Death Penalty of Sreifa
8. Death Penalty of Chenek
9. Death Penalty of Chereg
10. Death Bidey Shamayim
11. Kares
12. Mitzvos of Eretz Yisrael
13. Mitzvos Tamidi 24/7
14. Mitzvos done in Yerushalayim

More details for each Mitzvah can be found on the 'Which Am I Cards' and the Book with all the 'Which Mitzvah Am I Clues' entitled 'The Taryag Detective.'

We now come to the meat of this Knowledge Map with the practical activities for learning Taryag Mitzvos.

---

137. There are a few exceptions where we did not use the exact lashon or Rambam, for example Mitzvos #70 and #71.
138. All these icons can be found in the Taryag Mitzvos Manual (page 44 of 2018 edition)

4.0
Practical Applications - Taryag Activities

The following activities provide multiple ways for the students to learn and review the Mitzvos according to the sequence of Rambam's 14 Sefarim and 83 Sub-Sections.

4.1a *Which Mitzvah is this picture?* (done with a partner).
Select about 5 -10 Mitzvos already learned, and place them in a pile facing down. Then with a partner, one student (we will call him Partner A) flips over the top card from the pile and asks Partner B to identify the Mitzvah. After Partner B identifies it, the card is placed at the bottom of the pile and Partner B now shows A the next Picture Card and asks which Mitzvah is it? They rotate till they know all 5-10 cards.

4.1b

Which Mitzvah is this picture? (done as class teams).
This is the same game as described in **4.1a** above, but instead of pairs quizzing their partner, the rebbe asks the entire class to identify the Mitzvah from the Picture he is holding or showing on screen. Rebbe can also split the class into teams and asks each team in turn to identify the Mitzvah from the Card he holds up or shows on screen.[139]

4.2a *Match My Code-Name !* (done with a Partner)
Select only 3 Mitzvos Picture Cards.[140] Lay them out facing up. Student A says out loud the Hebrew Code Name for one of the three Mitzvos, partner B has to point to its Matching Picture Card. For example, Partner A calls out "Ahavas Hashem," Partner B point to the Picture Card of Ahavas Hashem. The partners should only do 3 cards at a time and add more as they are ready for the challenge of more than 3 at a time.

4.2b Partner B has a turn to call out loud a Hebrew Code Name and Partner A has to point to the correct Picture Card. Rotate till they complete all three 3 cards and select the next 3 cards.

4.3a *Match My Hebrew Description Card*[141] *to My Picture* !
Lay out 3 Picture Cards facing up. Partner A reads out loud the Rambam's Hebrew Description Card and Partner B has to point to the correct Picture Card. (They should do this with a pile of 3 Mitzvos at a time and add more as they are ready for the challenge)

4.3b Select 3 Picture Cards & their equivalent Hebrew Description Cards & Code Name Cards.
Partner A places on the table the Hebrew Description Card facing up, and Partner B finds its equivalent Picture Card and the equivalent Hebrew Code Name Card to place next to the Hebrew Description Card.

---

139. Using the digital version of the Mitzvos makes for easy display on a screen, smart board, computer screen or lap top. The digital version is specially helpful for children to review on their own.
140. The reason we recommend only three is because the mind can easily remember three items without a system of recall. As the student's memory muscles improve, they can add more cards.
141. These are the cards with Rambam's Hebrew description of each Mitzvah.

4.4a *Match My English Description to My Hebrew Code Name* ![142]

Partner A calls out the English Description and Partner B Pulls out or points to the Hebrew Code Name Card. (They should do this with a pile of 3 Mitzvos at a time and add more as they are ready for the challenge)

4.4b Partner A places on the table the English Description Card (e.g. Be a Kiddush Hashem) and Partner B has to find its equivalent Hebrew Code Name (קדוש ה') and place it next to the English Description Card.

(They should do this with a pile of 2-3 Mitzvos at a time and add more as they are ready for the challenge)

4.5a *Match My Passuk Card to My Picture!*

Select 3 Picture cards and their equivalent Passuk Cards. Partner A reads out loud the Passuk Card and Partner B points or find from the to the equivalent Picture.

4.5b Partner A places down a Passuk Card, reads it out loud and Partner B has to find the equivalent Picture Card and place it next to the Passuk Card.

4.6 Review Time:

With a partner or on his own, student matches previously learned Mitzvah Cards with the Hebrew Code Name and its equivalent English Description Card.

4.7 3-Card Match:
Match My Hebrew Description Card to My Hebrew Code Name Card[143] *&*
My Picture Card![144]

4.8 *Match My Passuk-Card to My Picture-Card!*

Select 5-10 Mitzvah Cards already learned and their Passuk Cards. Lay out the 5-10 Mitzvah Cards facing up. Partner A reads out loud a Passuk Card & Partner B pulls out the matching Picture Card (for more of a challenge, Partner B can pull out or point to the Code Name and English Description Card too!).

4.9 4 - Card Match: *Match My Passuk Card to My Hebrew Code-Name and Hebrew & English Description Cards*!

Using same 5-10 Mitzvah cards laid facing up as in 4.8. Partner A reads out loud a Passuk Card & Partner B has to find and match its equivalent Hebrew Code Name Card, English Description Card, Hebrew Description Card and Passuk Card.

4.10 *Match All Cards to My Passuk!*

Lay out randomly all the different Matching Cards for 5-10 Mitzvos on a surface, facing up. Partner A calls out a Passuk card and partner B has to find and place the Picture Card which matches that Passuk next to that Passuk Card. Then Partner B reads a Passuk Card and Partner A has to find and place the correct matching Picture card. They rotate till they complete that group of Mitzvos or that section of the 83 Sub-Sections of Rambam.

---

142. Note that you will only do this if the student/s are reading English well enough to understand.
143. Note that you will only do this if the student/s are able to translate the Hebrew word description.
144. The student working alone has to find these cards from a pile of Mitzvah cards that have been shuffled and then laid on a table surface or work area for him to arrange according to their matching cards. Another way would be to pair with a partner and race between them to see how fast they can match all the correctly matching cards (timing themselves with a timer). With a bit of creative thinking, the children and teacher will come up with many different ways of reviewing the details of each Mitzvah.

4.11 *Match My Code-Name Card to My Hebrew Description Card!*

Partner A calls out a Hebrew Code Name and Partner B has to find the Hebrew Description Card to match. Then Partner B calls out a Hebrew Code Name and Partner A has to find the matching Hebrew Description Card.

4.12 *Match My English Description Card to All My Matches!*

Partner A reads out loud the English Description Card and Partner B has to find and match every card relating to that description.[145] Then Partner B has his turn to read out loud an English Description Card and Partner A has to find and match every card relating to that description.

4.13 *Matrix All The Mitzvah Cards for My Sub-Section of Rambam!*

Matrix all the cards for that section of Rambam.

A. Start by placing down the Icon Card for that section of Rambam.

B. Now lay out (horizontally) beneath the icon card all the Mitzvah Picture cards of that section (if there is room on table, or do in batches of 10 cards).

Identify every matching card to be placed beneath the Picture Card.

So, for example, the Picture Card for Emuna would have placed beneath it:
1. The Hebrew Code Name 'Emuna,' then
2. The English Description Card (Know Hashem Exists) and then beneath that card -
3. The Hebrew Description Card and beneath that -
4. The Passuk Card. Do the same for each Picture card till you have matrixed all of Yesodei HaTorah (10 Mitzvos).

4.14 *Self-Assessment Time.*

Fill in the Assessment Sheet for Taryag Mitzvos of Hilchos Yesodei HaTorah.[146]

4.15 Repeat 4.13 for the next Section of Rambam (Hilchos Deos).

4.16 Fill in the Assessment Sheet for Taryag Mitzvos of Hilchos Deos and continue matrixing each section of the 83 Sub-sections of Rambam. This would be equivalent to another 81 Activities.

4.17 Make a siyum for every 100 Mitzvos or for each completed Sefer of Rambam (14 Siyumim!).

---

145. That means Partner B has to find 1. The Picture Card, 2. The Hebrew Code Name, 3. The Passuk, 4. The Hebrew Description Card.
146. The Assessment Sheets for demonstrating Mastery of that Section of Rambam are available from www.breakththroughchinuch.com. A sample of that sheet is printed at the end of this document, if you do not have it in your document, please contact us and we will email you a generic sample from which you can make your own copies.

5.0 Taryag Detective - Which Mitzvah Am I?

The goal in 5.0 is for the students to learn how to **teach themselves more details of the Mitzvos** they know and even new Mitzvos.

This will be achieved by the Rebbe first role modeling how to use the Which Mitzvah Am I Cards and Taryag Detective Book. (This can be viewed on the Disc #2). After about 5-10 Mitzvos of role modeling, the students should be good to go on their own.

Using the Which Mitzvah Am I Cards / Taryag Detective Book, we will now describe ways children can be actively engaged in learning more details about the Mitzvos they already know.

For the students to fully benefit from this section, we highly encourage the teacher read the introduction to the Taryag Detective Book and watch the DVD on Taryag Mitzvos Applications Disc #2 corresponding to this section 5.0.

Note that the rebbe can begin reading clues from The Taryag Detective and Which Mitzvah Am I Cards for Mitzvos he knows the students already know. He does not have to wait till they know all 613 Mitzvos to start section 5.0.

5.1 For the Teacher: Read the introduction to The Taryag Detective.

5.2 Select Mitzvos the student/s have learned.[147] e.g Tefillin Shel Rosh & read the clues of those Mitzvos.

5.3 Role model reading the clues for about 5 - 10 Mitzvos after which the students should know how to read the clues themselves.

5.4 When role modeling, read one clue, then a second clue but before reading the third clue, quickly re-read the first two clues. Read the fourth clue and then read the first three before reading the fifth clue, etc. This repetition insures increased retention. If the children's body language suggests they are losing focus, then only repeat all the clues after every 3 clues.

5.5 After the above role modeling of clue reading, the students should pair into partners and the Reading Partner A reads the clues of a Mitzvah and the Listening Partner B has to answer (at the end of the clues) **Which Mitzvah Am I? Then they rotate** (the listening partner becomes the clue reader).

5.6 If you know a specific student has low self-esteem in learning, then invite him to select the Mitzvos <u>he wants</u> you to read the clues of. Or, announce to the class that when learning the clues with a partner, they should first select the Mitzvos they are familiar with.

5.7 Have the students fill in the Mastery Assessment Chart for the Taryag Mitzvos they master.
6.0

---
147. See the Taryag Manual Ch. #4 for a list of over 100 of the most familiar Mitzvos.

The Taryag Mitzvos Reference Book.

This is not an activity, it is a resource for the students to cross reference the Mitzvos as they appear according to the numbering system of **Rambam's** listing[148] and that same Mitzvah as it appears in Sefer **HaChinuch**. It also cross references the name of the Parsha, Chapter number and verse where it appears in Chumash.

This reference chart can also be found at the back of Sefer Mitzvos HaMishna. Showing the students the Taryag Mitzvos Reference Book is a tool for them to use when they begin matrixing the Mitzvos in 7.0 below.

7.0
Matrix Taryag Mitzvos as they appear in Chumash

This method of organizing the Mitzvos follows Sefer HaChinuch. A full list of the Mitzvos found in each Parsha is in the Knowledge Map for Building Block #2, Taryag Mitzvos, Part III.[149] You can also direct the students to find the Mitzvos of each Parsha in the table of contents of Sefer HaChinuch.[150]

Note that section 13.0 below addresses learning Taryag Mitzvos according to the Chapter number of that Mitzvah using the Memory System of Mental Mapping and Mental Palaces.

7.0 is Matrixing 613 Mitzvos in the order they appear in the Chumash only, if the students are ready for the Mental Mapping games in 13.0, then you should look at 13.0 before doing 7.1 in order for them to retain their learning of which Mitzvah is in which Perek of Chumash.

7.1 Matrix[151] the 3 Mitzvos in Chumash Bereishis

7.2 Matrix the 20 Mitzvos found in Parshas Bo.[152]

This means laying out all 14 Mitzvos in Chapter #12 beneath an index card with פרשת בא written on it as a name label. Then beneath that label would be two more cards, one with **Chapter #12** written on it and the other with **Chapter #13**. The the student would lay out the 14 Mitzvah picture cards beneath the label for Chapter 12 and the 6 Mitzvah Picture Cards beneath the label for Chapter 13. These are all the 20 Mitzvos listed in Parshas Bo.

The remaining activities from 7.3 to 7.37 instruct you in matrices for the remainder of the entire Chumash.

---

148. This refers to the 14 Sefarim and their 83 Sub-Sections.
149. Available from www.breakthroughchinuch.com.
150. Sefer Poel Tzedek from the Shach printed in Rabbi Bluth's sefer Chanoch L'Naar also provides a precise listing of every Mitzvah as listed by Sefer Hachinuch. It's available from Rabbi Bluth, 600 East 8th Street, Brooklyn NY 11218. Feldheim also published a sefer called Madrich L'Taryag Mitzvos which also lists the Mitzvos as they appear in the Torah. It also cross references the same Mitzvah in Rambam, Shulchan Aruch and Smag.
151. 'Matrix' means to lay out the cards of Chumash Bereishis in sequence. So for example, each of the three Mitzvos in Chumash Bereishis are in different Parshios. The first Mitzvah to father children is in Parshas Bereishis. The second Mitzvah of Bris Mila is in Lech Lecha and the third Mitzvah, Gid HaNasheh is in Vayishlach. So Matrixing these three Mitzvos would mean laying them out beneath a name label of the parsha it is found in.
152. Parshas Bo contains the first Taryag Mitzvah found in Chumash Shemos. 14 Mitzvos in Chapter 12 and 6 Mitzvos in Chapter 13.

7.3 Take a photo of the student's Matrix of that Parsha for his portfolio.[153]

7.4 Matrix the one Mitzvah in Parshas Beshalach.[154]

7.5 Matrix the 17 Mitzvos in Parshas Yisro.

7.6 Matrix the 53 Mitzvos in Parshas Mishpatim.

7.7 Matrix the 3 Mitzvos in Parshas Terumah.

7.8 Matrix the 7 Mitzvos in Parshas Tetzaveh.

7.9 Matrix the 9 Mitzvos in Parshas Ki Tissa.

7.10 Matrix the 1 Mitzvah in Parshas Vayakhel.

7.11 Matrix the 3 Mitzvos in Parshas

7.12 Matrix the 3 Mitzvos in Parshas

7.13 Matrix the 16 Mitzvos in Parshas Vayikra

7.14 Matrix the 18 Mitzvos in Parshas Tzav.

7.15 Matrix the 17 Mitzvos in Parshas Shemini.

7.16 Matrix the 7 Mitzvos in Parshas Tazria.

7.17 Matrix the 11 Mitzvos in Parshas Metzora.

7.18 Matrix the 28 Mitzvos in Parshas Acharei Mos.

7.19 Matrix the 50 Mitzvos in Parshas Kedoshim.

7.20 Matrix the 63 Mitzvos in Parshas Emor.

7.21 Matrix the 24 Mitzvos in Parshas Behar.

7.22 Matrix the 12 Mitzvos in Parshas Bechukosai.

7.23 Matrix the 18 Mitzvos in Parshas Nasso.

7.24 Matrix the 5 Mitzvos in Parshas Behalosecha.

7.25 Matrix the 3 Mitzvos in Parshas Shlach.

7.26 Matrix the 9 Mitzvos in Parshas Korach.

7.27 Matrix the 3 Mitzvos in Parshas Chukas.

7.28 Matrix the 6 Mitzvos in Parshas Pinchas.

7.29 Matrix the 2 Mitzvos in Parshas Mattos.

7.30 Matrix the 6 Mitzvos in Parshas Massai.

7.31 Matrix the 1 Mitzvos in Parshas Devarim.

7.32 Matrix the 12 Mitzvos in Parshas VaEtchanan.

7.33 Matrix the 8 Mitzvos in Parshas Ekev.

7.34 Matrix the 55 Mitzvos in Parshas Re'eh.

7.35 Matrix the 41 Mitzvos in Parshas Ki Tetze.

7.36 Matrix the 6 Mitzvos in Parshas Ki Savo.

7.37 Matrix the 2 Mitzvos in Parshas Vayelech.

---

153. The photos could be collected for a project to be stapled as a book or scroll/banner or album of Taryag Mitzvos. Or else just collected as part of his portfolio of work he has done that year.

154. This means, lay out the Picture Card for Techum Shabbos (#90) with its supporting materials, the Code Name Card, the Hebrew & English Description Cards and the Passuk Card all laid beneath the Picture card.

8.0
Matrix Taryag Mitzvos according to the Human Anatomy

This order of the Mitzvos follows Sefer Chareidim. Note for the teacher: A full list of Mitzvos for each part of the anatomy is provided in the appendices of the Taryag Mitzvah Manual.[155]

8.1 *"Howdy Partner!"* **Divide class into pairs. Now go to 8.2.**

8.2 *Draw My Body !*
One student lies down on a large sheet of paper and his partner draws the outline of his body.

8.3 *This is Why I Have A Body!*
The partners take turns with one Mitzvah card at a time[156] and decide which part of the body it is performed by.[157]

8.4 They place that card on that part of the body outline.
Here is a list of the 11 parts of the body identified by Sefer Chareidim:

8.5 1. **Mitzvos of the Mind**[158]
8.6 2. **Mitzvos of the Hands**[159]
8.7 3. **Mitzvos of the Legs**[160]
8.8 4. **Mitzvos of the Head**
8.9 5. **Mitzvos of the Eyes**[161]
8.10 6. **Mitzvos of the Ears**[162]
8.11 7. **Mitzvos of the Nose**[163]
8.12 8. **Mitzvos of the Mouth**[164] **- Speech**
8.13 9. **Mitzvos of the Mouth - Eating**[165]
8.14 10. **Mitzvos of entire body**
8.15 11. **Mitzvos of the Brit**[166]

---

155. Please note that Sefer Chareidim covers the Mitzvos applicable nowadays (279 Mitzvos). He also lists Mitzvos not counted in Rambam, so for example, he lists Tamim Tihyeh Im Hashem (Dev.18:13) as one of the 613 and as a Mitzvah of the mind, Rambam does not count it in his list of 613. The Taryag Mitzvos Manual provides a list for all 613 Mitzvos and which part or parts of the body they are performed by. Contact us at www.breakthroughchinuch.com for more information.
156. Start with Mitzvos the children already know and are familiar with. You can use the list in Chapter 4 of the Taryag Mitzvos Manual as a guide.
157. Note: some Mitzvos could be identified as belonging to more than one limb. e.g. the Mitzvah of Ahavta L'Rei'acha Kamocha may be placed on the brain as indeed it is a Mitzvah that begins with thought, while one student may place it on the hand he is doing an act of Hessed, as when lending a toy to a friend which is done with the hand. Another student might say it is done with the feet because he walks to visit a sick friend. Let the student decide this with minimum help from the teacher. Later you can ask why they think a particular Mitzvah is done with this part of the body.
158. See Sefer Chareidim, Ch. 9 for list of Asehs and Ch. 21 for list of Lo Taasehs done with the mind. Sefer Chareidim has a total of 51 Mitzvos done in thought. There are about 68 Mitzvos out of 613 done with the mind.
159. See Sefer Chareidim, Ch. 16, 17 & 29.
160. See Sefer Chareidim, Ch. 18, 19 & 31.
161. See Sefer Chareidim, Ch. 10 & 22.
162. See Sefer Chareidim, Ch. 11 & 23.
163. See Sefer Chareidim, Ch.15 & 28.
164. See Sefer Chareidim, Ch. 12, 13, 14, 24, 25, 26 & 27.
165. Ibid.
166. See Sefer Chareidim, Ch. 20 & 32.

9.0 Miscellaneous Matrixes

This section, 9.0 is an excellent opportunity for the teacher to reach a student Al Pi Darko. The children are invited to list different ways the Mitzvos can be organized or classified. Their answers are clues for the Al Pi Darko Teacher to recognize specific interests the child might gravitate to and then that is a chance to let that student identify the Mitzvos related to his choice.

9.1 Out of The Box ways to categorize Taryag Mitzvos

Ask the class to make a list of different ways to organize the Mitzvos. In other words, sort the Mitzvos into categories other than the four most known classifications.[167] Here are some examples:

1. **Chukim**
2. **Mishpatim**
3. **Applicable today**
4. **Bein Adam L'Chavero**
5. **Bein Adam L'Makom**
6. **Eretz Yisrael**
7. **Weapons**
8. **Food**
9. **Animals**
10. **Baking**
11. **Cooking**
12. **Music**
13. **Tamidi**[168]
14. **Shemen Zayit**
15. **Magic**
16. **Clothes**
17. **Only Men**
18. **Only Women**
19. **Only kohanim**
20. **Only Kohen Gadol**
21. **Only Shevet Levi**
22. **Only a King**
23. **Fire**
24. **Trees**
25. **Construction/Building**
26. **Olive Oil**

[**Please note** - If you want a tailored chart listing the Mitzvos in any of these or other categories, let us know and we will provide you a list of all the Mitzvos related to that topic].

---

167. The four most common classifications are 1. Sefer HaMitzvos (Dividing the Mitzvos according Aseh and Lo Taaseh). 2. The Mishneh Torah (14 Sefarim with 83 Sub-Sections). Sefer HaChinuch (according to the sequential appearance of each Mitzvah in the weekly Parshios). 4. Sefer Chareidim (Mitzvos performed by different parts of the Human Anatomy).
168. Contstant Mitzvos that apply every moment of one's life. There are six famous ones, but in reality, there are closer to 40 total! See Appendices to The Taryag Mitzvos Manual.

10.0 *My Own Taryag Mitzvah Cards!*
Students Create their own Taryag Mitzvah Cards.
Ask the student/s to select a favorite Mitzvah/Mitzvos from the Stick-Figure Taryag Mitzvos.[169]

10.1 Using index cards, invite the student/s to draw their own illustration of their favorite Mitzvos.
See DVDs on Applications of Taryag Mitzvos Disc #5 (section 10.0) where you will see examples of first grade children's artwork. After you see these examples, you and your students will see how simple and easy this is. This activity is a perfect match for children who are artistic and have a good eye, but even children who are not known for being particularly artistic will surprise themselves with how well they can do this activity.

10.2 Turn his illustrations into a Personal Album/Banner Project.[170]
After the student has illustrated his favorite Mitzvos on a number of index cards, ask if he would like to stick them into an album or make a banner, or put the cards into his own album (using a photo album to insert his cards).

10.3[171] My Own Taryag Mitzvos Book
Ask the student if he wants to make his/her own Illustrated Taryag Mitzvos Book. *See the DVD Applications for Taryag Mitzvos for samples of a child's Illustrated book.* **The student would illustrate one Mitzvah per page.**

10.4 My Own Illustrated Banner/Scroll of the Mitzvos
This can be a banner or scroll illustrating Mitzvos of the student's own choice. It can either follow Rambam's listing, or the Chinuch or Sefer Chareidim, or a list of the Mitzvos the child selects which is of interest to him/her self. For example: Animals in Taryag Mitzvos, or Mitzvos related to animals, or food, or money, or bein adam l'chavero, etc.

11.0 *Reveal What You Know! - The Mitzvah-Clue Game.*[172]
The following game can be done as a class game where each student is playing for himself, or you split the class into partners[173] or teams.

11.1 Call out a Mitzvah (e.g. Live in a Sukkah 7 days)

11.2 Activate a 2-Minute Timer

11.3 Students write as many details they recall which relate to this Mitzvah. For example: A sukkah needs kosher S'chach, 3 walls, need to eat, drink and sleep in the Sukkah, etc.

11.4 When 2 minutes end, students take turns to read to the class one item they each wrote and rotate around the class.[174] (each new detail can be listed on the board by the teacher).

---

169. Asking the students to make their own picture/drawing of a Mitzvah is much easier from the set of Stick Picture version than the Photo version of Taryag.
170. Please note that in the DVD version of The Applications of Taryag Mitzvos, this is numbered 10.1.
171. Please note that in the DVD version of The Applications of Taryag Mitzvos, this is numbered 10.2.
172. Thanks to Rabbi Simcha Cohen who shared this idea which he did with his students.
173. Either they can choose their own partners, or the teacher can pair them, or use a lottery to decide who is paired with who.
174. If your class uses incentives, one could award one point to the entire class for every single new, additional detail. The points would be part of a broader incentive program where every X number of points equals a dollar toward a charity which the class have predetermined they would collect for. Parents would be asked to contribute toward a fund from which the charity dollars are distributed. Or else the points can be counted toward a class treat (Pizza or ice-cream party) or a class trip.

11.5 Continue rotating till all new details have been exhausted and written on the board.

11.6 Call out another Mitzvah and follow steps 11.2 till 11.5 again.

11.7 Students take turns to call out a Passuk to the class or their partner and the rest of the class or his partner have to say which Mitzvah that Passuk refers to.

11.8 In pairs, one student calls out a Mitzvah (e.g Tefillin Shel Rosh) and his partner has to say **the number of the Perek it is found in.** For example "Devarim Chapter #6." If they know the Parsha name it is in, they can add that too (e.g Parshas V'Etchanan). This exercise is for the students who have done the Memory system for the Chapters of the Mitzvos (see 13.0 below on Mental Mapping and Mental Palaces of Taryag Mitzvos).

12.0 <u>*Taryag Chevrusos - Mitzvah Quiz Games*</u>

12.1 **Pair the students** *(they can either choose their own partners, or the teacher can pair them, or use a lottery to decide who is paired with who).*

12.2 They read out loud all the clues from one of the Mitzvos in The Which Mitzvah Am I Cards or Taryag Detective Book.

12.3 Each partner takes a turn asking their partner to say 3 details he remembers from the Which Mitzvah Am I Card they just read.

12.4 They write down the 3 details.

12.5 They look at the Which Mitzvah Am I Card to check off the items on their own list.

12.6 Now they do the same as 12.3 for another 3 details of the same Mitzvah.

12.7 Do the same as 12.2 - 12.6 above to another Mitzvah.

12.8 Do the same as 12.2 - 12.6 above to another Mitzvah for a total now of 3 Mitzvos.

12.8 <u>*Reveal What you Know!*</u>
After 3 Mitzvos, ask all the partners to join together in the class. Appoint a student to read out the Code Name of one of the Mitzvos learned between all the Chevrusos. The two partners who learned that Mitzvah now have to tell the class 6 details they recall without looking at their list. If they miss any details, don't tell them which they missed, give them a clue instead. The Appointee reads another Code Name and the Chevrusos who learned that Mitzvah now tell the rest of the class 6 details they remember without looking at their list. Continue till you cover all the class members.

12.9 <u>*Find All My Matching Information !*</u>
Pair the students *(they can either choose their own partners, or the teacher can pair them, or use a lottery to decide who is paired with who).*

12.10   Each pair select and lay out 10 Picture Cards facing up.

12.11   One partner reads the Hebrew Code Name of one of the ten Mitzvos and the other partner has to say which Mitzvah it is and points to the correct picture card.[175]

12.12   One partner reads the English Description Card and the other partner has to say which Mitzvah it is and and points to or picks up the correct picture card.

12.13   One partner reads the Hebrew Description Card and the other says which Mitzvah it is and points to or picks up the correct picture card.

12.14   One Partner reads out a Passuk and the other has to identify the correct Mitzvah by pointing to or picking up the correct picture card.

12.15   Rotate Chevrusos till both know all 10 cards.

Advanced Level for Taryag Chevrusos (use same 10 cards as 12.10 above)
12.16   Pair the students.[176]

12.17   One partner reads the Hebrew Description Card and the other has to say the Passuk.

12.18   Rotate till both partners know all the Passukim on all 10 cards.

12.19   One partner reads a Passuk and the other says which Perek in Chumash it is in.

12.20   Rotate till both partners know all the Perakim for all 10 cards.

13.0   *Where Am I in The Torah?*
Mental Mapping/Palaces - Memorize Where each Mitzvah is in The Torah.
This section is for children who have been introduced to the Memory Systems described in Building Block #6 or to the Chumash Story Line Memory System found on the Discs #3 & #4 (of Building Block #3). This exercise is probably for 3rd Graders and older.

13.1   For the teacher: Watch the DVD of Taryag Mitzvos Applications, Disc #5 which describes how to 'Mentally Map' Mitzvos in your mind.

13.2   *Map A Mitzvah*
On the class room white board, trace the outline of the very classroom the children are in right now. Make very simple illustrations inside the classroom outline for major items in the class, e.g. The door, windows, shelves, cupboards, pictures, posters, cubby, desk configuration, etc,.

---
[175]. Note this is not exactly the same as activities done in 4.0 because here you are dealing with ten Mitzvos at a time, while in 4.0 a similar activity was done with 1-3 Mitzvos at a time.
[176]. Either they choose their own partners, or the teacher can pair them, or use a lottery to decide who is paired with who.

Each one of the items you outline will be a location to which you will associate a specific Mitzvah. This is called 'Mental Palaces' or 'Mental Mapping.' You identify a room that is already familiar to all the students in the class and then map out the outline of the room and identify all the main items in the room.

13.3 Assign the classroom a chapter number from which you are going to memorize Taryag Mitzvos.

So for example, the first chapter in Chumash that has more than one Mitzvah[177] is Parshas Bo, Chapter 12. It has 14 Mitzvos. So assign your classroom as Chapter 12.

13.4 Ask the students to identify the first Mitzvah in Chapter 12.[178]

13.5 *Press Your Imagination Button!*

Starting from the entrance door to the class, assign the first Mitzvah in Chapter 12 to that door and associate the Mitzvah in a most unusual way. For example, the first Mitzvah in Chapter 12 is Bet Din announces the New Moon, Rosh Chodesh, based on its sighting from two witnesses. Using your creative imagination, give the children your funny version of association between the entrance door and this Mitzvah. For example, see two witnesses sticking their heads through the door into the class and then see both their necks stretch across the class to the nearest window, smash through the window and they shout together "we see the new moon!"

13.6 Call on several students at random to describe in their own words the funny story you just made. They are now repeating the imagery they created in their own mind based on your description of your creative imagination!

13.7 Take the stick Picture #129 of Kiddush HaChodesh and stick it to the door inside the classroom outline on the white board (alternatively you can stick it on the actual door of the classroom or both!). Either way, you are 'Mapping' out the Mitzvos in the classroom.

13.8 Ask the class to identify the next Mitzvah in Chapter 12, Parshas Bo.[179]

The next Mitzvah is Shechitas Korban Pesach after Midday of Erev Pesach.

13.9 Identify the next item in the classroom as mapped on the white board.

Let's say it's the classroom clock next to the door. Using your creative imagination, give the children your funny version of an association between the clock and Shechitas Korban Pesach. For example, see a lamb's head crash through the clock face and announce "Chatzot Hayom, time to Shecht me!" then the clock's hands slice the neck of the lamb's head sticking out the clock face and see the blood drip down the clock and down the wall. If you want to add humor, you could have the lamb complain "*that was a real pain in the neck*!"

---

177. Chumash Bereishis only has 3 Mitzvos total, each in a different chapter so you do not need to assign an entire room in your mind for one Mitzvah.
178. Show them how to use the Taryag Mitzvos Reference Book or the table of contents of Sefer HaChinuch for the sequence of Mitzvos in every Parsha of Chumash.
179. Show them references they can use to find where the Mitzvos are in each Parsha. They can use the table of contents of Sefer HaChinuch, or Poel Tzedek of The Shach. They can find it from The Taryag Mitzvos Reference Book.

13.10 Call on several students at random to describe in their own words the funny story you just gave as well as the previous one. As the two or three students you call upon repeat the story, all the other students listening are reviewing the same Mitzvos by default!

13.11 Take the stick Picture Card of Mitzvah #404 and place it on or above the class clock in your classroom outline on the white board or the actual class clock (or both).

13.12 Ask the class to identify the next Mitzvah in Chapter 12, Parshas Bo.
The next Mitzvah is Eating the Korban Pesach on the night of Pesach.

13.13 Identify the next item in the classroom you mapped on the white board.
Let's say it's a shelf of books. Using your creative imagination, give the children your funny version of association between the shelf of books and Eating the Korban Pesach. See yourself feeding a Kezayit measure of meat from the Korban Pesach and holding it in your palm in front of the book shelf, see the books fighting to eat the meat in your hand, they open themselves and snap closed their pages on the Kezayit of meat and gobble it all up, see yourself feeding another Kezayit and the books rushing off the shelf to open and close themselves on the meat in your palm.

13.14 Call on several students at random to describe in their own words the funny story you just gave as well as the previous two.

13.15 Take the stick Picture Card of Mitzvah #408 and place it on the book shelf in your classroom outline on the white board or the actual book shelf (or both).

13.16 When you finish locating all 14 Mitzvos in your classroom, ask the students to make a list of other rooms in Yeshiva/school/home/places they are extremely familiar with.
This list will be used as 'Mental Palaces' and 'Mental Mapping.' For example, other rooms in the school, all the rooms in their home, their shul, their grandparents home, friends homes, bungalow colony, etc, etc.

13.17 Show the students how you can remove the picture from the drawing you made of the classroom outline and write in its place the numbers 1-14 for the 14 Mitzvos in that Chapter. So for example, you will write #1 in the illustration of the door on the classroom outline on the white board and a number #2 on the Clock and #3 on the Book Shelf, etc.

13.18 Instruct the students to:
A. Copy the outline you have on the board onto graph paper and
B. Write at the top of their chart - Chapter #12 Parshas Bo.
C. Make a chart at the bottom of the page with 1-14 and the assigned Mitzvah to that number.
Now they have a full page of all the Mitzvos in Chapter 12 of Bo.

13.19 They can do the same for all the future 'Mental Maps' they draw till they have their own file/portfolio of all the Chapters in Chumash.

13.20 Ask the students to select specific rooms in the school they can allocate for the next chapter in Shemos which have Mitzvos. Chapter 13 in Bo has 6 Mitzvos. Tell them to assign the number 13 to that room.

13.20 Instruct them to work alone or in pairs and draw an outline of room #13 with all its major furnishings as done in 13.2 above. (Since there are 6 Mitzvos in this chapter/room, they only need to identify 6 items in the room to associate all 6 Mitzvos of that Chapter).

13.21 Direct them to do all the steps in 13.2-13.8 above and start building their own file of all the chapters in Chumash.

Once the students understand the template of steps 13.2 - 13.8, they can do this by themselves. If you have shown them how to find the Mitzvos in the table of contents of Sefer HaChinuch, they can plot the Mitzvos themselves using 'Mental Mapping' of other rooms in the school or their homes or shuls they are familiar with.

It should not take more than three or four times for you to give your own examples of how to associate the Mitzvah with the next item in the class till you can ask the students if they are ready to make up their own funny associations.

For your information, all 613 Mitzvos are plotted in a total of 77 Chapters out of the 209 Chapters in all Chumash.[180] That means that to 'Mentally Map' the entire Chumash, you only need to allocate 77 rooms in your mind from the many homes and buildings you are already familiar with. It may also interest you to know that 25 chapters from these 77 only have as few as 1-3 Mitzvos. So really, you only have to assign 52 rooms. You can also assign the front of a neighbors house on your street or a local park and its layout for locating Mitzvos. You can even assign Mitzvos to places in your car! The sky is the limit with your imagination.

A word of caution, these funny stories really do work. Your brain has to create its own file for something it never saw before. Your imagination is your mind's eye and is as impressionable as if you actually saw what your mind imagined. This being the case, you want the children to use their imagination with the following cautions:
1. The images they think of should not be disrespectful to anything Kadosh &
2. Not disrespectful to anyone.

---

180. Although there are technically 209 Chapters in the entire Chumash, the Mitzvos are bunched in different chapters and in most chapters there are no Mitzvos at all. In the entire Chumash Bereishis there are only 3 Mitzvos from all 613 out of 50 Chapters.

14. Taryag Mitzvos Photo Cards

The Taryag Mitzvos Photo Cards have the following 14 additional details to the Stick Picture Card. They include icons for:

1. Men
2. Women
3. Kohen
4. Kohen Gadol
5. Malkus
6. Death Penalty of Skila
7. Death Penalty of Sereifa
8. Death Penalty of Chereg (Sword)
9. Death Penalty of Chenek
10. Missa Bidei Shamayim
11. Kares
12. Mitzvos of Eretz Yisrael
13. Mitzvos Tamidi 24/7
14. Mitzvos done in Yerushalayim

14.0 *What's That Photo in the Window? Game*

Materials needed for this activity:

1. 6" X 4" envelopes
2. Pair of scissors.
3. Red colored pencil
4. Green colored pencil
5. Pen/Pencil

14.1 Using envelopes[181] that accommodate the photo cards of Taryag Mitzvos (4" x 6"), cut out a window in the middle of the face of the envelope to then insert the Mitzvah Card you are using.

14.2 With only the photo part of the card showing, the student has to identify as many of the correct icons for this photo and draw those icons on his own index card.

14.3 For additional challenge, the student can write the Hebrew Description of the Mitzvah, the **English Description and Passuk.** For even more challenge, for those students who are ready, they can also write the chapter where that Mitzvah is found.

14.4 Do the same as 14.1 - 14.3 for each section of the 83 sub-sections or for the favorite Mitzvos of that particular student.

PUBLIC REQUEST:

If you or your students come up with your own very engaging activities and games with the Mitzvos Cards, please let us know or send an email or short video clip of your activity and we would be delighted to include it, in your name, in future editions of the Application's Knowledge Map.

---

181. You can just as easily use card stock and fold it over the Photo Card of Taryag and cut a window in the card to only show the photo beneath. Then insert the photo card under the window.

15.0 *Build your own Class Taryag Mitzvos Library*

We strongly recommend either a classroom library or at least a school library of the book list below for both teacher and students to have many resources to expand their Taryag Mitzvos career!

1. Six Constant Mitzvos, Rabbi Mordecai Plaut, Feldheim Press.
2. Taryag Tales, 613 Stories Based on Taryag Mitzvos.[182]
3. The Taryag Companion, Rabbi Jack Abramowitz.[183]
4. The Horeb, Rabbi Samson Raphael Hirsch.[184]
5. The Encyclopedia of the Taryag Mitzvoth, The Taryag Foundation[185]
6. Yahadus, 5 Volumes. Colorful and comprehensive description of 613 Mitzvos.[186]
7. Sefer Chareidim
8. Kitzur Sefer Chareidim
9. Sefer Chanoch L'Naar (includes reprint of Poel Tzedek of the Shach)[187]
10. Kitzur Sefer HaChinuch, Published by Feldheim.
11. Smag (Sefer Mitzvos Gedolos from Rav Moshe M'Coucy).
12. Sefer HaMitzvos of Rambam
13. Yad Hazakah of Rambam, Moznaim Press.[188]
14. Sefer HaChinuch.[189]
15. Sefer Mitzvos HaKitzir, The Chafetz Chaim, Feldheim Press.[190]
16. Madrich to Taryag Mitzvos, Feldheim Press.[191]

---

182. Published by Toras Chaim Ltd.
183. Available from Amazon.com
184. Translated by Dayan I Grunfeld. Available on Amazon.com
185. Distributed by Israel Bookshop, 501 Prospect Street, Lakewood, NJ 08701. Tel: 732-901-4012
186. Published by Living Lessons, 1375 Coney Island Avenue, #207. Brooklyn, NY 11230. Tel: 347-709-8660. inconclusiveness or
187. Available from Rabbi Hamelech Bluth 600 East 8th Street, Brooklyn, NY 11218.
188. An English Edition runs about 30 volumes with excellent foot notes, written by Rabbi Eliyahu Tougher, also available from Moznaim Press.
189. Scroll published 10 volumes with translation and excellent foot notes for further research.
190. The Chafetz Chaim wrote a brief summary of all 279 Mitzvos applicable nowadays. Feldheim printed an English facing translation.
191. This is a reference book of all 613 Mitzvos and where they are found in Sefer HaChinuch, The Rambam's Yad Chazaka, Sefer HaMitzvos, Shulchan Aruch and a listing of where Rambam differs to Rambam.

Knowledge Map B:

How to Memorize Taryag Mitzvot According to the Rambam

There are two methods for memorizing Taryag Mitzvot.

Method #1 is to memorize the Mitzvot according to the list of **Rambam** in Mishneh Torah.

Method #2 is to memorize the Mitzvot according to the chapter number in **Chumash**.[192]

The method for memorizing the Mitzvot according to Rambam is described in the Taryag Mitzvot Manual,[193] and in the following knowledge map we will give you the step by step process of learning and teaching them.

STEP ONE
Teach yourself the Mitzvot most familiar to you and your student

Below (Pages 4-7) is a list of the more familiar Mitzvot as well as others that are very easy to teach using the Taryag Picture cards in Building Block #3 of Taryag Mitzvot.[194] There are many Mitzvot that are less familiar, but a simple picture will create a deep enough impression that you and the student will immediately remember that Mitzvah when you or he sees the picture again.[195]

In the list below (Pages 4-7) a number appears to the far right of the Code Name to indicate which number this Picture Card is in the Taryag Mitzvot Manual. This number is the same as the numbered Taryag Animations, so you can direct the children to watch that number Mitzvah.

- 1.1   Teach yourself the first 10 Mitzvot listed below.[196]
- 1.2   Teach yourself the next 10 Mitzvot 11-20 listed below.
- 1.3   Select a partner and review together the first 20 cards in random sequence and say out loud the Code Name for that Mitzvah. So, for example, if you pull out the picture of a Heart and the word Yisrael printed inside the heart, you have to say out loud "Love other Jews," or your own words "Ahavat Yisrael." Finish all the 20 cards, then shuffle the cards and now your partner does the same.
- 1.4   Teach yourself the next 10 Mitzvot 21-30 listed below.
- 1.5   Teach yourself the next 10 Mitzvot 31-40 listed below.

---

192. Sefer HaChinuch numbers the Mitzvot from 1-613 as they appear in sequence in Chumash.
    This system is not useful as a reference because the only sefer that references the Mitzvot according to their number is Sefer HaChinuch and Minchat Chinuch. However, knowing which Parsha and actual perek in Chumash a particular Mitvzah appears is very useful for quickly finding Mitzvot and cross-referencing. Indeed, this has become the prevailing reference system since printing. So we are teaching here a memory system for knowing the perek every Mitzvah is in.
193. Page 28-29 in The Taryag Mitzvot Manual 2015 edition.
194. See www.breakthroughchinuch.com for list of products under Building Block of Chinuch #3, Taryag Mitzvot.
195. Watch DVD #2 of Taryag Mitzvot, Building Block #2, which shows how to teach over 100 Mitzvos in less than an hour.
196. On the back of each Picture card is a brief explanation of that Mitzvah. If the Mitzvah is not obvious from the picture, then read the back of the picture. These 121 have been selected because of their familiarity or because the picture is so telling, it immediately triggers off which Mitsvah it is. So for example, if you see a picture of a man writing a Sefer Torah, it will trigger off in your mind the Mitzvah to write a Sefer Torah. When you see a picture of a man with a crown on his head writing a Sefer Torah, you will immediately remember the Mitzvah for a Jewish King to write a Sefer Torah.

- 1.6 Select a partner and review together the first 40 cards in random sequence and say out loud the code word/s for that Mitzvah. So, for example, if you pull out the picture of a Jew learning Torah, you have to say 'The Mitzvah to learn and teach Torah." Finish all the 20 cards, then shuffle the cards and now your partner does the same.
- 1.7 Teach yourself the next 10 Mitzvot 41-50 listed below.
- 1.8 Teach yourself the next 10 Mitzvot 51-60 listed below.
- 1.9 Select a partner and review together the first 60 cards in random sequence and say out loud the code word/s for that Mitzvah. So, for example, if you pull out the picture of destroying Chametz, you say out loud "The Mitzvah to destroy Chametz." Finish all the 60 cards, then shuffle the cards and now your partner does the same.
- 1.10 Teach yourself the next 10 Mitzvot 61-70 listed below.
- 1.11 Teach yourself the next 10 Mitzvot 71-80 listed below.
- 1.12 Select a partner and review together the first 80 cards in random sequence and say out loud the code word/s for that Mitzvah. Finish all the 80 cards, then shuffle the cards and now your partner does the same. The entire activity should should take less than two minutes.
- 1.13 Teach yourself the next 10 Mitzvot 81-90 listed below.
- 1.14 Teach yourself the next 10 Mitzvot 91-100 listed below.
- 1.15 Select a partner and review together the first 100 cards in random sequence and say out loud the code word/s for that Mitzvah. Finish all the 100 cards, then shuffle the cards and now your partner does the same. The entire activity should should take between 2-3 minutes.
- 1.16 Teach yourself the next 10 Mitzvot 101-110 listed below.
- 1.17 Teach yourself the next 12 Mitzvot 111-122 listed below.
- 1.18 Select a partner and review together the first 100 cards in random sequence and say out loud the code word/s for that Mitzvah. Finish all the 122 cards, then shuffle the cards and now your partner does the same. The entire activity should should take about 3 minutes.

List of 122 Most Familiar Mitzvot

Here is the list of familiar Mitzvot that you are being asked to teach yourself and your student/s. They are simple to recall because the picture easily reminds you which Mitzvah it is.[197]

1.	Hashem is One	3
2.	Love Hashem	4
3.	Have Emuna in Hashem	1
4.	Love other Jews	13
5.	Love the convert	14
6.	Tzitzit	84
7.	Tefilin shel Rosh	79
8.	Tefilin Shel Yad	80
9.	Shema	76
10.	Tefila	77
11.	Kiddush & Havdala	91
12.	Mezuza	81
13.	Live in a Sukkah seven days	117
14.	Listening to the Shofar	116
15.	Shake the Lulav	118
16.	Learn and Teach Torah	22
17.	Show Kavod to Talmidey Chachamim	23
18.	Don't hate another Jew	15
19.	Don't speak Lashon Hara	19
20.	Don't embarrass someone	17
21.	Kibud Av V'Em	584
22.	Keep your promises	214
23.	Don't wear Shaatnez. (wool and linen together)	238
24.	Give Tzedaka	250
25.	Don't refuse to give Tzedaka	251
26.	Do Teshuva for Aveiros	75
27.	Return lost object to its owner	480
28.	Return a stolen object	478
29.	Don't harm someone else's body	481
30.	Don't hurt people with words	501
31.	Don't hurt a convert with words	503
32.	Take chala from the dough	273
33.	Don't kill	482
34.	Don't kidnap	473
35.	Don't steal	467

---

197. Using the picture cards of Taryag Mitzvos you will be able to teach many more Mitzvos than just those the child is familiar with. That's because the picture 'speaks a thousand words,' meaning it prints the information in the mind of the child at a much deeper level of penetration than just teaching the information verbally. Because many of the Mitzvos listed above are part of the child's cultural environment and Jewish calendar, you are maximizing the likelihood of the child remembering the Mitzvah and enjoying learning about them.

36.	Don't rob	474
37.	Don't serve Avoda Zara	28
38.	Destroy Avoda Zara	53
39.	Don't let a Witch or Wizard live	552
40.	Lend money to the poor	526
41.	Don't do Melacha on Shabbos	88
42.	Don't do Melacha on the 1st day of Pesach	97
43.	Don't do Melacha on the 7th day of Pesach	99
44.	Don't do Melacha on Shavuos	101
45.	Don't do Melacha on Rosh Hashana	103
46.	Don't do Melacha on Yom Kippur	93
47.	Fast on Yom Kippur	94
48.	Don't do Melacha on the 1st day of Sukkos	105
49.	Don't do Melacha on the 7th day of Sukkos	107
50.	Rest on Shabbos	87
51.	Rest on the 1st day of Pesach	96
52.	Rest on the 7th day of Pesach	98
53.	Rest on Shavuos	100
54.	Rest on Rosh Hashana	102
55.	Rest on Yom Kippur	92
56.	Rest on 1st day of Sukkos	104
57.	Rest on 7th day of Sukkos	107
58.	Count the Omer	384
59.	Destroy Chametz on Erev Pesach	109
60.	Eat Matza on first night of Pesach	114
61.	Don't eat Chametz 7 days	110
62.	Tell story of Yetzias Mitzrayim, 1st night of Pesach	115
63.	Don't cut Peos of the head	68
64.	A man cannot wear women's clothes	70
65.	A woman cannot wear men's clothes	71
66.	Don't make a tattoo on your skin	72
67.	Birkas Kohanim	78
68.	Birkas Hamazon	85
69.	Write a Sefer Torah	82
70.	A King must write his own Sefer Torah	83
71.	Bris Mila	86
72.	Don't eat Treif meat	190
73.	Know which animals are Kosher	176
74.	Know which birds are Kosher	177
75.	Know which fish are kosher	178
76.	Know which locusts are kosher	179
77.	Don't eat blood	192
78.	Don't eat flying insects	183
79.	Don't eat crawling insects	184

80.	Don't eat water insects	187
81.	Don't eat worms in fruit	186
82.	Don't eat maggots	185
83.	Don't eat milk and meat together	195
84.	Don't cook meat and milk together	196
85.	Shecht an animal in a kosher way	204
86.	Don't marry a non-Jew	162
87.	Don't steal someone elses wife (adultery)	160
88.	Don't live as married to a father (Mishkav Zachur)	158
89.	Don't live as married to another man	157
90.	Don't live as married to an uncle	159
91.	Don't marry your mother	139

(We use the word 'marry' here in reference to arayus, and all the next 17 examples below)

92.	Don't marry your step-mother	140
93.	Don't marry a sister	141
94.	Don't marry a half-sister	142
95.	Don't marry a granddaughter (son's daughter)	143
96.	Don't marry a granddaughter (daughter's daughter)	145
97.	Don't marry a daughter	144
98.	Don't marry a mother and daughter	146
99.	Don't marry a mother and granddaughter (mother and her son's daughter)	147
100.	Don't marry a mother and granddaughter (mother and daughter's daughter)	148
101.	Don't marry your aunt (father's sister)	149
102.	Don't marry your aunt (mother's sister)	150
103.	Don't marry your aunt (Uncle's wife)	151
104.	Don't marry your daughter-in-law	152
105.	Don't marry your sister-in-law (brother's wife)	153
106.	Don't marry your sister-in-law (your wife's sister)	154
107.	A man cannot marry an animal	155
108.	A woman cannot marry an animal	156
109.	Make a Ma'aka (fence around a flat roof)	494
110.	Don't leave things in places a person could trip	493
111.	Help another Jew unload heavy things	496
112.	Help others to load their heavy things.	497
113.	Do business honestly, according to Torah law	499
114.	Don't cheat in business	500
115.	Don't cheat a convert in business	502
116.	Pay your day worker on time	518
117.	Don't delay paying your worker	519
118.	Don't muzzle an animal while it is ploughing	523
119.	A Jewish King cannot have more than 18 wives	591
120.	A Jewish King cannot have too many horses	594
121.	A Jewish King cannot have too much money	595

Step Two
Assign a Code Name for each Mitzvah the students learn.

2.1
Teach yourself the Hebrew Code Names for the first 10 Mitzvot. You will find these 'Code Names' on the front of each card and also in the Taryag Mitzvah Manual. Right now you are still teaching yourself the 122 Mitzvot listed as 'the most familiar.' So check out the number of each Mitzvah in the list of 122 against which number it is in the Manual. For example, in the list of the 122 Mitzvot, the first one is 'Hashem is One.' The corresponding number of that Mitzvah in the Taryag Manual is #3. So in the Manual you will see the Hebrew Name word of that Mitzvah is אחד.

2.2   Teach yourself the Hebrew Code Words for the next 10 Mitzvot, 11-20.
2.3   Teach yourself the Hebrew Code Words for the next 10 Mitzvot, 21-30.
2.4   Teach yourself the Hebrew Code Words for the next 20 Mitzvot, 31-40.
2.5   Teach yourself the Hebrew Code Words for the next 20 Mitzvot, 41-60.
2.6   Test yourself (best with a partner and take turns) by shuffling the 60 cards and pull one out at a time, cover the place where the Hebrew code word is and based on the picture, say the code word. For example, if you pull out a picture of the cover of a bencher, call out "ברכת המזון."
2.7   Teach yourself the Hebrew Code Words for the next 20 Mitzvot, 61-80.
2.8   Teach yourself the Hebrew Code Words for the next 20 Mitzvot, 81-100.
2.9   Teach yourself the Hebrew Code Words for the next 20 Mitzvot, 101-122.
2.10 Test yourself (best with a partner and take turns) by shuffling the 122 cards and pull one out at a time, cover the place where the Hebrew code word is and based on the picture, say the code word.

Step Three
Organize The Mitzvot

3.1
Ask yourself (or your student) how many different ways can you organize the Mitzvot? Keep asking yourself the same question till you/your partner/student come up with the four main methods of organizing the Mitzvot.[198] They are:

1. Rambam in Sefer HaMitzvot   - Listed in two groups of Aseh and Lo Ta'aseh.
2. Rambam in Mishneh Torah   - Bunched according to categories.
3. Sefer HaChinuch   - Listed according to sequential appearance in Chumash.
4. Sefer Chareidim   - Listed according to parts of the body.

The goal in 3.1 is for you to come up with these ideas yourself. When teaching 3.1 to children, you want them to figure these methods out themselves and *then* you can reveal to them that these are in fact the four main methods.[199]

---

198. There are many more ways than these four. One could divide the Mitzvot into 'Bein Adam L'Chavero and Bein Adam LaMakom, or into Mitzvot which apply nowadays or into Mitzvot which are Chukim and which are Mishpatim, etc,.
199. Challenge the students to organize the Mitzvos themselves. *Bring to class the following Seforim: 1. Sefer HaMitzvos of the Rambam, 2. One of the*

Memorize The Names of The 14 Books of Rambam

Before learning the actual Mitzvot in sequence, first you will teach yourself the order of the 14 Books of Rambam.[200] These are the 14 major categories Rambam lists all the Mitzvot under. Each of the 14 has sub-categories, 83 in total. The Taryag Mitzvot are plotted under these 83 sub-categories of the 14 books. For now, learn the icons for each of the 14 books. These are found in the DVD of Building Block #2 of Taryag Mitzvah Training. You can also find these icons in the Taryag Manual at the end of Chapter 6. (See page 40 of this document for a sample).

3.2

Memorize the first 3 icons of Rambam's 14 Books. They are Sefer Mada, Ahava and Zemanim. See the icon for each of these stacked upon each other. The first icon is for Sefer מדע and is an image of the 10 Commandments with their famous slit in the middle, as often seen in depictions of the Aseret Hadibrot on top of the Aron Hakodesh in shuls. (like two inverted letters UU right next to each other). Then see the icon for Sefer אהבה which is simply a heart. In your mind, place the heart inside the slit of the Aseret Hadibrot icon. Now take the icon of Sefer זמנים which is a clock, and place it atop the heart icon and you have stacked the icons for the first three Sefarim of fourteen. This memory system is known as 'stacking.'

3.3

Memorize the next three icons of Rambam's 14 Books; Nashim, Kedusha and Hafla'ah. Our icons for these three sefarim are a stick figure of an Isha for Sefer נשים, a Kiddush cup as an icon for Sefer קדושה and a mouth as the icon for Sefer הפלאה.[201] Now stack each one of these icons on top of each other beginning with the Isha atop the icon of the clock for Zmanim. Now place a kiddush cup on top of the head of the Isha. Now see the mouth of the cup talking, making oaths and nedarim!

3.4

Review the first 6 books of Rambam from memory only. (Even if you can only recall the books because you are seeing their icons stacked one atop the other, you will eventually know all the books without using these icons as simanim).

Sefarim of Rambam's Yad Chazaka, Mishnah Torah, 3. One copy of Sefer HaChinuch and 4. One copy of Sefer Chareidim. Once you have taught the children about a hundred Mitzvos or more with the pictures, and they know them really well, you can then ask the children to think of ways to organize the Mitzvos. Let them surprise you...and they will! For example, ask: 'Children, what ways can you think of to help us sort the Mitzvos? Are their some piles we could make of one type of Mitzvah and another pile for a different type of Mitzvah?" One kid will probably tell you that we can separate the Mitzvos into two piles, one pile of the dos and another of the dont's. Then you can say *"Wow, Moshe! You just had the same idea as Rambam!"* Now walk to the 6,000-year time line on the classroom wall and show them where Rambam lived. if you can have an actual **Sefer HaMitzvos** of the Rambam for this lesson, pull it out in view of the children and show the class how the Rambam thought of the same idea as Moshe over here. Moshe will feel so happy and he will feel a personal connection to Rambam. Another student might suggest sequencing the Taryag Picture cards in the order of the Mitzvos as they appear in the Torah. That is your cue to say *"Wow! Mordecai, you have the same idea as Sefer HaChinuch!* And show the class your **Sefer HaChinuch**. Again, walk over to the Time Line and show them when the Author of Sefer HaChinuch lived and where. He lived soon after the Rambam and also from Spain. Next, ask the students if there are any other ways they can think of to sort and arrange the Mitzvos. At some point, one student will offer to sort them out according to bunches, or categories. Then you can show them how Rambam did exactly that in his other, much bigger work on Taryag Mitzvos, the **Mishnah Torah**. Again, pull out a copy or show them an entire set and again, walk to the Time Line reminding where and when Rambam lived. Don't be surprised if eventually one student figures out how to make piles of Mitzvos according to the part of the body which does that Mitzvah. That's your cue to introduce **Sefer Chareidim**, which indeed, lists the Mitzvos of the Torah according to the bodypart it is performed by.

200. Also known as The Mishneh Torah and Yad Hazaka.

201. Sefer Hafla'ah refers to Mitzvot which are vocal declarations, or functions of our mouths, such as oaths, promises, Shavuos, Nedarim and the vocal declaration of a Nazir or one who vocally declares his property Hekdesh. So we selected the picture of a mouth as an icon for Hafla'ah. In remembering the sequence of Sefarim, you can pretend the 'mouth' of the cup is saying promises and oaths. See this in your mind, see the 'lip' of the Kiddush cup mouthing oaths and promises.

3.5

Review the first 6 books of Rambam backwards (see the lip of the mouth of the kiddush cup (Hafla'ah), then the kiddush cup (Kedusha), then the Isha beneath the Kiddush Cup (Nashim), then the clock beneath the isha (Zmanim), then the heart beneath the clock (Ahava) and lastly the Aseret Hadibrot icon beneath the heart for Sefer Mada. You may ask why are you learning the order backwards? Actually there is no real specific need to know the sefarim in reverse order, it is more an exercise in flexing your memory muscles and showing you that this particular system of memorizing through stacking, your brain is able to see where the information is in both forward and backward order. This helps your mind see the context of each item in its relationship to the other items.

3.6

Memorize the next three icons of Rambams' books. We us 'seeds' as an icon for Sefer Zeraim. An icon of the Mizbayach for Sefer Avoda. Lastly an icon of Smoke (coming off the top of the Mizbayach) for Sefer Korbanot. Now see seeds coming out the mouth of the kiddush cup (remember the mouth is Sefer Hafla'ah, so now the seeds are directly associated with the mouth of the cup). Then see the seeds land on the ramp of the Mizbayach (connecting your mind to Sefer Avoda) and lastly see smoke coming off the top of the Mizbayach (Sefer Korbanot).

3.7

Review the first 9 books of Rambam by memory.

3.8

Review all 9 books backwards.

3.9

Memorize the next 3 icons of Rambams' books. They are an icon of a Mikveh for Sefer Tahara. An icon of a smashed up car for Nezikin and an icon of a dollar bill for Kinyan. Stack these three atop the smoke of Sefer Korbanot. How? Well, best use your imagination, but here is our version. See the smoke rising from the Mizbayach and heating a Mikveh suspended in midair above the smoke. Now see a car crash into the Mikveh and crack the mikveh floor open and concertina the car. See $100 dollar bills flying out the car sun roof. Or if you prefer, you can have a time bomb as the icon of Nezikin and see it in the Mikveh explode, blowing up the Mikveh and see hundred dollar bills come flying out the bomb in all directions. The main idea is that you create simanim, or icons in your mind that are closely connected to each other as you stack them, and make the connection unusual, because that is what will stick in your mind.

3.10

Review the first 12 books of Rambam.

3.11

Review the frist 12 books backward.

3.12

Memorize the last two icons of Rambams' books. We use a weighing scale as an icon for Mishpatim and a Bais Din of three judges sitting behind a table as an icon for Shoftim. Now stack the Scale atop of the flying hundred dollar notes. See the flying dollars landing on both scales and see the notes piling onto the scales. Then see the three judges reach over their table and their arms stretching beyond their normal length sweeping the hundred dollar bills off the scales (if you want to add that the judges motivation is because Dayanim should not love money so they cannot easily be bribed). So now you have all 14 icons stacked.

3.13

Say out loud all the story of your icons from beginning to end with a partner. If your partner is learning them too, have him take a turn after you. Otherwise the purpose of the partner is to check your order of icons as they come up in the story. Your story would sound something like this: The Aseret Hadibrot has a HEART inserted in the slit between the two luchot. On top of the heart is a CLOCK (if you want to make the connection stronger, make a funny connection, like black ink dripping from the hour hand onto the red heart and discoloring the red heart). On top of the clock is standing a LADY (whose dress covers the numbers at the top of the clock so you cannot read the time properly). On top of the lady's head, she is balancing a very large KIDDUSH CUP and the MOUTH of the cup is talking non stop oaths and promises and out of the mouth come flying SEEDS which land on the ramp of the MIZBAYACH (and immediately sprout into fruit trees). On top of the Mizbayach there is SMOKE ascending into the sky and heating up a MIKVEH. Inside the Mikveh is a TIME BOMB, the wire is on fire and when the fire reaches the end of the wire, the bomb explodes and hundreds of ONE HUNDRED DOLLAR NOTES come flying out the bomb and land on both sides of SCALES and extra long arms of three JUDGES keep wiping the hundred dollar notes off the scales because they are interfering with their ability to judge the case at hand.

Chart of 14 books of Rambam stacked here

3.14

Review the icons and say what each icon is a siman for:

1. Aseret Hadibrot = Sefer Mada
2. Heart = Sefer Ahava
3. Clock = Sefer Zmanim
4. Isha = Sefer Nashim
5. Kiddush Cup = Sefer Kedusha
6. Mouth of Cup = Sefer Hafla'ah
7. Seeds = Sefer Zeraim
8. Mizbayach = Sefer Avoda
9. Smoke = Sefer Korbanot
10. Mikveh = Sefer Tahara
11. Bomb = Sefer Nezikin
12. Hundred dollar notes = Sefer Kinyan
13. Scales = Sefer Mishpatim
14. Bet Din of 3 Judges = Sefer Shoftim

3.15

Review all 14 books in order without saying the story, just the names of the books.

1. מדע
2. אהבה
3. זמנים
4. נשים
5. קדושה
6. הפלאה
7. זרעים
8. עבודה
9. קרבנות
10. טהרה
11. נזיקין
12. קנין
13. משפטים
14. שופטים

Step 4
Memorize Rambam's List of The Taryag Mitzvot

BOOK 1 Sefer Mada

Book 1 of Rambam is Sefer Mada, lists 5 categories, they are Hilchot:
1. Yesodei HaTorah/Fundamentals of Monotheism
2. Deot/Laws of Thinking & Excellence of Character
3. Talmud Torah/How to learn and teach Torah
4. Akum/Laws of Idol Worship
5. Teshuva/Laws of Personal Transformation. Teach yourself the first 3 Mitzvot.

4.1   Study the first three Picture Cards and their Hebrew and English Code Names.[202] So that would be: Emuna, Zulato, Echad. אמונה - זולתו - אחד.[203]

4.2   Teach yourself the next 2 Mitzvot and their Code Names. יראת ה' & אהבת ה' See the Code Names on the actual picture cards or check them in the list of Taryag Mitzvot in the manual.

4.3   Review the first five Code Names for the first five Mitzvot from memory.

4.4   Teach yourself the next 3 Mitzvot and their Code Names: That means look at the picture cards 6,7 & 8 and their essay on the back of the card and the Hebrew Code Name on the front. They are קדוש ה' - חילול ה' - לאבד.

4.5   Review the first 8 Mitzvot by heart.

4.6.   Teach yourself the next 2 Mitzvot 9-10 and their Code Names. See the code names on the actual picture cards or check them in the list of Taryag Mitzvot in the manual. Now you have learned all 10 Mitzvot in **Hilchot Yesodei HaTorah**.

4.7   Review from memory Mitzvot 1-10 in sequence. Best if you can do every review with a partner who is learning the Mitzvot with you because that adds a stronger level of commitment.

4.8   Teach yourself Mitzvot 11-12 of **Hilchot Hilchot Deot**.[204]

4.9   Teach yourself Mitzvot 13-14 and their Code Names.

4.10   Review with your partner Mitzvot 1-14 and their Code Names.[205]

4.11   Teach yourself Mitzvot 13-14 and their Code Names.

4.12   Review all the Mitzvot 1-14 and their Code Names.

4.13   Teach yourself Mitzvah 15 and its Code Name.

4.14   Teach yourself Mitzvot 16-17 and their Code Names.

4.15   Review Mitzvot 1-17 and their Code Names.

4.16   Teach yourself Mitzvot 18-19 and their Code Names.

4.17   Teach yourself Mitzvot 20-21 and their Code Names.

---

202. You will recall that in the DVD of Building Block #6 (You did watch it...right?!...just checking!) that we explained how the mind best contains information in sequence when it is not more than 3-4 items in a row. Even up to 5 items the mind can hold onto the order of all five. But from 5-8 items, most people cannot remember in sequence without a system to link them together. It is note worthy that Rambam actually 'bunches' the vast majority of Mitzvot in obvious association with each other in a range of 2-3 Mitzvot, and sometimes up to 5, but rarely more than 5. In the Taryag Manual, we have made a space between the numbering of the Mitzvot where we saw there was an obvious break in bunching within each list of Mitzvot in each of the 83 sub-categories of the 14 books of Rambam. All this is explained in the Manual.

203. Read the back of each card to learn more about the Mitzvah, specially if you are not very familiar with that Mitzvah.

204. There are 11 Mitzvot in this category. They are bunched in pairs of two Mitzvot at a time.

205. It will not take long, merely seconds! You will surprise yourself. The message here is that constant review of what you already know will deepen your kinyan, mastery of the entire 613 headlines.

4.18 Review all the Mitzvot from 1-21 and their Code Names.

4.19 Teach yourself the only two Mitzvot in **Hilchot Talmud Torah** and their Code Names.

4.20 Review from memory Mitzvot 1-23 and their Code Names.

4.21 Teach yourself Mitzvot 24-26 in **Hilchot Ovdei Kochavim**[206] with their code Names. REMEMBER to always learn the essay on the back of the picture card. We will learn much more details of each Mitzvah when we have finished learning the 613 Headlines.

4.22 Teach yourself Mitzvot 27-28 and their Code Names.

4.23 Teach yourself Mitzvot 29-31 and their Code Names. These three Mitzvot are bunched because they relate three ways to make an idol.

4.24 Teach yourself Mitzvot 32-35 and their Code Names. These four Mitzvot are bunched because they all relate to an Ir Hanidachat, a city which served Avoda Zara.

4.25 Teach yourself Mitzvot 36-4 and their Code Names. These six Mitzvot are bunched together because they all relate to the laws of a missionary.

4.26 Review Mitzvot 24-41 and their Code Names.

4.27 Review Mitzvot 1-41 and their Code Names.

4.28 Teach yourself Mitzvot 47-49 and their Code Names.[207]

4.29 Teach yourself Mitzvot 50-52 and their Code Names.[208]

4.30 Teach yourself Mitzvot 53-55 and their Code Names.[209]

4.31 Teach yourself Mitzvot 56-59 and their Code Names.[210]

4.32 Teach yourself Mitzvot 60-62 and their Code Names.

4.33 Teach yourself Mitzvot 63-67 and their Code Names.

4.34 Review Mitzvot 24-67 and their Code Names.

4.35 Review Mitzvot 1-67 and their Code Names.

4.36 Teach yourself Mitzvot 68-69 and their Code Names. Both these Mitzvot are paired together because they are related to the hairstyles of Avoda Zara.

4.37 Teach yourself Mitzvot 70-71 and their Code Names.[211]

4.38 Teach yourself Mitzvot 72-74 and their Code Names.[212]

4.39 Review Mitzvot 224-64 and their Code Names.

4.40 Review all the Mitzvot from 1-74 and their Code Names.

4.41 Teach yourself Mitzvah 75 in **Hilchot Teshuva**.

4.42 Review all the Mitzvot from 1-75 and their Code Names.

4.43 Here is a great exercise, write out from memory all 75 Code Names!

Congratulations! You should know by heart 75 Mitzvot by now, that is over

---

206. There are 51 Mitzvot in Hilchot Akum or otherwise known as Ovdei Kochavim, literally Star worshippers. All 51 are bunched in clusters of mostly 3-4 Mitzvot at a time, sometimes even 5 in a go because they are all associated to the same topic. In one case, you have 6 Mitzvot in a row because they are all about the laws of a Meissit, a Missionary.

207. These three are related, try to understand by yourself why they are bunched together. Our reasoning is because 47-49 are acts of Avoda Zara one does oneself.

208. These three Mitzvot are related, try to understand by yourself why they are bunched together. Our reasoning is that the previous three were actual acts of Avoda Zara done with the body, while these three (50-52) acts of Avoda Zara are making use of a column or mosaic stone or tree to place Avoda Zara upon or next to.

209. These three are bunched because they refer to the Mitzvah to destroy Avoda Zara completely and not even enjoy their accessories.

210. Note how these Mitzvot are bunched because they all relate to ways to distance ourselves from Avoda Zara.

211. These two are paired together because they relate to styles of clothes that lead to Aveiros. Chazal tell us that Avoda Zara was really a camouflage for Issurei Arayos. See Sanhedrin 63b -

אמר רב יהודה אמר רב: יודעין היו ישראל בעבודה זרה שאין בה ממש, ולא עבדו עבודה זרה אלא להתיר להם עריות בפרהסיא.

212. What do these three Mitzvot have in common? We reasoned that they all relate to acts which Ovdei Kochavim did to their skin.

10% of 613! Are you pleasantly surprised how easy this is?

You have completed the first book of the 14 books of Rambam, Mazal Tov. If you would like to treat yourself and your learning partner to a small siyum for reaching this milestone, you would be fulfilling the Mitzvah learning Torah with Simcha. Go for it! Please remember, the purpose of memorizing the 613 Mitzvot is preparing your mind to have 613 files for your future learning to be filed into, and you will be learning more details for each Mitzvah as you progress through this program.

BOOK 2 Sefer Ahava

You are starting **Book 2, Sefer Ahava**. Rambam lists 6 Categories under Sefer Ahava. They are Hilchot:
1. Kriat Shema/Daily Recital of The Shema
2. Tefila & Birkat Kohanim
3. Tefilin, Mezuza and Sefer Torah
4. Tzitzit
5. Berachot
6. Brit Mila

Total count of 11 Mitzvot in Sefer Ahava.

All 11 Mitzvot are shared between these 6 categories of Sefer Ahava.
It is called the book of Ahava because these Mitzvot stand out in both our open declaration of our Love to Hashem and He gave us these Mitzvot to show His love to us.

5.1   Teach yourself Mitzvot 76-78, Shema, Tefila & Birkat Kohanim, with their Code Names.[213]
5.2   Teach yourself Mitzvot 79-81 and their Code Names.[214]
5.3   Teach yourself Mitzvot 82-83 and their Code Names.[215]
5.6   Teach yourself the next 5 Mitzvot, 82-86 and their code words.
5.7   Review Mitzvot 76-86 with their Code Names.
5.8   Review all 1-86 Mitzvot by heart with their Code Names.
5.9   Review the names of all the 14 books of Rambam.
5.10 Since you really do know all 86 by heart, give yourself the extra boost of confidence by writing out all 86 Code Names, surprise yourself, go on!

---
213. Note that these three Mitzvot are part of two of the categories of Hilchot Kriat Shema and Hilchot Tefila and Birkat Kohanim.
214. 79-81 are obviously bunched together because they are part of Hilchot STaM (Sefer Torah, Tefilin and Mezuza) which are amongst the very few Mitzvot of Taryag which are recorded in writing. As you learn more Mitzvot, you will be able to identify other Mitzvot which have to be written, can you think of any right now? (Sota, Ketuva, Gittin, any others?)
215. Obviously bunched together because they are the only two times there is a Mitzvah to write a Sefer a Torah.

BOOK 3 Sefer Zemanim

You are starting **Book 3, Sefer Zemanim**. Rambam lists 10 categories under Sefer Zemanim, they are Hilchot:

1. Shabbat
2. Eruvin
3. Shivat Assor (Yom Kippur)
4. Shvitat Yom Tov
5. Chametz & Matza

With a total count of 35 Mitzvot in Sefer Zemanim.

6.1   Teach yourself Mitzvot 87-91 in **Hilchot Shabbat** and their Code Names.

6.2   Teach yourself The Mitzvah Derabanan of Eruvin[216] in **Hilchos Eruvin**.

6.3   Now teach yourself Mitzvot 92-95 in **Hilchot Yom Kippur** & their Code \ Names.

6.4   Review Mitzvot 87-95 and their Code Names.

6.5   Review by memory all Mitzvot from 1-95.

6.6   Teach yourself Mitzvot 96-107 in one shot! That all 12 Mitzvot in **Hilchos Shvitat Yom Tov**.[217]

6.7   Review Mitzvot 87-107 with their Code Names.

6.8   Review all the Mitzvot from 1-107, say them all out loud with a partner.

Congratulations, you know over 20% of 613 Mitzvot! Hey, be honest, it was not that painful! How does it feel to know you know!? Are you motivated to keep going? Great!

6.9   Teach yourself Mitzvot 108-110 in **Hilchos Chametz Umatzah**.

6.10 Teach yourself Mitzvot 111-115 with their Code Names.

6.11 Review all the Mitzvot you know so far, from 1-115.

6.12 Teach yourself Mitzvot 116-118, and their Code Names.

6.13 Review Mitzvot 108-118 with their Code Names.

6.14 Teach yourself Mitzvot 116-118 which represent **Hilchot Shofar, Sukkah & Lulav**.

6.15 Teach yourself Mitzvot 119-121 which represent **Hilchot M'Chatzit Hashekel, Kiddush HaChodesh & Taanit**.

6.16 Review Mitzvot 87-121 with their Code Names.

6.17 Review all the Mitzvot from 1-121 with their Code Names.

6.18 Review the names of all 14 books of Rambam.

6.19 Teach yourself the two Mitzvot D'rabanan associated with Sefer Zemanim, **Chanukah and Purim**.

6.20 Hhhm, how about checking you REALLY know it! Write out all 121 Code Names....you know you can. No excuses! What! You can't read your own hand writing! Likely story!

Mazal Tov. If you have learned this far with a partner, we suggest you make a simple siyum with your learning partner.

---

216. Note that Eruvin is not numbered because it is not part of Taryag.

217. See how we have bunched them into 6 pairs since each Yom Tov has both the Aseh of resting on Yom Tov and the Lo Ta'aseh of not doing Melacha. You already know the sequence of the Yomim Tovim starting with Pesach, Shavuot, Rosh Hashana, Sukkot and Shemini Chag Atzeret, it will be easy for you to memorize all 6 pairs and their code names as found in the manual because they are sequenced according to their appearance in the calendar.

BOOK 4 Sefer Nashim

You are starting **Book 4, Sefer Nashim**. Rambam lists 5 Categories under Sefer Nashim. They are Hilchot:
1. Ishut/Marriage
2. Gerushin/Divorce
3. Yibum & Chalitza
4. Naarah Betula/ Laws of a Maidin & Virgin Wife
5. Sota/Laws of an Adulterous Wife

Total count of 17 Mitzvot in Sefer Nashim

7.1 Teach yourself Mitzvot 121-125 in **Hilchot Ishut**, and their Code Names.

7.2 Teach yourself the only two mitzvot 126-127 in **Hilchot Gerushin**, and their Code Names.

7.3 Review Mitzvot 121-127 by heart with their Code Names.

7.4 each yourself Mitzvot 128-130 in **Hilchot Yibum V'Chalitza**, with their Code Names.

7.5 Teach yourself Mitzvot 131-135 in **Hilchot Naara Betula** and their Code Names.

7.6 Teach yourself Mitzvot 136-138 in **Hilchos Sota** and their Code Names.

7.7 Review all the Mitzvot in Sefer Ishut, 121-138 with their Code Names.

7.8 Review all the Mitzvot from 1-138 and their Code Names.

7.9 Yes! Your favorite exercise! Write out all the Code Names from 1-138!

BOOK 5 Sefer Kedusha

Now you are starting **Book 5, Sefer Kedusha**. Rambam lists three Categories in Sefer Kedusha. They are Hilchot:
1. Issurei Bi'ah/Forbidden marriages[218] & relationships
2. Ma'achalot Assurot/Forbidden foods
3. Shechita

With a total count of 70 Mitzvot in Sefer Kedusha.

8.1   Teach yourself Mitzvot 139-141 of **Hilchot Issurei Bi'ah**, 139-142 and their Code Names.
8.2   Teach yourself Mitzvot 143-145 and their Code Names.
8.3   Review 139-145 by heart.
8.4   Teach yourself Mitzvot 146-148 and their Code Names.
8.5   Teach yourself Mitzvot 149-152 and their Code Names.
8.6   Review all the Mitzvot so far in Issurei Bi'ah, 139-152.
8.7   Review all the Mitzvot from 1-152.
8.8   Teach yourself Mitzvot 149-151 and their Code Names.
8.9   Teach yourself Mitzvot 152-154 and their Code Names.
8.10 Review all of 139-154 by heart.
8.11 Teach yourself Mitzvot 155-156 and their Code Names.
8.12 Teach yourself Mitzvot 157-159 and their Code Names.
8.13 Teach yourself Mitzvot 160-162 and their Code Names.
8.14 Review all Mitzvot from 139-162.
8.15 Teach yourself Mitzvot 163-165 and their Code Names.
8.16 Teach yourself Mitzvot 166-168 and their Code Names.
8.17 Teach yourself Mitzvot 169-171 and their Code Names.
8.18 Teach yourself Mitzvot 172-175 and their Code Names.
8.19 Review all the Mitzvot from 139-172.
8.20 Review all the Mitzvot from 1-172.
8.21 Teach yourself Mitzvot 176-179 of **Hilchot Ma'achalot Assurot** & their Code Names. Remember to learn the essays on the back of each card.
8.22 Teach yourself Mitzvot 180-182 and their Code Names.
8.23 Review Mitzvot 176-182.
8.24 Teach yourself Mitzvot 183-187 and their Code Names.
8.25 Review Mitzvot 176-87 and their Code Names.
8.26 Teach yourself Mitzvot 188-190 and their Code Names.
8.27 Teach yourself Mitzvot 191-193 and their Code Names.
8.28 Teach yourself Mitzvot 194-196 and their Code Names.
8.29 Review all Mitzvot from 176-196.

---

218. When teaching young children the Mitzvot of Issurei Bi'ah, we have followed the advice of R'Eliyashav z"l who said to use the terminology of 'it is assur **to live as married to**....' This is usually sufficient for children without going into further detail. If you want to learn more about 'when and how to talk to children about the birds and the bees' we have a lecture with that title which can be listened to on www.jewishinspiration.com under the series of 'Successful Parenting.' There is also a special chapter devoted to this subject at the end of the Taryag Mitzvot Manual (Chapter 12).

8.30   Review all Mitzvot from 1-196.

8.31   Teach yourself Mitzvot 197-199 and their Code Names.

8.32   Teach yourself Mitzvot 200-203 and their Code Names.

8.33   Review all Mitzvot from 176-203.

You have now finished all 38 Mitzvot of Ma'achalot Assurot. Well done! You have also covered over one third of Taryag Mitzvot!! Anyone for a siyum?

8.34   Now teach yourself the only 4 Mitzvot in **Hilchot Shechita**, 204-208 and their Code Names.

8.35   Review by heart these four Mitzvot 204-208.

8.36   Review by heart all the Mitzvot from 1-208.

8.37   Review all the names of the 14 books of Rambam.

8.38   Just a suggestion! Write out all 208 Code Names from memory! Go on! You can do it!

BOOK 6 Sefer Hafla'ah

You are now starting **Book 6, Sefer Hafla'ah** which lists the Mitzvot we perform with our mouths. Specifically verbal commitments.

Rambam lists 4 Categories under Sefer Hafla'ah. They are Hilchot:
1. Shavuot/Oaths
2. Nedarim/Promises
3. Nazirut/Laws of a Nazir
4. Erchin & Charamim/Evaluations & Dedications

With a total count of 25 Mitzvot in Sefer Hafla'ah.

9.1 Teach yourself Mitzvot 209-210 in **Hilchot Shavuot**. Study the back of the cards for more details.[219]

9.2 Teach yourself Mitzvot 211-213 and their Code Names.

9.3 Now starts **Hilchot Nedarim**. Teach yourself the next 3 Mitzvot 214-216 and their Code Names.

9.4 Review all the Mitzvot in Sefer Hafla'ah so far, that's 209-216.

9.5 Now start **Hilchot Nazir**. It has a total of 10 Mitzvot. Teach yourself the next 3 Mitzvot 217-218 and their Code Names.

9.6 Teach yourself Mitzvot 219-223 and their Code Names.[220]

9.7 Teach yourself the last 3 Mitzvot in Nazir, 224-226 and their Code Names.

9.8 Review all the Mitzvot in Sefer Hafla'ah, from 209-226.

9.9 Review all the Mitzvot from 1-226.

9.10 Teach yourself Mitzvot 227-231 of **Hilchot Erchin V'Charamim** and their Code Names.[221]

9.11 Review all the Mitzvot in Sefer Hafla'ah from 209-231.

9.12 Review all the Mitzvot from 1-231 and their Code Names.

9.13 Review the names of all 14 books of Rambam.

9.14 For the tough of heart only: You guessed! Write out 1-231 Code Names!

---

219. Remember, at this time we are building the filing system in the mind to later contain more details.
220. Note how these are a bunch of 5 Mitzvot in a row which are easily associated for the fact that they are all forbidden items to a Nazir because of their wine derivative.
221. This is the last book in Sefer Hafla'ah. The first five Mitzvot are bunched together because they all relate to a Kohen estimating the value of a person or property being donated to the Bet Hamikdash.

BOOK 7 Sefer Zeraim

You are now starting **Book 7. Sefer Zeraim**. It deals with all the Taryag Mitzvot relating to agriculture. Rambam list 7 sections in Sefer Zeraim. They are Hilchot:

1. Kilayim / Laws of forbidden mixtures.
2. Matnat Aniyim / Agricultural Gifts for the Poor
3. Teruma / Agricultural Tax to the Kohen
4. Maaser Rishon / Agricultural Tax to the Levi
5. Maaser Sheni & Neta Reva'i / Gift of 1/10 for oneself and 4th Yr Produce
6. Bikkurim and Other Gifts for the Kohanim
7. Shemitta & Yovel

10.1 Teach yourself all five Mitzvot in **Kilayim**, 234-238 and their Code Names.

10.2 Teach yourself Mitzvot 239-248 in **Hilchot Matnat Aniyim** and their Code Names.

Your 'memory Muscles' should be getting a pretty good work out by now! You should be noticing that you are more confident in taking on larger numbers of Mitzvot and committing their Code Names to memory. If any of these exercises ask too much from you, then reduce the number of Mitzvot you learn to smaller amounts. There is no race or pressure, just go at your own pace.

10.3 Teach yourself Mitzvot 249-251 and their Code Names.
10.4 Review all the Mitzvot so far in Zeraim, 234-251 and their Code Names.
10.5 Review all the Mitzvot from 1-251 and their Code Names.
10.6 Teach yourself Mitzvot 252-254 of **Hilchot Terumah** & their Code Names.
10.7 Teach yourself Mitzvot 255-259 and their Code Names.[222]
10.8 Review all 8 Mitzvot of Hilchot Terumah, from 252-259.
10.9 Review all the Mitzvot so far in Sefer Zeraim, 234-259.
10.10 Review all Mitzvot from 1-259 with their Code Names.
10.11 Teach yourself Mitzvah 260, the only Mitzvah in **Hilchot Maaser Rishon**.
10.12 Teach yourself Mitzvot 261-264 of **Hilchot Maaser Sheni** with their Code Names.
10.13 Teach yourself Mitzvot 265-267 and their Code Names.
10.14 Teach yourself Mitzvot 268-269 of **Hilchot Neta Revai** and their Code Names.
10.15 Review Mitzvot 261-269 and their Code Names.
10.16 Review Mitzvot 234-269 and their Code Names.
10.17 Review all the Mitzvot from 1-269 and their Code Names.
10.18 Teach yourself Mitzvot 270-272 of **Hilchot Bikurim** and their Code Names.
10.19 Teach yourself Mitzvot 273-275 of **Hilchot Sh'ar Matnot Kehuna**.
10.20 Teach yourself Mitzvot 276-278 and their Code Names.
10.21 Review Mitzvot 270-278 and their Code Names.
10.22 Review Mitzvot 234-278 and their Code Names.

---
222. These 5 are bunched together because they list all the people forbidden to eat Terumah.

10.23 Teach yourself Mitzvot 279-281 of **Hilchot Shemitta** and their Code Names.
10.24 Teach yourself Mitzvot 282-284 and their Code Names.
10.25 Teach yourself Mitzvot 285-287 and their Code Names.
10.26 Teach yourself Mitzvot 288-290 of **Hilchot Yovel** and their Code Names.
10.27 Teach yourself Mitzvot 291-293 and their Code Names.
10.28 Teach yourself Mitzvot 294-296 and their Code Names.
10.29 Review Mitzvot 279-296 and their Code Names.
10.30 Teach yourself Mitzvot 297-300 and their Code Names.
10.31 Review Mitzvot 279-300 and their Code Names.
10.32 Review all of Sefer Zeraim from 234-300 and their Code Names.
10.33 Review all the Mitzvot from 1-300 and their Code Names.
10.34 Review all the names of the 14 books of Rambam.
10.35 Genius! You know exactly what this last exercise without being asked. If you really don't know, okay, then you can look at the footnote below![223]

Hey! You are almost half way through Taryag Mitzvot! Consider celebrating with some chocolate (you define 'some')! Oh! By the way, you have just completed book 7 of the Rambam, so you may as well finish the leftover chocolate! What left overs?

---
223. Write in sequence 1-300 Code Names!

BOOK 8 Sefer Avoda

You are now about to start **Book 8, Sefer Avodah**, instructions related to service in the Bait Hamikdash. Rambam lists 9 categories under Sefer Avoda. They are Hilchot:

1. Bet Bechira / Laws of The Temple.
2. Keley Hamikdash & Ha'Ovdim Bo / Furnishings and the workers
3. Bi'at Hamikdash / Laws of Entering the Temple Site
4. Issurei Mizbayach / Forbidden Offerings
5. Maaseh HaKorbanot / Laws of Offerings
6. Tamidim & Mussafim / Daily & Additional Offerings
7. Pesulei Mukdashim / Offerings which became Invalid
8. Avodat Yom Hakippurim / Yom Kippur in The Bet Hamikdash
9. Me'ila / Misuse of Temple Property

With a total count of 103 Mitzvot.

11.1 Teach yourself Mitzvot 301-303 and their Code Names.
11.2 Teach yourself Mitzvot 304-306 and their Code Names.
11.3 Teach yourself Mitzvot 307-309 of **Hilchot Keley Hamikdash v'Haovdim Bo** and their Code Names.
11.4 Teach yourself Mitzvot 310-313 and their Code Names.
11.5 Review Mitzvot 301-313 and their Code Names.
11.6 Teach yourself Mitzvot 314-317 and their Code Names.
11.7 Teach yourself Mitzvot 318-320 and their Code Names.
11.8 Review Mitzvot 301-320 and their Code Names.
11.9 Review all the Mitzvot from 1-320 and their Code Names, well done!
11.10 Teach yourself Mitzvot 321-323 of **Hilchot Bi'at Hamikdash** & their Code Names.
11.11 Teach yourself Mitzvot 324-325 and their Code Names.
11.12 Teach yourself Mitzvot 326-330 and their Code Names.
11.13 Teach yourself Mitzvot 331-335 and their Code Names.
11.14 Review Mitzvot 321-335 and their Code Names.
11.15 Review Mitzvot 301-335 and their Code Names.
11.16 Teach yourself Mitzvot 336-337 of **Hilchot Issurey Mizbayach** and their Code Names.
11.17 Teach yourself Mitzvot 336-337 and their Code Names.
11.18 Teach yourself Mitzvot 338-342 and their Code Names.[224]
11.19 Review Mitzvot 336-342 and their Code Names.
11.20 Teach yourself Mitzvot 346-349 and their Code Names.
11.21 Review Mitzvot 336-349 and their Code Names.
11.22 Teach yourself Mitzvot 350-354 of **Hilchot Maaseh Korbanot**.
11.23 Teach yourself Mitzvot 355-358 and their Code Names.
11.24 Review Mitzvot 350-358 and their Code Names.

---

224. These 5 Mitzvot are bunched because they all relate to not offering blemished animals on the Mizbayach.

11.25 Teach yourself Mitzvot 359-360 and their Code Names.

11.26 Teach yourself Mitzvot 361-364 and their Code Names.

11.27 Review Mitzvot 350-364 and their Code Names.

11.28 Teach yourself Mitzvot 365-368 and their Code Names.

11.29 Teach yourself Mitzvot 369-372 and their Code Names.

11.30 Review Mitzvot 350-372 and their Code Names.

11.31 Review Mitzvot 301-372 and their Code Names.

11.32 Review all the Mitzvot from 1-372 and their Code Names.

11.33 Teach yourself Mitzvot 373-376 of **Hilchot Tamidiim uMusafim**.

11.34 Teach yourself Mitzvot 377-377-379 and their Code Names.

11.35 Teach yourself Mitzvot 380-385 and their Code Names.

11.36 Teach yourself Mitzvot 386-391 and their Code Names.

11.37 Review Mitzvot 373-391 and their Code Names.

11.38 Review Mitzvot 301-391 and their Code Names.

11.39 Review all the Mitzvot from 1-391 and their Code Names.

11.40 Teach yourself Mitzvot 392-395 of **Hilchot Pesuley Hamukdashim**.

11.41 Teach yourself Mitzvot 396-399 and their Code Names.

11.42 Review Mitzvot 392-399 and their Code Names.

11.43 Teach yourself Mitzvah 400 in **Hilchot Avodat Yom Hakippurim** and its Code Name.

11.44 Teach yourself Mitzvot 401-403 of **Hilchot Meila**, and their Code Names.

11.45 Review Mitzvot 400-403 and their Code Names.

11.46 Review Mitzvot 301-403 and their Code Names.

11.47 Yes! you are right again! Write out the Code Names for 1-403 Mitzvot. *You know it's good for your memory muscles. Plus, you no longer have an excuse of what to do with your mind when waiting in traffic, or on line at the cashier, or waiting to board your plane, or waiting on line at security or at the bank......Hhmm, maybe knowing Taryag baal peh really will fill in some gaps in my life!*

Well done! You are passed 400 Mitzvot! That means you have pretty much reached two thirds of the way to the finish line!! Time for chocolate would you not agree?!

BOOK 9 Sefer Korbanot

You are about to start **Book 9, Sefer Korbanot**. Sefer Avoda covered all the Mitzvot pertaining to the service in the Bet Hamikdash, Sefer Korbanot relates to the 39 Mitzvot for the various Korbanot. Rambam lists 5 categories in Sefer Korbanot. They are Hilchot:

1. Hilchot Korban Pesach
2. Korban Chagiga
3. Korban Bechorot
4. Shegagot
5. Mechussrey Kapara
6. Temura

With a total count of 39 Mitzvot.

12.1   Teach yourself Mitzvot 404-406 of **Hilchot Korban Pesach** & their Code Names.
12.2   Teach yourself Mitzvot 407-409 and their Code Names.
12.3   Teach yourself Mitzvot 410-411 and their Code Names.
12.4   Teach yourself Mitzvot 412-414 and their Code Names.
12.5   Review Mitzvot 404-414 and their Code Names.
12.6   Teach yourself Mitzvot 415-519 and their Code Names.
12.10 Review Mitzvot 404-419 and their Code Names.
12.11 Teach yourself **Hilchot Korban Chagiga**, Mitzvot 420-422 & Code Names
12.12 Teach yourself Mitzvot 423-425 and their Code Names.
12.13 Review Mitzvot 420-425 and their Code Names.
12.14 Review Mitzvot 404-425 and their Code Names.
12.15 Teach yourself **Hilchot Bechorot** Mitzvot 426-428 and their Code Names.
12.16 Teach yourself Mitzvot 429-430, the two Mitzvot of Maaser Behema.
12.17 Review Mitzvot 426-430 and their Code Names.
12.18 Review Mitzvot 404-430 and their Code Names.
12.19 Review all the Mitzvot 1-430 and their Code Names.
12.20 Teach yourself **Hilchot Shegagot**, Mitzvot 431-433 and their Code Names.
12.21 Teach yourself Mitzvot 434-435 and their Code Names.
12.22 Teach yourself Mitzvot 436-439 in **Hilchot M'chuserey Kapara**
12.23 Teach yourself Hilchot Temura, Mitzvot 440-442 and their Code Names.
12.24 Review 436-442 and their Code Names.
12.25 Review all the Mitzvot in Sefer Korbanot, Mitzvot 404-442 & Code Names.
12.26 Review all the Mitzvot 1-442 and their Code Names.
12.27 Review the names of all 14 books of Rambam.
12.28 We'll spare you this time!

BOOK 10 Sefer Tahara

You are starting **Book 10, Sefer Tahara**. Rambam lists 5 categories of Mitzvot in Sefer Tahara with a total of 20 Mitzvot.

13.1 Teach yourself the only Mitzvah 443 in **Hilchos Tumat Met**.
13.2 Teach yourself the only 2 Mitzvot 444-445 in **Hilchot Para Aduma**.
13.3 Teach yourself Mitzvot 446-449 in **Hilchot Tumat Tzara'at** and their Code Names.
13.4 Teach yourself Mitzvot 450-543 and their Code Names.
13.5 Review Mitzvot 443-453 and their Code Names.
13.6 Review Mitzvot 404-453 and their Code Names.
13.7 Teach yourself all 4 Mitzvot in **Hilchot Temei Mishkav Umoshav**, 454-457 and their Code Names.
13.8 Teach yourself all 3 Mitzvot in Hilchot Sh'ar Avot HaTumah, 458-460 and their Code Names.
13.9 Teach yourself the Mitzvah D'rabanan of Tumat Avodah Zara. Note this is not numbered because it is not included in Taryag.
13.10 Teach yourself the 1 Mitzvah 461 in **Hilchot Tumat Achalin** (that's also its Code Name).
13.11 Teach yourself the Mitzvah D'rabanan of Tumat Keilim. Note that this Mitzvah is not numbered because it is not included in Taryag, though interestingly, it occupies the most chapters in a single masechta of Keilim, 30 perakim.
13.12 Teach yourself the last Mitzvah in Sefer Tahara, 462 of **Hilchot Mikvaot**, and its Code Name.
13.13 Review Mitzvot 443-462 and their Code Names.
13.14 Review Mitzvot 401-462 and their Code Names.
13.15 Review Mitzvot 1-462 and their Code Names.
13.16 Review the names of all 14 Books of Rambam.

BOOK 11 Sefer Nezikin

You are starting **Book 11, Sefer Nezikin**. Rambam lists 5 categories of Mitzvot in Sefer Nezikin. They are Hilchot:

1. Nizkei Mammon / Laws of Monetary Compensation for Damages
2. Geneiva / Laws of Stealing
3. Gezeila & Aveida / Laws of Theft, Lost & Found
4. Chovel & Mazik / Laws of Physical Harm & Damage
5. Rotze'ach and Shemirat Nefesh / Laws of Murder & Protecting Lives

With a total of 36 Mitzvot.

14.1 Teach yourself Mitzvot 463-466 in **Hilchot Nizkei Mamon** & Code Names.
14.2 Teach yourself Mitzvot 467-468 of **Hilchot Geneiva** and their Code Names.
14.3 Teach yourself Mitzvot 469-471 and their Code Names.
14.4 Teach yourself Mitzvot 472-473 and their Code Names.
14.5 Review Mitzvot 463-473 and their Code Names.
14.6 Teach yourself Mitzvah 474 of Hilchot Gezeila and Aveida & Code Name.
14.7 Teach yourself Mitzvot 475-477 and their Code Names.
14.8 Teach yourself Mitzvah 478 and its Code Name.
14.9 Teach yourself Mitzvot 479-480 and their Code Names.
14.10 Review Mitzvot 474-480 and their Code Names.
14.11 Review Mitzvot 463-480 and their Code Names.
14.12 Teach yourself Mitzvah 481 of **Hilchot Chovel and Mazik**.
14.13 Teach yourself Mitzvot 482-485 of **Hilchot Rotze'ach** & Code Names.
14.14 Teach yourself Mitzvot 486-488 and their Code Names.
14.15 Teach yourself Mitzvot 489-490 and their Code Names.
14.16 Teach yourself Mitzvot 491-492 and their Code Names.
14.17 Review Mitzvot 482-492 and their Code Names.
14.18 Review Mitzvot 463-492 and their Code Names.
14.19 Teach yourself Mitzvot 493-495 and their Code Names.
14.20 Teach yourself Mitzvot 496-498 and their Code Names.
14.21 Review Mitzvot 482-98 and their Code Names.
14.22 Review Mitzvot 463-498 and their Code Names.
14.23 Review all the Mitzvot from 1-498 and their Code Names.
14.24 Review the names of all 14 books of Rambam.
14.25 Please, if your wrist can *hand*le it, write out the Code Names for 498 Mitzvot. It's very healthy for your brain! Its' called 'Brain Gain.'

BOOK 12 Sefer Kinyan

You are starting **Book 12 Sefer Kinyan**. Rambam lists 3 categories in Sefer Kinyan. (One of the three is Mitzvot D'rabanan). They are Hilchot:

1. Mechira / Sales.
2. D'rabanan - Zechia, Matana, Shechenim, Sheluchim and Shutfim.
3. Avadim / How to treat Servants.

With a total count of 18 Mitzvot.

15.1   Teach yourself Mitzvot 499-501 of **Hilchot Mechira** & their Code Names.
15.2   Teach yourself Mitzvot 502-503 and their Code Names.
15.3   Review Mitzvot 499-503 and their Code Names.
15.4   Teach yourself the next three Mitzvot D'rabanan which have no number because they are not included in Taryag.
15.5   Teach yourself Mitzvot 504-508 of **Hilchot Avadim** and their Code Names.
15.6   Teach yourself Mitzvot 509-510 and their Code Names.
15.7   Teach yourself Mitzvot 511-513 and their Code Names.
15.8   Review Mitzvot 504-513 and their Code Names.
15.9   Teach yourself Mitzvot 514-516 and their Code Names.
15.10 Review Mitzvot 504-516 and their Code Names.
15.11 Review Mitzvot 499-516 and their Code Names.
15.12 Review Mitzvot 463-516 and their Code Names.
15.13 Review Mitzvot 301-516 and their Code Names.
15.14 Review all the Mitzvot from 1-516 and their Code Names.
15.15 Review the names of all 14 books of Rambam.
15.16 We'll get you on the next one! Enjoy the break!

Congratulations! You have reached 5/6 of Taryag. Guess what we recommend you do to celebrate? (you are not allowed more than 18 guesses!)

BOOK 13 Sefer Mishpatim

You are about to start **Book 13 Sefer Mishpatim**.
Rambam lists 5 Categories of Mitzvot. They are Hilchot:

1. Sechirut / Rentals.
2. Sh'iela and Pikadon / Borrowing & Collateral.
3. Malveh and Loveh / Lending & Borrowing.
4. To'en and Nitan / Claims & Defence.
5. Nachalot / Inheritance.

With a total count of 23 Mitzvot.

16.1   Teach yourself Mitzvot 517-519 of **Hilchot Sechirut** & their Code Names.
16.2   Teach yourself Mitzvot 520-522 and their Code Names.
16.3   Teach yourself Mitzvot 523 and its Code Name.
16.4   Review Mitzvot 517-523 and their Code Names.
16.5   Teach yourself Mitzvot 524-525 of Hilchot Sh'eila & Pikadon and their Code Names.
16.6   Teach yourself Mitzvot 526-528 of **Hilchot Malveh and Loveh** and their Code Names.
16.7   Review Mitzvot 517-528 and their Code Names.
16.8   Teach yourself Mitzvot 529-533 and their Code Names. These 5 Mitzvot are bunched together because they all relate to the laws of a Mashkon, a security deposit.
16.9   Teach yourself Mitzvot 534-537 and their Code Names. These 4 Mitzvot are bunched together because they all relate to loans with interest.
16.10 Review Mitzvot 526-537 and their Code Names.
16.11 Review Mitzvot 517-537 and their Code Names.
16.12 Teach yourself Mitzvah 538 in **Hilchot To'en & Nitan** and its Code Name.
16.13 Teach yourself Mitzvah 539 in **Hilchot Nachalot** and its Code Name.
16.14 Review Mitzvot 517-538 and their Code Names.
16.15 Review Mitzvot 463-538 and their Code Names.
16.16 Review Mitzvot 1-538 and their Code Names.
16.17 Review the names of the 14 books of Rambam.
16.18 You know what? It's really up to you!

BOOK 14 Sefer Shoftim

You are about to start Book 14 Sefer Shoftim. *Yes, it is the last book! Almost there!* Rambam lists 5 categories of Mitzvot in Sefer Shoftim with a total of 74 Mitzvot. They are Hilchot:

1. Sanhedrin / Supreme Court
2. Edut / Testimony
3. Mamrim / Obedience to Authority
4. Avel / Mourning
5. Melachim and Milchamoteychem / laws of King & laws of War.[225]

17.1   Teach yourself Mitzvot 540-544 of **Hilchot Sanhedrin** & their Code Names.
17.2   Teach yourself Mitzvot 545-548 and their Code Names. These 4 are bunched together because they are 4 types of death penalties.
17.3   Teach yourself Mitzvot 549-551 and their Code Names. These 3 are bunched together because they relate to the laws of hanging.
17.4   Teach yourself Mitzvah 552 and its Code Name.
17.5   Teach yourself Mitzvot 553-554 and their Code Names. These 2 Mitzvot relate to lashes.
17.6   Teach yourself Mitzvot 555-556 and their Code Names.
17.7   Teach yourself Mitzvot 557-562 and their Code Names. All these Mitzvot relate to how a Dayan on Bet Din judges.
17.8   Teach yourself Mitzvot 563-565 and their Code Names.
17.9   Teach yourself Mitzvot 566-569 and their Code Names.
17.10 Review Mitzvot 540-569 and their Code Names.
17.11 Teach yourself Mitzvot 570-572 in **Hilchos Edut** & their Code Names.
17.12 Teach yourself Mitzvot 573-575 with their Code Names. These 3 are bunched together because they are all invalid witnesses.
17.13 Teach yourself Mitzvot 576-577 with their Code Names.
17.14 Review Mitzvot 570-577 and their Code Names.
17.15 Review Mitzvot 540-577 and their Code Names.
17.16 Review all the Mitzvot from 1-577 and their Code Names.
17.17 Teach yourself Mitzvot 578-579 of **Hilchot Mamrim** & their Code Names.
17.18 Teach yourself Mitzvot 580-581 and their Code Names.
17.19 Teach yourself Mitzvot 582-585 and their Code Names. These 4 are bunched together because they all relate to our relationship with our parents.
17.20 Teach yourself Mitzvah 586 and its Code Name.
17.21 Teach yourself Mitzvot 587-590 in **Hilchot Avel** and their Code Names.
17.22 Review Mitzvot 578-590 and their Code Names.
17.23 Review Mitzvot 540-590 and their Code Names.
17.24 Teach yourself Mitzvot 591-592 in **Hilchot Melachim** & their Code Names.
17.26 Teach yourself Mitzvot 593-595 and their Code Names. These three Mitzvot are bunched since they describe the 3 items a King must not have in excess.

---

225. In the original printing of Rambam, there is an added section called 'the laws of Melech HaMashiach.' That section was taken out by the Christian censors but has been reprinted in many new editions of the Rambam.

17.27 Teach yourself Mitzvot 596-597 and their Code Names.

17.28 Teach yourself Mitzvot 598-600 and their Code Names. These 3 Mitzvot are bunched because they all relate to waging war against Amalek.

17.29 Teach yourself Mitzvot 601-603 and their Code Names.

17.30 Review Mitzvot 591-603 and their Code Names.

17.31 Teach yourself Mitzvot 604-606 and their Code Names.

17.32 Teach yourself Mitzvot 607-609 and their Code Names. These 3 Mitzvot are bunched because they relate to exemptions at war time.

17.33 Teach yourself Mitzvot 610 and its Code Name.

17.34 Teach yourself Mitzvot 611-613 and their Code Names. These 3 Mitzvot are bunched because they relate to the laws of a Yafet Toar.

17.35 Review Mitzvot 591-613 and their Code Names.

17.36 Review Mitzvot 540-613 and their Code Names.

17.37 And now the moment you have worked so hard toward: Review all the Mitzvot 1-613 and their Code Names.

17.38 Dance and sing with joy for completing the headlines of all Taryag Mitzvot!

17.39 Make a siyum and invite your family and friends. Tell them they can do this too!

Knowledge Map C:

How to Memorize the Taryag Mitzvot According to the Sefer Hachinuch

Part I - How To Memorize Taryag Mitzvot - The Chinuch's List

Till now, you have learned a Memory System for three Limudim:
1. The Map of Chumash, the headline of what is in each chapter of the entire Chumash.[226]
2. The 14 Books of Rambam, and then you learned a method to recall all
3. The 613 Mitzvot based on the 14 major categories and 83 sub-categories.

Now we will focus on a second method of memorizing Taryag Mitzvot. Here you will learn:
How to remember which chapter of the Chumash every Mitzvah is in.
This memory system is called 'Mental Palaces' or as we call it 'Mental Mapping.'
You have learned about this idea in the Training DVDs on Building Block #6 Memory (right you remember watching them?!).

1. Mental Mapping Your Home
'Mental Mapping' is a method of using physical places you are already intimately familiar with. For example, you know the exact lay out of your home. You know exactly what is where as you enter your front door, where the hallway is, the dining room, living room, stairs to the second floor, the kitchen, the bathroom, the den, the laundry room, etc. You see, you have gone through your home so many thousands of times, you have a total 'mental map' in your mind of its precise layout. You know all these rooms and all the main furnishings of each room too. You know exactly where the chairs, tables, couch, windows, etc, are located.

2. Assign a Number to Each Room in Your Mental Map.
This Memory system uses these rooms in your mental map for you to assign a number to a specific room. So for example, let's assume the first room you enter in your home is the living room. We will assign number 12 to this room. In our memory system, you recall that 12 is TiN.[227] You may want to make a funny association with the word TiN with the entrance to your living room. It might be that the door of your living room has been removed and replaced with a metal door made of TiNs of TuNa (TuNa is also 12) and that you have to be very careful because some of the TiNs are open with TuNa spilling on your living room floor.

---
226. As outlined in Knowledge Map for Building Block #3, The Story Line of Chumash.
227. See pages 10-13 in the Chumash Memory-System Control Book for the full explanation as well as the Hebrew version of assigning numbers on pages 14-15. This was also covered on page 3 in this document.

3. Locate the 1st Mitzvah of that Chapter number in your Mental Map Room.

Now take the 14 Mitzvot in Chapter 12 of Shemot, Parshat Bo, and as you walk through your dining room in your mind's eye, make a funny association in the mind that connects each Mitzvah with that item in the living room. Remember to plot each Mitzvah in sequence as you walk through your living room. After a few reviews of where each of the 14 Mitzvot are in the living room, you will remember that all these 14 Mitzvot are in Chapter 12 (TiN - TuNa). For example, take the first Mitzvah in chapter 12 of Shemot, Kiddush HaChodesh. Let's assume that you enter your living room and you turn left, the first furnishing is a couch. Now see two men standing on your couch pointing to a slither of Moon that is sticking out a crack in your living room ceiling (the moon crashed through your living room ceiling). This outlandish image should be enough to trigger off the Mitzvah of Kiddush HaChodesh (which requires two witnesses giving Edut, testimony that they saw the new moon).

Next Mitzvah: Shecht the Korban Pesach

Continue walking around your living room and assume the next item is a fire place. Great! The next Mitzvah in sequence in chapter 14 is Slaughtering the Korban Pesach. So use your imagination to associate the Mitzvah of Korban Pesach with the fire place in your living room! My suggestion would be to see the Korban Pesach on a spit being bar-b-q'd whole with the Shechita knife still stuck in its neck. Can you smell the delicious smell of schwama? If you want to add more drama to your image, see Mitzri neighbors banging hard on your window with their teeth grinding and falling out their mouths as they protest you roasting one of their gods. If you want, add them pointing at the roasted lamb screaming 'oh my god!!!.[228] Are you getting the hang of this mental mapping?

Next Mitzvah: Eating the Korban Pesach

Go to the next item in your living (going from the left side and traveling in sequence around your living room in your mind's eye). Perhaps you have an armchair. The next Mitzvah after Shechting and roasting the Korban Pesach is 'Eating the Korban Pesach.' So now you have to associate eating the Korban Pesach with your armchair. This should not be too hard. How about you see yourself leaning on your left side wearing a kittel (it's Seder night) and your family are standing on line while you use a three foot long pruning fork to slice off a kezayit of the Korban Pesach (or a Kezayit of the armchair!) and pass it to your family members waiting on line for each one to receive a slice of a kezayit of the korban pesach. Can you see yourself lying down while you chew your kezayit and pass a slice to your wife and children?

Next Mitzvah: Don't Eat the Korban Pesach raw (partially roasted) or cooked.

Now go to the next item in your living room. Perhaps it's a coffee table next to your armchair. The next Mitzvah in Chapter 12 is the issur not to eat the Korban Pesach raw, or not fully roasted or cooked in water. The Onesh if one does violate this is Lashes. So imagine seeing a neighbor standing on your coffee table, leaning down on a stove he set up on your coffee table and he is cooking a lamb in a pot on the stove! See boiling water spill over the stove onto your living room floor! See him cut off a leg of his boiled but still raw lamb and eat it, see a Shaliach Bet Din with a long beard standing on the shoulders of your neighbor whipping him lashes for eating the Korban Pesach cooked and not roasted.

---

228. According to the Zohar, Parshat Bo, the sight of seeing their god, the lamb being roasted whole was more painful than all the Makkot combined! The Zohar says the onlooking Mitzri neighbors grit their teeth from anger and anguish that they had wasted their lives worshipping this defenceless lamb that indeed, their teeth fell out from the pressure!

Go around the rest of your living room, associating each next Mitzvah with whatever is next in your room. There are for sure more than 14 items in your living room, you can include paintings, the chandelier, book case, shtender, reading light, etc. Each Mitzvah is associated to the next item and before you know it, you have memorized all 14 Mitzvot in chapter 12 of Shemot. Then you go to the next room in your house, it might be an adjoining dining room. Assign chapter 13 to your dining room and simply locate the 6 Mitzvot in chapter 13 to 6 different items in your dining room.

You actually have many 'Mental Maps' in your mind. You know the exact layout of the home of your childhood, and the home of a close friend, or several homes of your neighbors. You have a mental map of your shul and the yeshiva you learn in or went to in your youth. Even the houses on your block may easily be printed on your mind and now you have another mental map! Hey, even the route from your home to shul and to work and back are mental maps waiting for you to use! You can take any Mitzvah in the Torah and locate a place for a chapter and do the same mental imaging we just did with you above. This is not 'stam' a gimick to remember chapter numbers and information associated to that number. You are actually memorizing Mitzvah information contained in your image. When you imagine two witnesses pointing to the sliver of the moon, your brain is imagining the actual facts of the Mitzvah of Kiddush HaChodesh. If you wanted to add more facts to the picture you could, but right now, your goal is creating headlines in the map of your mind. [229] Your goal now is only the outline of Taryag Mitzvot within the Chumash structure, not details of each Mitzvah. Your brain will automatically 'file' future details in the files of your brain you are creating with your memory systems.

In Part II below, you will find a list of all the Mitzvot in the order in which they appear in Chumash, precisely which Chapter they are found. This list will help you with your 'Mental Mapping' because it is the list you will use to map each Mitzvah in sequence in the Mental Map of your house, or rooms in your house as outlined in the paragraphs above.

This list also cross references the exact number of the same Mitzvah as found in Rambam and your Taryag Manual so you can easily reference the Mitzvah. The first number refers to the Mitzvah as numbered in Sefer HaChinuch, the second number after the slash sign is the number of that Mitzvah as found in Rambam. For example the first Mitzvah is **Peru Urevu, to father children**. This description is immediately followed by two numbers - 1/125. The first number '1' refers to the number of the Mitzvah as listed in Sefer HaChinuch and the next number, '125', is Mitzvah number 125 in your Taryag Mitzvot Manual of Rambam's list.

May the memorization of Taryag Mitzvot give you the great Zechut of being able to review all Taryag Mitzvot every day and counted as having kept all 613 Mitzvot every day! Amen.[230] Still more, may you be Zoche to have many students memorize Taryag Mitzvot and endear them to The Ribbono Shel Olam through their learning of His Mitzvot and enable them to become veritable Talmidei Chachamim, Amen.

---

229. Later, if you want to add an image of the witnesses being interrogated and the Sanhedrin in the lishkas Hagazit declaring the new moon, you can, but we do not recommend you do that now because you may overload yourself with details which will be covered when you learn Mishna Rosh Hashana.

230. See introduction to the Taryag Mitzvot Manual citing The Ben Ish Chai in Parshat VaEtchana, who claims that by reviewing Taryag Mitzvot once a day you receive reward as though you fulfilled all 613 Mitzvot!

Part II - List of all The Mitzvot in every Parsha of The Torah

Part II contains the following four pieces of information:
1. Name of the Parsha
2. The Number of the Chapter and Number of Mitzvot in that chapter
3. The English description of the Mitzvah.
4. After the English description of each Mitzvah are 2 numbers divided by a back slash (/). The first number is the reference number as found in Sefer HaChinuch and the second number is the number of that Mitzvah as found in Rambam (and your manual). So, for example, **4/408** means Mitzvah number 4 in Sefer HaChinuch and number 408 in Rambam's Mishneh Torah. This list will help you cross reference the two lists of the Rambam and Chinuch as well as guide you in creating the funny story as you travel through your Mental Palaces/Maps in your mind as explained in Part III above (pages 65 - 68).

Sefer Bereishit has a total of 3 Mitzvot.

Bereishit 1:28   **1 Mitzvah**
A Jewish man has to father children. 1/125.

Lech Lecha 17:12   **1 Mitzvah**
Do Brit Milah on the 8th day of every Jewish baby boy. 2/86.

Vayishlach 32:33   **1 Mitzvah**
Don't eat the Gid Hanasheh sinew of the thigh. 3/194.

Sefer Shemot has a total of 111 Mitzvot.

Bo
Ch. 12   14 Mitzvot
1. Calculate the beginning of every Rosh Chodesh. 4/120.
2. Shecht the Korban Pesach on the 14th of Nissan after midday. 5/404.
3. Eat meat of the Korban Pesach with Matzah and Marror. 6/408.
4. Don't eat the Korban Pesach meat raw or boiled. 7/410.
5. Don't leave any meat of the Korban Pesach till morning. 8/417.
6. Destroy all Chametz on Erev Pesach. 9/109.
7. Eat Matzah on the first night of Pesach. 10/114.
8. Chametz should not be found all 7 seven days. 11/113.
9. Don't eat mixtures of Chametz. 12/111.
10. A Mumar cannot eat the Korban Pesach. 13/412.
11. A Toshav or Hired Worker cannot eat the Korban Pesach. 14/415.
12. Don't remove Korban Pesach meat from the group's area. 15/411.
13. Don't break any bones of the Korban Pesach. 16/415.
14. An Arel cannot eat the Korban Pesach. 17/414.

Ch. 13   6 Mitzvot

1. A 1st born sheep, goat or cow is reserved for the Kohen. 18/426.
2. Don't eat Chametz all 7 days of Pesach. 19/110.
3. Chametz should not be seen all 7 days. 20/112.
4. Tell the story of Yetziat Mitzrayim on the 1st night of Pesach. 21/115.
5. Buy back a 1st born donkey with a lamb to a Kohen. 22/277.
6. Break the 1st born donkey's neck if it's not redeemed. 23/278.

Beshalach
Ch. 16   1 Mitzvah

1. Don't walk outside the city boundary. 24/90.

Yitro
Ch. 18   17 Mitzvot

1. Know Hashem exists. 25/1.
2. Know there are no other powers except Hashem. 26/2.
3. Don't make Avoda Zara for yourself. 27/29.
4. Don't serve idols in the four ways we serve Hashem. 28/28.
5. Don't serve Avoda Zara, even to throw stones at it. 29/27.
6. Don't mention Hashem's Name for no reason. 30/210
7. Declare Shabbat as special with Kiddush and Havdalah. 31/91.
8. Don't do Melacha on Shabbat. 32/88.
9. Respect your father and your mother. 33/584.
10. Don't murder. 34/482.
11. Don't marry another man's wife. 35/160.[231]
12. Don't kidnap. 36/473.
13. Don't swear falsely in Hashem's Name. 37/209.
14. Don't even think of ways to get what belongs to others. 38/476.
15. Don't make full human statues, even for decorations. 39/31.
16. don't build the Mizbayach using steps. 40/302.
17. Don't ascend the Mizbayach using steps. 41/303.

Mishpatim
Ch. 21 13 Mitzvot.

1. Follow the laws of buying an Eved Ivri. 42/504.
2. The buyer of a Jewish girl servant must marry her or marry her to his son. 43/512.
3. Buy back a Jewish girl servant to return her to her family. 44/511.
4. A master cannot sell his Jewish maidservant. 45/513.
5. A husband has to give food, clothes and time to his wife.[232] 46/124.

---

231. The actual לא תעשה refers to ביאה but in English we are using the term 'married' when teaching younger children around the age of 6-8. When teaching young children the Mitzvot of Issurei Bi'ah, we have followed the advice of R'Eliyashav z"l who said to use the terminology of 'it is assur **to live as married to**….." This is usually sufficient for children without going into further detail. If you want to learn more about 'when and how to talk to children about the birds and the bees' we have a lecture with that title which can be listened to on www.breakthroughchi under the second series of 'Successful Parenting.'

232. The word עונה refers to cohabitation, we are using the word 'time' since the details of this Mitzvah are not needed at a young age and there are

6. Follow the laws of the death penalty of Cheneck. 47/548.
7. Don't hit your father or your mother. 48/583.
8. Bet Din must judge cases of bodily harm and damage to property. 49/481.
9. Follow the laws of death penalty of Sayif. 50/547.
10. Bet Din must judge the cost of damage by a goring ox. 51/463.
11. Don't eat the meat of a condemned ox, שור הנסקל. 52/189.
12. Judge cost of damages to an animal or person who fell into a pit. 53/465.
13. Bet Din must enforce consequences for stealing. 54/468.

Ch. 22   19 Mitzvot.
1. Just the cost of damage caused by an animal eating or walking on other people's property. 55/464.
2. Judge cost of damage caused by fire. 56/466.
3. Follow the laws of an unpaid guard. 57/525.
4. Bet Din must judge all types of cases of one person making a claim against another. 58/538.
5. Follow the laws of a hired worker and hired guard. 59/517.
6. Follow the laws of a borrower. 60/524.
7. A Mefateh must pay three fines. 61/131.
8. Bet Din must not let a witch or wizard live. 62/552.
9. Don't insult a Ger Tzedek with words. 63/503.
10. Don't overcharge or underpay for merchandise. 64/500.
11. Don't hurt adults or children who have nobody to defend them. 65/18.
12. Lend money to the poor. 66/526.
13. Don't pressure him for payment if you know he does not have money to pay you back. 67/527.
14. Don't even be a witness, a guarantor, sofer or middle man on a loan of Ribit. 68/536.
15. Don't curse Hashem. 69/26.
16. Don't curse judges. 70/567.
17. Don't curse a king or Nasi. 71/568.
18. Don't give Terumah and Maaser in the wrong order. 72/254.
19. Don't eat a Treifa animal. 73/190.

Ch. 23   21 Mitzvot.
1. A Judge must not listen to a testimony till both sides are present. 74/566.
2. A Baal Aveira cannot testify in court. 75/574.
3. A majority of 2 Judges is required to give the death penalty. 76/543.
4. A Judge cannot switch verdict from innocent to guilty. 77/544.
5. If Judges disagree, decide the case by a majority vote. 78/542.
6. A Judge must not show favor to a poor man at a trial. 79/558.
7. Help remove a heavy load from an animal even though it belongs to someone you hate. 80/496.
8. A Judge must not decide a guilty verdict because the accused is a Choteh. 81/560.
9. Don't give the death penalty only based on circumstantial evidence. 82/555.
10. A Judge must not accept bribes. 83/565.
11. Disown your produce grown in Shemitta. 84/284.

Mefarshim that define עונה as 'time' and even 'a home' from the language of מעונה, abode.

12. Rest on Shabbat. 85/87.
13. Don't swear in the name of Avoda Zara. 86/46.
14. Don't persuade a city to follow Avoda Zara. 87/32.
15. Celebrate every Yom Tov in the Bet Hamikdash with the Korban Chagiga. 88/421.
16. Don't shecht the Korban Pesach while you still own Chametz. 89/405.
17. Don't leave the Emurim fats of the Korban Pesach overnight. 90/406.
18. Separate the Bikkurim first fruits for the Kohanim in the Bet Hamikdash. 91/270.
19. Don't cook milk and meat together. 92/196.
20. Don't make agreements with people who serve Avoda Zara. 93/56.
21. Don't let anyone who serves Avoda Zara live in Eretz Yisrael. 94/58.

Teruma
Ch. 25 3 Mitzvot.
1. Build a Bet Hamikdash. 95/301.
2. Don't remove poles from the Aron. 96/313.
3. Bake the Lechem Hapanim. 97/381.

Tetzaveh
Ch. 27 1 Mitzvah.
1. Light the Menorah every day. 98/378.

Ch. 28 3 Mitzvot.
1. Kohanim must wear bigdei Kehuna during their Avoda. 99/318.
2. The Choshen must not be loose. 100/320.
3. Don't tear the Me'il gown. 101/319.

Ch. 29 1 Mitzvah.
1. Kohanim must eat Kodshei Kodshim meat of the Chatat & Asham inside the Azara. 102/356.

Ch. 30 2 Mitzvot.
1. Burn Ketoret every day. 103/377.
2. Burn only Ketoret on the Golden Mizbayach. 104/311.

Ki Tissa
Ch. 30 6 Mitzvot.
1. Give a donation of half a Shekel every year to the Bet Hamikdash. 105/119.
2. A Kohen must wash his hands and feet before doing Avoda. 106/331.
3. Prepare the Shemen Hamishcha. 107/307.
4. Don't use the Shemen Hamishcha on a non-Kohen. 108/309.
5. Don't reproduce the exact same formula of Shemen Hamishcha. 109/308.
6. Don't reproduce the exact same formula of the Ketoret. 110/310.

Ch. 34 3 Mitzvot.
1. Don't drink wine used for Avoda Zara. 111/203.
2. Rest the land in Shemitta, the 7th year. 112/279.
3. Don't eat milk and meat together. 113/195.

Vayakhel
Ch. 35 1 Mitzvah.
1. Bet Din cannot give the death penalty on Shabbat. 114/89.

Sefer Vayikra has a total of 249 Mitzvot.

Vayikra
Ch. 1   1 Mitzvah.
1. Follow the laws of the Korban Olah. 115/350.

Ch. 2   4 Mitzvot.
1. Follow the laws of the Korban Mincha. 116/361.
2. Don't burn Se'or or Dvash on the Mizbayach. 117/347.
3. Don't leave out salt from any Korban. 118/349.
4. All Korbanot must be salted. 119/348.

Ch. 4   2 Mitzvot.
1. Sanhedrin brings a Chatat Bet Din for a mistaken ruling. 120/435.
2. An individual brings a Korban Chatat for an accidental Chet. 121/431.

Ch. 5   9 Mitzvot.
1. Whoever knows evidence must testify in Bet Din. 122/570.
2. For 4 known Aveirot, bring a Korban Oleh V'Yored. If wealthy, a sheep. If poor, a bird or Korban Mincha. 123/434.
3. Don't completely split the Chatat Ha'off. 124/354.
4. Don't add oil to the Minchat Choteh. 125/362.
5. Don't add Levona to the Minchat Choteh. 126/363.
6. Misuse of Hekdesh property pays fine of full price plus 1/5. 127/401.
7. Bring an Asham Talui if he not sure he did a Chet. 128/432.
8. Return a stolen item or its value to its owner. 129/478.
9. Bring an Asham Vadai if for sure he did a Chet. 130/433.

Tzav
Ch. 6   9 Mitzvot.
1. Remove ashes from the Mizbayach every day. 131/376.
2. Light a fire on the Mizbayach every day. 132/374.
3. Don't extinguish the fire on the Mizbayach. 133/375.
4. Kohanim must eat the remains of the Korban Mincha. 134/366.
5. Don't bake a Mincha as Chametz. 135/365.

6. The Kohen Gadol must bring a Korban Mincha every morning and afternoon. 136/379.
7. The Korban Mincha of a Kohen cannot be eaten. 137/364.
8. Follow the laws of the Korban Chatat. 138/352.
9. Don't eat meat of the Chatat Hapenimi whose blood is brought in the Kodesh. 139/353.

Ch. 7   9 Mitzvot.

1. Follow the laws of the Korban Asham. 140/355.
2. Follow the laws of the Korban Shelamim. 141/359.
3. Don't let a Korban become Notar after final burning time. 142/394.
4. Burn Notar, left over Korbanot. 143/398.
5. Don't eat a Korban brought with the wrong thoughts, called Pigul. 144/393.
6. Don't eat Korbanot that became Tameh. 145/396.
7. Burn all Korbanot which became Tameh. 146/399.
8. Don't eat Chelev. 147/193.
9. Don't eat blood. 148/192.

Shemini
Ch. 10 4 Mitzvot.

1. A Long haired Kohen must not enter the Bet Hamikdash. 149/322.
2. A Kohen must not enter the Bet Hamikdash with torn clothes. 150/323.
3. Don't leave the Bet Hamikdash during the Avoda. 151/325.
4. A Kohen must not enter the Bet Hamikdash drunk. 152/321.

Ch. 11 13 Mitzvot.

1. Learn to identify signs of Kosher animals. 153/176.
2. Don't eat unkosher animals. 154/180.
3. Learn to identify the signs of Kosher fish. 155/178.
4. Don't eat non-Kosher fish. 156/182.
5. don't eat non-Kosher birds. 157/181.
6. Learn to identify Kosher Locusts. 158/179.
7. Follow laws of Tumah caused by contact with the 8 Sheratzim. 159/459.
8. Follow the laws of Tumah caused by contact with foods and liquids. 160/461.
9. Follow laws of Tumah caused by contact with a Neveila. 161/458.
10. Don't eat crawling creatures. 162/184.
11. Don't eat worms in fruit. 163/186.
12. Don't eat water insects. 164/187.
13. Don't eat maggots. 165/185.

Tazria
Ch. 12 3 Mitzvot.

1. Follow the laws of Tumah caused by childbirth. 166/455.
2. Follow the laws of Tumat Met. 167/443.
3. After giving birth, a mother brings a Korban Yoledet. 168/437.

Ch. 13 4 Mitzvot.
1. Follow the laws of Tzara'at. 169/446.
2. A Metzorah must not shave signs of Tzara'at from his skin. 170/448.
3. A Metzorah must publicize his Tumah. 171/449.
4. Follow the laws of Tzara'at on clothing. 172/452.

Metzora
Ch. 14 5 Mitzvot.
1. Follow the rules to make a Metzorah Tahor. 173/450.
2. Shave all hair of a Metzorah before Tahara in a Mikveh. 174/451.
3. Every Tameh person must immerse in a Mikveh. 175/462.
4. A Metzorah brings a Korban Metzorah. 176/439.
5. Follow the laws of Tzara'at on houses. 177/453.

Ch. 15 6 Mitzvot.
1. Follow the laws of Tumah of a Zav. 178/457.
2. A Zav brings a Korban Zav. 179/439.
3. Follow the laws of Tumah caused by Shichvat Zera. 180/460.
4. Follow the laws of Nidda. 181/454.
5. Follow the laws of Tumah of a Zava. 182/456.
6. A Zava brings a Korban Zava. 183/436.

Acharei Mot
Ch. 16 2 Mitzvot.
1. A Kohen cannot enter the Bet Hamikdash if he is not doing Avoda. 184/324.
2. Follow the order of Avoda on Yom Hakippurim. 185/400.

Ch. 17 2 Mitzvot.
1. Don't shecht Korbanot outside the Azara. 186/371.
2. After Shechita, cover the blood of a Chaya or bird. 187/206.

Ch.18 24 Mitzvot.
1. Don't have physical contact with any forbidden women. 188/175.
2. A man cannot marry his father. 189/158.
3. A man cannot marry his mother. 190/139.
4. A man cannot marry his step-mother. 191/140.
5. A man cannot marry his sister. 192/141.
6. A man cannot marry his granddaughter (son's daughter) 193/143.
7. A man cannot marry his granddaughter (daughter's daughter) 194/145.
8. A man cannot marry his daughter. 195/144.[233]
9. A man cannot marry his half sister. 196/142.
10. A man cannot marry his aunt (father's sister). 197/149.
11. A man cannot marry his aunt (mother's sister). 198/150.

---
233. Actually derived from a Kal V'Chomer and Gezera Shav. See Sefer HaChinuch Mitzvah 195.

12. A man cannot marry his uncle. 199/159.
13. A man cannot marry his aunt (uncle's wife). 200/151.
14. A man cannot marry his daughter in law. 201/152.
15. A man cannot marry his sister in law (brother's wife). 202/153.
16. A man cannot marry a mother and her daughter. 203/146.
17. A man cannot marry a mother & her granddaughter (her son's daughter). 204/147.
18. A man cannot marry a mother and her granddaughter (her daughter's daughter). 205/148.
19. A man cannot marry his sister in law (wife's sister). 206/154.
20. Don't be close to a Nidda. 207/161.
21. Don't pass children in the fire of Molech. 208/49.
22. A man cannot marry a man. 209/157.
23. A man cannot marry an animal. 210/155.
24. A woman cannot marry an animal. 211/156.

Kedoshim
Ch. 19 48 Mitzvot.
1. Fear your father and your mother. 212/585.
2. Don't think about Avoda Zara or find out how to do it. 213/24.
3. Don't make Avoda Zara to sell to others. 214/30.
4. Don't eat Notar after the allowed time. 215/395.
5. Don't harvest Peah, the corner of your field. 216/240.
6. Leave Peah, a corner of the field for the poor. 217/239.
7. Don't collect Leket of the field. 218/242.
8. Leave Leket of the field for the poor. 219/241.
9. Don't gather Ollelos, small bunches of grapes of the vineyard. 220/244.
10. Leave Ollelos, small bunches of grapes of the vineyard for the poor. 221/ 243.
11. Don't pick up Peret, fallen or unformed grapes. 222/246.
12. Leave Peret, fallen or unformed grapes, for the poor. 223/245.
13. Don't steal money or property. 224/246.
14. Don't deny possession of collateral. 225/211
15. Don't make a Shavua to deny a monetary claim. 226/212.
16. Don't swear falsely in Hashem's Name. 227/209.
17. Don't hold onto your worker's salary or refuse to pay a debt. 228/475.
18. Don't rob. 229/474.
19. Don't delay payment of your worker's salary. 230/519.
20. Don't curse another Jew. 231/569.
21. Don't put a stumbling block in front of the blind or take advantage of someone's ignorance. 232/493.
22. A Judge must not pervert justice. 233/561.
23. A Judge must not show favor to a rich or powerful man at a trial. 234/559.
24. A Judge must treat both side equally in court. 235/563.
25. Don't speak Lashon Hara. 236/19.
26. Don't stand by and do nothing when someone's life is in danger. 237/489.
27. Don't hate other Jews. 238/15.

28. Gently correct other Jews. 239/16.
29. Don't embarrass others. 240/17.
30. Don't take revenge. 241/20.
31. Don't keep remembering other people's mistakes. 242/21.
32. Love every Jew. 243/13.
33. Don't crossbreed animals. 244/236.
34. Don't plant two different seeds together. 245/234.
35. Don't eat Orla, fruit of a tree in its first three years. 246/200.
36. Neta Reva'i, fourth year produce can only be eaten in Yerushalayim like Maaser Sheni. 247/268.
37. Don't be a Ben Sorer Umoreh. 248/586.
38. Don't be superstitious. 249/60.
39. Don't read the future using astrology. 250/62.
40. Men must not shave their hair from the sides of their head. 251/68.
41. Men must not shave any of the five corners of their beard. 252/69.
42. don't tattoo the skin. 253/72.
43. Show Yirah, reverence for the Bet Hamikdash. 254/304.
44. Don't consult an Ov. 255/65.
45. Don't consult a Yidoni. 256/66.
46. Respect Torah teachers. 257/23.
47. Don't cheat with scales and weights. 258/470.
48. Make sure your scales and weights are exact. 259/469.

Ch. 20   3 Mitzvot.

1. Don't curse your father or your mother. 260/582.
2. Follow the laws of the death penalty of Sereifa. 261/546.
3. Don't copy the customs or clothing of people who follow Avoda Zara. 262/59.

Emor

Ch. 21 15 Mitzvot.

1. A Cohen must not become Tameh except for his closest relatives. 263/590.
2. Mourn close relatives. Even Kohanim can become Tameh for their closest relatives. 264/587
3. A Kohen Tameh who toveled, still cannot enter the Bet Hamikdash till after sundown. 265.330.
4. A Kohen may not marry a Zona. 266/173.
5. A Kohen may not marry a Challala. 267/174.
6. A Kohen may not marry a divorcee. 268/172.
7. A Kohen must be treated special. 269/316.
8. A Kohen Gadol cannot be under the same roof as a dead body. 270/589.
9. A Kohen Gadol must not become Tameh, even for his closest relatives. 271/587.
10. A Kohen Gadol must only marry a Betula. 272/171.
11. A Kohen Gadol may not marry a widow. 273/169.
12. A Kohen Gadol must not act as married to a widow even if they don't get married with a Ketuba. 274/170.
13. A wounded Kohen cannot do Avoda. 275/333.
14. Even a temporarily wounded Kohen cannot do Avoda. 276/334.
15. A wounded Kohen cannot enter the Bet Hamikdash. 277/332.

Ch. 22   19 Mitzvot.

1. A Kohen Tameh may not do Avoda. 278/329.
2. A Kohen Tameh may not eat Terumah. 279/258.
3. A Zar, non-Kohen may not eat Terumah. 280/255.
4. Hired workers of a Kohen cannot eat Terumah. 281/256.
5. A Kohen Arel may not eat Terumah.[234] 282/257.
6. A Challala must not eat Terumah. 283/259.
7. Don't eat Tevel foods. 284/202.
8. Don't reserve a wounded animal for a Korban. 285/337.
9. Only bring Korbanot with no wounds. 286/336.
10. Don't make a wound on a Korban. 287/343.
11. Don't sprinkle the blood of a wounded Korban. 288/339.
12. Don't Shecht a wounded animal for a Korban. 289/338.
13. Don't burn the fats of a wounded Korban. 290/340.
14. Don't make a person or animal a Sariss. 291/168.
15. Don't bring temporarily wounded Korban of Goyim. 292/342.
16. Any Korban must be at least eight days old. 293/345.
17. Don't Shecht a mother animal and her child on the same day. 294/205.
18. Don't be a Chillul Hashem. 295/7.
19. Be a Kiddush Hashem. 296/6.

Ch. 23[235]   29 Mitzvot.

1. Rest on the 1st day of Pesach. 297/96.
2. Don't do Melacha on the 1st day of Pesach. 298/97.
3. Bring a Korban Musaf on Pesach. 299/383.
4. Rest on the 7th day of Pesach. 300/98.
5. Don't do Melacha on the 7th day of Pesach. 301/99.
6. Bring the Omer of the 2nd day of Pesach. 302/384.
7. Don't eat bread from Chadash (new grain). 303/197.
8. Don't eat parched grain (Kali) from Chadash, new grain. 304/198.
9. Don't eat early ripened grain called Karmel. 305/199.
10. Count 7 weeks from the 2nd day of Pesach till Shavuot. 306/385.
11. Bring Shtei Halechem with the Korban Mussaf on Shavuot. 307/387.
12. Rest on Shavuot. 308/100.
13. Don't do Melacha on Shavuot. 309/101.
14. Rest on Rosh Hashana. 310/102.
15. Don't do Melacha on Rosh Hashana. 311/103.
16. Bring a Korban Mussaf on Rosh Hashana. 312/388.
17. Fast on Yom Kippur. 313/94.

---

234. This Mitzvah is one of the 613 but is not learned directly from a verse but rather a Gezeira Shav from Ex. 12:45 which forbids an Arel to eat from the Korban Pesach and Yevamot 70a explains we have a Kabbala that this Issur has a 'parallel application' (Gezeira Shav) to an Arel Kohen eating Terumah.

235. Some people find it unnecessary to use the 'mental mapping' for the majority of Mitzvot in this chapter. The reason why is because most of them are related to the days of rest and of not doing melacha of the Yomim Tovim. That means one's brain can easily put all such related Mitzvot under the one heading of chapter 23. Similar to Chapter 18 in Vayikra where the vast majority of Arayos are found.

18. Bring a Korban Mussaf on Yom Kippur. 314/389.
19. Don't do Melacha on Yom Kippur. 315/93.
20. Don't eat or drink on Yom Kippur. 316/95.
21. Rest on Yom Kippur from Melacha. 317/92.
22. Rest on the 1st day of Sukkot. 318/104.
23. Don't do Melacha on the 1st day of Sukkot. 319/105.
24. Bring a Korban Mussaf on Sukkot. 320/390.
25. Rest from Melacha on Shemini Chag Atzeret. 321/106.
26. Bring a Korban Mussaf on Shemini Chag Atzeret. 322/391.
27. Don't do Melacha on Shemini Chag Atzeret. 323/107.
28. Shake the Lulav and Etrog all 7 days of Sukkot. 324/118.
29. Live in a Sukkah all 7 days of Sukkot. 325/117.

Behar
Ch. 25 23 Mitzvot.
1. Don't work the land in Shemitta. 326/280.
2. Don't work with trees in Shemitta. 327/281.
3. Don't harvest Sefichim (wild crops) in the usual way in Shemitta. 328/282.
4. Don't collect Nezirim (wild grapes) in the usual in Shemitta. 329/283.
5. Sanhedrin counts 7 cycles of 7 years till Yovel. 330/288.
6. Blow Shofar on the 10th of Tishrei in the Yovel year. 331/290.
7. Sanhedrin must declare Yovel (the 50th year) as Kodesh. 332/289.
8. Don't work the land in Yovel (the 50th year). 333/291.
9. Don't harvest Sefichim (wild crops) in the usual way in Yovel. 334/292.
10. Don't pick Nezirim (wild grapes) in the usual way in Yovel. 335/293.
11. Buy and sell according to the Torah laws of business. 336/499.
12. Don't overcharge or underpay for merchandise. 337/500.
13. Don't hurt anybody with words. 338/501.
14. Don't sell land in Eretz Yisrael as a permanent sale. 339/295.
15. Return land and homes to original owners in Yovel. 340/294.
16. Follow the laws of Batei Arei Choma (houses in walled cities), 1 year right to buy back. 341/296.
17. The fields of Shevet Levi must remain theirs before and after Yovel. 342/300.
18. Don't borrow money and pay Ribit (interest). 343/534.
19. Don't give degrading work to an Eved Ivri. 344/508.
20. Don't sell an Eved Ivri the same way a slave is sold. 345/505.
21. Don't give harsh work to an Eved Ivri. 346/506.
22. An Eved Canaani must work forever, he does not go free after 6 years or Yovel. 347/514.
23. Don't allow a gentile to give an Eved Ivri harsh work. 348/507.

Ch. 26 1 Mitzvah
1. Don't bow down on an Even Maskit (smooth mosaic stone). 349/51.

Bechukotei

Ch. 27 12 Mitzvot.

1. Estimate Erchei Adam (human value) as a money gift to Hekdesh (the Bet Hamikdash). 350/227.
2. Don't substitute a new animal for an already reserved Korban. 351/440.
3. Both a new animal and the original Korban are Kodesh. 352/441
4. Estimate Erchei Beheima (animal value) as a money gift to Hekdesh. 353/228.
5. Estimate Erchei Batim (house value) as a money gift to Hekdesh. 354/229.
6. Estimate Erchei Sadot (field value) as money gift to Hekdesh. 355/230.
7. Don't switch one Korban for another type of Korban. 356/442.
8. Follow the laws of Cherem, dedicated property to Hekdesh. 357/231.
9. Don't sell Cherem, property donated to Hekdesh. 358/232.
10. Don't redeem Cherem, property donated to Hekdesh. 359/233.
11. A Jewish farmer must give Maaser Beheima from his sheep, goats and cows to a Kohen. 360/429.
12. Don't buy back Maaser beheima. 361/430.

Sefer Bamidbar has a total of 50 Mitzvot.

Naso

Ch. 5   6 Mitzvot

1. Someone Tameh has to leave the Bet Hamikdash. 362/326.
2. Someone Tameh cannot enter the Har Habayit. 363/328.
3. Admit mistakes and correct them. 364/75.
4. Follow the laws of Sotah. 365/136.
5. Don't add oil to the Sotah's Mincha. 366/137.
6. Don't add Levona to the Sotah's Mincha. 367/138.

Ch. 6   11 Mitzvot

1. A Nazir must not drink wine. 368/219.
2. A Nazir must not eat grapes. 369/220.
3. A Nazir must not eat Tzimukim, raisins. 370/221.
4. A Nazir must not eat Hartzanim, grape seeds. 371/222.
5. A Nazir must not eat Zagim, grape skins. 372/223.
6. A Nazir must not cut his hair. 373/218.
7. A Nazir must let his hair grow. 374/217.
8. A Nazir must not be under the same roof as a dead body. 375/224.
9. A Nazir must not touch a dead body. 376/225.
10. A Nazir must shave all his body hair when he brings a Korban Nazir. 377/226.
11. Kohanim bless Jewish people daily. 378/78.

Ch. 7   1 Mitzvah

1. The Levi'im transport the Aron on their shoulders. 379/312.

B'haalotecha
Ch. 9   4 Mitzvot
1. Shecht the Korban Pesach Sheni on the 14th of Iyyar. 380/407.
2. Eat meat of the Korban Pesach with Matzah and Marror. 381/408.
3. Don't leave any meat of the Korban Pesach Sheni till the morning. 382/418.
4. Don't break bones of the Korban Pesach Sheni. 383/416.

Ch. 10   1 Mitzvah
1. Fast and cry out in times of trouble. 384/121.

Shelach
Ch. 15   3 Mitzvot
1. Separate the Challa portion of dough for the Kohen. 385/273.
2. Tie Tzitzit to all 4 cornered garments. 386/84.
3. Don't trust everything you think and see. 387/25.

Korach
Ch. 18   9 Mitzvot
1. Guard the Bet Hamikdash. 388/305.
2. A Levi cannot do the Avoda of another Levi or Kohen. 389/315.
3. A Non-Kohen must not do any Avoda in the Bet Hamikdash. 390/335.
4. Don't leave the Bet Hamikdash unguarded. 391/306.
5. Do Pidyon Haben, buy back a first born son with money to a Kohen. 392/276.
6. Don't buy back a first born sheep, goat or cow from the Kohen. 393/428.
7. Levi'im must work in the Bet Hamikdash. 394/314.
8. A farmer gives Maaser Rishon to a Levi each year. 395/260.
9. The Levi must give Terumat Maaser (1/10 of his Maaser Rishon) to the Kohen. 396/253.

Chukat
Ch. 19   3 Mitzvot
1. Follow the laws of the Parah Aduma. 397/444.
2. Follow the laws of Tumat Met. 398/443.
3. Follow the laws of Tahara for a Tumat Met (sprinkling Mei Nidda waters on a Tamei Met to make him Tahor. 399/445.

Pinchas
Ch. 27   1 Mitzvah
1. Follow the laws of Yerusha and the order of who inherits first, second, etc. 400/539.

Ch. 28   4 Mitzvot
1. Offer 2 lambs for the Korban Tamid every day. 401/373.
2. Bring a Korban Mussaf on Shabbat of 2 extra lambs. 402/380.
3. Bring a Korban Mussaf on Rosh Chodesh. 403/381.
4. Bring a Korban Mussaf on Shavuot. 404/386.

Ch. 29   1 Mitzvah
1. Hear the Shofar blown on the 1st day of Tishrei. 405/116.

Mattot
Ch. 30   2 Mitzvot
1. Follow the laws of how to cancel a Neder or Shavua. 406/216.
2. Don't break a promise. 407/215.

Masa'ai
Ch. 35   6 Mitzvot
1. Give Shevet Levi 48 cities and the surrounding fields. 408/299.
2. Don't execute a murderer before he stands trial. 409/486.
3. An unintentional killer must escape to an Ir Miklat, city of safety. 410/484.
4. A witness cannot also be the judge in a case which could have the death penalty. 411/572.
5. Don't accept Kofer money to free a convicted murderer. 412/483.
6. Don't accept Kofer money from the accidental murderer instead of him going to an Ir Miklat, city of safety. 413/485.

Sefer Devarim has a total of 200 Mitzvot

Devarim
Ch. 1   2 Mitzvot
1. Don't select judges who are not expert Talmidei Chachamim. 414/541.
2. A Judge must not let the fear of threats from a violent offender sway his decision. 415/564.

Va'Etchanan
Ch. 5   1 Mitzvah
1. Don't desire anything belonging to someone else. 416/477.

Ch. 6   8 Mitzvot
1. Know that Hashem is One. 417/3.
2. Love Hashem. 418/4.
3. Learn and Teach Torah. 419/22.
4. Say the Shema every morning and night. 420/76.
5. Strap Tefilin on the arm. 421/80.
6. Wear Tefilin on the head. 422/79.
7. Fix a Mezuza on each door post. 423/81.
8. Don't over test Hashem or His Navi. 424/10.

Ch. 7   3 Mitzvot
1. Destroy the 7 Nations of Canaan. 425/596.
2. Don't show favor to those who serve Avoda Zara. 426/50.
3. Don't marry a non-Jew. 427/162.

Ekev
Ch. 7   2 Mitzvot
1. Don't benefit from ornaments of Avoda Zara. 428/55.
2. Don't benefit from Avoda Zara. 429/54.

Ch. 8   1 Mitzvah
1. Bless Hashem after eating bread. 430/85.

Ch. 10   5 Mtizvot
1. Love a Ger Tzedek. 431/14.
2. Be in awe of Hashem. 432/5.
3. Thank, praise and ask things from Hashem every day. 433/77.
4. Be close to Hashem by being close to Tzadikim & Talmidei Chachamim. 434/12
5. Confirm the truth with a Shavua. 435/213.

Re'eh.
Ch. 12   18 Mitzvot
1. Destroy Avoda Zara. 436/53.
2. Don't destroy an item with Hashem's Name on it. 437/8.
3. Bring to the Bet Hamikdash every Korban Neder and Nadava on the first available Yom Tov. 438/367.
4. Don't Shecht Korbanot outside the Azara. 439/371.
5. Bring all Korbanot to the Bet Hamikdash. 440/369.
6. Buy back Korbanot which became Passul. 441/344.
7. Don't eat Maaser Sheni grains outside Yerushalayim. 442/265.
8. don't eat Maaser Sheni wine outside Yerushalayim. 443/266.
9. Don't eat Maaser Sheni oil outside Yerushalayim. 444/267.
10. A Kohen cannot eat a 1st born sheep, goat or cow outside Yerushalayim. 445/427.
11. Don't eat the Kodshei Kodshim meat of the Chatat and Asham outside the Azara. 446/357.
12. Don't eat the meat of the Korban Olah. 447/351.
13. Don't eat Kodshei Kalim meat before sprinkling their blood. 448/360.
14. Kohanim must not eat Bikkurim outside Yerushalayim. 449/271.
15. Don't avoid giving the Levi'im their Maaserot on Yom Tov. 450/424.
16. Must Shecht an animal before eating its meat. 451/204.
17. Don't a limb from a living animal. 452/191.
18. Bring all Korbanot from outside Eretz Yisrael to the Bet Hamikdash. 453/370.

Ch. 13   13 Mitzvot
1. Don't add to the 613 Mitzvot. 454/580.
2. Don't delete any of the 613 Mitzvot. 455/581.
3. Don't listen to a Navi Sheker. 456/43.
4. Don't love a missionary. 457/37.
5. Don't stop hating a missionary. 458/38.
6. Don't save a missionary's life. 459/39.

7. Don't say anything in a missionary's defence. 460.40.
8. Don't avoid giving testimony against a missionary. 461/41.
9. Don't persuade anyone to serve Avoda Zara. 462/36.
10. Carefully examine the witnesses. 463/571.
11. Burn an Ir Hanidachat, a city which served Avoda Zara. 464/33.
12. Don't rebuild an Ir Hanidachat. 465/34.
13. Don't benefit from an Ir Hanidachat. 466/35.

Ch. 14   8 Mitzvot
1. Don't tear the skin in mourning. 467/73.
2. Don't tear our hair or make a bald spot in mourning. 468/74.
3. Don't eat a Korban which is Passul or has a wound. 469/392.
4. Learn to identify Kosher birds. 470/177.
5. Don't eat flying insects. 471/183.
6. Don't eat a Kosher animal not slaughtered according to Halacha. 472/188.
7. A farmer has to separate Maaser Sheni for himself. 473/261.
8. Give Maaser Oni to the poor in years 3 & 6 of Shemitta. 474/249.

Ch. 15   10 Mitzvot
1. Don't pressure the borrower to pay back the loan in Shemitta. 475/286.
2. Pressure a non-Jew to pay back a loan. 476/528.
3. Cancel all loans in Shemitta. 477/285.
4. Don't refuse to give charity. 478/251.
5. Give charity. 479/250.
6. Don't refuse to lend money Erev Shemitta. 480/287.
7. Don't send an Eved Ivri away empty handed. 481/510.
8. Give an Eved Ivri generous gifts when he goes free. 482/509.
9. Don't do Melacha with animals reserved for Korbanot. 483/402.
10. Don't sheer wool of sheep reserved for Korbanot. 484/403.

Ch. 16   6 Mitzvot
1. Don't eat Chametz from midday of the 14th of Nissan. 485/108.
2. Don't leave the meat of the Korban Chagiga later than the 16th of Nissan. 486/419.
3. A non-Kohen cannot eat Kodshei Kodshim meat.[236] 487/358.
4. Be B'Simcha on Pesach, Shavuot and Sukkot. 488/422.
5. Be seen in the Bet Hamikdash on Pesach, Shavuot and Sukkot. 489/420.
6. Don't come to the Bet Hamikdash all 3 times a year without a Korban Olat Riah. 490/423.

Shoftim
Ch. 16   3 Mitzvot
1. Select judges for Bet Din. 491/540.
2. Don't plant Asheira trees in the courtyard of the Bet Hamikdash. 492/52.
3. Don't build a Matzeiva - stand for Avoda Zara. 493/50.

---
236. This is the Mitzvah according to Rambam and he derives it from Ex. 29:33. However, Sefer HaChinuch counts here a Mitzvah not to eat the Korban Pesach on a Bama, a Private Altar. Rambam does not count this in Taryag.

Ch. 17   10 Mitzvot

1. Don't bring a temporarily wounded animal for a Korban. 494/341.
2. A Jew must follow the rulings of the Sanhedrin. 495/578.
3. Don't act differently than the rulings of the Sanhedrin. 496/579.
4. Only select a Jewish King. 497/591.
5. Don't select a convert to be a king. 498/592.
6. A King must not have too many horses. 499/594.
7. Don't live in Egypt permanently. 500/601.
8. A King must not have too many wives. 501/593.
9. A King must not have too much gold and silver. 502/595.
10. A King must write a second Sefer Torah. 503/83.

Ch. 18   16 Mitzvot

1. Shevet Levi has no portion in Eretz Yisrael. 504/297.
2. Shevet Levi has no share in the spoils of war. 505/298.
3. Gift the stomach, 2 cheeks and shoulder to the Kohen. 506/274.
4. Give Teruma Gedola to a Kohen. 507/252.
5. Gift Reishit Hagez, the first sheering of a sheep to a Kohen. 508/275.
6. All 24 shifts of Kohanim work on all 3 Yomim Tovim. 509/317.
7. Don't go into a trance to see the future (לקסום). 510/61.
8. Bet Din must not let a Witch or Wizard live. 511/552.
9. Don't say magic spells. 512/63.
10. Don't consult an Ov. 513/65.
11. Don't consult a Yidoni. 514/66.
12. Don't try to contact the dead. 515/67.
13. Listen to a real Navi of Hashem. 516/9.
14. Don't give false Nevua in Hashem's Name. 517/44.
15. Don't say Nevua in the name of Avoda Zara. 518/42.
16. Don't be afraid to kill a Navi Sheker. 519/45.

Ch. 19   5 Mitzvot

1. Set aside Cities of Safety and clearly mark the road signs to the nearest Arei Miklat. 520/490.
2. A Judge must not pity a murderer at trial by giving a lesser punishment. 521/557
3. Don't move a boundary marker. 522/472.
4. Don't accept the testimony of one witness. 523/573.
5. Give false witnesses the same punishment they would have caused the accused. 524/577.

Ch. 20   5 Mitzvot

1. Don't panic and retreat during battle. 525/610.
2. Select a special Kohen to speak to the soldiers before battle. 526/607.
3. Offer a peace agreement to a city under siege. 527/602.
4. Don't let any of the 7 Nations of Canaan remain alive. 528/597.
5. Don't destroy fruit trees during a siege. 529/604.

Ch. 21   2 Mitzvot
1. Break the Egla Arufa's neck after an unsolved murder. 530/491.
2. Don't work or plant the ground where the Egla Arufa was killed. 531/492.

Ki Tetze

Ch. 21   6 Mitzvot
1. A Jewish soldier must follow the laws of a Yafet Toar. 532/611.
2. Don't sell a Yafet Toar into slavery. 533/612.
3. Don't keep a Yafet Toar to be your maid. Either marry her of free her. 534/613.
4. Someone who curses Hashem or worships Avoda Zara gets Skila following by hanging. 535/549.
5. Don't delay burial overnight. 536/551.
6. Bury the executed on the same day as execution. 537/550.

Ch. 22   21 Mitzvot
1. Return a lost object. 538/480.
2. Don't ignore a lost object. 539/479.
3. Don't pass by without helping unload an animal's heavy packages, and help re-loading. 540/598.
4. Help others load their animal. 541/497.
5. Women must not wear men's clothing. 542/71.
6. Men must not wear women's clothing. 543/70.
7. Don't take a mother bird from her chicks. 544/207.
8. Send away the mother bird before taking the chicks. 545/208.
9. Make a guard rail around flat roofs. 546/494.
10. Don't leave objects lying around that could be dangerous. 547/493.
11. don't plant different grains or beans together in a vineyard. 548/235.
12. Don't eat Kilayaim seeds planted in a vineyard. 549/201.
13. Don't work different animals together. 550/237.
14. Don't wear Shaatnez, a mixture of wool and linen together. 551/238.
15. Marry a lady with a Ketuba and Kiddushin. 552/122.
16. A Motzi Shem Ra must remain married to his wife. 553/134.
17. A Motzi Shem Ra cannot divorce his wife. 554/135.
18. Follow the laws of the death penalty of Skila. 555/545.
19. Don't punish an Anuss. 556/556.
20. A M'aness must marry her. 557/132.
21. A M'aness cannot divorce her. 558/133.

Ch. 23   20 Mitzvot

1. A Sariss cannot marry a Jew. 559/167.
2. A Mamzer must not marry a Jew. 560/166.
3. A Jewess may not marry a man from Amon or Moav. 561/163.
4. Don't offer peace to Ammon and Moav during a siege. 562/603.
5. A Jew may marry a 3rd generation convert from Edom. 563/165.
6. A Jew may marry a 3rd generation Egyptian convert. 564/164.
7. Someone Tameh cannot enter the Bet Hamikdash. 565/327.
8. Prepare bathroom areas when going to war. 566/605.
9. Every soldier must have a small shovel to dig with. 567/606.
10. Don't send back a non-Jewish slave who fled to Eretz Yisrael for safety. 568/515.
11. Don't hurt hurt a runaway non-Jewish slave with words. 569/516.
12. Don't marry without a Ketuba and Kiddushin. 570/123.
13. Don't bring an animal used to pay a Zona or an animal traded for a dog. 571/346.
14. Don't borrow money and pay Ribit, interest. 572/535.
15. Borrow and lend money with Ribit to non-Jews. 573/537.
16. Don't delay bringing a Korban Neder or Nedava. 574/368.
17. Keep your promise. 575/214.
18. Allow workers to eat from grown produce while they walk between rows. 576/520.
19. A worker must not take more than he can eat. 577/522.
20. While at work, a worker may not eat from the crops. 578/521.

Ch. 24   15 Mitzvot

1. Divorce with a Kosher Get. 579/126.
2. Don't remarry one's ex-wife after she divorced her second husband. 580/127.
3. In the first year of marriage, a husband does no military service or communal service. 581/609.
4. A soldier who just married, built a house or planted a vineyard must return home. 582/608.
5. Don't demand Keilim used for food as a Mashkon. 583/533.
6. A Metzora must not remove signs of Tzaraat. 584/447.
7. Someone owed money cannot take a Mashkon by force. 585/529.
8. Don't delay returning a Mashkon. 586/531.
9. Return a Mashkon when it is needed by its owner. 587/530.
10. Pay your worker's salary on time. 588/518.
11. Relatives cannot testify. 589/575.
12. A judge must not favor an orphan or convert in a trial. 590/562.
13. Don't demand a Mashkon from a widow. 591/532.
14. Leave Shikcha, forgotten bundles of stalks of grain for the poor. 592/247.
15. Don't go back to collect Shikcha, forgotten bundles of stalks of grain. 593/248.

Ch. 25   12 Mitzvot
1. Bet Din must whip the Choteh. 594/553.
2. Don't whip more than the lashes decided by Bet Din. 595/554.
3. Don't muzzle an ox while it is treading grain. 596/523.
4. A widow must not remarry outside her husbands' brothers until Chalitza. 597/130.
5. Do Yibum. 598/128.
6. Do Chalitza. 599/129.
7. Save the person being chased even by taking the life of the Rodef. 600/487.
8. Don't pity the Rodef. 601/488.
9. Don't even own inaccurate scales and weights even if they are not being used. 602/471.
10. Remember what Amalek did to the Jewish people when we came out of Egypt. 603/599.
11. Wipe out the descendants of Amalek. 604/598.
12. Don't forget Amalek's evil attack on Benei Yisrael. 605/600.

Ki Tavo
Ch. 26   5 Mitzvot
1. Read the Torah portion when you bring Bikkurim. 606/270.
2. Say Vidui Maaser in 4th and 7th years of Shemitta. 607/269.
3. Before buriel, an Onen mourner must not eat Maaser Sheni. 608/264.
4. Don't eat Maaser Sheni if Tameh. 609/263.
5. If a farmer buys back Maaser Sheni with money, he must spend it on food, drink and oil in Yerushalayim. 610/262.

Ch. 28   1 Mitzvah
1. Learn and copy Hashem's ways. 611/11.

Ch. 31   2 Mitzvot
1. Every single Jew must gather inside the Azara on Motzei Yom Tov rishon of Sukkot at the end of Shemitta. 612/425.
2. Each Jewish man has to write a Sefer Torah. 613/82.

Knowledge Map D:

Anatomy of the Mitvot:
Which Mitzvot are Done with Which Part of the Body

Kol Atzmotai Tomarna - Mi Kamocha?

Introduction

This booklet is part of the Taryag Mitzvos Building Block of Chinuch #2. This program uses Rambam's list of the Taryag Mitzvos as the main list for teaching children, as fully explained in the Taryag Teacher Manual. We also teach how to memorize the Taryag Mitzvos according to Rambam and Sefer HaChinuch, all of which is outlined in the DVD Teacher Training Videos.[237]

This is a reference work which lists Taryag Mitzvos according to the parts of the body by which they are performed. This booklet is like a control chart for children who are learning to identify which of the Taryag Mitzvos Picture Cards match which limb of the body. Now they have a reference book to rely upon to check their findings.

Sefer Chareidim famously lists those Mitzvos which apply nowadays according to the body part it is performed by. He did not list all Taryag. This list relies on his listing and has added the Mitzvos of all Taryag as well.[238]

We have also added a list of those Mitzvos performed by the entire body and not just a particular limb. Another addition you will find in this booklet is a list of Mitzvos done by the mind that constantly apply. Though it is true that Sefer HaChinuch identifies only six constant Mitzvos, it happens to be that there are over fifty in total. We have not found any source for why Sefer HaChinuch did not include the many more constant Mitzvos, including those he himself lists.[239]

Finally, we have given you lists of those Mitzvos where Ramban, SMaK, SMaG, the B'HaG and Sefer Yereim differ to the Rambam. We have also put a lot of effort into providing you with sources so that your more studious students can do their own research.

---

237. Available from www.breakthroughchinuch.com
238. Sefer Zoveach Todah of R' Mordecai Itzvan in his introduction explains that Sefer Chareidim left out many Mitzvos DeOraissa and Derabanan that apply nowadays, and even more Mitzvos Min HaTorah were left out of his list that are a Machlokes HaPoskim. See also Sefer Eved HaMelech from the Gaon and Tzadik Rebi Shmuel Huminer z"l who lists still more Mitzvos that are not part of Taryag but are nevertheless Mitzvos found in NaCh which count as Mitzvos. R' Isser Zalman Meltzer z"l wrote his own Haskama to Sefer Eved HaMelech and encouraged readers to learn from it every day, something he himself did.
239. For example, Sefer HaChinuch counts לֹא תִתְאַוֶּה - 'Don't desire other people's property' as one of Taryag (Dev. 5:18). Yet he does not count is as constant Mitzvah even though it applies every moment. And so too the Mitzvah of Deveikus in Hashem, as well as many others. My close friend Rabbi Dovid Wax shlita, Founder of the famous Taryag Foundation asked this very question (of why Sefer HaChincuh only counts six constant Mitzvos when it is clear that there are many many more) to the following Gedolim: R'Elyashiv z"l, Rav Vozner z"l, Rav Noach Weinberg z"l, and Yibadel L'Chaim, Rav Chaim Kaniefsky shlita, who themselves agreed there are many more than six constant Mitzvos and do not know why Sefer HaChinuch only singled out six. Sefer Chareidim lists 10 constant Mitzvos.

Who better than Eliyahu HaNavi himself to tell us to serve Hashem with every part of our body? [240]

All your body parts should do whatever Hashem requests of you as it says -

שפכי כמים לבך נכח פני ה'

מה מים הללו רבים לכל באי עולם (לעשות בהם כל רצונם - ישועות יעקב) כך בכל איבריו צריך אדם לעשות רצונו של הקב"ה.

Hashem wants us to love Him with all our **מאד**[241] which shares the same letter as **אדם** - Man[242]. In other words, Hashem wants us to love Him with all our body and with all our talents.[243]

You will notice two columns of numbers to the far left. The first number tells you the sequence of numbering for Mitzvos of that part of the body. The second column of numbers gives you the reference number for that Mitzvah in our listing of Rambam's Mitzvos as found in the Teacher Manual and the Student's Edition of Taryag Mitzvos and of course the picture cards of Taryag Mitzvos. This will help you or your student to easily reference which Mitzvah card to look for when identifying the Mitzvos done with that part of the body.

Enjoy your journey through the anatomy of the Mitzvos!

---

240. Tanna Debey Eliyahu Raba 18:21
241. Dev. 6:5.
242. The Shelah HaKadosh.
243. Just like אדם comes from the אדמה so too, man has potential like the earth, to produce great benefit for mankind.

Mitzvos of The Mind

1. 1. Emuna
2. 2. Zulato
3. 3. Echad
4. 4. Ahavas Hashem
5. 5. Yiras Hashem
6. 6. Kiddush HaShem
7. 7. Chilul HaShem
8. 9. Listen to a Navi Emes.
9. 11. Emulate Hashem.
10. 12. Be close to Talmidei Chachaim.
11. 13. Love Jews.
12. 14. Love converts.
13. 15. Don't hate other Jews
14. 20. Don't take revenge
15. 21. Don't remember other people's mistakes.
16. 22. Learn Torah
17. 23. Respect Torah Teachers.
18. 24. Don' think about Avoda Zara.
19. 25. Don't trust everything you think and see.
20. 37. Don't love a missionary.
21. 38. Don't stop hating a missionary.
22. 40. Don't judge a missionary favorably.
23. 57. Don't show favor to those who serve Avoda Zara.
24. 60. Don't be superstitious
25. 75. Do Teshuva.
26. 76. Recite Shema with Kavana.
27. 77. Tefila with Kavana.
28. 85.   Birkas Hamazon.
29. 109. Destroy Chametz (because it Bitul B'Lev counts)
30. 120 Calculate the beginning of every Rosh Hodesh.
31. 176. Learn and identify which are Kosher animals.
32. 177. Learn and identify which are Kosher birds.
33. 178. Learn and identify which are Kosher fish.
34. 179. Learn and identify which are Kosher locust.
35. 247. Forgotten sheaves should be left behind.
36. 251. Don't refuse to give Tzedaka.
37. 304 Have Yirah for the Bais Hamikdash.
38. 316. A Kohen must be treated special.
39. 337. Don't designate a Baal Moom. a wounded animal as a Korban.[244]
40. 393. Don't eat Pigul (the actual thought of Pigul is what causes the Kodshim food to forbidden to be eaten).

---

244. Hekdesh is done with either the Mouth or Thought/The Mind. Shavuos 26b.

41. 422. Be B'Simcha on Pesach, Shavuos & Sukkos.
42. 463. A Judge must calculate the cost of damage caused by a Goring Ox.
42. 464 A Judge must calculate the cost of damage caused by an animal eating other's property.
43. 465. A Judge must calculate the cost of damage to a person or animal who fell in a pit.
44. 466. A Judge must calculate the cost of damage caused by fire.
45. 469. Make sure your scales and weights are exact.
46. 470. Don't cheat with scales and weights.
47. 476. Don't think of ways to get what belongs to others.
48. 477. Don't think thoughts of jealousy.
49. 479. Don't ignore a lost object.
50. 488. Don't pity a Rodef.
51. 538. Bais Din must judge all types of cases of litigation.
52. 544. A Judge cannot switch verdict from innocent to guilty.
53. 545. Follow the laws of the death penalty of Skila.
54. 555. Don't give the death penalty based on circumstantial evidence.
55. 557. A Judge must not pity a murderer or violent person at a trial
56. 558. A Judge must not show any favor to a poor man at a trial.
57. 559. A Judge must not show favor to a rich or powerful man at a trial.
58. 560. A judge must not decide a guilty verdict because the accused is a known Rasha.
59. 561. A Judge must not pervert justice.
60. 562. A Judge must not favor a convert or orphan in a trial.
61. 563. A Judge must treat both sides equally in court. Also this Mitzvah is for every Jew to judge others favorably.
62. 564. A Judge must not let fear of threats from a violent offender sway his decision.
63. 566. Don't believe Lashon Hara.
64. 584. Respect your father and mother.
65. 585. Fear your father and mother.
66. 587. Mourn closest relatives.[245]
67. 599. Remember what Amalek did to Beney Yisrael when we came out of Egypt.
68. 600. Don't forget Amalek's evil attack on Beney Yisrael.
69. 610. Don't let thoughts of fear make you panic in war and retreat.

---

245. Aveilus is a Mitzvah done with one's thoughts. Throughout Aveilus one is not allowed to learn Torah or go to work in order not to be מסיח דעת, let one's mind be distracted from the Aveilus. Min HaTorah, this only applies to the first day. This is also a Mitzvah done with the entire body because one sits on the floor and mourns.

Mitzvos of the Eyes

1. 24. Don't look at Avoda Zara.
2. 25. Don't trust what your eyes see.
3. 84. Look at your Tzitzit.[246]
4. 112. Chametz should not be seen on your property.
5. 120. Calculate the New Moon based on the sighting of witnesses.
6. 176. Identify the signs of Kosher animals.
7. 177. Identify the signs of Kosher birds.
8. 178. Identify the signs of Kosher fish.
9. 179. Identify the signs of Kosher Locusts.
10. 446. Kohen identifies signs of Tzaraas on skin of the Metzorah.
11. 452. Kohen identifies signs of Tzaraas on clothing.
12. 453. Kohen identifies signs of Tzaraas on houses.
13. 454. Identify Tumas Nidda.
14. 455. Identify Tumas Yoledes.
15. 456. Identify Tumas Zava.
16. 457. Identify Tumas Zav.
17. 479. Don't turn your eyes away from a lost object.
18. 489. Don't watch an injustice and do nothing.
19. 570. Give testimony for what you saw.

Mitzvos of the Ears

1. 9. Listen to a Navi Emes.
2. 12. Listen to your teachers.[247]
3. 38. Don't listen to a missionary.[248]
4. 43. Don't listen to a Navi Sheker.
5. 76. Listen to yourself reciting Shema.[249]
6. 85. Listen to your recital of Birkas Hamazon.[250]
7. 116. Listen to the Shofar blow on Rosh Hashana.
8. 538. Listen to claims of both sides in court.
9. 566. Don't listen to Lashon Hara/Don't listen to a claim without the defendant present.
10. 571. Judges must listen carefully to answers of witnesses.
11. 573. Don't listen to the evidence of a single witness.
12. 578. A Jew must follow the rulings of the Sanhedrin.[251]
13. 579. Listen to the words of Sanhedrin and our Chachamim.[252]
14. 586. Don't be a Ben Sorer U'Moreh who does not listen to his parents.

---

246. Sefer Chareidim and SMaK both count looking at your Tzitzit as a separate Mitzvah to 'wearing' them.
247. The Mitzvah of לדבק בו according to Rambam, means associate closely with Talmidei Chachamim in order to learn from their ways. This includes 'listening' to their advice and paying close attention to what they say.
248. In the Mitzvah to not stop hating a missionary, the Torah writes it in a lashon of וְלֹא תִשְׁמַע אֵלָיו - "Don't listen to him." This indicates that by not listening to someone, you show disdain to them, as they do not even exist! This is the ultimate hatred, because talking to someone you hate still shows you acknowledge they exist, but to not listen and ignore them is still more degrading.
249. Lechatchila one should hear what one is saying.
250. Lechatchila one should hear what one is saying.
251. Sefer Chareidim lists this is a Mitzvah done with the ears as it is a Mitzvah to listen to the Dayanim in every generation.
252. Rambam describes the Mitzvah as "שלא יסור מדבריהם" - "Don't deviate from their words" also means to only listen to them and not the yetser hara or anyone who disputes them.

Mitzvos of the Nose

1. 54. Not to benefit from Avoda Zara or any of its accessories, this includes smelling their aromas.
2. 160. The Issur of Eshet Ish is learned from the verse (Ex.20:13) לא תנאף, which includes all types of נאוף, including the Issur to smell the perfume of a forbidden Isha.[253]

Miderabanan:

1. Assur to smell fruit on Shabbos and Yom Tov while it is attached to the tree incase one comes to detach it.
2. Mitzvah to smell Bessamim, spices on Motzei Shabbos in Havdalah.

---

253. The connection between the Passuk and the issur of smelling the perfume of an Eshet Ish is derived from the fact that the word נאוף shares the same root as אף which means 'nose.' So לא תנאף can be read as 'don't smell.'

Mitzvos of the Mouth - Throat/Speech/Eating

1. 1. Emuna. When you speak words of Emuna you get this Mitzvah.
2. 2. Zulaso. When you say no other power exists except Hashem.
3. 3. Echad, when you say words showing you believe Hashem is The Only Power.
4. 4. Ahavas Hashem. When you say you love Hashem.
5. 5. Yiras Hashem
6. 6. Kiddush Hashem
7. 7. Chilul Hashem.
8. 10. Don't over test a Navi Emes by asking him to do more miracles after he has already established he is a Navi Emes.
9. 11. Emulate Hashem.[254]
10. 13. Ahavas Yisrael, every kind word/appreciation/compliment/words of gratitude are included in this Mitzvah.
11. 14. Ahavas HaGer. This includes every kind word, compliment, words of encouragement and appreciation, gratitude.
12. 16. Tochacha.
13. 17. Not to embarrass another person.
14. 18. Don't hurt sensitive people with words (Almana and Yasoma).
15. 19. Rechilus and Lashon Hara.
16. 22. Learn & teach Torah.
17. 23. Give Kavod to Talmidei Chachamim.[255]
18. 24. Don't inquire after Avoda Zara.
19. 26. Don't curse Hashem.
20. 32. Don't persuade a city to follow Avoda Zara.
21. 36. Don't missionize.
22. 37. Don't show Ahava to a missionary with words.
23. 40. Don't say anything in defence of a missionary.
24. 41. Don't hold back from saying anything that will incriminate a missionary.
25. 42. Don't prophecy in the name of Avoda Zara.
26. 44. Don't give false Nevua in Hashem's Name.
27. 46. Don't make a Shavua in the name of Avoda Zara.
28. 56. Don't make agreements with idol worshippers.
29. 57. Don't show favor to idol worshippers.
30. 59. Don't speak like Akum, speak with clean language.[256]
31. 60. Don't be superstitious.
32. 61. Don't tell the future after going into a trance.
33. 62. Don't engage in Astrology.
34. 63. Don't mutter incantations/magic spells.
35. 64. Don't speak to the dead.
36. 65. Don't consult an Ov.

---

[254]. Sefer Chareidim lists this as a Mitzvah done with the mouth.

[255]. Sefer Chareidim claims סתם כבוד בדיבור (Kizur Chareidim, 6th perek).

[256]. The Mitzvah is not to go in their ways, this would include dress, behavior and ways of speaking. In Mitzrayim, one of the ways we retained our identity was not adopting the language of our host nation, we spoke :Lashon Hakodesh amongst ourselves and retained our Hebrew names.

37. 66. Don't consult a Yidoni.
38. 75. Say Vidui as part of the Mitzvah of Teshuva.
39. 76. Recite Shema.
40. 77. Talk to Hashem in Tefila.[257]
41. 78. Kohanim bless the Jewish people every day.[258]
42. 85. Bless Hashem with Birkas Hamazon.
43. 91. Recite Kiddush Friday night to make Shabbos Kadosh & recite Havdalah.[259]
44. 95. Don't eat or drink on Yom Kippur.
45. 108. Don't eat Chametz after midday on 14th of Nissan.
46. 110. Don't eat Chametz all 7 days.
47. 111. Don't eat a mixture of Chametz.
48. 114. Eat Matzah on the first night of Pesach.
49. 115. Tell the story of Yetziat Mitzrayim on first night of Pesach.
50. 120. Bais Din declare Rosh Chodesh.
51. 121. Fast from eating and drinking and cry out in times of trouble.
52. 134. Motzi Shem Ra, husbands accuses his wife of not being faithful.[260]
53. 136. Sota drinks water, denies accusation or admits her Aveira.
54. 175. Don't kiss a forbidden Isha.
55. 180. Don't eat non-kosher animals.
56. 181. Don't eat non-kosher birds.
57. 182. Don't eat non-kosher fish.
58. 183. Don't eat flying insects.
59. 184. Don't eat crawling creatures/insects.
60. 185. Don't eat maggots.
61. 186. Don't eat worms in fruit.
62. 187. Don't eat water insects.
63. 188. Don't eat a Neveila.
64. 189. Don't eat a condemned ox.
65. 190. Don't eat a Treifa animal.
66. 191. Don't eat a limb torn from a kosher animal.
67. 192. Don't eat blood.
68. 193. Don't eat non-kosher fats called Chelev.
69. 194. Don't eat the Gid Hanasheh, sinew of the thigh.
70. 195. Don't eat milk and meat together.
71. 197. Don't eat bread from Chadash.
72. 198. Don't eat parched (Kali) grain from Chadash.
73. 199. Don't eat early ripened grain (Karmel) from Chadash.
74. 200. Don't eat Orla produce.

---

257. Sefer Chareidim offers that Tefila is a Mitzvah done with the mind and mouth, and he also lists the hands because a person is meant to pray to Hashem with his hands against his heart as a servant stands before his master. See also Shabbos 40a and Rambam, Hilchos Tefila, Perek 5, Halacha 4. See also Shulchan Aruch, Orach Chayim #95. It appears that Sefer Chareidim reasons that the hands are part of Tefila because the Passuk tells us to 'Serve Him' - ולעבדו which indicates we should stand before Hashem like a servant whose hands are humbly positioned against his heart when standing before his master. So his extrapolation is from the language of עבדות, 'servitude.' See also Smag, Aseh #19.
258. Sefer Chareidim lists Birkas Kohanim as a Mitzvah done with the mouth, the legs and the hands.
259. Sefer Chareidim counts Havdalah as a separate Aseh of Taryag whereas Rambam counts both Kiddush and Havdalah as one Mitzvah.
260. Sefer Chareidim.

75. 201. Don't eat Kilayim seeds planted in a vineyard.
76. 202. Don't eat Tevel.
77. 203. Don't drink wine used for Avoda Zara.
78. 209. Don't say a Shevuas Sheker.
79. 210. Don't say Hashem's Name in vain.
80. 211. Don't deny possession of a Pikadon, collateral.
81. 212. Don't deny a monetary claim.
82. 213. Say a Shavuas Emes.
83. 214. Fulfil your Neder.
84. 215. Don't break a promise, Neder.
85. 216. Nedarim and Shavuos should be nullified with a verbal cancellation.
86. 219. A Nazir must not drink wine.
87. 220. A Nazir must not eat grapes.
88. 221. A Nazir must not eat raisins.
89. 222. A Nazir must not eat grape seeds.
90. 223. A Nazir must not eat grape skins.
91. 227. Declaring a person's worth as a gift to the Bais Hamikdash.
92. 228. Declaring the worth of an animal as a gift to the Bais Hamikdash.
93. 229. Declaring the worth of a house as a gift to the Bais Hamikdash.
94. 230. Declaring the worth of a field as a gift to the Bais Hamikdash.
95. 231. Declare ones possessions as a gift to the Bais Hamikdash.[261]
96. 255. A Zar, non Kohen cannot eat Teruma.
97. 256. Hired workers of a Kohen cannot eat Teruma.
98. 257. An Arel cannot eat Teruma.
99. 258. A Kohen Tameh cannot eat Teruma.
100. 259. A Challala cannot eat Teruma.
101. 263. Don't eat Maaser Sheni in a state of Tumah.
102. 264. Don't eat Maaser Sheni if one is an Onen.
103. 265. Don't eat Maaser Sheni grains outside Yerushalayim.
104. 266. Don't eat Maaser Sheni wine outside Yerushalayim.
105. 267. Don't eat Maaser Sheni Oil outside Yerushalayim.
106. 268. Only eat Neta Revai produce with the same laws as Maaser Sheni.
107. 269. Recite Vidui Maaser on 4th and 7th years.
108. 271. Kohanim cannot eat Bikkurim outside Yerushalayim.
109. 272. Read the Torah portion at the presentation of Bikkurim.
110. 285. Cancel all loans in Shemitta.[262]
111. 286. Don't pressure a borrower to pay back a loan.
112. 288. Sanhedrin count 7 groups of 7 years.
113. 289. Sanhedrin declare 50th year of Yoval as Kadosh.
114. 290. Blow Shofar on the 10th of Tishrei in Yovel year.

---

[261]. Sefer HaMitzvos L'Rambam, Mitzvah #145, the Torah requires Bais Din to judge cases of Charamim, dedicated property to Hekdesh. Sefer Chareidim, 4:44 claims that the Mitzvah to judge monetary cases is a Mitzvah done with the mouth, and while Sefer Chareidim only deals with Mitzvos done nowadays, nevertheless it is logical to deduce that all other Mitzvos of judgement of monetary matters is also dependent on the mouth. Rabbi Avraham Waldman Shlita.

[262]. Sefer Chareidim counts this as a Mitzvah done with the mouth.

115. 295. Don't sell land in Eretz Yisrael as a permanent sale.[263]
116. 296. Follow the laws of Batei Arei Choma.[264]
117. 299. Give Shevet Levi 48 Cities and surrounding fields.[265]
118. 316. A Kohen must be treated special.[266]
119. 337. Don't verbally designate a wounded animal for a Korban.[267]
120. 343. Don't make a wound on a Korban.[268]
121. 350. Verbally dedicate a Korban Olah.
122. 351. Don't eat the meat of the Olah.
123. 352. Verbally dedicate a Korban Chatat.
124. 353. Don't eat the meat of any Chatos HaPenimi.
125. 355. Verbally dedicate a Korban Asham.
126. 356. Kohanim eat meat of Chatat and Olah in the Mikdash area.
127. 357. Kohanim cannot eat meat outside the Azarah.
128. 358. A Zar, non-Kohen cannot eat Kodshim meat.
129. 359. Verbally designate a Korban Shelamim.
130. 360. Don't eat meat of the Kodshei Kalim before sprinkling their blood.
131. 364. Don't eat the Mincha of the Kohen Gadol.
132. 366. Kohanim eat the left overs of the Mincha.
133. 385. Count Sefiras Haomer.
134. 392. Don't eat meat of Kodshim which is Passul or had a blemish.
135. 393. Don't eat meat which is Pigul.
136. 394. Don't let a Korban become Notar.[269]
137. 395. Don't eat meat which is Notar.
138. 396. Don't eat Korbanos which became Tameh.
139. 397. In a state of Tumah one cannot eat Kodshim.
140. 408. Eat meat of the Korban Pesach with Matzah and Maror.
141. 409. Eat meat of the Korban Pesach Sheni on the 15th of Iyar.
142. 410. Don't eat the meat of the Korban Pesach raw or boiled.
143. 412. A Mumar cannot eat the Korban Pesach.
144. 413. A Toshav or hired worker cannot eat the Korban Pesach.

---

263. See Hasagat HaRamban to Sefer HaMitzvos of the Rambam, Lo Taaseh #227, Ramban says the Issur is to verbally declare - "הריני מוכרה לך לעולם". Heard from Rabbi Avraham Waldman Shlita. See Rambam, Hilchos Shemittah & Yovel, Ch. 12:15.
264. Sefer HaMitzvos L'Rambam, Mitzvah #145, the Torah requires Bais Din to judge cases of Charamim, dedicated property to Hekdesh. Sefer Chareidim, 4:44 claims that the Mitzvah to judge monetary cases is a Mitzvah done with the mouth, and while Sefer Chareidim only deals with Mitzvos done nowadays, nevertheless it is logical to deduce that all other Mitzvos of judgement of monetary matters is also dependent on the mouth. Rabbi Avraham Waldman Shlita.
265. See Sefer HaChinuch, Parshas Masai, Mitzvah #408, this is a Mitzvah upon the entire Jewish People to fulfil, and done through the leaders. Assumably this Mitzvah is done with the Mouth where the leaders tell the Levi'im to inherit their land, similar to Sefer Chareidim who learns that the Mitzvah of giving ones inheritance to the next generation, Nachala, is done with the Mouth.
266. Sefer Chareidim lists this Mitzvah as performed with the mouth. So when speaking with respect to a Kohen, giving him priority to be called up Rishon to the Sefer Torah and recite Zimun.
267. Hekdesh is done with either the Mouth or Thought/Mind. Shavuos 26b.
268. Sefer Chareidim lists this Mitzvah as performed with the mouth because if the Korban is wounded, it will become forbidden to be eaten with the mouth.
269. Since the Mitzvah is to eat the meat of Kodshim before it becomes Notar, one could deduce the Mitzvah of Notar is related to the Mouth. This can be deduced from the Mitzvah La Taaseh of not leaving a dead person not buried overnight. Sefer Chareidim counts this Mitzvah as done with the Hands. So too, with leaving in one's possession weights and measures which are not accurate as a Lo Taaseh done with the Hands. One could deduce from these two examples of Sefer Chareidim that the limb with which one does the Issur is also the very limb of the body one avoids doing that very same Issur. Thus, the Issur of Notar depends on the Mouth since it is the Mouth that is meant to eat the Kodshim to avoid the Issur of Notar (Rabbi Avraham Waldman).

145. 414. An Arel cannot eat the Korban Pesach.
146. 417. Don't leave any meat of the Korban Pesach till morning.[270]
147. 418. Don't leave any meat of the Korban Pesach Sheni till morning.[271]
148. 419. Don't leave any meat of the Korban Chagiga later than the 16th of Nissan.
149. 421. Celebrate Yom Tov in the Bais Hamikdash with eating meat from the Korban Chagiga.
150. 422. Be Happy on the three Yomim Tovim by eating meat and drinking wine.
151. 426. A First Born sheep, goat or cow is verbally designated for the Kohen.
152. 427. Kohen cannot eat a first born sheep, goat or cow outside Yerushalayim.
153. 446. A Kohen verbally declares a Metzora as Tameh.
154. 449. A Metzorah must publicize his Tumah.
155. 452. Follow the laws of Tzara'as on clothing (The Kohen declares it Tameh).
156. 453. Follow the laws of Tzara'as on houses (The Kohen declares it Tameh).
157. 463. Bais Din give a verdict on damages done by a goring ox.
158. 464. Bais Din give a verdict on damage caused by an animal eating other's property.
159. 465. Bais Din give a verdict on damages to a person or animal who fell into a pit.
160. 466. Bais Din give a verdict on damages caused by fire.
161. 489. Don't stand by and do nothing if someone's life is in danger.[272]
162. 495. Don't put a stumbling block in front of a blind person or take advantage of their ignorance.[273]
163. 499. Buy and sell according to the Torah laws of business.[274]
164. 501. Don't hurt anybody with words.
165. 503. Don't hurt a Ger Tzedek with words.
166. 505. Don't sell an Eved Ivri in the same way a slave is sold, this includes calling out loud "slave for sale."
167. 508. Don't give degrading work to an Eved Ivri, this includes not give verbal instructions to do degrading work.
168. 516. Don't hurt with words a run away non-Jewish slave who fled to safety in Eretz Yisrael.
169. 520. Allow workers to eat from grown produce while they walk between rows.
170. 521. While at work, a worker may not eat from the crops.
171. 525. Follow the laws of an unpaid guard, Shomer Chinum.[275]
172. 527. Don't pressure a poor man to pay back a loan if you know he does not have the money to

---

270. Since the Mitzvah is to eat the meat of Kodshim before it becomes Notar, one could deduce the Mitzvah of Notar is related to the Mouth. This can be deduced from the Mitzvah La Taaseh of not leaving a dead person unburied overnight. Sefer Chareidim counts this Mitzvah as done with the Hands. So too, with leaving in one's possession weights and measures which are not accurate as a Lo Taaseh done with the Hands. One could deduce from these two examples of Sefer Chareidim that the limb with which one does the Issur is also the very limb of the body one avoids doing that very same Issur. Thus, the Issur of Notar depends on the Mouth since it is the Mouth that is meant to eat the Kodshim to avoid the Issur of Notar.

271. Since the Mitzvah is to eat the meat of Kodshim before it becomes Notar, one could deduce the Mitzvah of Notar is related to the Mouth. This can be deduced from the Mitzvah La Taaseh of not leaving a dead person unburied overnight. Sefer Chareidim counts this Mitzvah as done with the Hands. So too, with leaving in one's possession weights and measures which are not accurate as a Lo Taaseh done with the Hands. One could deduce from these two examples of Sefer Chareidim that the limb with which one does the Issur is also the very limb of the body one avoids doing that very same Issur. Thus, the Issur of Notar depends on the Mouth since it is the Mouth that is meant to eat the Kodshim to avoid the Issur of Notar.

272. Sefer Chareidim counts this as a Mitzvah of the mouth (in addition to being a Mitzvah done by the mind and hands and body) when one has good advice to save someone and is silent.

273. Sefer Chareidim counts this as a Mitzvah of the mouth when one gives bad advice to another.

274. Sefer Chareidim counts this as a Mitzvah of the mouth.

275. This Mitzvah is done by Bais Din who judge such cases. Since it is a monetary case and Sefer Chareidim already established that all cases of business disputes are decided by the mouth of the judge, thus, this Mitzvah of judging cases of a Shomer Chinum is also done by the mouth.

pay you back yet. This includes not harassing him with words.
173. 528. Pressure a non-Jew to pay back a loan. This includes asking for payment.
174. 532. Don't demand a Mashkon from an Almana.
175. 533. Don't demand Keilim used for food as a Mashkon.
176. 536. Don't act as a witness with a loan of Ribis.[276]
177. 538. Bais Din must judge (and therefore pass verdict) all cases of litigation.
178. 539. Laws of Inheritance.[277]
179. 540. Select judges for Bais Din.[278]
180. 541. Don't select judges who are not expert Talmidei Chachamim.[279]
181. 542. If judges disagree, decide the case by a majority vote.[280]
182. 544. A judge cannot switch verdict from innocent to guilty.
183. 545. Follow the laws of the death penalty by Skila, this includes the verbal declaration of Bais of a verdict of guilt and the named death penalty.
184. 546. Follow the laws of the death penalty of Sereifa. This means the mouth of the guilty person is forced open to swallow molten lead.
185. 547. Follow the laws of the death penalty of Sayif. This means severance with a sword of the head from the body at the neck. The neck being the extension of the mouth.
186. 548. Follow the laws of the death penalty of Chenek. This means choking by strangulation around the neck which is the extension of the mouth.
187. 552. Bais Din must not let witch or wizard live.[281]
188. 553. Bais Din whip the Choteh. Malkus is given at the verbal count of a Shaliach Bais Din.
189. 555. Don't give a guilty verdict involving the death penalty based on circumstantial evidence.
190. 556. Don't give any verdict of guilt and punishment to the victim of rape.
191. 557. A judge may not give a less severe penalty because he pities the murderer.
192. 558. A judge must not give a favorable verdict because he favors a poor man at a trial.
193. 559. A judge must not give a favorable verdict because he favors a rich or powerful man at a trial.
194. 560. A judge must not decide a guilty verdict because the accused is a Choteh.
195. 561. A judge must not pervert justice.
196. 562. A judge must not give a favorable verdict because he favors a convert or orphan in a trial.
197. 563. A judge must treat both sides equally in court, this includes how he speaks to each side.
198. 564. A judge must not let fear of threats from a violent offender sway his decision.
199. 567. Don't curse a judge.
200. 568. Don't curse a King or Nasi.
201. 569. Don't curse another Jew.
202. 570. Whoever knows evidence must testify in Bais Din.
203. 571. Carefully examine the witnesses by asking many questions.
204. 572. A witness cannot also be a judge in a case which could have the death penalty.
205. 573. Don't accept the testimony of one witness.

---

276. Sefer Chareidim counts this as a Mitzvah of the mouth.
277. Sefer Chareidim counts this as a Mitzvah of the mouth.
278. Sefer Chareidim counts this as a Mitzvah of the mouth.
279. Sefer Chareidim counts this as a Mitzvah of the mouth.
280. Sefer Chareidim counts this as a Mitzvah of the mouth.
281. This is a Mitzvah done with the Mouth because Bais Din give the guilty verdict verbally.

206. 574. A Baal Aveira is Pasul to testify.
207. 575. Relatives are Pasul to testify.
208. 576. Don't give a false testimony.
209. 577. False witnesses receive the punishment they would have caused the accused. This can only happen because they gave false testimony (with their mouths).
210. 580. Don't add to the 613 Mitzvos (includes not making claims there is another Mitzvah, as when claiming there are five compartments in Tefilin).
211. 581. Don't delete any of the 613 Mitzvos (includes verbally claiming there are less than 613).
212. 582. Don't curse your father or mother.
213. 584. Respect your father and mother.[282]
214. 585. Fear your father and mother. This includes not arguing with them or raising one's voice at them or contradicting them.
215. 586. Don't be a Ben Sorer Umoreh.
216. 591. Only select a Jewish King. This was done by the Sanhedrin[283] and Navi who poured[284] the Shemen Hamishcha on his forehead and declared him the new king.
217. 592. Don't select a convert to be a king.[285]
218. 593. A king must not have too many wives.[286]
219. 599 Remember what Amalek did to the Jewish people when we came out of Egypt. This remembering is done with the mouth.[287]
220. 600. Select a special Kohen to speak to the soldiers before battle. He gave a speech with words of encouragement and another speech listing the four types of soldiers exempt from battle.
221. 602. Offer peace to an enemy under siege.[288]
222. 603. Don't offer peace to Amon or Moav.[289]

---

[282]. Sefer Chareidim counts this as a Mitzvah of the mouth. He claims the עיקר כבוד הוא בפה - the main way of showing parents respect is with our mouths, how we speak, in a gentle voice, respectful tone, happy voice, etc. Sefer Chareidim also counts doing this Mitzvah with the legs as when one stands for a parent, or with ones hands as when we give them food and drink. He also claims this Mitzvah is done with the mind because respect is indeed an attitude born in thought.

[283]. See Sefer HaChinuch Mitzvah #547, the Jewish king is only appointed by the Mouth of Bais Din. The Mitzvah to appoint a Jewish King includes having Kavod and Morah, respect and awe for him. These are two Mitzvos that apply to respecting and having awe for one's parents, and from that Mitzvah of honoring and fearing parents we learn to respect and fear a king. Thus this Mitzvah is also done with the Mind because respect and fear and Mitzvos of the Mind. See Sefer Chareidim 1:27 and paragraphs 35-38. He also deduces from the Mitzvah to honor parents with one's hands and body to do the same for a Jewish king, thus this Mitzvah is also done with the hands and all the body. He makes the same extension of legs, since one must stand for ones parents, so too one must stand for a king, thus the legs are also limbs that do this Mitzvah.

[284]. The pouring of the Shemen HaMishcha was done with the hands of the Bais Din or Navi, so this Mitzvah was also done with the hands. See Rambam Hilchos Melachim, 1:7.

[285]. Sefer Chareidim counts this as a Mitzvah done with the Mouth. It includes not appointing a convert for any position of authority over Yisrael.

[286]. The act of marriage is accomplished through the mouth when the groom says the words הרי את מקודשת לי. The act of Kiddushin is also done through a Shtar or Kessef, a marriage document or money, both of which are given into the hand of the wife, so this Mitzvah is also a Mitzvah done by the hand. The fact that she is also acquired through ביאה means this Mitzvah is also done with the Bris. Lastly, since she can only be married with her consent, this Mitzvah is also done with the mind. See Kiddushin 9b, - צריך לכתוב השטר מדעתה ולשמה.

[287]. Sefer Chareidim counts this as a Mitzvah of the mouth. We also make a public, verbal declaration of this Mitzvah to remember when we read the Torah of Parshat Zachor.

[288]. This Mitzvah can be done with the mouth, as was the case when Moshe Rabeynu sent an agent to King Sichon to offer peace. Or else it can also be done by hand as in the case of Yehoshua who sent letters offering peace to the kings of Canaan.

[289]. Waging war can be done through the mouth or by written document which would be written by hand and delivered by hand.

Mitzvos of the Hands

1. 23. Respect Torah Teachers.[290]
2. 27. Don't serve Avoda Zara, even to throw stones.[291]
3. 28. Don't serve idols in the 4 ways we serve Hashem.[292]
4. 29. Don't make a Pessel for yourself.
5. 30. Don't make a Pessel for others.
6. 31. Don't make a full human statue.
7. 33. Burn an Ir Hanidachas.
8. 34. Don't rebuild an Ir Hanidachas.
9. 39. Don't save the life of a Missionary.
10. 45. Don't be afraid to kill a Navi Sheker.
11. 47. Don't do an act of Ov.
12. 48. Don't do an act of Yidoni.
13. 49. Don't pass children through the fire of Molech.
14. 50. Don't build a stand for Avoda Zara.
15. 51. Don't bow down on an Even Maskis.[293]
16. 52. Don't plant trees in the courtyard of the Bais Hamikdash.
17. 53. Destroy Avoda Zara.
18. 54. Don't benefit from Avoda Zara.
19. 55. Don't benefit from ornaments of Avoda Zara.
20. 56. Don't make agreements with people who serve Avoda Zara.[294]
21. 58. Don't let anyone who serves Avoda Zara live in Eretz Yisrael.[295]
22. 59. Don't copy the customs or clothing of people who serve Avoda Zara.
23. 61. Don't go into a trance to see the future.
24. 67. Don't perform acts of magic, Kishuff.
25. 68. Men must not shave their Peos.
26. 69. Men must not shave any of the five corners of their beard.
27. 70. Men must not wear women's clothing.
28. 71. Women must not wear men's clothing.
29. 72. Don't tattoo the skin.
30. 73. Don't tear the skin in mourning.
31. 74. Don't tear out hair in mourning.
32. 78. Birkas Kohanim.[296]
33. 79. Tefilin on the head.
34. 80. Tefilin on the arm.
35. 81. Mezuza.
36. 82. Writing a Sefer Torah.
37. 83. A king writing a Sefer Torah.

---

290. Sefer Chareidim also count this Mitzvah is being done with the mind, the legs, as when you stand for a Talmid Chacham, and the hands as when you serve them a drink or give them something the ask for or need.
291. Sefer Chareidim adds that the entire body and legs also do this Aveira.
292. Sefer Chareidim adds that the entire body and legs also do this Aveira.
293. Sefer Chareidim adds that the entire body also does this Aveira.
294. Agreements are made by shaking hands and writing documents.
295. This Mitzvah is done with all the body.
296. Sefer Chareidim counts the mouth and hands in this Mitzvah too.

38. 84. Tzitizis.[297]
39. 86. Do Bris Mila.
40. 87. Rest on Shabbos.[298]
41. 88. Don't do Melacha on Shabbos.[299]
42. 89. Bais Din cannot give Onesh on Shabbos.
43. 92. Rest on Yom Kippur.
44. 93. Don't do Melacha on Yom Kippur.
45. 96. Rest on the first day of Pesach.
46. 97. Don't do Melacha on the first day of Pesach.
47. 98. Rest on the 7th day of Pesach.
48. 99. Don't do Melacha on the 7th day of Pesach.
49. 100. Rest on Shavuos.
50. 101. Don't do Melacha on Shavuos.
51. 102. Rest on Rosh Hashana.
52. 103. Don't do Melacha on Rosh Hashana.
53. 104. Rest on the first day of Sukkos.
54. 105. Don't do Melacha on the first day of Sukkos.
55. 106. Reset on Shemini Chag Atzeres.
56. 107. Don't do Melacha on Shemini Chag Atzeres.
57. 109. Destroy Chametz from midday of 14th of Nissan.
58. 112. Chametz should not be seen on seven days of Pesach.[300]
59. 113. Chametz should not be found in your domain for seven days.[301]
60. 117. Live in a Sukkah 7 days.
61. 118. Shake Lulav and Esrog all 7 days of Sukkos in the Bais Hamikdash.
62. 119. Give half a Shekel donation every year.
63. 124. Don't hold back food, clothes and time from one's wife.[302]
64. 131. A Mefateh pays three fines.
65. 137. Don't add oil to a Sota's Mincha.
66. 138. Don't add Levona spices to a Sota's Mincha.
67. 168. Don't make a person or animal a Sariss.
68. 175. Don't have physical contact with any forbidden women.
69. 196. Don't cook milk and meat together.[303]
70. 204. Shecht an animal before eating.[304]
71. 205. Don't Shecht a mother animal and its child on the same day.[305]

---

297. Sefer Chareidim counts the making of Tzitzis with the hand and also the entire body because one wears it over the majority of one's chest and back. He also counts this as a Mitzvah done with the eyes because he counts looking at one's Tzitzis in order to remember all Taryag Mitzvos as a separate Mitzvah. SMaK also counts looking at Tzitzis as one of the Taryag Mitzvos.
298. Sefer Chareidim counts Resting on Shabbos from Melacha as a Mitzvah done with the hands. He does not offer a reason. Perhaps the fact that Melacha is done with the hands, the desistance of Melacha is thus the hands desisting from Melacha and thus considered a Mitzvah related to the hands.
299. Sefer Chareidim counts desisting from Melacha on Shabbos as a Mitzvah done with the hands.
300. Sefer Chareidim counts this Mitzvah as done with the hands. He does not count this Mitzvah as a Mitzvah done with the eyes.
301. Sefer Chareidim counts this Mitzvah as done with the hands.
302. Sefer Chareidim counts this Mitzvah as done with the hands.
303. Sefer Chareidim counts this Mitzvah as done with the hands.
304. Although the act of Shechita is done with the hands, Sefer Chareidim counts this as a Mitzvah also done with the mouth because without the act of Shechita one could not eat any meat.
305. Sefer Chareidim counts this Mitzvah as done with the hands.

72.	206.	Cover the blood after Shechita of a Chaya or bird.[306]
73.	207.	Don't take a mother bird from her chicks.
74.	208.	Send away the mother bird before taking the chicks.[307]
75.	214.	Keep your promise.[308]
76.	218.	A Nazir must not cut his hair.
77.	225.	A Nazir must not touch a dead body.
78.	226.	A Nazir must shave all his body hair when he brings a Korban.
79.	234.	Don't plant two different seeds together.
80.	235.	Don't plant two different grains together in a vineyard.
81.	236.	Don't crossbreed animals.[309]
82.	237.	Don't make two different animals work together.
83.	238.	Don't wear Shaatnez.
84.	239.	Leave Peah for the poor.[310]
85.	240.	Don't harvest Peah, leave it for the poor.
86.	241.	Leave Leket for the poor.
87.	242.	Don't collect Leket.
88.	243.	Leave Ollelos for the poor.
89.	244.	Don't gather Ollelos.
90.	245.	Leave Peret for the poor.
91.	246.	Don't pick up Peret.
92.	248.	Don't go back to collect a forgotten bundle of stalks of grain.
93.	249.	Give Maaser Oni to the poor.
94.	250.	Give Tzedaka.[311]
95.	252.	Give Teruma Gedola to a Kohen.
96.	253.	The Levi must give Terumas Maaser to a Kohen.
97.	254.	Don't Teruma and Maaser in the wrong order.
98.	260.	The farmer gives Maaser Rishon to a Levi.
99.	261.	A farmer has to separate Maaser Sheni for himself.
100.	262.	Pidyon Maaser Sheni.
101.	270.	Separate Bikkurim fruits for the Kohanim.
102.	273.	Separate Challa for a Kohen.
103.	274.	Give the Zeroah, Lechayim and Keiva to a Kohen.
104.	275.	Give Reishis HaGeiz to a Kohen.
105.	276.	Do Pidyon Haben for a first born son with money to a Kohen.[312]
106.	277.	Do Pidyon Peter Chamor for a 1st born donkey with a lamb to a Kohen.
107.	278.	Break the neck of the Peter Chamor if it is not redeemed.
108.	279.	Rest the land in Shemitta.

---

306. Sefer Chareidim counts this Mitzvah as done with the hands and davka not the feet because to cover the blood with the feet shows disrespect for the Mitzvah.
307. Sefer Chareidim counts this Mitzvah as done with the hands and all the body.
308. Sefer Chareidim counts this Mitzvah as done with the hands.
309. Sefer Chareidim counts this Mitzvah as done with the hands.
310. *Sefer Chareidim only counts Mitzvos that apply nowadays, however, one could deduce from Sefer Chareidim 5:15, that leaving Peah is a Mitzvah Derabanan.*
311. Sefer Chareidim adds that this Mitzvah is also done with the mind because one should give with Simcha and a לב טוב - with good intent.
312. Sefer Chareidim counts this Mitzvah as done with the hands and all the body.

109.	280.	Don't work the land in Shemitta.
110.	281.	Don't do work to tress in Shemitta.
111.	282.	Don't harvest Sefichim in Shemitta.
112.	283.	Don't collect Nezirim in Shemitta.
113.	284.	Disown your produce grown in Shemitta.
114.	287.	Don't refuse to lend money Erev Shemitta.
115.	291.	Don't work the land in Yovel.
116.	292.	Don't harvest wild crops, Sefichim in Yovel.
117.	293.	Don't pick Nezirim, wild grown grapes in Yovel.
118.	295.	Don't sell land as a permanent sale in Eretz Yisrael.
119.	297.	Shevet Levi has no portion in the land.
120.	298.	Shevet Levi has no share in the spoils of war.
121.	300.	Fields of Shevet Levi cannot be sold.[313]
122.	301.	Build a Bais Hamikdash.
123.	302.	Don't build the Mizbayach with stones cut with metal.
124.	305.	Guard the Bais Hamikdash.
125.	306.	Don't leave the Bais Hamikdash unguarded.
126.	312.	Shevet Levi transport the Aron on their shoulders.
127.	313.	Don't remove the poles from the Aron.
128.	314.	Levi'im must work in the Bais Hamikdash.
129.	315.	A Levi cannot do the Avoda of another Levi or Kohen.
130.	317.	All 24 Mishmaros, shifts of Kohanim work all 3 Yomim Tovim.
131.	318.	Kohanim must wear Bigdei Kehuna during their Avoda.
132.	319.	Don't tear the Me'il gown.
133.	320.	The Choshen must not be loose.[314]
134.	329.	A Kohen Tameh must not do Avoda.
135.	331.	A Tevul Yom must not do Avoda.[315]
136.	331.	A Kohen must wash his hands and feet before doing Avoda.
137.	333.	A wounded Kohen cannot do any Avoda.[316]
138.	334.	A temporarily wounded Kohen cannot do any Avoda.[317]
139.	335.	A non-Kohen must not do any Avoda.
140.	336.	Only bring Korbanos with no wounds.
141.	338.	Don't Shecht a Baal Moom, wounded animal for a Korban.
142.	339.	Don't sprinkle the blood of a Korban Baal Moom.
143.	340.	Don't burn the fats of a Baal Moom.
144.	341.	Don't bring a temporarily wounded animal as a Korban.
145.	342.	Don't bring a temporarily wounded animal of Goyim.
146.	343.	Don't make a wound on a Korban.[318]

---

[313]. See Sefer HaChinuch, Parshas Behar, Mitzvah #342, and Rashi to Makot 12a - "דאין בוניו בית במגרש" - "ד"ה: תיפוק ליה"

[314]. See Sefer HaChinuch, Parshas Tetzaveh, Mitzvah #100, one received Malkus for undoing or loosening the Choshen from its fasteners during the Avoda. Untying and loosening is done with the Hands.

[315]. The Avodah for a Kohen was Kabalas Dam, Zerika, Haktara, Kemitza, Nisuch HaYayin and Holacha. All but the last are done with the hands. Holacha is done with the feet.

[316]. The Avodah for a Kohen was Kabalas Dam, Zerika, Haktara, Kemitza, Nisuch HaYayin and Holacha. All but the last are done with the hands.

[317]. The Avodah for a Kohen was Kabalas Dam, Zerika, Haktara, Kemitza, Nisuch HaYayin and Holacha. All but the last are done with the hands.

[318]. Sefer Chareidim counts this Mitzvah as done with the hands and adds that it is also done with the mouth because if he inflicts a wound on this

147. 344. Redeem Korbanos which became Passul.
148. 345. Bring a Korban after it is at least 8 days old.
149. 346. Don't bring an animal used for paying a Zona or that was traded for a dog.
150. 347. Don't burn yeast or Devash on the Mizbayach.
151. 348. All Korbanos must be salted.
152. 349. Don't leave out salt from any Korban.
153. 350. Follow the laws of the Korban Olah.
154. 352. Follow the laws of the Korban Chatos.
155. 354. Don't completely split the Chatos Ha'Off.
156. 355. Follow the laws of the Korban Asham.
157. 361. Follow the laws of the Korban Mincha.
158. 362. Don't add oil to a Minchas Choteh.
159. 363. Don't add Levona spices to a Minchas Choteh.
160. 365. Don't bake a Mincha as Chametz.
161. 367. Bring every Korban Neder and Nedava to the Bais Hamikdash.
162. 368. Don't delay bringing a Korban Neder or Nedava.
163. 371. Don't Shecht Korbanos outside the Azara.
164. 372. Don't bring Korbanos outside the Azara.
165. 373. Bring the Korban Tamid every day.
166. 374. Light Aish on the Mizbayach every day.
167. 375. Don't extinguish the fire on the Mizbayach.
168. 376. Remove ashes from the Mizbayach every day.
169. 377. Burn Ketores every day.
170. 378. Light the Menorah every day.
171. 379. Kohen Gadol brings his Korban Mincha every day.
172. 380. Bring the Korban Mussaf of Shabbos.
173. 381. Bake the Lechem Hapanim.
174. 382. Bring the Korban Mussaf of Rosh Chodesh.
175. 383. Bring the Korban Mussaf of Pesach.
176. 384. Bring the Omer on 2nd day of Pesach.
177. 386. Bring the Korban Mussaf of Shavuos.
178. 387. Bring the Shtei Halechem.
179. 388. Bring Korban Mussaf on Rosh Hashana.
180. 389. Bring Korban Mussaf on Yom Kippur.
181. 390. Bring Korban Mussaf on Sukkos.
182. 391. Bring Korban Mussaf on Shemini Chag Atzeret.
183. 394. Don't let a Korban become Notar.[319]

Korban it becomes אסור באכילה.

319. Sefer Chareidim counts Mitzvah #88 to desist from doing Melacha on Shabbos as a Mitzvah related to the hands. I am assuming this may be the same reason why the Mitzvah of not doing Melacha on Shabbos is listed by Sefer Chareidim as a Mitzvah related to the hands. However, since the Mitzvah is to eat the meat of Kodshim before it becomes Notar, one could deduce the Mitzvah of Notar is related to the Mouth. This can be deduced from the Mitzvah La Taaseh of not leaving a dead person unburied overnight. Sefer Chareidim counts this Mitzvah as done with the Hands. So too, with leaving in one's possession weights and measures which are not accurate as a Lo Taaseh done with the Hands. One could deduce from these two examples of Sefer Chareidim that the limb with which one does the Issur is also the very limb of the body one avoids doing that very same Issur. Thus, the Issur of Notar depends on the Mouth since it is the Mouth that is meant to eat the Kodshim to avoid the Issur of Notar.

184. 398. Burn Notar.
185. 399. Burn all Korbanos which became Tameh.
186. 400. Follow the order of Avoda on Yom Kippur.
187. 401. Misuse of Hekdesh property pays Meila fine.
188. 402. Don't do Melacha with animals reserved for Korbanos.
189. 403. Don't sheer the wool of sheep reserved for Korbanos.
190. 404. Shecht the Korban Pesach.
191. 405. Don't Shecht the Korban Pesach while owning Chametz.
192. 406. Don't leave Emurim fats of the Pesach Korban over night.[320]
193. 407 Shecht the Korban Pesach Sheni.
194. 411. Don't remove meat of the Korban Pesach from the group area.
195. 415. Don't break any bones of the Korban Pesach.
196. 416. Don't break any bones of the Korban Pesach Sheni.
197. 421. Celebrate every Yom Tov in the Bais Hamikdash with the Korban Chagiga.
198. 423. Don't come to the Bais Hamikdash on Yom Tov without a Korban Riyah.
199. 424. Don't avoid giving the Levi'im their Maaseros on Yom Tov.
200. 426. A first born sheep, goat or cow is reserved for the Kohen.[321]
201. 428. Don't buy back the first born sheep, goat or cow.
202. 429. Separate Maaser Beheima from sheep, goats and cows
203. 430. Don't buy back Maaser Beheima.
204. 431. Bring a Korban Chatos.
205. 432. Bring an Asham Talui.
206. 433. Bring a Korban Olah V'Yored.
207. 435. Sanhedrin bring a Korban for a mistaken ruling.
208. 436. A Zava brings a Korban.
209. 437. A Yoledes brings a Korban.
210. 438. A Zava brings a Korban.
211. 439. A Metzorah brings a Korban.
212. 440. Don't substitute a new animal for an already reserved Korban.
213. 442. Don't switch one Korban for another type of Korban.
214. 443. Follow the laws of Tumas Meis.
215. 444. Follow the laws of the Para Aduma.
216. 445. Sprinkle the Mei Nidda to Metaher a Tamei Meis.
217. 446. Follow the laws of Tzaraas.
218. 447. A Metzorah must not remove signs of Tzaraas.
219. 448. A Metzorah must not shave of Tzaraas from his skin.
220. 450. Follow the rules of making a Metzorah Tahor.
221. 451. Shave all hair of a Metzora before Tahara in a Mikveh.
222. 452. Follow the laws of Tzaaras on clothes.
223. 453. Follow the laws of Tzaraas on houses.
224. 454. Follow the laws of Nidda.
225. 456. Follow the laws of Tumas Zava.

---

320. Burning the fats is done with the hands. So too, leaving the fats on the Mizbayach passed its time is an Issur violated by the Hands.
321. Sefer Chareidim counts this as a Mitzvah done with the mouth as well as the hands and all the body.

226. 457. Follow the laws of Tumas Zav.
227. 458. Follow the laws of Tumas Neveila.
228. 459. Follow the laws of Tumas Shemoneh Sheratzim.
229. 460. Follow the laws of Tumas Shichvas Zera.
230. 461. Follow the laws of Tumas Ochlim and Mashkin.
231. 462. Every Tameh person must immerse in the Mikveh.
232. 467. Don't steal money or property.
233. 469. Make your scales and weights exact.
234. 470. Don't cheat with scales and weights.
235. 471. Don't even own inaccurate scales and weights, even if not used.[322]
236. 472. Don't move a boundary marker.
237. 473. Don't kidnap.
238. 474. Don' rob.
239. 475. Don't keep your worker's salary or refuse to pay a debt.
240. 478. Return a stolen item to its owner.
241. 479. Don't ignore a lost object.[323]
242. 480. Return a lost object.
243. 481. Bais Din must judge cases of bodily harm and damage to property.[324]
244. 482. Don't murder.
245. 483. Don't accept money to free a convicted murderer.
246. 485. Don't accept money from an accidental murderer instead of him fleeing to a city of safety, an Ir HaMiklat.
247. 486. Don't execute a murderer before he stand trial.
248. 487. Save a Nirdaf even if it means harming or killing the Rodef.
249. 489. Don't be a bystander when someone's's life is in danger.[325]
250. 490. Set aside cities of safety and clearly mark the roads to the nearest Arei Miklat.
251. 491. Break the Egla Arufa's neck.
252. 492. Don't work or plant the ground where the Egla Arufa was killed.
253. 493. Don't leave objects lying around which can be dangerous.[326]
254. 494. Make a guard rail around flat roofs.
255. 496. Help remove a heavy load from an animal even though it belongs to someone you hate.
256. 497. Help others load their animals.
257. 498. Don't pass by without helping unload an animal's heavy packages and help re-loading.
258. 499. Buy and sell according to the Torah laws of business.[327]
259. 500. Don't overcharge or underpay for merchandise.[328]

---

322. Sefer Chareidim counts this as a Mitzvah done with the hands.
323. Sefer Chareidim interestingly counts this Mitzvah as performed both by the mind (pretending one cannot see the lost object) and the hands. He does not explain the reason this is related to the hands.
324. Sefer Chareidim points out that from the moment a person lifts his 'hand' to strike his fellow, he is labeled a Rasha and is Pasul to give testimony. It appears that even though the actual Mitzvah here is upon Bais Din to adjudicate justice which is done through deliberation (Mind) and their verbal verdict (Mouth), Sefer Chareidim seems to take the position of defining this Mitzvah as done by the hand because that is the origin for why the accused is in Bais Din in the first place, he did harm or damage with his hands.
325. Sefer Chareidim counts this Mitzvah as done with the hands as well as with the mouth.
326. Sefer Chareidim counts this Mitzvah as done with the hands.
327. Sefer Chareidim counts this Mitzvah as done with the mouth, we assume that because many acts of acquisition require lifting or pulling with the hands, this Mitzvah is also done with the hands.
328. Sefer Chareidim counts this Mitzvah as done with the hands and the whole body.

260. 502. Don't cheat a Ger Tzedek in business.
261. 504. Follow the laws of buying an Eved Ivri.
262. 505. Don't sell an Eved Ivri the same way a slave is sold.[329]
263. 506. Don't give an Eved Ivri harsh work.
264. 507. Don't allow a gentile to give an Eved Ivri harsh work.[330]
265. 508. Don't give an Eved Ivri degrading work.
266. 509. Give an Eved Ivri generous gifts when he goes free.
267. 510. Don't send away an Eved Ivri empty handed.
268. 511. Buy back a Jewish girl servant to return her to her family.
269. 513. A master cannot sell his Jewish maidservant.
270. 514. An Eved Canaani must work forever.[331]
271. 515. Don't send back a non-Jewish slave who fled to Eretz Yisrael for safety.[332]
272. 518. Pay your workers salary on time.
273. 519. Don't delay payment of your worker's salary.[333]
274. 520. Allow workers to eat from grown produce while they walk between rows.
275. 521. While at work, a worker must not eat from the crops.
276. 522. A worker must not take more than he can eat.
277. 523. Don't muzzle an ox while it is treading grain.
278. 528. Pressure a gentile to pay back a loan.
279. 529. Don't take a Mashkon by force.
280. 530. Return a Mashkon when its owner needs it.
281. 531. Don't delay returning a Mashkon.
282. 532. Don't demand a Mashkon from a widow.
283. 533. Don't demand Keilim used for food as a Mashkon.
284. 534. Don't lend and charge Ribis.
285. 535. Don't borrow money and pay Ribis.
286. 537. Borrow and lend money with Ribis to gentiles.
287. 543. Don't give the death penalty with only a majority vote of one.
288. 545. Follow laws of Skila.
289. 546. Follow laws of Sereifa.
290. 547. Follow laws of Sayif.
291. 548. Follow laws of Chenek.
292. 549. Hang those who got Sekila for cursing Hashem or serving Avoda Zara.
293. 550. Bury the executed on the same day of execution.

---

329. See Sefer HaChinuch, Parshas Behar, Mitzvah #345, one should not sell an Eved Ivri on the platform designated for selling ordinary slaves. This would be done with the Hands. Sefer HaChinuch continues in the Shoresh of the Mitzvah to add that this way of selling an Eved Ivri violates showing respect for a fellow Jew and thus is also a Mitzvah done with the Mind. Also, calling out to people passing by "Slave for sale" also denigrates the Eved Ivri and would thus be a violation done with the Mouth too.
330. See Sefer HaChinuch Mitzvah #348, if a Jew sees a gentile working a Jew with back breaking work, and he has the power in his hands to prevent him but does not do so, violates this Issur. The expression 'ויש כח בידו למונעו ולא מנעו, עובר על לאו זה'
331. See Sefer HaChinuch. Mitzvah #347, if his Jewish master places Tefilin on the head of his Eved, the Eved Canaani goes free. The fact that the violation of the Issur to not let him free is done with the hands by putting Tefilin on him, demonstrates that the way to keep him forever is done with the same limb (as explained several times). This Mitzvah is also done with the Mouth because if the master marries his Eved Canaani to Bat Chorin, or asks him to read three Passukim in a Sefer Torah in front of a Minyan, he goes free.
332. See Sefer HaChinuch, Mitzvah #568, If one violates this Issur by grabbing him and returning him to his original master, he violates this Mitzvah. The language of grabbing indicates this Mitzvah is done with the hands and the rest of the body - ותפסו והשיבו אל אדוניו עבר על לאו זה. וזה לשון ספר החינוך שם: ...
333. Sefer Chareidim counts this Mitzvah as done with the hands.

294. 551. Don't delay burial overnight.
295. 553. Bais Din must whip the Choteh.
296. 554. Don't whip more than the number of lashes decided by Bais Din.
297. 555. Don't give the death penalty only based on circumstantial evidence.
298. 556. Don't punish an Anuss.
299. 565. A judge must not accept bribes.
300. 577. Give false witnesses the same punishment they would have caused the accused to receive.
301. 580. Don't add to the 613 Mitzvos.[334]
302. 581. Don't delete any of the 613 Mitzvos.
303. 583. Don't hit your father or your mother.
304. 586. Don't be a Ben Sorer Umoreh.
305. 588. A Kohen Gadol must not become Tameh Meiss even for his closest relatives.
306. 589. A Kohen Gadol cannot be under the same roof as a dead body.
307. 590. A Kohen must not become Tameh except for his 7 closest relatives.
308. 591. Only select a Jewish King.[335]
309. 594. A king must not have too many horses.[336]
310. 595. A king must not have too much gold and silver.[337]
311. 596. Destroy the seven nations of Canaan.
312. 597. Don't let any of the seven nations of Canaan remain alive.
313. 598. Wipe out the descendents of Amalek.
314. 602. Offer peace to a city under siege.[338]
315. 603. Don't offer peace to Amon or Moav.[339]
316. 604. Destroy fruit trees during a siege.
317. 605. Prepare bathroom areas when going to war.
318. 606. Every soldier must have a small shovel to dig with.
319. 607. Select a special Kohen to speak to the soldiers before war.[340]
320. 612. Don't sell a Yefes Toar into slavery.
321. 613. Don't keep a Yefes Toar to be your maid.

---

334. Sefer Chareidim counts this Mitzvah as done with the hands.
335. Since the Sanhedrin or a Navi would poor the Shemen HaMishcha on the new King's forehead, this Mitzvah is thus done by the hand. Note that not all kings needed actual anointing, so it may not always have applied.
336. Acquiring horses requires a formal Kinyan, which is done by picking up the animal, or pulling it, or with the transference of a written deed, or money, all of which are done with the Hand (Shulchan Aruch, Choshen Mishpat, 197:1
337. All coins of gold or silver are bought and sold in the same way all movable items are acquired, through a formal Kinyan of picking up the money or pulling it toward oneself or by exchange of hands. A king also has the right to place taxes on his people which are collected by hand. These taxes cover all military expenses and government expenses (Rambam, Hilchos Melachim, 4:1).
338. Just like Yehoshua sent letters to all the kings of Canaan, offering options of peace, leave the land or battle. Alternatively, this Mitzvah can also be done with the mouth just like Moshe Rabeinu sent an agent with the verbal message of a peace overture to King Sichon.
339. Waging war is done either by mouth or by hand. Here, the refusal to make peace is the inverse of both the mouth and hand.
340. The appointment of the Kohen Mashuach was done by pouring the Shemen Hamishcha on his head. The pouring was done by hand and thus a Mitzvah of the hand. See Sefer HaChinuch that this is also a Mitzvah done with the mouth because the Kohen Mashuach was specially selected in order to speak to the troops at the border and again before battle.

Mitzvos of the Head

1. 68. Men must not shave the Peos of their head.
2. 70. Men must not wear head wear of women.
3. 71. Women must not wear head wear of men.
4. 72. Don't Tattoo the skin.[341]
5. 74. Don't tear out hair in mourning.[342]
6. 79. Wear Tefilin on the head.
7. 175. Don't have physical contact with any forbidden women.
8. 217. A Nazir must let the hair of his head grow.
9. 218. A Nazir must not cut the hair of his head.
10. 238. Don't wear a head gear of Shaatnez.
11. 309. Don't pour Shemen HaMishcha on a Zar.
12. 318. Kohanim wear Bigdei Kehuna which includes a special head covering.
13. 322. A long haired Kohen must not enter the Bais HaMikdash.
14. 451. A Metzorah has to shave all the hair from his entire body before Tahara in a Mikveh. This includes the hair of his head.

---

341. This includes the head even though most tattoos are on other limbs.
342. This issur includes not making a bald spot on the head from tearing out hair.

Mitzvos of the Legs

1. 23. Respect Torah teachers.[343]
2. 27. Don't serve Avoda Zara. Even to throw stones at it.
3. 28. Don't serve Avoda Zara in the 4 ways we serve Hashem.
4. 51. Don't bow down on smooth stone.
5. 58. Don't let Ovdei Avoda Zara live in Eretz Yisrael.
6. 90. Don't walk outside the city boundary.
7. 136. Follow the laws of Sota.
8. 175. Don't have physical contact with any forbidden women.
9. 224. A Nazir must not be under the same roof as a corpse.
10. 248. Don't go back to collect a forgotten bundle of stalks of grain.
11. 250. Give Tzedaka.[344]
12. 280. Don't work the land in Shemitta.
13. 281. Don't work the trees in Shemitta.
14. 282. Don't harvest sefichim in Shemitta.
15. 283. Don't collect Nezirim, wild grapes in usual way in Shemitta.
16. 284. Disown your produce grown in Shemitta.
17. 291. Don't work the land in Yovel.
18. 292. Don't harvest Sefichim in Yovel.
19. 293. Don't pick wild grown grapes in Yovel.
20. 297. Shevet Levi has no portion in Eretz Yisrael.
21. 298. Shevet Levi has no share in the spoils of war.
22. 301. Build a Bais Hamikdash.
23. 303. Don't ascend the Mizbayach using steps.
24. 305. Guard the Bais HaMikdash.
25. 306. Don't leave the Bais HaMikdash unguarded.
26. 314. Levi'im must work in the Bais HaMikdash.
27. 315. A Levi cannot do the Avoda of another Levi or Kohen.
28. 317. All 24 shifts of Kohanim work on the 3 Chagim.
29. 321. A drunk Kohen must not enter the Bais HaMikdash.
30. 322. A long haired Kohen must not enter the Bais HaMikdash.
31. 323. A Kohen must not enter the Bais HaMikdash with torn clothes.
32. 324. A Kohen cannot enter the Heichal if not doing Avoda.
33. 325. Don't leave the Bais HaMikdash during the Avoda.
34. 326. Someone Tameh must leave the Bais HaMikdash.
35. 327. Someone Tameh cannot enter the Bais HaMikdash.
36. 328. Someone Tameh cannot enter the Har HaBayit.
37. 330. A Kohen Tameh after Tevila cannot enter the Bais HaMikdash till after sun down.
38. 331. A Kohen must wash his hands and feet before doing Avoda.
39. 332. A wounded Kohen cannot enter the Bais HaMikdash.

---

343. Sefer Chareidim lists this Mitzvah as done with the legs as when one stands for a Talmid Chacham. He also counts this as a Mitzvah of the Mind, because respect is an attitude, and also a Mitzvah done with the Hands as when we serve a Talmid Chacham and lastly with all the body.

344. Since we should be Rodef Tzedaka and Hessed, one may deduce that this Mitzvah is performed with the help of the feet (author's opinion). Sefer Chareidim does not list Tzedak as done with the feet, though he does list Tzedaka as done with the Hand and with a Lev Tov and B'Simcha.

40. 341. Don't bring a temporarily wounded animal for a Korban.
41. 342. Don't bring a wounded animal of Goyim for a Korban.
42. 345. Bring a Korban after it is 8 days old.
43. 346. Don't bring an animal used to pay a Zona or that was traded for a dog.
44. 350. Follow the laws of the Korban Olah.
45. 352. Follow the laws of the Korban Chatos.
46. 355. Follow the laws of the Korban Asham.
47. 357. Don't eat Kodshei Kadshim meat outside the Azara.
48. 367. Bring every Korban Neder and Nedava to the Bais Hamikdash on the first available Yom Tov.
49. 368. Don't delay bringing a Korban Neder or Nedava.
50. 369. Bring all Korbanos to the Bais HaMikdash.
51. 370. Bring all Korbanos from outside Eretz Yisrael to the Bais Hamikdash.
52. 371. Don't Shecht Korbanos outside the Azara.
53. 372. Don't bring Korbanos outside the Azara.
54. 373. Offer two lambs for the Korban Tamid every day.
55. 374. Light a fire on the Mizbayach every day.
56. 375. Don't extinguish the fire on the Mizbayach.
57. 376. Remove ashes from the Mizbayach every day.
58. 377. Burn Ketores everyday.
59. 378. Light the Menorah every day.
60. 379. Kohen Gadol has to bring a Mincha every morning and afternoon.
61. 380. Bring Korban Mussaf on Shabbos.
62. 382. Bring Korban Mussaf on Rosh Chodesh.
63. 383. Bring Korban Mussaf on Pesach.
64. 384. Bring the Omer on the 2nd day of Pesach.
65. 386. Bring the Korban Mussaf on Shavuos.
66. 387. Bring Shtei HaLechem with Korban Mussaf on Shavuos.
67. 388. Bring Korban Mussaf on Rosh Hashana.
68. 389. Bring Korban Mussaf on Yom Kippur.
69. 390. Bring Korban Mussaf on Sukkos.
70. 391. Bring Korban Mussaf on Shemini Chag Atzeret.
71. 400. Follow the order of Avoda on Yom Kippur.
72. 402. Don't Melacha with animals reserved for Korbanos.
73. 411. Don't take the Korban Pesach meat from the group area.
74. 420. Be seen in the Bais Hamikdash 3 times a year.
75. 421. Celebrate every yom Tov in the Bais HaMikdash with the Korban Chagiga.
76. 423. Don't come to the Bais HaMikdash 3 times a year without a Korban Olas R'iya.
77. 425. Mitzvas Hakhel.
78. 427. Kohen cannot eat first born sheep, goat or cow outside Yerushalayim.
79. 429. Separate Maaser Beheima.
80. 431. Bring a Korban Chatos.[345]

---

345. Most of the acts of bringing any Korban was done with the hands (egg Shechita, Kabalas Dam, Zerika, Haktara) but Holacha, walking to the Mizbayach with the blood was also one of the steps of the Avoda (pun intended!). So it was done with the legs.

81. 432. Bring a Korban Asham Talui.
82. 433. Bring a Korban Asham Vadai.
83. 434. Bring a Korban Oleh Ve'Yored when applicable.
84. 435. Sanhedrin bring a Chatos Bais Din for a mistaken ruling.
85. 436. Zava brings a Korban Zava.
86. 437. A Yoledes brings a Korban Yoledes.
87. 438. A Zav brings a Korban Zav.
88. 439. A Metzora brings a Korban Metzora.
89. 444. Follow the laws of Para Aduma.
90. 445. Follow the laws of sprinkling Mei Nidda water.
91. 446. Follow the laws of Tzaraas.
92. 450. Follow the rules to make a Metzora Tahor.
93. 453. Follow the laws of Tzaraas on houses.
94. 454. Follow the laws of Nidda.
95. 455. Follow the laws of Tumah caused by childbirth.
96. 456. Follow the laws of Tumah of a Zava.
97. 457. Follow the laws of Tumah of a Zav.
98. 458. Follow the laws of Tumah caused by a Neveila.
99. 459. Follow the laws of Tumah caused by the 8 Sheratzim.
100. 460. Follow the laws of Tumah caused by Shichvat Zera.
101. 462. Every Tameh person must immerse in a Mikveh.
102. 467. Don't steal money or property.
103. 472. Don't move a boundary marker.
104. 474. Don't rob.
105. 484. Manslaughter must escape to a city of safety.
106. 487. Save the Nirdaf.
107. 489. Don't stand still when someone's life is in danger.
108. 496. Help remove a heavy load from an animal, even if it belongs to someone you hate!
109. 497. Help others load their animal.
110. 498. Don't walk by without helping unload an animal's heavy packages.
111. 570. Whoever knows evidence must testify in Bais Din.[346]
112. 587. Mourn for closest relatives.
113. 588. A Kohen Gadol must not become Tameh.
114. 589. A Kohen Gadol cannot be under the same roof as a corpse.
115. 601. Don't return to live in Egypt permanently.
116. 608. Soldiers in their first year of marriage return from battle.
117. 609. Soldiers in their first year of marriage do not go to war.
118. 610. Don't panic and retreat during battle.

---

346. Sefer Chareidim counts this as a Mitzvah done with the Legs because a witness must stand when giving testimony. Obviously it is also a Mitzvah done with the Mouth too.

Mitzvos of the Bris

1. 86. Bris Mila
2. 122. Marry with a Ketuba and Kiddushin.
3. 123. Don't marry without a Ketuba and Kiddushin.
4. 124. A Husband must not hold back time[347] from his wife.
5. 125. A Jewish man has to father children.
6. 127. Don't remarry one's ex wife after she divorced her 2nd husband.
7. 128. Do Yibum.
8. 130. A widow must not remarry outside her husband's brothers till Chalitzah.
9. 132. A Ma'aness must marry her.
10. 133. A Ma'aness cannot divorce her.[348]
11. 134. A Motzei Shem Ra must remain married.
12. 135. A Motzei Shem Ra cannot divorce his wife.
13. 139. Mother.
14. 140. Step-mother
15. 141. Sister.
16. 142. Half-sister.
17. 143. Granddaughter (son's daughter)
18. 144. Daughter
19. 145. Granddaughter (daughter's daughter)
20. 146. Mother & her daughter.
21. 147. Mother & her granddaughter.
22. 148. Mother & her granddaughter.
23. 149. Aunt.
24. 150. Aunt.
25. 151. Aunt.
26. 152. Daughter-in-law.
27. 153. Sister-in-law (brother's wife).
28. 154. Sister-in-law (wife's sister).
29. 155. A man cannot live as married with an animal.
30. 156. A woman cannot live as married with an animal.
31. 157. A man cannot marry a man.
32. 158. A man cannot marry his father.
33. 159. A man cannot marry his uncle.
34. 160. Don't live as married with another man's wife.
35. 161. Don't be close to a Nidda.
36. 162. Don't marry a non-Jew.
37. 164. Don't marry an Egyptian convert till 3rd generation.
38. 165. Don't marry a convert from Edom till 3rd generation.
39. 166. A Mamzer must not marry a Jew.
40. 167. A Saris cannot marry a Jew.
41. 169. A Kohen Gadol cannot marry a widow.

---

347. The Mitzvah of Onah is being translated here as 'time' though most Rishonim translate it as the Mitzvah of intimacy in marriage.
348. Sefer Chareidim counts this as a Mitzvah of the Bris because he has to remain married, since he cannot divorce her.

42. 170. A Kohen Gadol cannot be with a widow even without a Ketuba & Kiddushin.
43. 171. A Kohen Gadol must only mary a Besula.
44. 172. A Kohen cannot marry a divorcee.
45. 173. A Kohen cannot marry a Zona.
46. 174. A Kohen cannot marry a Chalala.
47. 175. Don't have physical contact with any forbidden women.
48. 257. A Kohen Arel must not eat Terumah.
49. 414. An Arel cannot eat the Korban Pesach.
50. 438. A Zav brings a Korban Zav.
51. 457. Follow the laws of Tumas Zav.
52. 460. Follow the laws of Tumas Shichvat Zera.
53. 593. A king must not have more than 18 wives.
54. 609. First year of marriage
55. 611. A Jewish soldier must follow the laws of a Yefas Toar.

Mitzvos of the entire Body

1. 23. Respect Torah scholars.
2. 28. Don't serve Avoda Zara in the 4 ways we serve Hashem.
3. 35. Don't benefit from an Ir Hanidachas.
4. 51. Don't bow on an Even Mashchis.
5. 54. Don't benefit from Avoda Zara.
6. 58. Don't let Ovdei Avoda Zara live in Eretz Yisrael.
7. 61. Don't go into a trance to see the future.
8. 70. Men must not wear ladies clothing.
9. 71. Women must not wear men's clothing.
10. 84. Wear Tzitzit.[349]
11. 117. Living in a Sukkah for seven days.
12. 175. Don't have physical contact with any forbidden women.
13. 225. A Nazir must not touch a dead body.
14. 226. A Nazir must shave his entire body hair when he brings his Korban.
15. 238. Don't wear Shaatnez.
16. 276. Do a Pidyon Haben for a first born son with money to a Kohen.[350]
17. 294. Return land and homes to original owners in Yovel.
18. 305 Guard the Bais HaMikdash.
19. 306. Don't leave the Bais HaMikdash.
20. 400. Follow the Avoda of Yom Kippur.
21. 426. Separate 1st born sheep, goats and cows for the Kohen.[351]
22. 443. Follow the laws of Tumas Meis.[352]
23. 448. A Metzora must not shave any signs of Tzaraas from his skin.
24. 450. Follow the rules to make a Metzora Tahor.
25. 454. Follow the laws of Nidda.
26. 455. Follow the laws of Tumah caused by childbirth.
27. 456. Follow the laws of a Tumas Zava.
28. 457. Follow the laws of Tumah of a Zav.
29. 458. Follow laws of Tumah caused by contact with a Neveila.
30. 459. Follow the laws of Tumah caused by the 8 Sheratzim.
31. 460. Follow the laws of Tumah caused by Shichvas Zera.
32. 462. Immerse in a Mikveh.
33. 467. Don't steal money or property.
34. 469. Make sure your scales and weights are exact.[353]
35. 473. Don't kidnap.
36. 474. Don't rob.
37. 482. Don't murder.[354]

---

[349]. Sefer Chareidim counts this as done with the entire body.
[350]. Sefer Chareidim counts this as done with the entire body. Presumable because the father holds his son in his arms, against his chest, supported by his legs and answers the Kohen's questions.
[351]. Sefer Chareidim counts this as done with the entire body.
[352]. Since no part of the body must have contact with a Meis, this Mitzvah applies to the entire body.
[353]. Sefer Chareidim counts this as done with the entire body.
[354]. Sefer Chareidim counts this as done with the entire body.

38. 487. Save a person being chased, even if you have to take the life of the Rodef.[355]
39. 489. Don't be a bystander when someone's life is in danger.
40. 496. Help remove a heavy load from an animal, even if belongs to someone you hate.
41. 497. Help others load their animals.
42. 580. Don't add to the 613 Mitzvos.[356]
43. 581. Don't delete any of the 613 Mitzvos.[357]
44. 587. Mourn close relatives.
45. 588. Kohen Gadol must become Tameh even for closest relatives.
46. 589. Kohen cannot be under the same roof as a corpse, except for closest relatives.

---

355. Sefer Chareidim counts this as done with the entire body.
356. Sefer Chareidim counts this as done with the entire body.
357. Sefer Chareidim counts this as done with the entire body.

Constant Mitzvos of the Mind.

The popular list for the constant Mitzvos of the Mind are known as 'The Six Constant Mitzvos.' They are mentioned in Mishna Berura in the second Biur Halacha in his work on Orach Chaim. He quotes Sefer HaChinuch who lists those six Mitzvos for which one receives reward for every moment one thinks about them. On closer examination of the most classic Rishonim who count the Taryag Mitzvos, it appears that there are closer to *50 Mitzvos which are constant*. I am most interested in any comments as to how the Chinuch decided to single out the six that he did, while other Rishonim have listed so many more than the popular six.[358]

1. Emuna in Hashem.[359]
2. Know there are no other powers beside Hashem.[360]
3. Love Hashem.[361]
4. Fear Hashem.[362]
5. Hashem is One.[363]
6. Don't follow your thoughts or eyes.[364]
7. Don't desire other people's possessions.[365]
8. Be Davuk to Hashem.[366]
9. Emulate Hashem.[367]
10. Remember Hashem.[368]
11. Don't forget Hashem.[369]
12. Be Tamim with Hashem.[370]
13. Don't forget Amalek.[371]

---

358. My close friend Rabbi Dovid Wax shlita of the famous Taryag Foundation asked this very question (of why Sefer HaChincuh only counts six constant Mitzvos when it is clear that there are many many more) to the Gedolim: R'Elyashiv z"l, Rav Vozner z"l, Rav Noach Weinberg z"l, and Yibadel L'Chaim, Rav Chaim Kaniefsky shlita, who themselves agreed there are many more than six constant Mitzvos and do not know why Sefer HaChinuch only singled out six. Sefer Chareidim lists 10 constant Mitzvos. See Sefer Zoveach Todah from R' Mordecai Itzvan in his introduction who explain that Sefer Chareidim left out many Mitzvos DeOraissa and Derabanan that apply nowadays, and even more Mitzvos Min HaTorah were left out of his list that are a Machlokes HaPoskim. See also Sefer Eved HaMelech from the Gaon and Tzadik Rebi Shmuel Huminer z"l who lists still more Mitzvos that are not part of Taryag but are nevertheless Mitzvos found in NaCh which count as Mitzvos. R' Isser Zalman Meltzer z"l wrote his own Haskama to Sefer Eved HaMelech and encouraged readers to learn from it every day, something he himself did.

359. Ex. 20:2. Dev. 5:6.
360. Ex. 20:3. Dev. 5:7.
361. Dev. 6:5. Dev. 11:22. Dev. 11:13.
362. Dev. 10:20. Dev. 8:6.
363. Dev. 6:4.
364. Num. 15:39.
365. Dev. 5:18.
366. Dev. 10:20 - וּבוֹ תִדְבָּק **וּלְדָבְקָה־בוֹ** - Dev. 30:20 - Dev. 11:22 - לְאַהֲבָה אֶת־יְהוָה אֱלֹהֶיךָ לִשְׁמֹעַ בְּקֹלוֹ **וּלְדָבְקָה־בוֹ** כִּי אִם־שָׁמֹר תִּשְׁמְרוּן אֶת־כָּל־הַמִּצְוָה הַזֹּאת אֲשֶׁר אָנֹכִי מְצַוֶּה אֶתְכֶם לַעֲשֹׂתָהּ לְאַהֲבָה אֶת־ה' אֱלֹקֵיכֶם לָלֶכֶת בְּכָל־דְּרָכָיו **וּלְדָבְקָה־בוֹ** Sefer Chareidim (chapter #9, Paragraph #10) lists this Mitzvah as referring to thinking about Hashem all the time. He quotes Chovos Halevavos (פתיחה שער אהבת ה') - here are his words there: וזה שענין הדביקה היא אהבה הנאמנה והלב השלם. לשונו הרמב"ן (על חומש דברים פ' י:כ) ובו תדבק: שתהא **זוכר השם יתברך תמיד**, לא תפרד מחשבתך ממנו בביתך ובלכתך בדרך ובשכבך ובקומך עד שיהיו דבריו לבני אדם בפיהו ובלשונו, ולבו איננו עמהם, אבל הוא לפני השם. This Mitzvah applies at all times and places and in every waking moment. Sefer Yereim also counts this as one of Taryag in Siman #407.

367. The Mitzvah to Emulate Hashem is learned from וְהָלַכְתָּ בִּדְרָכָיו (Dev. 28:9) which means to go in Hashems' ways, to emulate His patience, kindness, compassion, etc. See also Gen.17:1. Dev. 11:22. Dev. 30:20.

368. Dev. 8:18 - וְזָכַרְתָּ אֶת־ה' אֱלֹקֶיךָ כִּי הוּא הַנֹּתֵן לְךָ כֹּחַ לַעֲשׂוֹת חָיִל. This is counted as a Mitzvah Aseh by Sefer Chareidim. See also Sefer Yereim, Siman #408 who counts this a one of Taryag. See also Ben Ish Chai, Chelek II, Parshas Ekev - שמצוה ויסוד וקיום העולם כולו שיהיה אדם חושק תמיד בכל הטובה אשר ישיג בעולם הזה שהם מאת השם יתברך ולא ממנו מעצמו. עיין שם לשונו הקדוש.

369. Ramban, Lo Taaseh, #41 - שלא לשכוח אמונת אלקות. It is derived from Dev. 6:12 הִשָּׁמֶר לְךָ פֶּן־תִּשְׁכַּח אֶת־ה' אֲשֶׁר הוֹצִיאֲךָ מֵאֶרֶץ מִצְרַיִם מִבֵּית עֲבָדִים - Also Smag & Sefer Chareidim count this Mitzvah as one of Taryag Mitzvos even though Rambam does not it. See also Dev. 8:11 & 9:7.

370. To be a Tam means to completely trust Hashem (Sefer Chareidim, Ch.9, Paragraph #21). This Mitzvah is derived from Dev. 18:13 - תָּמִים תִּהְיֶה עִם ה' אֱלֹקֶיךָ. Ramban, Aseh #7, Sefer Chareidim (Ch.9:21), the Smag and Rabeynu Yona (Shaar Gimel, Paragraph #17) & Sefer Yereim (Siman #431) all count this as one of Taryag even though Rambam does not. See also Gen.17:1 & Yehoshua 24:14, Tehilim 62:9 - בִּטְחוּ בוֹ בְכָל־עֵת. See also Mishley 3:5 - בְּטַח אֶל־ה' בְּכָל־לִבֶּךָ.

371. Dev. 25:19 - **לֹא תִּשְׁכָּח** תִּמְחֶה אֶת־זֵכֶר עֲמָלֵק מִתַּחַת הַשָּׁמָיִם. Rambam, Ramban, Smag, Smak, Sefer Chareidim all agree this is one of Taryag.

14. Don't forget what happened to Korach.[372]
15. Don't forget Hashem spoke to us at Matan Torah.[373]
16. Don't forget our ungrateful complaining in the Midbar.[374]
17. Love every Jew.[375]
18. Love every Ger Tzedek.[376]
19. Remember the day of Shabbos.[377]
20. Remember Yetziat Mitzrayim.[378]
21. Remember what Hashem did to Paroh & Egypt.[379]
22. Remember you were slaves in Mitzrayim.[380]
23. Remember all the 613 Mitzvos.[381]
24. Don't forget the 613 Mitzvos.[382]
25. Look at your Tzitzit to remember all 613 Mitzvos.[383]
26. Don't plan to get other people's possessions.[384]
27. Remove unnecessary thoughts from your mind.[385]

---

[372]. Num. 17:5 - וְלֹא־יִהְיֶה כְקֹרַח וְכַעֲדָתוֹ. This is counted as one of Taryag by Ramban, Lo Taaseh #25 - לא לחלוק על הכהונה ולא להחזיק במחלקת. Smak Siman #132 also counts it and adds that it also means a person should not be a Baal Machloket - שלא יהיה אדם בעל מחלקת. Sefer Yereim counts in Siman #357. Rambam does not count it.

[373]. Dev. 4:9-10 - רַק הִשָּׁמֶר לְךָ וּשְׁמֹר נַפְשְׁךָ מְאֹד פֶּן־תִּשְׁכַּח אֶת־הַדְּבָרִים אֲשֶׁר־רָאוּ עֵינֶיךָ וּפֶן־יָסוּרוּ מִלְּבָבְךָ כֹּל יְמֵי חַיֶּיךָ וְהוֹדַעְתָּם לְבָנֶיךָ וְלִבְנֵי בָנֶיךָ: יוֹם אֲשֶׁר עָמַדְתָּ לִפְנֵי ה' אֱלֹקֶיךָ בְּחֹרֵב. Ramban, Lo Taaseh #2 counts this in Taryag. Rambam does not. Remembering national revelation at Har Sinai is one of the Ten Zechiros listed at the end of Shachris in every standard Siddur.

[374]. Dev. 9:7-8 - זְכֹר אַל־תִּשְׁכַּח אֵת אֲשֶׁר־הִקְצַפְתָּ אֶת־ה' אֱלֹקֶיךָ בַּמִּדְבָּר לְמִן־הַיּוֹם אֲשֶׁר־יָצָאתָ ׀ מֵאֶרֶץ מִצְרַיִם עַד־בֹּאֲכֶם עַד־הַמָּקוֹם הַזֶּה מַמְרִים הֱיִיתֶם עִם־ה': וּבְחֹרֵב הִקְצַפְתֶּם אֶת־ה' וַיִּתְאַנַּף ה' בָּכֶם לְהַשְׁמִיד אֶתְכֶם. Sefer Chareidim and Ramban, Aseh #6 both count this as one of Taryag Mitzvos. Ramban counts it as an Aseh to remember our defiance and ingratitude, while Sefer Chareidim counts it as a Lo Taaseh not to forget our impudence. Rambam does not count this in his list of Taryag.

[375]. Lev. 19:18. This is a Mitzvah to think of the virtues in another Jew which will cause you to feel love for that person. It applies every time you have such thoughts.

[376]. Dev. 10:19 - וַאֲהַבְתֶּם אֶת־הַגֵּר כִּי־גֵרִים הֱיִיתֶם בְּאֶרֶץ מִצְרָיִם. See also Lev. 19:34. All agree this is one of Taryag.

[377]. Ex. 20:8 - זָכוֹר אֶת־יוֹם הַשַּׁבָּת לְקַדְּשׁוֹ. See Rashi there - (ביצה טו.) תְּנוּ לֵב לִזְכּוֹר תָּמִיד אֶת יוֹם הַשַּׁבָּת, שֶׁאִם נִזְדַּמֵּן לְךָ חֵפֶץ יָפֶה תְּהֵא מַזְמִינוֹ לְשַׁבָּת. See also Sefer Chareidim (Kitzur version) whose lashon is ופשוטו של מקרא שתמיד יהיה יום שבת שגור בפיו. See also Sefer Yereim, Siman #410 where lists one of Taryag Mitzvos is to have awe for Shabbos - מורא שבת. He explains the way we have awe for Shabbos is by having thoughts of how he intends to give Kavod to Shabbos and to avoid Melacha on Shabbos and to tremble at the thought of violating the day Hashem gave us to alone with our Creator.

[378]. Dev.16:3 - זָכוֹר אֶת־הַיּוֹם הַזֶּה אֲשֶׁר יְצָאתֶם מִמִּצְרַיִם מִבֵּית עֲבָדִים כִּי בְּחֹזֶק יָד הוֹצִיא ה' אֶתְכֶם.. See also Ex. 13:3 - לְמַעַן תִּזְכֹּר אֶת־יוֹם צֵאתְךָ מֵאֶרֶץ מִצְרַיִם כֹּל יְמֵי חַיֶּיךָ. זְכוֹר אֶת הַיּוֹם הַזֶּה. לִמֵּד שֶׁמַּזְכִּירִין יְצִיאַת מִצְרַיִם בְּכָל יוֹם. See Rashi on this Passuk who cites the Mechilta מזה. See also Shenos Eliyahu from the Vilna Gaon on Berachos 1:5 who explains the opinion of Ben Zoma that one must remember Yezias Mitzrayim all the days of your life to mean both day and night time - הלילות, כל ימי חייך, הימים, ימי חיי, ימי חייך. (דברים טז:ג) לְמַעַן תִּזְכֹּר אֶת־יוֹם צֵאתְךָ מֵאֶרֶץ מִצְרַיִם כֹּל יְמֵי חַיֶּיךָ - says the Gra - מובן כל היום כולו אף בלילה בכלל, כלומר תמיד יש מצוה לזכור יציאת מצרים - 'It is understood that the meaning here is that Ben Zoma means the entire period of a whole today, that includes the night of that day too. In other words, there is a constant Mitzvah to recall the Exodus.' The Smak in Aseh #110 agrees remembering Yetzias Mitzrayim is one of Taryag.

[379]. Dev. 7:18 the passuk warns us not to fear our enemies, then the verse continues to tell that instead of thinking thoughts of fear, we should recall what Hashem did to Paroh - לֹא תִירָא מֵהֶם זָכֹר תִּזְכֹּר אֵת אֲשֶׁר־עָשָׂה ה' אֱלֹקֶיךָ לְפַרְעֹה וּלְכָל־מִצְרָיִם.

[380]. Dev. 24:18 - וְזָכַרְתָּ כִּי עֶבֶד הָיִיתָ בְּמִצְרַיִם וַיִּפְדְּךָ ה' אֱלֹקֶיךָ מִשָּׁם. Sefer Chareidim, Ch.9, Mitzvah 27 counts this as one of Taryag, so does Rabeynu Yona. See also Dev. 5:15 - וְזָכַרְתָּ כִּי עֶבֶד הָיִיתָ. See also Dev.16:12 - וְזָכַרְתָּ כִּי־עֶבֶד הָיִיתָ בְּמִצְרָיִם. See also Dev. 15:15 - אֱלֹקֶיךָ ה' וַיִּפְדְּךָ מִצְרַיִם בְּאֶרֶץ הָיִיתָ עֶבֶד כִּי וְזָכַרְתָּ בְּאֶרֶץ מִצְרָיִם.

[381]. Num. 15:39 - וּזְכַרְתֶּם אֶת־כָּל־מִצְוֹת ה' וַעֲשִׂיתֶם אֹתָם. And Num.15:40 - וְהָיָה לָכֶם לְצִיצִת וּרְאִיתֶם אֹתוֹ. לְמַעַן תִּזְכְּרוּ וַעֲשִׂיתֶם אֶת־כָּל־מִצְוֹתָי. The predicate in the command to remember all the Mitzvos is one has a Mitzvah to know them first in order to then remember them. There is no logic in commanding us to remember something we have not learned.

[382]. Dev. 8:11 - הִשָּׁמֶר לְךָ פֶּן־תִּשְׁכַּח אֶת־ה' אֱלֹקֶיךָ לְבִלְתִּי שְׁמֹר מִצְוֹתָיו וּמִשְׁפָּטָיו וְחֻקֹּתָיו אֲשֶׁר אָנֹכִי מְצַוְּךָ הַיּוֹם.

[383]. Smak learns from Num. 15:39 - וְהָיָה לָכֶם לְצִיצִת וּרְאִיתֶם אֹתוֹ וּזְכַרְתֶּם אֶת־כָּל־מִצְוֹת ה' וַעֲשִׂיתֶם אֹתָם - that the purpose of looking at one's Tzitzit is to remember all Taryag Mitzvos, so he counts the actual looking at one's Tzitzit as a Mitzvah of Taryag. One can argue that since the Mitzvah of Tzitzit is a day time Mitzvah and not applicable at night, the Smak's Mitzvah to look at the Tzitzit is also only applicable every second of the day time and therefore not a Mitzvah Tamidi, that applies at all times.

[384]. Ex. 20:14 - לֹא תַחְמֹד בֵּית רֵעֶךָ לֹא־תַחְמֹד אֵשֶׁת רֵעֶךָ וְעַבְדּוֹ וַאֲמָתוֹ וְשׁוֹרוֹ וַחֲמֹרוֹ וְכֹל אֲשֶׁר לְרֵעֶךָ. This Mitzvah is also found in Dev. 5:18 - וְלֹא תַחְמֹד אֵשֶׁת רֵעֶךָ. All Rishonim agree this is one of Taryag. It is a Mitzvah of the mind that applies at all times.

[385]. Sefer Chareidim counts this as one of Taryag, derived from Dev. 10:16 - וּמַלְתֶּם אֵת עָרְלַת לְבַבְכֶם - which means 'to cut off extra thoughts.' The term Orlat HaLev refers to mind that is blocked (see Rashi in reference to the Orla of trees in the first three years - Lev.19:23 - וַעֲרַלְתֶּם עָרְלָתוֹ. וְנֶעֱרָלִים. אָטוּם, יְהֵא אָטוּם וְנִסְתָּם מִלְּהָנוֹת מִמֶּנּוּ. See also Rashi on Jer.9:25 that Orlah Oznam means blocked ears from hearing the truth. Orla means 'blocked.' So Orlat HaLev means a mind that is blocked from the Emet of Torah, Hashem's clarity. Our Aveiros block our mind from thinking straight (Sota

28. Don't think bad thoughts.[386]
29. Be Tzanuah.[387]
30. Do Teshuva.[388]
31. Be happy in all your Avodas Hashem.[389]
32. Count your blessings.[390]
33. Avoid Aveiros.[391]
34. Don't think about Avoda Zara.[392]
35. Don't be arrogant.[393]
36. Be Humble.[394]

3a). Radak in Sefer Sherashim translates Orla as a term of 'extra' - ערלה הוא לשון מיותר. Based on the Radak's definition, the Mitzvah to cut off one's Orlat HaLev refers to removing the extra thoughts (Yetzer Hara). Worry, anxiety, fear are all thought which go against the Mitzvah of Emuna, trusting Hashem, being Tamim with Hashem (Dev.18:13) and are counted as 'extra' overweight thinking! The Torah wants me to pay attention to my thoughts so that I can remove the thoughts that are non-reality thoughts.

386. Dev.20:10 - וְנִשְׁמַרְתָּ מִכֹּל דָּבָר רָע. Chazal derive from this Passuk that one should not have forbidden thoughts during the day which could lead to seeing Keri at night - (Avoda Zara 20b) שלא יהרהר אדם ביום ובא לידי קרי בלילה. The same Gemora (Avoda Zara 20a) adds that this Passuk is a warning not to look at beautiful Isha, even is she is single, or a married lady even if she is ugly, or ladies clothing that is striking, or stare at animals when they are mating. All these are possible causes for forbidden thoughts. This Mitzvah applies every waking second. It is counted as one of Taryag by the Smak, Sefer Chareidim & Ramban (Lo Taaseh #62). Rambam does not count this in Taryag, perhaps Rambam saw it as part of the Lo Taaseh of וְלֹא תָתוּרוּ אַחֲרֵי לְבַבְכֶם וְאַחֲרֵי עֵינֵיכֶם (Num.15:39) while Smak, Sefer Chareidim and Ramban count וְנִשְׁמַרְתָּ מִכֹּל דָּבָר רָע in addition to וְלֹא תָתוּרוּ and thereby gaining reward for the fulfillment of both these Mitzvos when avoiding forbidden thoughts. It is noteworthy to add that Hashem only asks us to control our thoughts because we are able to. He could not ask of us the impossible. Thus the logic here is most revealing, Hashem's very command to keep our minds clean of Hirhurim Raim is predicated on the fact that He made us able to choose our next thought, always. No exceptions. Nobody is beyond controlling their thoughts. See Dev. 30:14.

387. This is counted by the Smak as one of Taryag. He learns it from Dev. 23:15 - וְהָיָה מַחֲנֶיךָ קָדוֹשׁ וְלֹא יִרְאֶה בְךָ עֶרְוַת דָּבָר - Smak derives from here that 'your Machaneh' should be Kadosh by your behavior of Tzniut in four instances: 1. The bathroom. 2. During intimacy. 3. When learning Torah and Davening. 4. Distance oneself from excretion an urine. He adds a fifth, that this includes not having Sefarim Chitzonim on one's home. Rambam does not count being Tzanua as one of Taryag. Neither does Sefer Chareidim or Ramban.

388. Sefer Chareidim, Ch. #9, Paragraph #34 writes that the main aspect of Teshuva is in our *mind*, the secondary aspect is our *verbal* Teshuva. See Shulchan Aruch, Even HaEzer, Siman #31:38 where a person known to be a total Rasha, and betrothed himself on condition he is a total Tzadik, the marriage is valid because שמא הרהר תשובה בלבו, perhaps he had a thought of Teshuva. We see that one thought of Teshuva counts in Hashem's dictionary to be reality. See also Num. 26:11 - וּבְנֵי קֹרַח לֹא מֵתוּ - Rashi cites Medrash Shocher Tov 45 - הֵם הָיוּ בָּעֵצָה תְּחִלָּה, וּבִשְׁעַת הַמַּחֲלֹקֶת הִרְהֲרוּ תְּשׁוּבָה בְלִבָּם, לְפִיכָךְ נִתְבַּצֵּר לָהֶם מָקוֹם גָּבוֹהַּ בַּגֵּיהִנֹּם וְיָשְׁבוּ שָׁם (מגילה יד.).

389. Dev. 28:47. The Passuk there singles out serving Hashem B'Simcha as the single most likely Mitzvah whose absence would be the cause for the 98 curses listed in the Torah. The Passuk also tells why we might fail to be happy in Hashem's Avoda - because we did not think about the good Hashem constantly does for us and act gratefully while we enjoyed His abundant blessings. Here is the verse in full: תַּחַת אֲשֶׁר לֹא־עָבַדְתָּ אֶת־ה' אֱלֹקֶיךָ בְּשִׂמְחָה וּבְטוּב לֵבָב - good thoughts, and 3. כל מֵרֹב - you see it refers to three items - 1. Not serving Hashem with Simcha, 2. With וּבְטוּב לֵבָב from the overwhelming abundance of blessings in my life. Rashi explains this last item to mean I was not grateful while I was enjoying so many blessings from Hashem. The bottom line is that even though none of the Rishonim actually count Simcha as one of the Taryag, all agree it is a Mitzvah from the Torah to be happy. See also Dev. 28:11 - וְשָׂמַחְתָּ בְכָל־הַטּוֹב אֲשֶׁר נָתַן־לְךָ ה' אֱלֹקֶיךָ - 'Be happy with all the good Hashem your Power of powers has gifted you.' The predicate in this instruction is simply that there is good in your life to be grateful and happy about! This Mitzvah applies every second of your life. Every time you think or say you are happy with Hashems' blessings, you attain this Mitzvah. Sefer Chareidim counts being happy during Tefila, learning Torah and doing Mitzvos as a Derabanan, derived from Tehilim, 100:2 - עִבְדוּ אֶת־ה' בְּשִׂמְחָה.

390. Dev. 28:47 - the last words in this verse tell us Hashem expects us to count our blessings while we have them - תַּחַת אֲשֶׁר לֹא־עָבַדְתָּ אֶת־ה' אֱלֹקֶיךָ בְּשִׂמְחָה וּבְטוּב לֵבָב מֵרֹב כֹּל. The two words מֵרֹב כֹּל are explained by Rashi to mean 'while I still had that abundance of good in my life' - מֵרֹב כֹּל. בְּעוֹד שֶׁהָיָה לְךָ כָּל טוּב.

391. Sefer Chareidim counts avoiding Aveiros as a Mitzvah from Taryag. He derives it from the two words וּבָחַרְתָּ בַּחַיִּים in Dev.29:19 - נָתַתִּי לְפָנֶיךָ הַבְּרָכָה וְהַקְּלָלָה וּבָחַרְתָּ בַּחַיִּים לְמַעַן תִּחְיֶה אַתָּה וְזַרְעֶךָ. This Mitzvah applies with every thought you have where you choose to think good thoughts and not Hirhurim Ra'im.

392. Rambam and all others agree (Smag & Smak) that not to think thoughts of Avoda Zara is one of Taryag. It is derived from Lev. 19:4 - אַל־תִּפְנוּ אֶל־הָאֱלִילִם - 'Don't turn (your mind) toward gods.' The Rishonim read the words 'Don't remove EL (Hashem) from your thoughts' - אל תפנו אל מדעתכם. This Mitzvah applies every moment of your life. The Zohar on Parshat Kedoshim says that R' Shimon Bar Yochai would apply this verse to not looking at beautiful ladies.

393. This is not counted by Rambam as one of Taryag but the Smak (יום א' מצוה כב /סימן רב) and Sefer Chareidim (Ch.#21, Paragraph 15), Rabeynu Yona (Shaar Gimel, Paragraph #34) do count it. They derive it from Dev. 8:12-14 - פֶּן־תֹּאכַל וְשָׂבָעְתָּ וּבָתִּים טוֹבִים תִּבְנֶה וְיָשָׁבְתָּ: וּבְקָרְךָ וְצֹאנְךָ יִרְבְּיֻן וְכֶסֶף וְאָמַרְתָּ בִּלְבָבֶךָ כֹּחִי וְעֹצֶם יָדִי עָשָׂה לִי. See also Dev. 8:17 - וְזָכַרְתָּ אֶת־ה' אֱלֹקֶיךָ כִּי הוּא הַנֹּתֵן לְךָ כֹּחַ לַעֲשׂוֹת חָיִל יד. וְרָם לְבָבֶךָ וְשָׁכַחְתָּ אֶת־ה' אֱלֹקֶיךָ הַמּוֹצִיאֲךָ מֵאֶרֶץ מִצְרַיִם מִבֵּית עֲבָדִים. The Smag (lo Taaseh #64) also lists not being arrogant as one of Taryag, he derives it from Dev. 8:11 - הִשָּׁמֶר לְךָ פֶּן־תִּשְׁכַּח אֶת־ה' אֱלֹקֶיךָ אֶת־הַחַיִל הַזֶּה. Chazal were most scathing of anyone who had even a trace of arrogance. Mar Zutra in Sota 5a says that someone who is arrogant deserves excommunication as the verse states in Mishley16:5 - תּוֹעֲבַת ה' כָּל־גְּבַהּ־לֵב - 'Anyone who has an arrogant mind is an abomination to Hashem!'

394. Sefer Yerei'im counts this as one of Taryag (Mitzvah #232). Sefer Yerei'im writes that he found this Mitzvah listed as one of Taryag in the Halachos of R; Yehudai Gaon but could not find a direct command in the Torah to be humble except from how the Torah itself praises this trait from the

37. Don't express anger.[395]
38. Don't leave the Torah.[396]
39. Judge Hashem righteously.[397]
40. Don't forget what Amalek did to us.[398]
41. Don't stop hating a Missionary.[399]
42. Don't hate your brother in your thoughts.[400]
43. Don't deviate from any of the Mitzvos.[401]
44. Constantly remember Hashem's kindness to your forefathers and yourself.[402]
45. Don't forget Emuna in Hashem.[403]
46. Accept upon yourself the yoke of Taryag Mitzvos.[404]

---

words in Num. 12:3 - וְהָאִישׁ מֹשֶׁה עָנָיו מְאֹד מִכֹּל הָאָדָם אֲשֶׁר עַל־פְּנֵי הָאֲדָמָה - he then lists a few other sources in Nach and Chazal for the great praise of humility but nevertheless relies on R' Yehudai Gaon and the derivation of the Torah's praise for Moshe Rabeynu for why this is one of Taryag. Humility is a born from thought, thus it is a Mitzvah of the mind and as such applies every waking moment of one's life. Every time we attribute any achievement as a pure gift from Hashem, we are attaining this Mitzvah.

395. This is not counted by Rambam but Sefer Chareidim does count it (Ch.#21, Paragraph 17). Sefer Chareidim cites the Zohar as counting this as a D'Oraissa where the Zohar (Parshas Tetzaveh) derives it from Ex. 34:17 - אֱלֹהֵי מַסֵּכָה לֹא תַעֲשֶׂה־לָּךְ - 'Don't make for yourself gods made of metal.' He reads the verse as a warning not to let one's Neshama be replaced with a Ruach Tumah. He also brings a support from Tehilim 81:10 - לֹא־יִהְיֶה בְךָ אֵל זָר - 'Don't let a strange power (god) be inside you.' Sefer Chareidim reads this passuk to mean, do not let anger turn you into your own Avoda Zara because rage is synonymous with Avoda Zara (Shabbos 105b). Anger being related to Avoda Zara means anger is really the opposite of Emuna. Thus, anger is correlated to the Issur of not having any other powers in front of Hashem - Ex. 20:3 - See Sichot HaRan #38 how anger is a complaint against Hashem because one is essentially saying 'this should not be happening to me!' Eliyahu HaNavi advised Rav Yehuda 'don't be angry and sin.' Meaning that anger leads is a sin and leads to more sins. The words he said were לא תרתח ולא תחטא (Berachos 29b).

396. Smak counts this עַל־פִּי הַתּוֹרָה אֲשֶׁר יוֹרוּךָ וְעַל־הַמִּשְׁפָּט אֲשֶׁר־יֹאמְרוּ as שלא לפרוש מן התורה one of Taryag (יום א', מצוה טו). He derives it from Dev. 17:11 - לְךָ תַעֲשֶׂה לֹא תָסוּר מִן־הַדָּבָר אֲשֶׁר־יַגִּידוּ לְךָ יָמִין וּשְׂמֹאל. Rambam learns from this verse the Lo Taaseh to deviate from the Oral Law as prescribed by the Chachamim of every generation. According to the Smak's reading of this verse, every second you refuse to be Porush from the Torah, you attain this Mitzvah.

397. The Smak (יום א', מצוה ה) and the Smag (Aseh #17) both count the Mitzvah to judge Hashem righteously as one of Taryag. The Smag adds that when people do Teshuva and find they experience more suffering than before they did Teshuva, they should not question Hashem but accept that Hashem is giving them suffering in this world for their mistakes before they did Teshuva. This is their chance to just Hashem righteously and in doing so with joy and gratitude will make their reward many times greater. See Rabbi Shalom Arush's books Garden of Miracles - Say Thank You Hashem and See Miracles, and his other book Garden of Gratitude. See also Shulchan Aruch, Orach Chaim, Siman #222:3 - חייב אדם לברך על הרע & Siman #230.5 where the Mechaber writes "כל דעביד רחמנא לטב עביד" לעולם ירגיל אדם לומר & בדעת שלמה ובנפש חפצה כשמברך בשמחה על הטובה

398. This is a Mitzvah of the mind and applies every moment of our lives. All Rishonim count this in Taryag. It is derived from Dev.25:19 - תִּמְחֶה אֶת־זֵכֶר עֲמָלֵק מִתַּחַת הַשָּׁמָיִם לֹא תִּשְׁכָּח. See Ex. 17:14-15.

399. All agree with

400. Lev. 19:17 - לֹא־תִשְׂנָא אֶת־אָחִיךָ בִּלְבָבֶךָ - all agree this is one of Taryag. It applies to thought and at all times.

401. Dev. 17:11 - לֹא תָסוּר מִן־הַדָּבָר אֲשֶׁר יַגִּידוּ לְךָ יָמִין וּשְׂמֹאל. All agree this is one of Taryag. It applies every moment of your life. Every thought, word and action that is a refusal to deviate from the Halacha is automatically this Mitzvah, listening to Chazal and remaining loyal to the Torah Sh'Baal Peh through following the words and advice of our Chachamim.

402. Sefer Chareidim, Ch. #9, Paragraph #23 counts this as one of Taryag. He derives it from Dev. 8:2-4 - וְזָכַרְתָּ אֶת־כָּל־הַדֶּרֶךְ אֲשֶׁר הוֹלִיכֲךָ ה' אֱלֹקֶיךָ זֶה אַרְבָּעִים שָׁנָה...וַיַּאֲכִלְךָ אֶת־הַמָּן...שִׂמְלָתְךָ לֹא בָלְתָה מֵעָלֶיךָ וְרַגְלְךָ לֹא בָצֵקָה זֶה אַרְבָּעִים שָׁנָה... Sefer Chareidim (ibid) adds that 'one can logically deduce with a Kal VaChomer, that if this Passuk instructs us to remember the kindness Hashem did for our forefathers in previous generations, how much more is every single Jew obligated to remember the kindnesses Hashem does for us every single moment, and to all of our nation, that He saves us from the nations of the world who consistently stand up against with intent to destroy us?' He continues - 'and so every individual Jew is obligated to remember the kindnesses Hashem has done for him from the moment of conception in his mother's womb! (this includes gratitude for not being aborted or a miscarriage, born healthy and still alive till today). These thoughts of are enough to humble oneself before Hashem and then turn to Hashem in complete Teshuva. Rabyenu Yona also counts this as one of Taryag (Shaar Gimel, Paragraph #17).

403. Dev. 6:12 - הִשָּׁמֶר לְךָ פֶּן־תִּשְׁכַּח אֶת־ה' אֲשֶׁר הוֹצִיאֲךָ מֵאֶרֶץ מִצְרַיִם מִבֵּית עֲבָדִים. Note that this Passuk is almost the exact inverse of the first of the Aseret Hadibrot which states Hashem is The One Power of all powers Who took us out of Mitzrayim, the house of slaves. And here we are being instructed to be careful not to forget Hashem Who took us out of the land of Mitzrayim. This Mitzvah is counted by Sefer Chareidim (Ch.#21, Paragraph #6-7). He derives from the double terminology of הִשָּׁמֶר לְךָ וּפֶּן that this Mitzvah is actually counted as two Lavim, two Mitzvos. The first הִשָּׁמֶר is counted as one of Taryag, the second term פֶּן counts as an Anaf Mitzvah. See also Rabeynu Yona (Shaar Gimel, Paragraph #27) who concurs. Sefer Chareidim concludes: 'So this (double terminology) means we are being commanded to remember constantly not to forget Hashem.'

404. Sefer Chareidim derives this from Dev.10:16 - וּמַלְתֶּם אֵת עָרְלַת לְבַבְכֶם - writes Sefer Chareidim on this Passuk (in his Hakdama) - וּמַלְתֶּם אֵת עָרְלַת לְבַבְכֶם - שרוצה לומר שיקבל וישמע כל המצות. This is not counted as one of Taryag but it is counted as a Mitzvah Min HaTorah and is therefore called an Anaf Mitzvah, the 'branch of a Mitzvah.' Rambam in Sefer HaMitzvos explains this in Shoresh Revi'i and gives this Mitzvah of listening and accepting the Yoke of all the Mitzvos as an Anaf Mitzvah. Seder Olam of Rebi Yossi Ben Chalafta counts the acceptance of the yoke of the Mitzvos a Mitzvah from the Torah that depends on thought. He derives it from Dev. 11:18 - וְשַׂמְתֶּם אֶת־דְּבָרַי אֵלֶּה עַל־לְבַבְכֶם - and stating that when we say these words in the second paragraph of Shema, we should commit to all Hashem's Mitzvos. Rabeynu Yona (Shaar Aleph, Paragraph #6) learns that one

258

47. Don't be afraid of your enemies.[405]
48. Kiddush Hashem.[406]
49. Tefila.[407]
50. Remember what Hashem did to Miriam.[408]
51. Yirah for Parents.
52. Kavod for Parents.
53. Yirah for Chachamim.[409]
54. Don't forget your learning.[410]

---

who refuses to commit to Hashem's Mitzvos is in the category of אָרוּר אֲשֶׁר לֹא־יָקִים אֶת־דִּבְרֵי הַתּוֹרָה־הַזֹּאת לַעֲשׂוֹת אוֹתָם וְאָמַר כָּל־הָעָם אָמֵן (Dev.27:26).

405. The Mitzvah not to fear ones enemies is derived from Dev.20:1 - כִּי־תֵצֵא לַמִּלְחָמָה עַל־אֹיְבֶךָ...לֹא תִירָא מֵהֶם כִּי־ה' אֱלֹקֶיךָ עִמָּךְ הַמַּעַלְךָ מֵאֶרֶץ מִצְרָיִם. This Mitzvah means don't retreat in battle (out of fear of the enemy). This Mitzvah obviously only applies at time of war, however, beyond Peshat level, the greatest enemy we have is not our physical enemy but our own Yetzer Hara who hides in our thoughts of Sina, Kina, Taava, Machloket, Netira, Nekama, Gaava and Anger, etc. So in this sense, the Torah is replete with many reminders not to fear our enemy, meaning here, don't fear your Yetzer Hara thoughts! This applies every moment of our lives! Why not fear the Yetzer Hara? Because Hashem is with you all the time - לֹא תִירָא מֵהֶם כִּי־ה' אֱלֹקֶיךָ עִמָּךְ and He is The One Who took us out of Egypt with extraordinary miracles and wonders, so too, He can take us out of our slavery to our Yetzer Hara, so don't be afraid of your own thoughts which try to seduce you into Aveiros. Hashem is with you, so thank Him for your Yetzer Hara because now you are able to become closer to Him and fulfil many of these Mitzvos of the mind in this list by not listening to the Yetzer! For more examples of Hashem warning us to not listen to the thought of fear, see Dev.3:2, 7:21, Num.21:34, Yehoshua 8:1, 10:8, 10:25, 11:6.

406. Lev. 22:32 - וְנִקְדַּשְׁתִּי בְּתוֹךְ בְּנֵי יִשְׂרָאֵל אֲנִי ה' מְקַדִּשְׁכֶם. Sefer Chareidim (Ch. #8, Paragraph 16) explains that even though the essential Mitzvah of Kiddush Hashem refers to giving up one's life and refuse to change faith Hass Veshalom, or refuse to do an act of murder, Avoda Zara or adultery, nevertheless, one also attains this great Mitzvah through thought! He explains that during the daily recital of Shema, when we say the words וְאָהַבְתָּ אֵת ה' אֱלֹקֶיךָ … וּבְכָל־נַפְשְׁךָ - and again in the second paragraph of Shema during the words - וּבְכָל־נַפְשְׁכֶם - if make an absolute commitment in your mind that if you if you are tested, you will happily give up your life rather than give into the Nissayon, this thought is counted as though you died עַל קִדּוּשׁ ה'. He adds, this applies to if you tell yourself you would prefer to give up all your money and possessions to avoid giving in to a test. Sefer Chareidim writes that we should be willing to die, just as Rabbi Akiva gave his life away with the joy of fulfilling the Mitzvah to love Hashem with all his soul (Berachos 61b), and so too Chana and her seven sons. Claims Sefer Chareidim, such thoughts are counted by Hashem as though you truly did give your life for Hashem and attained the greatest level of Kiddush Hashem. He says this is the practise of Tzadikim every day when they have this thought in mind. He cites the Zohar (Parshas Balak) which advises we should have the thought of dyeing for Hashem while saying the letter Dalet of אחד in Shema. The Zohar writes that anyone who has in mind to die for Hashem rather than deny His Achdus (Being The Only One Power in all the universe) is counted as though he actually gave his life for Hashem. This thought is recommended davka when saying Shema, however, you attain it anytime you think these thoughts (Tzitel Katan). So you could be waiting on line in a store or at a red light or while boarding a plane, and in your mind you are telling yourself you gladly die for Hashem with all four Misass Bais Din, you attain the Mitzvah of Kiddush Hashem in that moment. Why would Hashem be so generous to give us so much reward for just thinking? Because He loves us so much!

407. Sefer Chareidim counts Tefila as a Taryag Mitzvah of the Lev/Mind (Ch.#9, Paragraph 17). Rambam, Smag, Smak, Sefer Yereim (Siman #406) and Ramban also counts Tefila in Taryag. We derive the Mitzvah of Tefila from Dev.10:20 - אֹתוֹ תַעֲבֹד and Dev. 11:13 - וּלְעָבְדוֹ בְּכָל־לְבַבְכֶם - claims Sefer Chareidim that Serving Hashem with all our thoughts applies to all 613 Mitzvos because all of us are Hashem's servants since He took us out of Mitzrayim to be His servants instead of Paroh or any other despot. Nevertheless, the Rishonim agree that these words 'to serve Hashem with all our thoughts' apply both to all 613 Mitzvos in general and also specifically to Tefila which is called Avoda Sh'B'Lev (Taanis, 2b & Sifri, Dev. 11:13). Smak also counts this as a Mitzvah of the Mind, because the Torah singles out the Lev in this Mitzvah. Rashbi in the Zohar (Parshas Pikudei 262a) 'when one comes before His Creator to and says his Tefila, but does not show Kavod to Him by saying the words of Tefila with his mind and heart, it would have been better if was not created!' Min HaTorah, there is no set time for Tefila, (Rambam, Hilchos Tefila, Ch.#1, Halacha 1-4) whenever you open your mouth and thank Hashem, praise Him, ask anything of Him, you attain this Mitzvah. Even if you do so in your mind. No thought is ever lost. Especially saying "Thank You" to Hashem and "I love You Hashem" are very powerful Tefilos because they have the power to cancel harsh decrees against us (see Rabbi Arush's Sefer Garden of Miracle, Say Thank You and See Miracles).

408. Dev. 24:9 - זָכוֹר אֵת אֲשֶׁר־עָשָׂה ה' אֱלֹקֶיךָ לְמִרְיָם בַּדֶּרֶךְ בְּצֵאתְכֶם מִמִּצְרָיִם - Sefer Chareidim (Ch.9, Paragraph 45) counts this as one of Taryag. The very previous verse is הִשָּׁמֶר בְּנֶגַע־הַצָּרַעַת לִשְׁמֹר מְאֹד - which Chazal explain means that Lashon Hara is what brought about the Tzaraas of Miriam. The Sifri derives that one should daily say this Passuk out loud and also in one's mind. Concludes Sefer Chareidim, 'It's Mitzvah Aseh to say out loud and also in one's mind every single day the account of Miriam and her punishment of Tzaraas in order to seal one's mouth and train oneself to have trepidation for speaking Lashon Hara.' The Chafetz Chaim (in Shmirat Halashon, 'ספר זכור למרים בפתיחה ובפרק א' and חלק א', שער תבונה פרק י"ב' ובסוף הספר פרק כ"ז) tells us the Mitzvah to remember how Miriam was stricken with Tzaraas because of Lashon Hara needs to articulated fully and with one's engaged in what one is saying. Reminding ourselves of the consequence Miriam got for Lashon Hara is something one can do any moment of the day or night and is thus a Mitzvah one attains every time we think it!

409. Sefer Yerei'im counts this as one of Taryag (Mitzvah #231). He cites the Gemora's derivation of this Mitzvah from Dev. 10:20 - אֶת־ה' אֱלֹקֶיךָ תִּירָא - which Chazal (Kiddushin 57a & Pesachim 22b) derive that the additional word אֶת comes to add 'fear for Chachamim.' Yirah is a Mitzvah of the mind, whenever one is in awe of Talmidei Chachamim, one attains this Mitzvah.

410. Sefer Yereim counts this as one of Taryag Mitzvos, Siman #359. He writes that what we learn should be on our mind constantly. His exact words are - דברי יוצרך - תן על לבך תמיד דכתיב (דברים ד:ט) רַק הִשָּׁמֶר לְךָ וּשְׁמֹר נַפְשְׁךָ מְאֹד פֶּן־תִּשְׁכַּח אֶת־הַדְּבָרִים אֲשֶׁר־רָאוּ עֵינֶיךָ וּפֶן־יָסוּרוּ מִלְּבָבְךָ כֹּל יְמֵי חַיֶּיךָ. He then quotes Chazal in Avos 3:8 - כָּל הַשּׁוֹכֵחַ דָּבָר אֶחָד מִמִּשְׁנָתוֹ, מַעֲלֶה עָלָיו הַכָּתוּב כְּאִלּוּ מִתְחַיֵּב בְּנַפְשׁוֹ, שֶׁנֶּאֱמַר (דברים ד), רַק הִשָּׁמֶר לְךָ וּשְׁמֹר נַפְשְׁךָ מְאֹד פֶּן־תִּשְׁכַּח אֶת־הַדְּבָרִים אֲשֶׁר רָאוּ עֵינֶיךָ. He concludes that יָכוֹל אֲפִלּוּ תָקְפָה עָלָיו מִשְׁנָתוֹ, תַּלְמוּד לוֹמַר (שם), וּפֶן יָסוּרוּ מִלְּבָבְךָ כֹּל יְמֵי חַיֶּיךָ, הָא אֵינוֹ מִתְחַיֵּב בְּנַפְשׁוֹ עַד שֶׁיֵּשֵׁב וִיסִירֵם מִלִּבּוֹ the fact that the Torah uses the language of פֶּן־תִּשְׁכַּח indicates it is a Lo Ta'aseh and thus one of Taryag Mitzvos. See also Menachos 99b where the Amoraim debate whether forgetting one's learning is one or even three violations. Rambam does not count 'forgetting one's learning' as a Lo

55. Remember your learning.[411]

In conclusion, we have listed over 50 Mitzvos of the Mind that can apply every second of one's life! It appears that Hashem's love for us is so immeasurable, that He gives us so many Mitzvos for a single thought of Emuna or love for Hashem. He loves us so much, He gives us the most Mitzvos when we are under stress and in the midst of a Nissayon and when we respond with Love for Hashem and Emuna and in that moment we attain the reward of over 50 other Mitzvos!

May the merit of learning the Taryag Mitzvos of the Mind activate tremendous Siyata Dishmaya from Hashem to learn His Torah with Kedusha and Tahara and inject in us a deep unswerving love for Hashem and His perfect Torah and love for His treasured nation, Am Yisrael, and may we all be worthy to greet Mashiach soon in our days when all Taryag Mitzvos will be reclaimed, Amen.

Taaseh, however, Sefer Yereim does, so does the B'HaG, SMaG (Laavim #13) & SMaK (Siman #15 and end of Siman #105). Shulchan Aruch HaRav explains why Rambam did not count it (Hilchos Talmud Torah, Ch. #3).

411. Sefer Yereim, Siman #414 counts remembering ones learning as one of Taryag. He writes that it apples constantly. Here are his words, we bolded and underlined the words which show he sees this as a constant Mitzvah: וְשִׁנַּנְתָּם אֶת־דְּבָרֶי אֵלֶּה - צוה הבורא ברוך הוא שישימו ישראל דברי תורה על לבם דכתיב (דברים יא:יח) וְשַׂמְתֶּם אֶת־דְּבָרַי אֵלֶּה עַל־לְבַבְכֶם, **פירוש** "שימה" **שיזכור דברי תורה וישימם על לבו תמיד** בהם בלבבו ויהגה "וְשִׁנַּנְתָּם" הלא למדת גדולתם של לומדי תורה שחושב אדם בדברי תורה וחושב בלבו מקיים מצות והוגיה **שמקיים מצות בכל עת**

Mitzvos listed in Ramban not counted by Rambam

There are a total of 70 Mitzvos where Ramban differs in the counting than Rambam. Many of the differences are where Ramban splits a command into two parts, counting each one as a separate Aseh or Lo Taaseh, while Rambam counts both parts of the command as one Mitzvah. For example, Rambam counts the Lo Taaseh not to anguish a widow or orphan as two examples of the same one Mitzvah, which means do no hurt those who are disadvantaged, like a widow and orphan who do not have advocates to defend them. Ramban takes the position that the Torah is listing two separate Mitzvos, don't hurt a widow, and also, don't hurt an orphan.[412] Whenever Ramban splits a Mitzvah into two, we have listed it as A and B.

1. Mitzvah to eat the meat of the Korban Pesach on the night of the 15th of Nissan.[413]
2. Not to eat the meat of the Korban Pesach when it is either A: raw or B: cooked.[414]
3. Don't benefit from the Petter Chamor before it is redeemed.[415]
4. Mitzvah to free an Eved Canaani if the owner caused the loss of an eye or tooth.[416]
5. Don't pain A: A widow or B: An orphan.[417]
6. Don't kill A: An innocent person or B: A Tzadik.[418]
7. Don't change the sequence of locating the Keilim in the Bais HaMikdash.[419]
8. Burn the Ketoret in A: the morning and B the late afternoon.[420]
9. Bring a Korban only from a domestic animal (Beheima), not from a non-domesticated animal (Chaya).[421]
10. Don't burn either A: Seor or B: Dvash on the Mizbayach.[422]
11. Bring all the Korbanos between the Korban Tamid of the morning and the Tamid of the afternoon.[423]
12. Don't eat a Korban that was slaughtered with the intent to eat it outside the Azara.[424] (Machshavas Chutz).
13. Distance yourself from a Beged that has a Nega Tzaraas on it.[425]
14. A Ben Sorer Umoreh should not eat like a glutton.[426]
15. Don't marry your daughter to anyone to whom the Kiddushin would not be valid.[427]
16. A Kohen must not A: Leave the Bais HaMikdash area while doing Avoda and B: Be מחלל את מקדש אלקיו.[428]

---

412. There are many more such examples as is explained briefly in these footnotes.
413. Ex. 12:8.
414. Ex. 12:9. Rambam counts both eating the meat of the Pesach raw or cooked as one Issur, while Ramban is counting these as two separate לאוים.
415. Ex. 13:13, Ramban deduces this using a Gezeira Shav from Egal Arufa.
416. Ex. 21:26-27. Rambam does not count this separately because he includes it in the Mitzvah to work an Eved Canaani forever (Mitzvah #514) (In Sefer HaChinuch, it is Mitzvah #347).
417. Ex.22:21. Rambam counts both as one Mitzvah, Ramban is counting them as two separate Mitzvos.
418. Ex. 23:7. Rambam counts this as one Mitzvah, Ramban counts them separately.
419. Ex. 23:13. This is not counted in Rambam as one of the 613.
420. Ex. 30:7. Rambam counts this as one Mitzvah, Ramban counts them as two.
421. Lev. 1:2.
422. Lev. 2:11. Rambam counts both of these as one Mitzvah, Ramban is counting them as two separate Mitzvos.
423. Lev. 6:5.
424. Lev.7:18.
425. Lev. 13:51.
426. Lev. 19:26. Ramban is learning from the words - לא תאכלו על הדם - both the warning of lashes and the death punishment from this one verse. Rambam understands that there is just one warning of the death penalty. The main content of this Mitzvah is learned in Dev. 21:18-21.
427. Lev. 19:29.
428. Lev. 21:12. Ramban is counting two Mitzvos in this verse, one Laav is to leave during the Avoda and the second Laav is the Chillul of Hashem's

17. Don't accept Shekalim from gentiles to pay for the Korbanos HaTzibur.[429]
18. A: Eat fruit of Shevi'is and B: Don't do business with fruit of Shevi'is.[430]
19. Maintain the life of a Ger Toshav,[431] save his life from danger and provide medical care.[432]
20. Return any Ribis you took from another Jew.[433]
21. Don't steal any Keley Shares (untensils used for Avoda in the Bais HaMikdash).[434]
22. Avoid any benefit from the hair of a Nazir.[435]
23. A Levi cannot serve in the Bais Hamikdash beyond the age of fifty.[436]
24. A: Separate Chalah from the dough and B: give it to the Kohen.[437]
25. A: Don't dispute the status of the Kehuna and B: Don't participate in Machlokes.[438]
26. The Kohanim must bring all the Korbanos exactly as instructed.[439]
27. A: Separate Maaser Rishon and B: Give it to the Levi.[440]
28. Separate Teruma from the best quality.[441]
29. The Levi'im must not give Terumas Maaser to the Kohen from inferior produce.[442]
30. Consult the Urim V'Tummim.[443]
31. Bring the Korban Tamid A: Every morning and B: every late afternoon.[444]
32. During a siege, the Jewish army must leave one side open for the enemy to escape.[445]
33. To A: Take ownership of Eretz Yisrael and B: Settle Eretz Yisrael.[446]
34. Don't spill innocent blood in Eretz Yisrael.[447]
35. A relative of the victim has a Mitzvah to chase the killer of his relative (after being convicted in Bais Din) and bring him to Bais Din to be killed or the Goel HaDam kills him himself.[448]
36. Don't provoke Edom to war.[449]
37. Don't provoke Moav to war.[450]
38. Don't provoke Amon to war.[451]

Bais HaMikdash, the desecration and disrespect in such an exit. Rambam counts both as one Lo Taaseh.
429. Lev. 22:25.
430. Lev. 25:6.
431. A Ger Toshav is a non-Jew living in Eretz Yisrael who committed to never serve Avoda Zara but still eats Tereifos.
432. Lev. 25:35.
433. Lev. 25:36.
434. Num. 4:20.
435. Num. 6:5.
436. Num. 8:25.
437. Num.15:20-21. Ramban counts two Mitzvos here, while Rambam counts both the separation of Challa from the dough and giving it to the Kohen as two parts of the same Mitzvah.
438. Num. 16:5 - וְלֹא־יִהְיֶה כְקֹרַח וְכַעֲדָתוֹ - Ramban deduces both Mitzvos from this verse, do not dispute the status of the Kohanim and do not be like Korach by joining Machlokes.
439. Num.18:7. Ramban includes seven separate Korbanos under one single Mitzvah for the Kohanim to follow the procedure for all Korbanos. Rambam, however, lists each one separately. 1. The Olah. 2. The Mincha. 3. The Chatat. 4. Asham Vadai. 5. Asham Talui. 6. Olah V'Yored. 7. The Shelamim.
440. Num. 18:24. Rambam counts both as part of the same Mitzvah.
441. Num. 18:29.
442. Num. 18:32.
443. Num. Num. 27:21.
444. Num. 28:4. Rambam counts both as part of the same Mitzvah.
445. Num. 31:7. It is interesting to note the reasoning offered to give the enemy an escape route is so they do fight for their lives and thus cause more casualties.
446. Num. 33:53.
447. Num. 35:34. This is in the context of the Mitzvah of Arei Miklat, setting aside cities of safety and refuge for unintentional manslaughter.
448. Num. 35:19.
449. Dev. 2:4-5.
450. Dev. 2:9.
451. Dev. 2:19.

39. Don't forget Divine Revelation at Har Sinai.[452]
40. Recite Shema every A: Morning and every B: Evening.[453]
41. Don't forget to have Emuna in Hashem's Omnipotence.[454]
42. Make an A: Aron and lid to B: Place the Luchos inside.[455]
43. Judge all cases of the death penalty.[456]
44. Don't eat the bird that was slaughtered to purify a Metzora.[457]
45. Eat A: The meat of the Bechor Beheima and B: Maaser Sheni, both in Yerushalayim.[458]
46. A: Separate Maaser Oni and B: Give it to the poor.[459]
47. Don't have thoughts of anguish when giving Tzedakah.[460]
48. Don't think thoughts of anguish when liberating an Eved Ivri.[461]
49. Only eat Terumah in a state of Tahara.[462]
50. Calculate leap years.[463]
51. A: At the moment of Shechita of a Korban, do not intend to eat it outside it's designated time or B: its physical boundary or C: Shecht a Korban Passul.[464]
52. Don't accept isolated testimonies in capital cases.[465]
53. A: Separate Terumah Gedola and B: Give it to a Kohen.[466]
54. Be Tamim with Hashem.[467]
55. Don't have compassion on a murderer.[468]
56. Don't go to battle if weak minded (רך לבב).[469]
57. Eat from the enemy's fruit trees during a siege.[470]
58. Don't benefit from the Egla Arufa.[471]
59. Don't give the portion assigned to a first born son to another brother.[472]
60. Give the first born son double portion in the father's inheritance.[473]

---

452. Dev. 4:9-10. This Mitzvah would be fulfilled every time one thought about it.
453. Dev. 6:7. Rambam counts both as part of the same Mitzvah.
454. Dev. 6:12. This Mitzvah would be fulfilled every time one thought about Emuna.
455. Dev. 10:11 & Ex. 25:16.
456. Dev. 13:6. Ramban is counting all four separate death penalties as one command to Bais Din to rule all such cases. Rambam on the other hand counts each of the four types of death penalties as separate Mitzvos. 1. Stoning - Skila,. 2. Burning - Sereifa. 3. Decapitation - Chereg. 4. Strangulation - Cheneck.
457. Dev. 14:12.
458. Dev. 14:23.
459. Dev. 14:28-29. Rambam counts both as one Mitzvah.
460. Dev. 15:10.
461. Dev. 15:18.
462. Dev. 15:22.
463. Dev. 16:1. Rambam does not list this separately, instead he includes it in the Mitzvah for Bais Din to determine every Rosh Chodesh (Ex. 12:2).
464. Dev. 17:1.
465. Dev. 17:1 Ramban means that if one witness saw a crime through one window, and another witness saw the same crime from a different window, but neither witnesses saw each other, their two testimonies are in isolation of each other cannot be counted in Bais Din as two witnesses seeing the same crime. Rambam counts this case as inclusive in the Mitzvah of one witness being invalid to testify in court (Mitzvah #573).
466. Dev. 18:4. Rambam counts both as one Mitzvah.
467. Dev. 18:13. Rashi ibid explains this to mean, be completely faithful (full of Emuna) in your reaction to what happens to you and be completely full of Emuna with whatever happens in the future, don't worry about the future. In Gen.17:1 where Rashi explains, be Shalem in all the Nissyonos I have sent you. See also Rashi Ex. 6:9. This Mitzvah is done in thought and applies every moment.
468. Dev. 19:13. It appears Rambam already counts this Mitzvah (#557) so it is not clear why Ramban lists this as one that differs from the Rambam's count. See Minchas Chinuch Mitzvah #521:1.
469. Dev. 20:8. Ramban counts this as a separate Mitzvah, that a soldier who is faint of heart, unable to face armed combat, as someone who may easily retreat and thus cause fear in the other Jewish soldiers. Rambam seems to count this in the Mitzvah not to retreat (#610).
470. Dev. 20:19. Ramban refers to the fruit trees within the Techum of the besieged city.
471. Dev. 21:8. It appears Rambam includes this in the overall Issur not to work the ground where the Egla is decapitated (see Mitzvah #492 in our manual of Taryag Mitzvos).
472. Dev. 21:16.
473. Dev. 21:17.

61. Don't marry A: An Amoni and B: Don't marry a Moavi.[474]
62. Don't have unclean thoughts at the time of war which could cause the Shechina to withdraw its protection of us during battle.[475]
63. Don't bring an animal Korban used to pay for A: The services of a Zona or B: An animal traded for a dog.[476]
64. Keep your word, whether a Shavua, oath, or Neder. Whether A Nidrei Gavoha (Promises to the Bais HaMikdash)[477] or B: Nidrei Issur (forbidding something upon oneself).[478]
65. Don't be intimate with one's wife after she was A: Mezaneh or B: After you divorced her, she remarried and divorced her second married.[479]
66. Bais Din must not permit a divorcee to re-marry his wife after she divorced her second husband.[480]
67. A newly married groom must not A: Join the army in his first year of marriage and B: He must not do any communal work in his first year of marriage.[481]
68. Remember both verbally and mentally what Hashem did to Miriam.[482]
69. A Yavam must not be intimate with the Yavama after he did Chalitza.[483]
70. Bless Birkat HaTorah.[484]

---

474. Dev. 23:4. Rambam counts both of these as the same Mitzvah (#163).
475. Dev. 23:10 - כִּי־תֵצֵא מַחֲנֶה עַל־אֹיְבֶיךָ **וְנִשְׁמַרְתָּ מִכֹּל דָּבָר רָע** - is taken to mean one should be careful in the day time not to have unclean thoughts about Nashim that could cause one to see Keri at night. In the context of battle, the Jewish soldiers depended on victory through the presence of the Shechina. Removal of the Shechina meant fatalities and possibly losing battle. The one item the Torah singles out for a soldier to avoid causing the Shechina to withdraw during battle is sinful/unclean thoughts. Ramban is counting this as a separate Mitzvah.
476. Dev. 23:19. Rambam counts both of these as one Mitzvah (see #346).
477. Ramban deduces Nidrei Gavoha from Dev. 23:24.
478. Ramban deduces Nidrei Issur from Num. 30:3.
479. Dev. 24:4. Rambam counts both cases in the one Mitzvah of not remarrying one's wife after she divorced her second husband (Mitzvah #127).
480. Dev. 24:4.
481. Dev. 24:5. Rambam counts both of these in the one Mitzvah (Mitzvah #609).
482. Dev.24:9. This Mitzvah to remember what happened to Miriam when she spoke Lashon Hara applies every moment of a person's life.
483. Dev. 25:9.
484. Dev. 32:3.

Mitzvos of the Smag[485] not counted by Rambam

Aseh:

1. To distance oneself from a Davar Sheker.[486]
2. To calculate the motions of the planets.[487]
3. To judge Hashem righteously.[488]

Lo Taaseh:

1. Don't be Porush from the Torah.[489] Even a Zaken Muflag.
2. Don't hug or kiss Avoda Zara idols or show any respect to them.[490]
3. Don't make a Pessel.[491]
4. Don't be arrogant.[492]
5. Don't curse oneself.[493]
6. A Kohen must not become Tameh by A: Contact with a corpse or B: By being in the tent of one.[494] (under the same roof).
7. Don't take a Mashkon from A: The upper or B: Lower part of a millstone.[495]
8. Neither A: A Patzua Daka or B: Karut Shofcha are allowed to marry a Jewish girl.[496]
9. An Arel cannot eat Maaser Sheni.[497]
10. Don't let one's daughter be intimate outside of marriage.[498]
11. Don't bring an animal Korban used to pay for A: The services of a Zona or B: An animal traded for a dog.[499]
12. Don't burn A: Seor, or B: Dvash.[500]
13. Not to eat the meat of the Korban Pesach when it is either A: raw or B: cooked.[501]
14. A Jewish lady is not allowed to marry a non-Jewish A: Amoni or B: Moavi.[502]

---

485. SMaG is an abbreviation for **S**efer **M**itzvos **G**edolos. Written by Rabbi Moshe M'Couci, one of the Baaley Tosafos frequently quoted in Shass Bavli in Tosafos.
486. Ex. 23:7. Sefer Yereim counts this too (Lo Taaseh #235) claiming that a sheker that does not lead to Ra is not forbidden by the Torah - שקר שאינו בא לידי רע לא הזהירה התורה.
487. Based on Dev. 4:6 - וּשְׁמַרְתֶּם וַעֲשִׂיתֶם כִּי הִוא חָכְמַתְכֶם וּבִינַתְכֶם לְעֵינֵי הָעַמִּים אֲשֶׁר יִשְׁמְעוּן אֵת כָּל־הַחֻקִּים הָאֵלֶּה וְאָמְרוּ רַק עַם־חָכָם וְנָבוֹן הַגּוֹי הַגָּדוֹל הַזֶּה - This Mitzvah is also listed by the BeHaG as one of Taryag.
488. Based on Dev. 8:5 - וְיָדַעְתָּ עִם־לְבָבֶךָ כִּי כַּאֲשֶׁר יְיַסֵּר אִישׁ אֶת־בְּנוֹ ה' אֱלֹקֶיךָ מְיַסְּרֶךָּ - This Mitzvah is also listed by the BeHaG as one of Taryag.
489. Dev. 4:9.
490. Ex. 20:5 - לא תעבדם.
491. Lev. 26:1.
492. Dev. 8:11-14. SMaK also counts this from Dev. 8:17. This is a constant Mitzvah, applicable every moment.
493. Dev. 4:9 - רַק הִשָּׁמֶר לְךָ וּשְׁמֹר נַפְשְׁךָ מְאֹד - though the context of the verse is to be exceedingly careful not to forget what happened at Har Sinai, nevertheless, this part of the verse has been understood by Rishonim and Achronim to also be the source for guarding ones health (see Kitzur Sh. Aruch. Ch. #32). Here, SMaG understands the verse more literally referring to ones soul, that in guarding ones soul, one must not curse oneself.
494. Lev. 21:1. Rambam counts both these as part of the same Mitzvah.
495. Dev. 24:6. This refers to not taking collateral against a loan that is something the borrower relies on for making a daily living, for example the grind mill he uses to grind flour. The verse mentions two parts to the mill, the lower and upper grinding stones. Rambam counts both as one Mitzvah (Mitzvah #533) while the SMaG counts each section of the mill as a separate prohibition for use as a Mashkon, collateral.
496. Dev. 23:2. Rambam counts both as one Mitzvah (#167).
497. Dev. 26:14.
498. Dev. 19:29. Ramban also counts this as one of Taryag (see #15 of the list of Ramban's differences above).
499. Dev. 23:19. Ramban also lists this as two Mitzvos (see #63 above in the Ramban's list) while Rambam counts both of these as one Mitzvah (see #346).
500. Lev. 2:11. See list of Ramban above #10 who also counts this as two Mitzvos. Rambam counts both of these as one Mitzvah.
501. Ex.12:9. See Ramban in his list above (#2) who also counts this as two Mitzvos while Rambam counts both eating the meat of the Pesach raw or cooked as one Issur.
502. Dev. 23:4. Ramban also counts these as two Mitzvos (Rambam counts both of these as the same Mitzvah - #163).

15. Don't hurt A: An Almana or B: An orphan.[503]
16. Don't be like Korach and his followers.[504]

Mitzvos in the SMaK not counted by **Rambam, Ramban, SMaG & B'HaG**

Aseh

1. Love Tochacha.[505]
2. Look at your Tzitzit.[506]
3. Destroy the names of Avoda Zara.[507]
4. Break the supporting pillars of Avoda Zara.[508]
5. Burn Asheira trees.[509]
6. Destroy the Bamos of Avoda Zara.[510]
7. Break into pieces the altars of Avoda Zara.[511]
8. To do Mitzvos beyond the letter of the law - לעשות לפנים משורת הדין.[512]
9. To be Tznius.[513]
10. To cause happiness to one's wife.[514]
11. Remind oneself of Yetzias Mitzrayim.[515]
12. To Pasken Halacha - lit. להורות.[516]
13. To bless food before eating.[517]
14. To do circumcision on oneself if one is an Arel yet not circumcised.[518]
15. To circumcise all members of one's household.[519]
16. To circumcise those you own through payment.[520]
17. To immerse Keilim bought from gentiles in a Mikveh.[521]
18. To make Havdalah on Motzei Shabbos and Yom Tov.[522]

---

503. Ex.22:21. Ramban (#5 above) also counts both as two separate Mitzvos. Rambam counts both as one Mitzvah (#18).
504. Num. 16:5 - וְלֹא־יִהְיֶה כְקֹרַח וְכַעֲדָתוֹ - Ramban (see list of Ramban above #25) deduces two Mitzvos from this verse, 1. do not dispute the status of the Kohanim and 2. do not be like Korach by joining Machlokes. It appears the SMaG refers more to not entering Machlokes.
505. Dev. 10:16 - וּמַלְתֶּם אֵת עׇרְלַת לְבַבְכֶם.
506. Num. 15:39 - וּרְאִיתֶם אֹתוֹ.
507. Dev. 12:3 - וְאִבַּדְתֶּם אֶת־שְׁמָם. This includes referring to Avoda Zara with names of disdain. This Mitzvah and the following four are all counted under the one Mitzvah in Rambam to destroy Avoda Zara (#53).
508. Dev. 7:5 - וּמַצֵּבֹתָם תְּשַׁבֵּרוּ.
509. Dev. 12:3 - וַאֲשֵׁרֵיהֶם תִּשְׂרְפוּן בָּאֵשׁ.
510. Num. 33:52 - כׇּל־בָּמוֹתָם תַּשְׁמִידוּ.
511. Dev. 12:3 - וְנִתַּצְתֶּם אֶת־מִזְבְּחֹתָם.
512. Ex. 18:20 - וְהוֹדַעְתָּ לָהֶם אֶת־הַדֶּרֶךְ יֵלְכוּ בָהּ וְאֶת־הַמַּעֲשֶׂה אֲשֶׁר יַעֲשׂוּן.
513. Dev. 23:15 - וְהָיָה מַחֲנֶיךָ קָדוֹשׁ וְלֹא־יִרְאֶה בְךָ עֶרְוַת דָּבָר - SMaK learns from here to act with Tznius in the toilet, intimacy, to be distanced from Tzoah and urine, as well be Tzanua when learning and davening.
514. Dev. 24:5 - וְשִׂמַּח אֶת־אִשְׁתּוֹ - Although the context of this verse is the Mitzvah of exemption from military and communal duties in Shana Rishona, the SMaK understands this part of the Passuk to refer to the full duration of marriage. SMaK's actual language is - לקיים עונה באשתו.
515. Dev. 16:3 - לְמַעַן תִּזְכֹּר אֶת־יוֹם צֵאתְךָ מֵאֶרֶץ מִצְרַיִם כֹּל יְמֵי חַיֶּיךָ.
516. Lev. 10:11 - וּלְהוֹרֹת אֶת־בְּנֵי יִשְׂרָאֵל אֵת כׇּל־הַחֻקִּים אֲשֶׁר דִּבֶּר ה' אֲלֵיהֶם בְּיַד־מֹשֶׁה.
517. Dev. 8:10 - וְאָכַלְתָּ וְשָׂבָעְתָּ וּבֵרַכְתָּ אֶת־ה' אֱלֹקֶיךָ עַל־הָאָרֶץ הַטֹּבָה אֲשֶׁר נָתַן־לָךְ. The SMaK is basing this Mitzvah from a Kal VaChomer made in the Gemora (Brachos 35a) on this Passuk, that if one is mandated to bless Hashem 'after' eating, then surely when one is hungry, one should bless Him just as you are about to satisfy your hunger! Shulchan Aruch and all other Poskim count blessings before eating as Miderabanan.
518. Gen. 17:14.
519. Gen. 17:13 - The SmaK includes the son of a Canaanite maid as derived from the words in this verse - הִמּוֹל ׀ יִמּוֹל יְלִיד בֵּיתְךָ.
520. This refers to circumcising an Eved Canaani, based on the words in Gen. 17:12 - יִמּוֹל לָכֶם כׇּל־זָכָר לְדֹרֹתֵיכֶם יְלִיד בָּיִת וּמִקְנַת־כֶּסֶף.
521. Num. 31:23 - כׇּל־דָּבָר אֲשֶׁר־יָבֹא בָאֵשׁ תַּעֲבִירוּ בָאֵשׁ וְטָהֵר אַךְ בְּמֵי נִדָּה יִתְחַטָּא וְכֹל אֲשֶׁר לֹא־יָבֹא בָּאֵשׁ תַּעֲבִירוּ בַמָּיִם.
522. Ex. 20:8 - זָכוֹר אֶת־יוֹם הַשַּׁבָּת לְקַדְּשׁוֹ. Rambam counts both Kiddush and Havdalah as one Mitzvah, we remember Shabbos and make it Kadosh through recital on wine which is Miderabanan but the actual recital of words of Kiddush and Havdalah are Min HaTorah based on this verse. The SMaK is counting Havdalah as a separate Mitzvah.

19. לפרוש מאשתו סמוך לוסתה.[523]
20. לפרוש מאשה שראתה באמצע תשמיש.[524]
21. Give a Ger Toshav a Neveila.[525]

Lo Taaseh

1. Don't think forbidden thoughts of Nashim during the day and cause one to see Keri by night, Hass Veshalom.[526]
2. Don't delay relieving the body.[527]
3. There should not be any Ervat Davar about you.[528]
4. Don't be alone with Nashim.[529]
5. Don't accept other gods as deities, even just to say such words is Assur.[530]
6. Don't do Melacha on Chol HaMoed.[531]
7. Don't do Melacha on the 14th of Nissan after midday.[532]
8. Don't resist giving testimony (to Bais Din).[533]

Mitzvos listed by Sefer Yereim[534] not counted by Rambam

1. Don't make your body disgusting (by eating insects of animals unbefitting for human consumption like rats and rodents). This Issur includes not delaying going to the bathroom.[535]
2. Eat three meals on Shabbos.[536]
3. Don't benefit from a dead body[537]
4. Clothe the naked.[538]
5. Bury the dead.[539]
6. Support your brother.[540]
7. Feed a Neveila to a Ger Toshav.[541]
8. Comfort mourners.[542]
9. Visit the sick.[543]

---

523. Lev. 15:31 - וְהִזַּרְתֶּם אֶת־בְּנֵי־יִשְׂרָאֵל מִטֻּמְאָתָם.
524. Lev. 1:19 - וְאֶל־אִשָּׁה בְּנִדַּת טֻמְאָתָהּ לֹא תִקְרַב
525. Dev. 14:21 - לֹא־תֹאכְלוּ כָל־נְבֵלָה לַגֵּר אֲשֶׁר בִּשְׁעָרֶיךָ תִּתְּנֶנָּה
526. Dev. 23:10 - כִּי־תֵצֵא מַחֲנֶה עַל־אֹיְבֶיךָ וְנִשְׁמַרְתָּ מִכֹּל דָּבָר רָע
527. Lev. 11:43 - אַל־תְּשַׁקְּצוּ אֶת־נַפְשֹׁתֵיכֶם
528. Dev. 23:15 - וְהָיָה מַחֲנֶיךָ קָדוֹשׁ וְלֹא־יִרְאֶה בְךָ עֶרְוַת דָּבָר - The SMaK understands this Passuk to include the Issur of saying words of Torah or Tefila if you can see Erva, which includes a Tefach of Erva of an Isha, or her hair uncovered.
529. Kiddushin 80b. See SMaG #126. The SMaK does not quote a verse for this Mitzvah.
530. Ex. 32:8 in reference to the Golden Calf when the Eruv Rav declared - עָשׂוּ לָהֶם עֵגֶל מַסֵּכָה וַיִּשְׁתַּחֲווּ־לוֹ וַיִּזְבְּחוּ־לוֹ וַיֹּאמְרוּ אֵלֶּה אֱלֹהֶיךָ יִשְׂרָאֵל אֲשֶׁר הֶעֱלוּךָ מֵאֶרֶץ מִצְרָיִם
531. Chagiga 18a & Pesachim 118a. SMaK does not quote a Passuk.
532. Pesachim 50a.
533. Lev. 5:1 - ...וְהוּא עֵד אוֹ רָאָה אוֹ יָדָע אִם־לוֹא יַגִּיד וְנָשָׂא עֲוֹנוֹ
534. Sefer Yereim was authored by R' Eliezer from Mitz, who was one of the Baaley Tosfos and a Talmid of Rabeyn Tam.
535. Sefer Yereim, Amud Sheni, Achilos. Siman 73.
536. Sefer Yereim, Amud Sheni, Achilos. Siman 92.
537. Sefer Yereim. Amud Shelishi. Issurei Hana'ah, Siman 113.
538. Sefer Yereim. Amud Revi'i. Issurei Mamon. Siman 153.
539. Sefer Yereim. Amud Revi'i. Issurei Mamon. Siman 154.
540. Sefer Yereim. Amud Revi'i. Issurei Mamon. Siman 155.
541. Sefer Yereim. Amud Revi'i. Issurei Mamon. Siman 172.
542. Sefer Yereim. Amud Chamishi. Issurim done to Shamayim and people but with no stealing or monetary benefit. Siman 219.
543. Sefer Yereim. Amud Chamishi. Issurim done to Shamayim and people but with no stealing or monetary benefit. Siman 220.

10. Bring joy to the Levi, Ger, Orphan and Widow.[544]
11. Make a bride happy.[545]
12. Have fear/awe for Chachamim.[546]
13. Be extremely humble.[547]
14. Distance yourself from anything Sheker.[548]
15. Don't be a Zaken Mamre.[549]
16. Don't say in your thoughts that your success comes from your own efforts. This also applies to Tzadikim not to think that any of their enemies fall to them, they should not think it's because of their righteous conduct.[550]
17. In addition to the Mitzvah to learn and teach Torah,[551] Sefer Yereim counts Lishmor V'La'assos too. That is, to remember what one learns and say it out loud.[552]
18. Complete all Hallel 18 days a year and one night.[553]
19. Recite Vidui on Yom Kippur.[554]
20. The Jewish King must read the Torah on Hakhel in front of the entire nation.[555]
21. Don't be like Korah.[556]
22. Don't forget your learning.[557]
23. Be careful not to forget Hashem.[558]
24. Don't pity the seven wicked nations when you conquer Eretz Yisrael.[559]
25. Don't bring Avoda Zara into your home.[560]
26. Don't refuse to do Teshuva.[561]
27. Don't let an Erva Davar be seen with you.[562]
28. Serve Hashem.[563]
29. To make yourself Davuk to Hashem.[564]

---

544. Sefer Yereim. Amud Chamishi. Issurim done to Shamayim and people but with no stealing or monetary benefit. Siman 227.
545. Sefer Yereim. Amud Chamishi. Issurim done to Shamayim and people but with no stealing or monetary benefit. Siman 228.
546. Sefer Yereim. Amud Chamishi. Issurim done to Shamayim and people but with no stealing or monetary benefit. Siman 231.
547. Sefer Yereim. Amud Chamishi. Issurim done to Shamayim and people but with no stealing or monetary benefit. Siman 232.
548. Sefer Yereim. Amud Chamishi. Issurim done to Shamayim and people but with no stealing or monetary benefit. Siman 235.
549. Sefer Yereim. Amud Hashishi. Issurim done with speech between oneself and Shamayim with speech but not people. Siman 240.
550. Sefer Yereim. Amud Hashishi. Issurim done between onself and Shamayim with speech but not people. Siman 251.
551. Rambam counts both learning and teaching Torah as one Mitzvah (Mada, Hilchos Talmud Torah 1.4, & Sefer HaChinuch Mitzvah #419).
552. Sefer Yereim. Amud Hashishi. Issurim done between onself and Shamayim with speech but not to people. Siman 257.
553. Sefer Yereim. Amud Hashishi. Issurim done between onself and Shamayim with speech but not to people. Siman 262.
554. Sefer Yereim. Amud Hashishi. Issurim done between onself and Shamayim with speech but not to people. Siman 263.
555. Sefer Yereim. Amud Hashishi. Issurim done between onself and Shamayim with speech but not to people. Siman 266.
556. Sefer Yereim. Amud Hashevi'i. Issurim done between onself and Shamayim without speech but not to people. Siman 357. It is not clear why Sefer Yereim counts this as a Mitzvah not done with ones mouth and not harming people. It would appear that avoiding Machlokes means being silent, so perhaps that is what Sefer Yereim means by counting not to be like Korach who did open his mouth and caused great harm in the death of all his followers.
557. Sefer Yereim. Amud Hashevi'i. Issurim done between onself and Shamayim without speech but not to people. Siman 359. This Issur is constant, it applies every waking moment of one's life.
558. Sefer Yereim. Amud Hashevi'i. Issurim done between onself and Shamayim without speech but not to people. Siman 360. He adds there that this includes remembering Hashem constantly and His Mitzvos.
559. Sefer Yereim. Amud Hashevi'i. Issurim done between onself and Shamayim without speech but not to people. Siman 362.
560. Sefer Yereim. Amud Hashevi'i. Issurim done between onself and Shamayim without speech but not to people. Siman 364.
561. Sefer Yereim. Amud Hashevi'i. Issurim done between onself and Shamayim without speech but not to people. Siman 365. He derives this from the verse in Dev. 10.16 - וּמַלְתֶּם אֵת עָרְלַת לְבַבְכֶם וְעָרְפְּכֶם לֹא תַקְשׁוּ עוֹד - meaning, do not be obstinate in refusing to even think of doing Teshuva. If he refuses such thoughts, he is in violation of this Lo Ta'aseh. The term עָרְלַת לְבַבְכֶם means to cut out ones extra thoughts that block one from changing our thinking to follow what Hashem asks us to think. See the list of Mitzvos of the Mind above.
562. Sefer Yereim. Amud Hashevi'i. Issurim done between onself and Shamayim without speech but not to people. Siman 392. He explains that this Mitzvah refers to not mentioning Hashem's Name or any דבר of קדושה in a place where Erva is present.
563. Sefer Yereim. Amud Hashevi'i. Issurim done between onself and Shamayim without speech but not to people. Siman 406. Sefer Yereim explains that 'Serving Hashem' לעבוד את השם means שילמדו ישראל את התורה ויעמלו בה ויתפללו לפניו...עיין שם עוד.
564. Sefer Yereim. Amud Hashevi'i. Issurim done between onself and Shamayim without speech but not to people. Siman 407. He explains this Mitzvah

30. To go in the ways of Hashem.[565]
31. Be in awe of Shabbos.[566]
32. Shmiras Shabbos.[567]
33. To enjoy Shabbos, delight in Shabbos.[568]
34. To think about words of Torah constantly.[569]
35. Ner Shabbos.[570]
36. A Dayan should judge with Tzedek.[571]
37. Be a Tam with Hashem. Completely trusting of Hashem.[572]
38. Make yourself Kadosh and you will become Kadosh.[573]
39. Yetzika - Pouring of Oil on a Korban Mincha.[574]
40. Belila - Mixing the oil with the flour of the Korban Mincha.[575]
41. Petitos - Breaking the Mincha into parts.[576]

צוה הקב"ה שידבק האדם בגרכי המקום...מה הקב"ה מבקר חולים וכול. He also adds that part of this Mitzvah is to be Davuk to Chachamim and their Talmidim. - in these words

565. Sefer Yereim. Amud Hashevi'i. Issurim done between onself and Shamayim without speech but not to people. Siman 408. Even though Rambam does indeed list this Mitzvah under the verse in Dev. 28:9 - וְהָלַכְתָּ בִּדְרָכָיו, we have still included this Mitzvah in this list because Sefer Yereim deduces this Mitzvah from a different verse, Devarim 8:6 - וְשָׁמַרְתָּ אֶת־מִצְוֹת ה' אֱלֹקֶיךָ **לָלֶכֶת בִּדְרָכָיו** וּלְיִרְאָה אֹתוֹ.

566. Sefer Yereim. Amud Hashevi'i. Issurim done between onself and Shamayim without speech but not to people. Siman 410. Sefer Yereim offers that in the same way Hashem instructed us to have Morah, awe and fear for the Kavod of the Bais HaMikdash, so too, He expects us to accord such awe and Kavod to Shabbos too. He deduces this from the fact that the awe of the Beis HaMikdash is juxtaposited right next to the Mitzvah to guard the Shabbos as in the verse Lev. 19:30 - אֶת־שַׁבְּתֹתַי תִּשְׁמֹרוּ וּמִקְדָּשִׁי תִּירָאוּ אֲנִי ה'. He then gives a definition for the מורא - awe of Shabbos, that it means a person thinks about how he can give Kavod to Shabbos and keep its Mitzvos, for it is Hashem one is trembling before in order not to violate His command not to do Melacha on Shabbos.

567. Sefer Yereim. Amud Hashevi'i. Issurim done between onself and Shamayim without speech but not to people. Siman 411. This Mitzvah is not the same as Rambam who lists 'resting on Shabbos' and 'not doing Melacha on Shabbos' as two separate Lavim. This Mitzvah listed by Yereim is to actually think about how you will protect Shabbos. Here are his words - ושמירה היא בלב...כך צוה לתת שמירת שבת על לבו. See also BeHaG, Aseh #46 who concurs that there is a Mitzvah to think about Shmiras Shabbos. The BeHaG explains this Mitzvah in more detail, explaining that the Shmira of Shabbos in one's mind refers to recognizing Hashem gave us Shabbos to remind us that He created the world from nothing, and that is our ikkar Emuna - שמירה בלב הוא כי השבת ניתן לנו להיות מופת על חידוש העולם שזו היא עיקר האמונה.

568. Sefer Yereim. Amud Hashevi'i. Issurim done between onself and Shamayim without speech but not to people. Siman 412. He deduces this Mitzvas Aseh as a Halacha LeMoshe MiSinai after which Yeshayahu attributed a Passuk to this Mitzvah - (Yishayahu 58:13) אִם־תָּשִׁיב מִשַּׁבָּת רַגְלֶךָ עֲשׂוֹת חֲפָצֶיךָ בְּיוֹם קָדְשִׁי **וְקָרָאתָ לַשַּׁבָּת עֹנֶג** לִקְדוֹשׁ ה'. Chazal define any food you personally enjoy as your Oneg Shabbos, even if it is a small amount but you enjoy it, then that is Oneg Shabbos for you and you attain this Mitzvas Aseh with that pleasure.

569. Sefer Yereim. Amud Hashevi'i. Issurim done between onself and Shamayim without speech but not to people. Siman 414. Here are his words - צוה פירוש "שימה" - שיזכור הבורא ברוך הוא, שישימו ישראל דברי תורה על לבם דכתיב "וְשַׂמְתֶּם אֶת־דְּבָרַי אֵלֶּה עַל־לְבַבְכֶם" (Dev. 11:18) which he explains means - דברי תורה וישמם על לבו תמיד ויהגה בהם כל שעה ושעה שחושב בלבו מקיים מצות "ושמתם את דברי...".

570. Sefer Yereim. Amud Hashevi'i. Issurim done between onself and Shamayim without speech but not to people. Siman 429. He counts Ner Shabbos based on Chazal (Shabbos 34a) that Ner Shabbos is a Mitzvah that relies on the Asmachta of the Passuk in Iyov 5:24 - וְיָדַעְתָּ כִּי־שָׁלוֹם אָהֳלֶךָ וּפָקַדְתָּ נָוְךָ וְלֹא תֶחֱטָא.

571. Sefer Yereim. Amud Hashevi'i. Issurim done between onself and Shamayim without speech but not to people. Siman 430. Sefer Yereim learns this from Devarim 1:16 (see Peirush Toafos Re'em on Sefer Yereim, foot note Aleph who identifies this is the correct verse) - וָאֲצַוֶּה אֶת־שֹׁפְטֵיכֶם בָּעֵת הַהִוא לֵאמֹר שָׁמֹעַ בֵּין־אֲחֵיכֶם **וּשְׁפַטְתֶּם צֶדֶק** בֵּין־אִישׁ וּבֵין־אָחִיו וּבֵין גֵּרוֹ. It appears that Rambam learns the same Mitzvah for Judges to judge righteously from Lev. 19:15 - לֹא־תַעֲשׂוּ עָוֶל בַּמִּשְׁפָּט לֹא־תִשָּׂא פְנֵי־דָל וְלֹא תֶהְדַּר פְּנֵי גָדוֹל **בְּצֶדֶק תִּשְׁפֹּט עֲמִיתֶךָ**.

572. Sefer Yereim. Amud Hashevi'i. Issurim done between onself and Shamayim without speech but not to people. Siman 431. Sefer Yereim counts this as one of Taryag as does Ramban and Sefer Chareidim, unlike Rambam who does not count it in Taryag. The verse this is derived from is Dev. 18:13 - **תָּמִים תִּהְיֶה** עִם ה' אֱלֹקֶיךָ. See Rashi there who who cites the Sifri and explains the Mitzvah refers to wholehearted trust in Hashem without worrying or speculating about the future, but rather accepting all that happens to a person with תמימות and in doing so, he will experience being close to Hashem - תמים תהיה עם ה' אלהיך. התהלך עמו בתמימות ותצפה לו ולא תחקור אחר העתידות, אלא כל מה שיבא עליך קבל בתמימות, ואז תהיה עמו ולחלקו.

573. Sefer Yereim. Amud Hashevi'i. Issurim done between onself and Shamayim without speech but not to people. Siman 434. This is a Mitzvah for every Jew to be Kadosh. The words of Sefer Yereim are - שיקדשו ישראל את הוא ברוך הבורא צוה את עצמם. He derives this from Parshas Shemini in Lev. 11:44 - קְדֹשִׁים. This is similar to Ramban's explanation in Parshas Kedoshim (Lev.19:2 - כִּי ה' אֱלֹקֵיכֶם **וְהִתְקַדִּשְׁתֶּם וִהְיִיתֶם קְדֹשִׁים** כִּי קָדוֹשׁ אָנִי). Sefer Yereim says this Mitzvah to a person not acting with any over-indulgence. His words are - שלא ינול אדם עצמו תִּהְיוּ כִּי קָדוֹשׁ אֲנִי ה' אֱלֹקֵיכֶם. ביותר, שהניוול הוא חסרון קדושה.

574. Sefer Yereim. Amud Hashevi'i. Issurim done between onself and Shamayim without speech but not to people. Siman 448. He counts this as its own Mitzvah in Taryag, Rambam counts this as part of the one Mitzvah of bringing a Korban Mincha.

575. Sefer Yereim. Amud Hashevi'i. Issurim done between onself and Shamayim without speech but not to people. Siman 449. He counts this as its own Mitzvah in Taryag, Rambam counts this as part of the one Mitzvah of bringing a Korban Mincha.

576. Sefer Yereim. Amud Hashevi'i. Issurim done between onself and Shamayim without speech but not to people. Siman 450. He counts this as its own Mitzvah in Taryag, Rambam counts this as part of the one Mitzvah of bringing a Korban Mincha.

42. Melichos - Salting the Korban Mincha.[577]
43. Tenufos - Waving the Korban Mincha.[578]
44. Hagashos - Touching the corner of the Mizbayach with the Keli of the Korban Mincha.[579]
45. Kemitzos - Removal of the Kemitza, hand full of dough from the Korban Mincha.[580]
46. Haktaros - Burning of the Kemitza of the Korban Mincha.[581]
47. Shechitat Kodshim and Chulin.[582]
48. Melikos - Cutting the neck of the Korban HaOff.[583]
49. Kabalas HaDam in a Keli Sharet. Receiving the blood of a Korban into a designated vessel in the Beis Hamikdash.[584]
50. Haza'os - The sprinkling of the blood on the Mizbayach.[585]

---

577. Sefer Yereim. Amud Hashevi'i. Issurim done between onself and Shamayim without speech but not to people. Siman 451. He counts this as its own Mitzvah in Taryag, Rambam counts this as part of the one Mitzvah of bringing a Korban Mincha.
578. Sefer Yereim. Amud Hashevi'i. Issurim done between onself and Shamayim without speech but not to people. Siman 452. He counts this as its own Mitzvah in Taryag, Rambam counts this as part of the one Mitzvah of bringing a Korban Mincha. Waving only applies to Log Shemen of the Korban Minchas Metzora, the Asham Metzorah, Minchas Bikkurim, Eimurei Shalmei Yachid with its chest and cheeks, the Shtei HaLechem and two Kivsei Atzeret.
579. Sefer Yereim. Amud Hashevi'i. Issurim done between onself and Shamayim without speech but not to people. Siman 453. He counts this as its own Mitzvah in Taryag, Rambam counts this as part of the one Mitzvah of bringing a Korban Mincha. See Siman 453 for the examples of which Menachos are brought to the Mizbayach's corner.
580. Sefer Yereim. Amud Hashevi'i. Issurim done between onself and Shamayim without speech but not to people. Siman 454. He counts this as its own Mitzvah in Taryag, Rambam counts this as part of the one Mitzvah of bringing a Korban Mincha. Kemitza is taken from types of Korban Mincha - Soles, Machvas, Marcheses, Chalos, Rekikim, Minchas Ovdei Kochavim, Minchas Nashim, Minchas HaOmer, Minchas Choteh & Minchas Kinaos.
581. Sefer Yereim. Amud Hashevi'i. Issurim done between onself and Shamayim without speech but not to people. Siman 455. He counts this as its own Mitzvah in Taryag, Rambam counts this as part of the one Mitzvah of bringing a Korban Mincha.
582. Sefer Yereim. Amud Hashevi'i. Issurim done between onself and Shamayim without speech but not to people. Siman 456. He counts this as its own Mitzvah in Taryag, Rambam counts this as part of the one Mitzvah of bringing each type of Korban. The Mitzvah to Shecht Chulin counted as its own Mitzvah by Rambam, so in this aspect of Shechita, the Yereim is not differing to Rambam's count.
583. Sefer Yereim. Amud Hashevi'i. Issurim done between onself and Shamayim without speech but not to people. Siman 457. Melikas HaOff, is the cutting of the Esophagus and Trachea with the thumb nail of the Kohen on the Korbanos of either the Olas HaOff or Chatas HaOff, each being either Shtei Torim or Shtei Beney Yona. Yereim is counting this one act of Melika as one of Taryag, while Rambam includes Melika as part of the Mitzvah to bring a Korban Olah or Chatas.
584. Sefer Yereim. Amud Hashevi'i. Issurim done between onself and Shamayim without speech but not to people. Siman 458. Kabalas HaDam is not counted as a separate Mitzva of Taryag in Rambam's listing because it is counted in the overall Mitzvah of the bringing of each individual Korban. Sefer Yereim counts it separately.
585. Sefer Yereim. Amud Hashevi'i. Issurim done between onself and Shamayim without speech but not to people. Siman 459. In Rambam, the sprinkling of blood from a Korban is not counted as a separate Mitzvah of Taryag, instead it is part of the overall Mitzvah of each Korban. Sefer Yereim counts the sprinkling as its own Mitzvah in Taryag.

Made in the USA
Las Vegas, NV
02 December 2021